Power Platform and Dynamics 365 CE for Absolute Beginners

Configure and Customize Your Business Needs

Sanjaya Prakash Pradhan

Apress®

Power Platform and Dynamics 365 CE for Absolute Beginners: Configure and Customize Your Business Needs

Sanjaya Prakash Pradhan
Ganjam, Odisha, India

ISBN-13 (pbk): 978-1-4842-8599-2   ISBN-13 (electronic): 978-1-4842-8600-5
https://doi.org/10.1007/978-1-4842-8600-5

Managing Director, Apress Media LLC: Welmoed Spahr
Acquisitions Editor: Smriti Srivastava
Development Editor: Laura Berendson
Coordinating Editor: Shrikant Vishwakarma
Copyeditor: Kezia Endsley

Cover designed by eStudioCalamar

Cover image designed by Pexels

Distributed to the book trade worldwide by Springer Science+Business Media LLC, 1 New York Plaza, Suite 4600, New York, NY 10004. Phone 1-800-SPRINGER, fax (201) 348-4505, email orders-ny@springer-sbm. com, or visit www.springeronline.com. Apress Media, LLC is a California LLC and the sole member (owner) is Springer Science + Business Media Finance Inc (SSBM Finance Inc). SSBM Finance Inc is a **Delaware** corporation.

For information on translations, please e-mail booktranslations@springernature.com; for reprint, paperback, or audio rights, please e-mail bookpermissions@springernature.com, or visit http://www.apress.com/rights-permissions.

Apress titles may be purchased in bulk for academic, corporate, or promotional use. eBook versions and licenses are also available for most titles. For more information, reference our Print and eBook Bulk Sales web page at http://www.apress.com/bulk-sales.

Any source code or other supplementary material referenced by the author in this book is available to readers on GitHub (github.com/apress).

Printed on acid-free paper

I dedicate this book to...

My father, for being my teacher during every step

My mother and my wife, for being my constant motivators

And finally to God, for his choicest blessings. Also I cannot forget my beloved Microsoft Dynamics community.

This book is for you all...

Table of Contents

About the Author

Sanjaya Prakash Pradhan is a Microsoft Dynamics 365 and Power Apps Business Applications MVP, as well as a Microsoft Certified Trainer (MCT) in Dynamics 365 CE and Power Apps. He is an experienced senior technical consultant, with 13+ years of experience in consulting and training. He has worked on numerous business system implementations. Sanjaya is currently working as a research and development industry solutions lead in an established worldwide business applications practice. Having led software projects in numerous industries, including BFS, healthcare, retail, and the public sector, he now works across all areas of the project lifecycle, from demonstrations to design, architecture, documentation, customization, and development. Sanjaya gets involved in the technical community by leading the Power Platform and Dynamics 365 user group in India, running technical events, and presenting technical and functional topics at conferences around the world. He is an MVP, MCT, community director, UG lead, speaker, trainer, blogger, author, podcaster, business advisor, and senior solution architect.

About the Technical Reviewer

 **Sanjaya Yapa** currently works as a Microsoft Dynamics CE/FS Solution Architect in Melbourne, Australia. He has more than 15 years of experience in the industry. He has been working with various Microsoft technologies since 2005 and possesses a wealth of experience in software development, team leadership, product management, and consultancy. He specializes in Power Platform, Dynamics 365 Customer Engagement, Field Services, Marketing, Azure Solution Development, and Application Lifecycle Management. Sanjaya is the author of *Customizing Dynamics 365* (Apress) and *Getting Started with Dynamics 365 Portals* (Apress), and the co-author of *Dynamics 365 Field Services* (Apress) and *Effective Team Management with VSTS and TFS* (Apress).

Acknowledgments

Thank you to the supporters of my Softchief Learn community. Any accomplishment requires the effort of many people and this work is no different. I thank my wife, whose patience and support was instrumental in accomplishing this task.

The dream of writing a good book is very different from actually finishing one. Since its initial draft, this book has undergone numerous revisions. At each revision, my reviewers provided me with priceless feedback. They continuously contributed, which has allowed the book to grow by adding fresh perspectives and refining existing ones.

I owe a debt of gratitude to every one of my reviewers, who contributed greatly with insightful comments, helpful suggestions, and insightful criticism of the draft chapters throughout the publication of this book. All of my reviewers are subject matter experts and leaders in their respective fields. Without their assistance, my writing would not have developed into the book you are currently reading.

I convey my gratitude to all the wonderful people I've encountered in my Microsoft Dynamics 365 and Power Platform career. These people supported, mentored, and trusted me with new challenges, helped me to find mistakes, and pushed my limits.

Introduction

This book is for users and developers who are starting a career in Power Apps and Dynamics 365. If you don't have any idea about how to work with Dynamics 365 and Power Platform, this is the book for you.

This book covers end-to-end, live projects with practice scenarios so that you can run through scenarios after learning about the topic at hand.

This is a hands-on manual for developing production-ready Power Apps and services. You'll do this by leveraging the rich ecosystem of the Power Platform less-code, no-code concept and Dynamics 365. This is important because real applications require many components, including security, deployment, customization, configuration, extensions, and more.

This book will give you practical, hands-on experience with the Dataverse, Power Apps, Power Automate, Power BI, Power Virtual Agent, and AI Builder. It also explains configuration and customization of plugins, custom workflows, security matrixes, and duplicate deletion rules with the core modules of Dynamics 365 CE overviews.

CHAPTER 1

Introduction: Microsoft Power Apps

Microsoft Power Apps is a trending, less-code and no-code business application development platform that comes with a suite of apps, services, and connectors. Its data platform provides a rapid development environment for building custom business applications that are fit for any business need. With the introduction of no-code, less-code app development, anyone can quickly build and share low-code apps with Microsoft Power Apps. The benefits of using Microsoft Power Apps are as follows:

- **Get started quickly**: Empower your team to start designing and releasing apps right away with pre-built templates, drag-and-drop ease, and speedy deployment and then iterate them as needed.

- **Build apps without compromising**: Give everyone the ability to create the apps they want with advanced features that were previously only available to professional developers, including built-in AI components.

- **Enable extensibility for developers**: Provide experienced developers with the tools they need to add Azure functions and custom connectors to proprietary or on-premises systems so they can effortlessly increase the app's capabilities.

Understanding Environments

From a developer's point of view, environments are instances, such as development, UAT, production, and so on, that businesses use to store, manage, and share data, apps,

© Sanjaya Prakash Pradhan 2022
S. Prakash Pradhan, *Power Platform and Dynamics 365 CE for Absolute Beginners*,
https://doi.org/10.1007/978-1-4842-8600-5_1

chatbots, and flows. You can also think of environments as containers that separate apps that have different security roles, security requirements, and target audiences.

In general, businesses can create multiple environments that manage data, apps, security roles, and users. Large organizations might have dev, SIT, ST, UAT, pre-prod, and production environments, for example. Small businesses might only have dev, UAT, and production environments. Figure 1-1 shows a typical business environment setup.

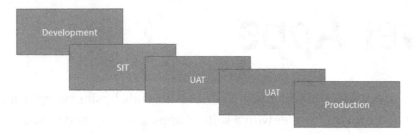

Figure 1-1. *Typical environments in common business implementations*

Every environment can contain flows, chatbots, solutions, AI Builders, data, and apps with security roles, users, and so on.

As a part of the subscription, a default environment is created automatically and shared by all users in that tenant. It's important to focus on understanding Power Apps for Dynamics 365 CE/CRM, so instead of using the default environment, you should create a new environment, called Trial (which is subscription-based). Trial environments are intended to support short-term testing needs and are automatically cleaned up after a short period of time. They expire in 30 days and are limited to one per user.

Understanding the Power Platform Architecture

Before going in-depth, you need to understand the architecture of Power Platform and Dynamics 365 Apps. The architecture in Figure 1-2 shows the Dynamics 365 Apps and Power Apps.

Note that the base concept of Power Apps is the environment. It stores all apps, Power Automate (previously called Flow), Power Virtual Agent, Power BI, and AI Builders in environments. Power Apps is divided into three categories—Canvas apps, model-driven apps, and Power Portals.

Dynamics 365 CE/CRM apps are model-driven apps with all the Power Apps capabilities backed by the Dataverse system.

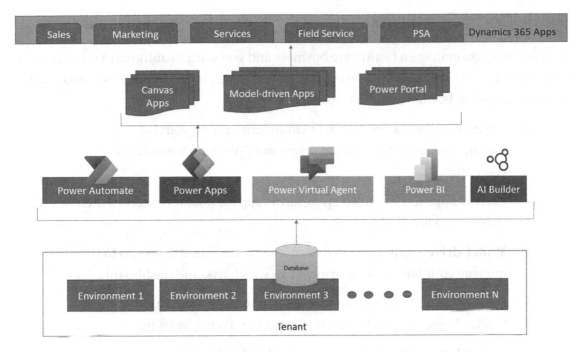

Figure 1-2. *Power Platform architecture*

Using Power Automate, you can configure automated flows using a cloud application with diversified connectors such as Salesforce, Outlook, Mailchimp, and sometimes a custom connector.

Power Apps can configure applications that are suitable for mobile devices. Canvas apps are suitable for designing apps targeted to mobile and tab devices that support multiple connectors. Model-driven apps can be used to define more complex apps leveraged by scripts and server-side code. Power Portal is intended for public-facing web portals so that public users can interact with the Dataverse without a license.

You can build Power Apps such as model-driven apps, Canvas apps, and Power Portals using the data stored in the Dataverse to build scalable applications fit to your business needs. Power Automate can be configured to automate day-to-day manual processes using the native Microsoft Dataverse and other Microsoft products or third-party applications. Data connectors are a new way of integrating diversified cloud and on-premise applications, ensuring less-code and no-code application development.

AI Builder is another Microsoft Power Platform capability that provides AI models that are designed to optimize your regular business processes. AI Builder enables your business to use artificial intelligence to automate processes. These models can be called from Power Apps and Power Automate with Dataverse data and other application data.

Real-World Scenario

Let's assume you manage a healthcare business and you want to automate your business processes. You can leverage the Power Platform low-code, less-code ecosystem to meet your business needs. Consider these example scenarios:

- **Dataverse**: You can create an environment to store your business data in the Dataverse. You can create multiple environments as you wish.

- **Canvas app**: You can develop a Canvas app for doctors to record their visits with a few clicks.

- **Model-driven app**: You can design a complex data-driven app to manage your business using forms, views, charts, and dashboards.

- **Power Portal**: You can capture patient appointment requests, feedback, records, and more, using a public-facing website.

- **Power Automate**: You can automate cloud tasks such as sending auto-emailers, sending reports to patients, and so on, without needing a department to manually handle medical reports.

- **Power Virtual Agents**: You can configure a digital chatbot that interacts with internal and external users to solve issues and answer queries without needing a real agent. For example, you can configure a chatbot to answer patient queries about doctor availability, report delivery times, and so on.

- **Power BI**: You can design dashboards and reports for your business strategy needs. You can report patients' and doctors' daily appointments in a dashboard and automate them by integrating them with other cloud apps.

- **AI Builder**: You can extract patient information from documents and identify patients' reports automatically.

This brief, real-world scenario shows how you can leverage the Power Platform ecosystem to solve your business needs.

Differences Between Power Apps and Dynamics 365 Apps

Power Apps is categorized into three types of apps:

- Canvas apps

- Model-driven apps

- Power Portals

Dynamics 365 CE/CRM apps are model-driven Power Apps. All capabilities of model-driven apps are inherited by Dynamics 365 CE/CRM apps, including the Sales Hub, the Customer Service Hub, Marketing for Dynamics 365, and Field Service and Project Service automation.

Dynamics 365 apps are built on model-driven Power Apps and you can build your custom apps as well. Dynamics 365 apps are created by Microsoft developers. Advanced features are used to meet common business needs that are not available in custom model-driven apps. You will learn about the details in later chapters.

How Power Apps Supports the Less-Code, No-Code Concept

Microsoft has reimagined the way to develop apps. The new less-code, no-code concept provides more flexibility for non-programmers to develop apps.

Microsoft Power Apps supports a drag-and-drop interface with easy-to-use built-in controls such as sliders, galleries, containers, icons, shares, and so on. It does not require any coding, which is why it's a no-code concept. For complex applications, though, the no-code concept is not enough. They require some sort of less-code, called *Power Fx,* to develop more dynamic apps. Power Fx are Excel formula-like scripts that you can use in Power Apps.

In general, you can use the no-code or less-code concept to develop Power Apps by connecting to the Dataverse and other diversified cloud applications through connectors.

The Power Fx Concept in Power Apps

Microsoft Power Fx is a free and open-source low-code, general-purpose programming language for expressing logic across the Microsoft Power Platform. Power Fx is inspired by the Excel formula. In Canvas apps Power Apps, you can use Power Fx to make the app more dynamic and complex. For more detailed information about Power Apps, go to the Microsoft site at `https://docs.microsoft.com/en-us/power-platform/power-fx/overview`.

The Power Fx example in Figure 1-3 demonstrates how to extract five characters from the right of a string that you pass in a text input control.

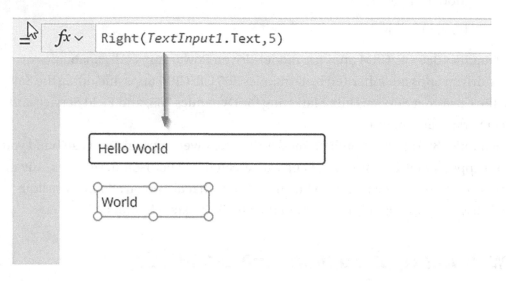

Figure 1-3. *Power Fx example*

Most logic can be reduced to one-liners, with plenty of expressiveness and control for more complex needs. The goal is to keep the number of concepts to a minimum—ideally no more than an Excel user would already know.

Power Fx Features

Power Fx is more popular in Power Apps, so this section looks at the Power Fx features in terms of its capabilities. Note the following key points about Power Fx:

- **Asynchronous**. All data operations in Power Fx are asynchronous in nature. The Power Apps developer doesn't need to explicitly specify this in the app.

- **Local and remote**. Whether it's a local or remote database or service, Power Fx uses the same syntax and functions for data. Power Fx automatically delegates what it can to the server to process filters and then sorts there more efficiently. Remember that delegation works in Power Fx only when the datasource supports delegation.

- **Excel syntax translation**. Excel is used by hundreds of millions of users, most of whom know that & is used for string concatenation. Power Fx uses & for concatenation as well, leveraging the knowledge Excel users already have.

Configuration vs Customization in the Power Platform

In the Power Platform, the configuration and customization terminology is defined by the nature of its app design. For example, if some sort of code is required to develop or design the app, it falls under customizations, but if it does not require any code, you can call it a configuration. Table 1-1 shows the differences between configuration and customization.

Table 1-1. *Differences Between Configuration and Customization*

Configuration	Customization
Table, fields, relationships configuration	Power Fx code addition
View, form, chart, dashboard designs	JavaScript code for Power Apps
Configuring flow	Writing plugins
Configuring chatbots	Writing custom workflow activities
AI model configuration	Writing console apps
Designing Power BI visualizations	Developing custom web apps

Enhancement Scopes in Power Apps

When the out-of-the-box application features are not enough to meet your business needs, you have to start thinking about enhancements to augment the default application behaviors. The diagram in Figure 1-4 explains the enhancement scopes available to developers and consultants in Power Apps for Dynamic 365 CE/CRM.

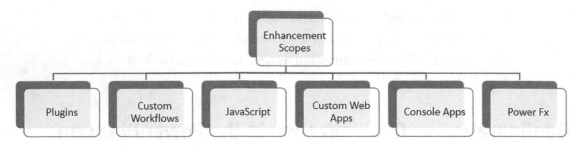

Figure 1-4. *Enhancement scopes*

You can enhance the application by using client-side and server-side code. Client-side code requires the JavaScript scripting language and server-side code requires the C#.Net programming language.

You can configure logic apps, service busses and endpoints, and Azure functions to make your Power Apps more powerful. For Azure integration, more details are available from the Microsoft site at `https://docs.microsoft.com/en-us/power-apps/developer/data-platform/azure-integration`.

Integration Concepts in Power Apps

Microsoft Power Apps can be easily integrated with native Microsoft applications such as Outlook, SharePoint, and OneDrive, as well as with third-party cloud applications such as web portals, Salesforce, and so on.

Using configurations, you can integrate native apps with Dynamics 365 CE/CRM apps. For third-party apps, you need to use connectors and server-side C# programming or client-side JavaScript. Figure 1-5 shows a typical integration diagram.

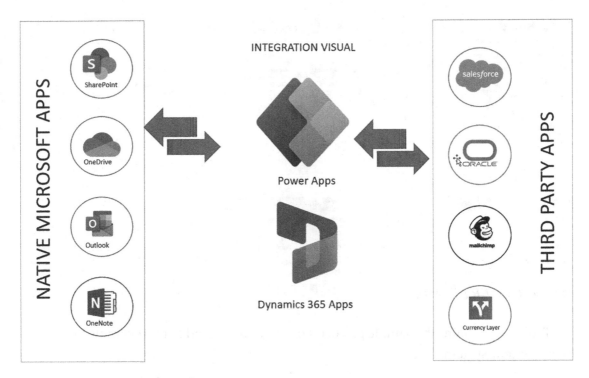

Figure 1-5. *Integration diagram*

Sample Domain and Project Analysis

This book focuses on giving practical business scenarios of Power Apps for Dynamics 365 CE/CRM, using a sample project called the Student Management System (SMS) implementation, which is part of an Education domain.

Let's first design the Entity Relationship (ER) diagram before going in-depth. In the diagram in Figure 1-6, there are five tables—Students, Payments, Payment Details, Courses, and Student Registered Courses. You can use existing out-of-the-box tables if your business needs are met that way, but this book focuses on creating new entities.

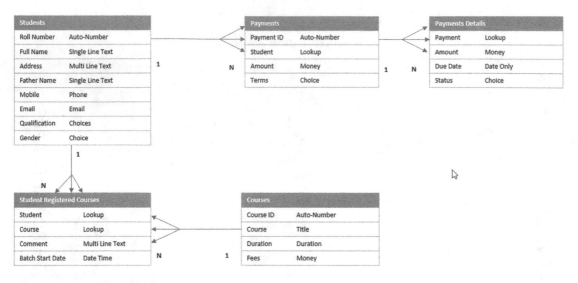

Figure 1-6. *ER diagram*

Table 1-2 explains the sample project requirements related to this example School Management System.

Table 1-2. *Sample User Stories*

Sl. No.	User Story	Solution
1	Systems should allow users to combine different configuration and customization components in a package so that they can be distributed to other environments.	Configure the Power Apps solution and add required components for packaging.
2	School management system must allow users to enter student information, such as roll number (auto-number), name, address, father's name, mobile, email address, and qualifications. System should capture course information and users should be able to record students joined for courses. The app must create payment information with term and payment details.	Solution components include tables, fields, forms, views, and relationships.

(continued)

Table 1-2. (*continued*)

Sl. No.	User Story	Solution
3	The system should display student-level total amount to be paid and the next renewal due date of the student after one year of joining.	The solution requires developers to configure rollup and calculated fields.
4	Mobile number and email should be mandatory when creating a student.	Use the business rules to solve this business need.
5	The system should allow associate courses for students; one student can have multiple courses and one course can be chosen by multiple students.	Configure relationships and relationship behaviors.
6	The system should be able to display courses by students joined and by joining date.	Configure charts for the solution.
7	The system should display a page to display all visualizations for a student.	Create a table-specific dashboard.
8	The system should include a portable application for the student management system with dashboards, tables, forms, etc.	Configure a model-driven app and customize a sitemap.
9	The app should be accessible only by sales people.	Manage roles for model-driven apps.
10	The system should configure a mobile device to enter student information by salesperson. Users should be able to create, update, read, and delete students from the app.	Configure a Canvas app for student entries.
11	Users should be able to search students and send emails to students from the mobile app.	Configure Canvas apps with an Outlook connector.
12	The system should display login user information in all screens of the mobile app.	Use global and local variables.

(*continued*)

Table 1-2. (*continued*)

Sl. No.	User Story	Solution
13	The system must have a public website through which new students can register and choose courses.	Configure Power Portal.
14	Students from the portal can create new course registration records, delete existing records, and update existing records.	Configure CRUD operations in Power Portal and then configure authentication and authorization.
15	The system must hide the father's name for the student when registering from the portal.	Use JavaScript and CSS to do the task.
16	The system must display the student's full name on the portal after they are logged in.	Use Liquid code for this requirement.
17	The system must provide a process to streamline the student onboarding process to capture general, communication, and course information.	Configure Business Process Flow using Power Automate.
18	As soon as a student is created, send a welcome email to them and create a task to collect payment from them three days after the student is created.	Use automated cloud flow through Power Automate.
19	The system should automatically send timesheet emails and links of the Power Portal to students to fill in the daily timesheet.	Use Scheduled Flow in Power Automate.
20	The system should fetch the latest currency exchange rates from a third-party WEB API currency layer and display it on the Canvas app.	Use Power Apps Trigger Flow.
21	Whenever a lead is created in the Dataverse with more than $50,000 annual revenue, send approval from the manager. After approval, update the lead for the qualification process.	Approvals in Power Automate.

(*continued*)

Table 1-2. (*continued*)

Sl. No.	User Story	Solution
22	The system should configure a Power Virtual Agent for public users so that the chatbot can capture user information and validate it against the Dataverse. If the user is not valid, create a contact in the Dataverse. Display Power Virtual Agent in an external website such as Power Portal or other websites.	Use Power Virtual Agent and call action.
23	The system should display student and course visualization dashboards in Power BI.	Configure Power BI.
24	The system should configure an AI Builder to process invoices to fetch data and push them in the Dataverse.	Use AI Builder.
25	The system should create personal settings walkthroughs in model-driven apps.	Model-driven apps settings.
26	The system should create advanced settings walkthroughs for Dynamics 365 CE/CRM apps.	Dynamics 365 CE/CRM Advanced Settings.
27	The system should configure users, security roles, teams, field security profiles, and hierarchy security.	Security Matrix Configuration.
28	The system should send an email on the payment due date to students when payment has not been received.	Use parallel wait in CRM workflows.
29	The system should provide a way to send reminder emails on-demand to student payments when are not paid after a certain time.	Develop custom workflow activities.
30	The system should automatically create payment details as soon as a payment is created. The line numbers will be the same as the terms selected in the payment and the amount should be divided equally.	Develop a plugin for this scenario.
31	The system should provide a button on the student form to create a payment record on demand by passing the required data.	Use a command button and form script.

(*continued*)

Table 1-2. (*continued*)

Sl. No.	User Story	Solution
32	The system should create a reusable action to send emails and create a task for lead on demand.	Configure custom action.
33	The system should create a report on leads and display leads by creation date.	Configure reports.
34	Users should be able to track email activities for students in Outlook.	Integrate Outlook with Dynamics 365.
34	Users should be able to upload student documents in SharePoint from Dynamics 365.	Integrate SharePoint with Dynamics 365.
35	The system should explain the sales model lifecycle in D365 and list the app's settings, the product catalog, and other settings available to the sales model.	Dynamics 365 Sales module in details.
36	The system should explain the marketing model lifecycle and app settings available for the marketing module.	Dynamics 365 Marketing (Legacy module in details).

These are the typical requirements that will be implemented throughout this book. Note that you must have an online trial version of Dynamics 365 CE/CRM Power Apps to implement these scenarios.

Subscribing to the 30-Day Free Trial Environment

Microsoft provides a 30-day free trial subscription to anyone who wants to learn about the features of Power Apps. Thirty days is sufficient to learn the basics, but if you want to extend the free trial version, you have to provide your credit card information. No money will be deducted; it's required just for user verification. To configure the trial version, use the following steps.

Navigate to the trial portal at `https://dynamics.microsoft.com/en-us/dynamics-365-free-trial/`. The landing page will list all the Dynamics 365 apps, such as Sales, Customer Service, Marketing, Project Service, and so on. Click the Try for Free button in Sales. Figure 1-7 shows the Dynamics 365 Sales free trial option.

Figure 1-7. *Dynamics 365 Sales free trial option*

It will open a popup where you provide your organization's email address. If you don't have an organization email address, just click Start Your Free Trial. It will display another option, called "Click Here to Set Up a New Trial Account Instead". Click the Click Here link and follow the instructions. Figure 1-8 shows the email options you'll see when accessing the trial.

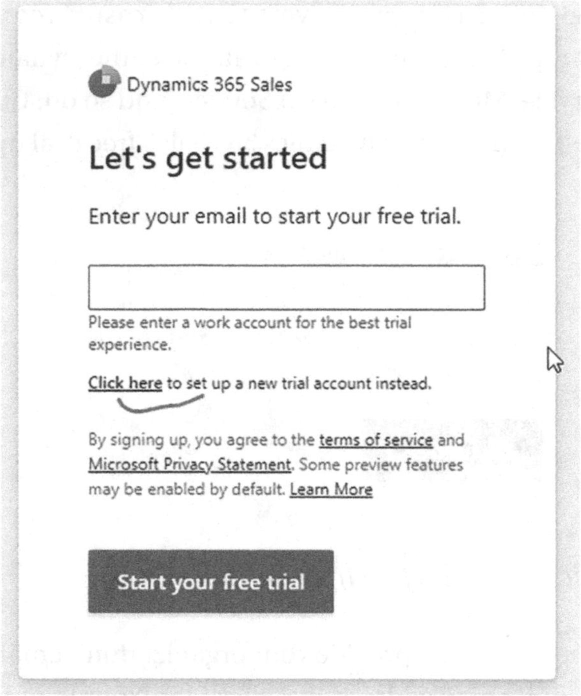

Figure 1-8. *Email options in free trial*

Now provide your personal email ID like Gmail, Yahoo! mail, or any domain you like and click Next. The email you provide is used for email communications related to your subscription. Figure 1-9 shows the getting started screen.

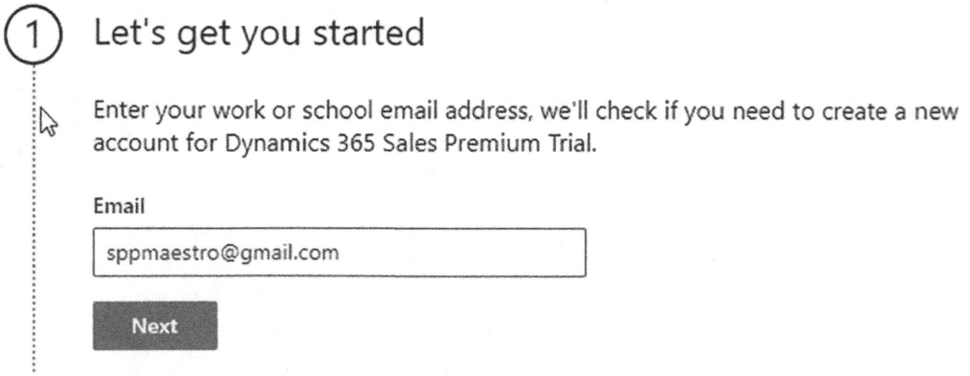

Figure 1-9. *Get started by providing a personal email*

The system will prompt you about your selected email. You can proceed by selecting the Set Up Account button. If you want to change the email, click the Not You? option. Figure 1-10 shows the setup account panel for trial.

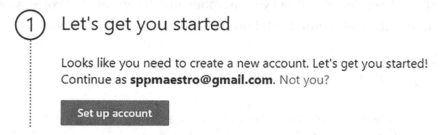

Figure 1-10. *Setup account panel*

The next step is to provide personal information like your first name, last name, phone number, company name, company size, and country and then click Next. Figure 1-11 shows the Tell Us About Yourself section.

② Tell us about yourself

First name
```
Sanjay
```

Middle name (Optional)
```
```

Last name
```
Prakash
```

Business phone number
```
8328865778
```

Company name
```
Softchief
```

Company size
```
1 person                                    ⌄
```

Country or Region
```
United States                               ⌄
```

Next

Figure 1-11. *The Tell Us About Yourself section*

The next step is to verify your phone number. Choose your country code and provide your mobile number. You can verify your number using the Text Me or Call Me option. If you choose the Text Me option, it will send a message with a code to your number. If you choose the Call Me option, it will call your number and the automated voice system will speak the code in the call. Figure 1-12 shows the mobile verification screen.

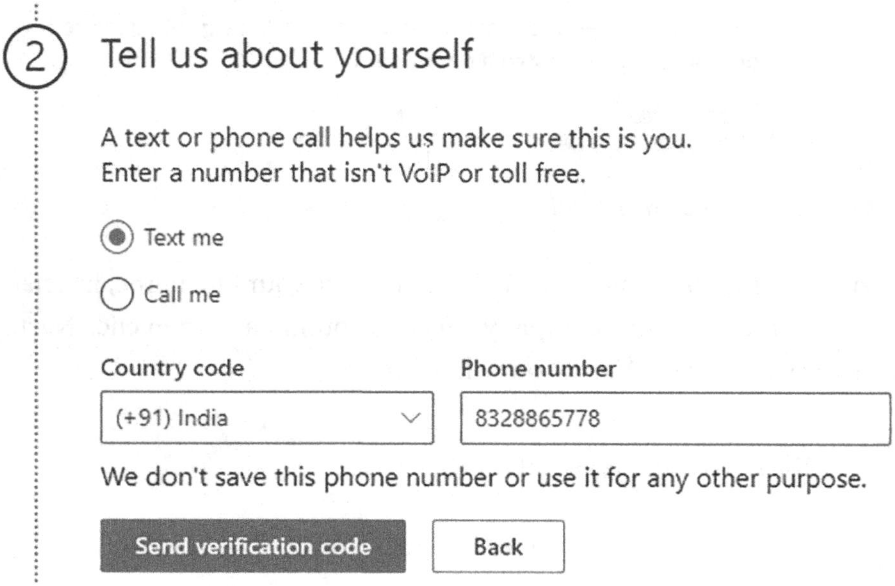

Figure 1-12. *Mobile verification screen*

After providing these details, click the Send Verification Code button. This will send a code to your mobile number. Supply that code and then click Verify. If you want to change your phone number, you can change do so and then re-verify at this stage. Figure 1-13 shows the OTP verification screen.

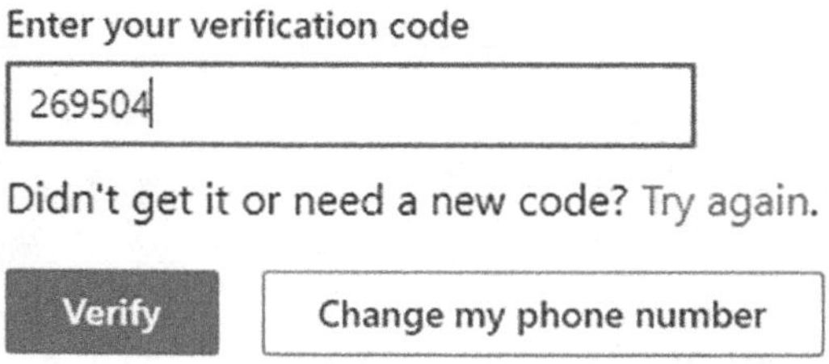

Figure 1-13. *OTP verification screen*

After your phone number has been verified, you need to provide sign-in information, like your username, domain name, and password. Complete this step by clicking Next. Figure 1-14 shows the sign-in option when subscribing to the trial version.

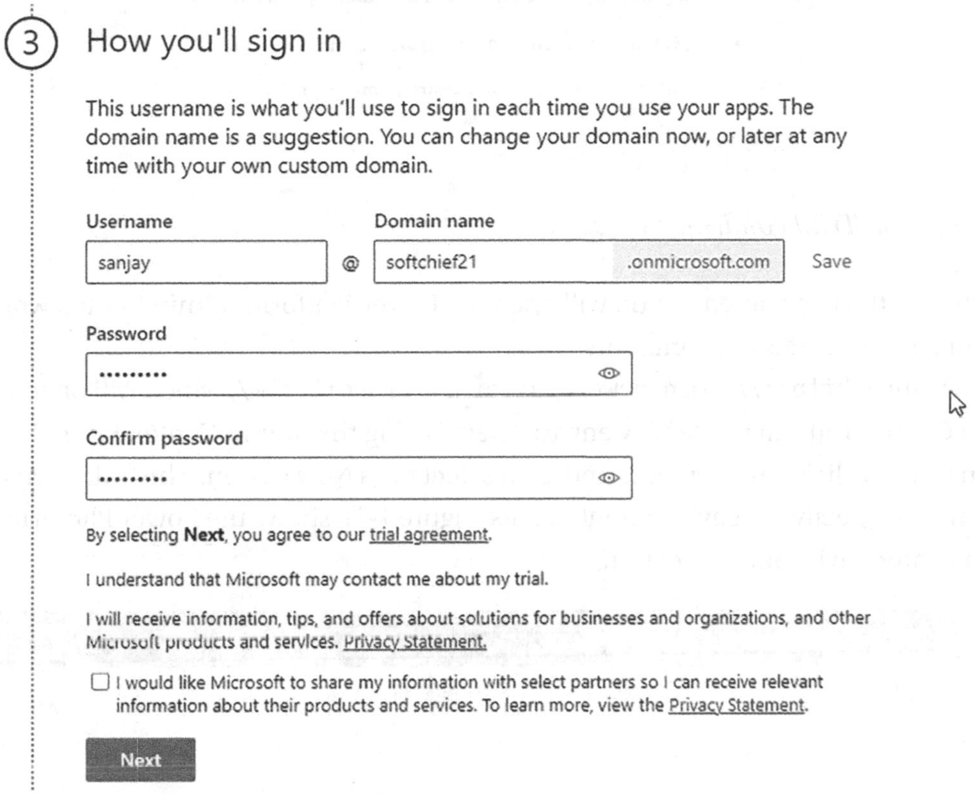

Figure 1-14. *Sign-in option in the trial version*

The next screen displays details about your username. Figure 1-15 shows this trial confirmation screen.

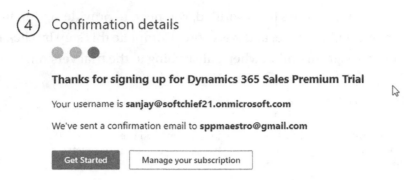

Figure 1-15. *Trial confirmation screen*

Clicking the Get Started option will open the Power Platform Admin Center, where you can configure new environments.

Navigate to `https://admin.powerplatform.microsoft.com/`, which will open the Admin Center. You can create new environments using the Admin Center. From the Admin Center, click Environments and then select the +New button. This will open the side panel to specify the environment details. Figure 1-16 shows the Power Platform admin center environment creation.

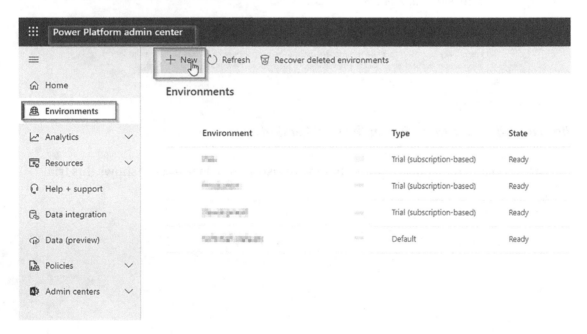

Figure 1-16. *Power Platform Admin Center environment creation*

Now you can create a new environment of the trial (subscription-based) type. In the last screen provided, you will find a side panel where you provide the environment details. If the popup is not showing, click the +New button on the environment list screen to open it. In the side popup screen, add the name of the environment (Development), set the Type to Trial (subscription-based), and set the Region to United States, which is the default. (You can choose your own region instead.) Now click Next. Figure 1-17 shows this environment-creation process.

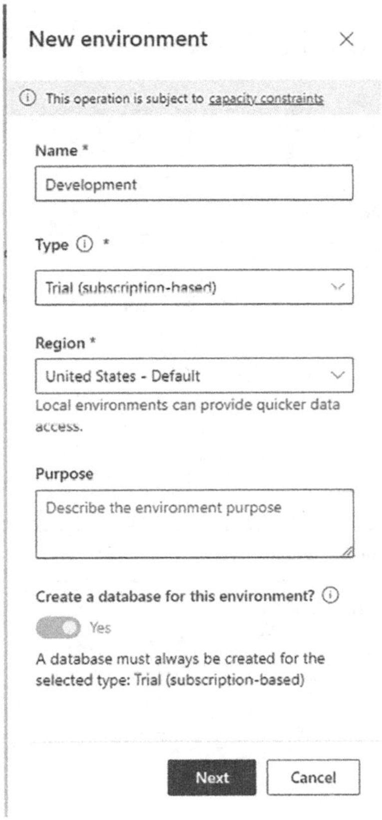

Figure 1-17. *Environment-creation process*

In the Next screen, choose a language. The default is English. If you want to use local languages for the user interface, choose Options from the Language dropdown. Choose a unique URL for the environment by using a custom domain.

After you provide a custom domain, it will appear like so:

```
<Custom Domain>.crm.dynamics.com
```

The custom domain will be automatically changed or selected per the region selected during the signup process. You can read the related information from Microsoft at `https://docs.microsoft.com/en-us/power-platform/admin/new-datacenter-regions`.

Next, choose the base currency your business uses. For example, you can choose USD if you are dealing with customers from the United States. Figure 1-18 shows the Add Database screen.

Figure 1-18. *Add Database screen*

As this book focuses on Dynamics 365 apps, keep the Enable Dynamics 365 Apps option enabled and, from the Automatically Deploy These Apps option, choose All Enterprise Applications. This option will automatically deploy all Dynamics 365 CE/CRM apps to your environment. You can also select the apps you want instead of selecting all enterprise applications. Figure 1-19 shows the Enable Dynamics 365 Apps screen.

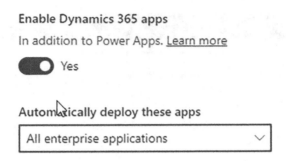

Figure 1-19. *Enable Dynamics 365 Apps*

If you want to restrict the environment to a security group only, you can choose the Security Group option.

When an environment is created with a Dataverse database or a Dataverse database is added to an existing environment, all users in the organization are automatically added to the environment unless a security group is selected as an access filter.

Automatically adding users to an environment takes time, especially if your organization is large and access to the environment isn't restricted to a security group. As a best practice, restrict access to your environment to a specific set of users by associating your environment to a security group. For more information, see the Microsoft site at `https://docs.microsoft.com/en-us/power-platform/admin/control-user-access`. Figure 1-20 shows the Security Group option.

Security group

Restrict environment access to people in this security group. Otherwise, everyone can access. Learn more

+ Select

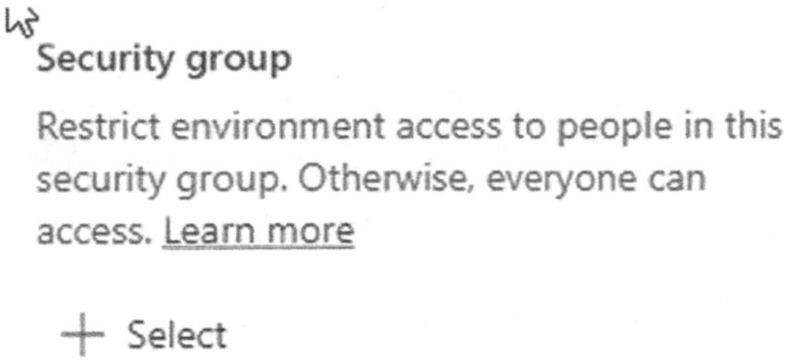

Figure 1-20. *Security Group option*

After completing these steps, click Save. The environment will be ready after a couple of seconds. You can see the status of the environment in the list, as shown in Figure 1-21.

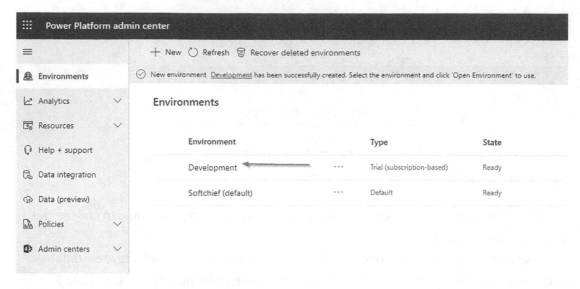

Figure 1-21. *The environment list*

Now you are ready to work on the environment. Go to a new tab on your browser and visit office.com. The credential will be validated automatically and you will see all your apps available on your home screen. Figure 1-22 shows all the Office apps.

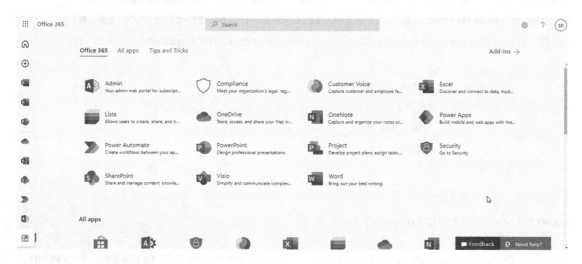

Figure 1-22. *Office apps*

Click the Power Apps icon to open the Power Apps screen. If it displays a popup, click Skip. In the top-right corner, you will see the Environment list. Choose your new environment. Figure 1-23 shows the environment switcher.

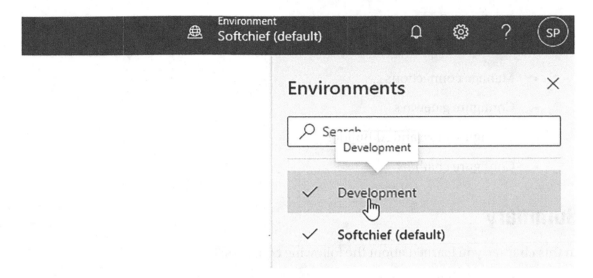

Figure 1-23. *The environment switcher*

After choosing the correct environment, you can create Power Apps, flows, chatbots, AI Builders, solutions, and more. Figure 1-24 shows the Power Apps home page.

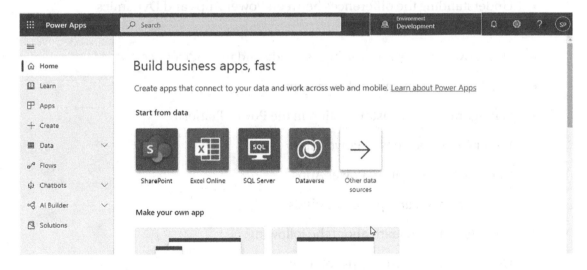

Figure 1-24. *The Power Apps home page*

Using the Power Apps screen, you can do the following:

- Configure solutions to encapsulate components

- Design Dataverse concepts

- Configure Canvas apps, model-driven apps, and Power Portals

- Configure dataflows

- Manage connections

- Configure gateways

- Configure Flow and AI Builder

- Configure chatbots

Summary

In this chapter, you learned about the following concepts:

- Understanding environments

- Subscribing to the 30-day free trial environment

- Understanding the Power Platform architecture

- Understanding the differences between Power Apps and Dynamics 365 Apps

- How Power Apps supports the less-code and no-code concepts

- The Power Fx concept in Power Apps

- Configurations vs. customization in the Power Platform

- Enhancement scopes in Power Apps

- Integration concepts in Power Apps

- Sample domain and project analysis

In the next chapter, you learn about the following:

- Understanding Power Apps solutions

- Working with table configurations and settings

- Working with columns, data types, calculated fields, and rollup fields

- Auto-number columns in the Dataverse

- Configuring relationships and relationship behaviors

- Working with business rules

- Configuring views for tables

- Table form design and layout

- Chart configuration and dashboard pinning

- Configuring table-specific dashboards

- Understanding alternate keys

- Working with data in the Dataverse

- Business scenarios, use cases, and implementations

CHAPTER 2

Working with Microsoft Dataverse

Microsoft Dataverse is a robust application platform that stores and manages all your business data in a tight security layer. The Dataverse is made up of tables and columns of business data. The Dataverse provides a standard set of Lead, Account, Contact, Opportunity, and Quote tables, which are used in common scenarios such as lead qualification and quote review. You can also configure custom tables to fit your specific business needs. You can use dataflow to import data into your table, by using Power Query with data transformation.

Microsoft Power Platform is made up of Power Apps, Power Automate, Power BI, and Power Virtual Agent, They can be configured to use the data stored in the Dataverse.

In this chapter, you learn about working with Dataverse tables, columns, and solutions. You learn about schema customization and how to configure forms, views, and relationships between tables.

Dynamics 365 and the Dataverse are closely related. Dynamics 365 applications such as sales, marketing, and services also use the Dataverse to store data. This enables you to build apps by using Power Apps and the Dataverse directly against your core business data, which is already used in Dynamics 365, without the need for integration.

Understanding Power Apps Solutions

Solutions are a great way to package configuration items and customization components to distribute to upstream environments. This ensures Application Lifecycle Management (ALM) for solution components in Power Apps. For example, if you want to develop a custom application and have the same application in other environments or if you want to share your app with source configurations, you can package all the components into

© Sanjaya Prakash Pradhan 2022
S. Prakash Pradhan, *Power Platform and Dynamics 365 CE for Absolute Beginners*,
https://doi.org/10.1007/978-1-4842-8600-5_2

a Power Apps solution. Then you can export them from the source environment and import them into the target environment.

Solutions can be exported from one environment and imported into any environment, but you should make sure the required components exist in the target environment. Figure 2-1 shows the solutions components.

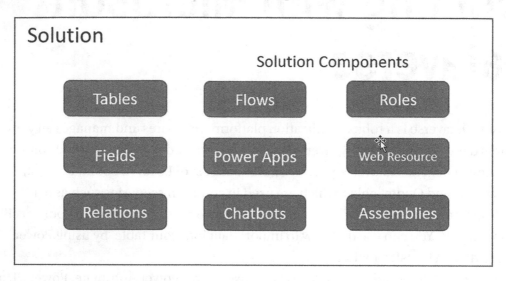

Figure 2-1. *Solution components*

Versions in Solution

Versions are important parts of solutions; they define which features are available in which version. The version format of a solution is comprised of four parts—Major, Minor, Build, and Release. In a general way, when you create a solution for a Major release, you increment the first digit; for Minor changes to an existing Major release, you increment the second digit; to prepare builds for a Minor release, you update the third digit; and for any hot fixes or if there are multiple releases to the same build, you update the last digit. The typical version format is shown in Figure 2-2.

Major	Minor	Build	Release
1	0	0	0

Figure 2-2. *Solution version format*

Create a New Solution

To create a new solution, you have to navigate to make.powerapps.com and provide the credentials. You will be directed to the Power Apps home page. Choose the environment you want to use to create the solution.

Click the Solutions option from the left navigation, which will display all the solutions that are part of the current environment. Now click the +New Solution command, which will open the New Solution Creation side panel. Figure 2-3 shows a solutions list and how to create a new solution.

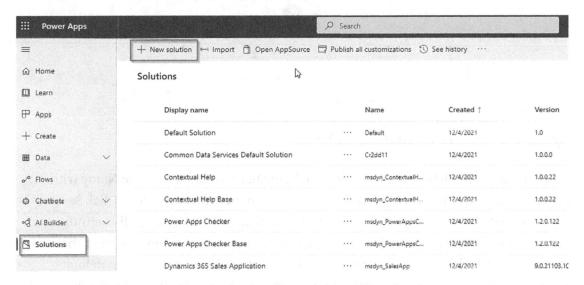

Figure 2-3. *Solutions view and creating a new solution*

Provide a Display name; the Name will be auto-populated. For Publisher, you can choose the default, but this example creates a new publisher by clicking the +New Publisher option. Figure 2-4 shows the solution information.

Figure 2-4. Solution details and information

In the New Publisher panel, provide the Publisher Display Name, the Name without a space, a Description, and a prefix that's a maximum of eight characters. Click Save.

Every solution requires a publisher to be associated with it. The publisher indicates who developed the app. For this reason, you should create a solution publisher that is meaningful and reflects the ownership of the solution. You can select the default publisher, but it is recommended that you create your own publisher to keep the components consistent in the app. Refer to the Microsoft site to understand the publisher creation process at `https://docs.microsoft.com/en-us/power-apps/maker/data-platform/create-solution#create-a-solution-publisher`. Figure 2-5 shows the publisher creation panel.

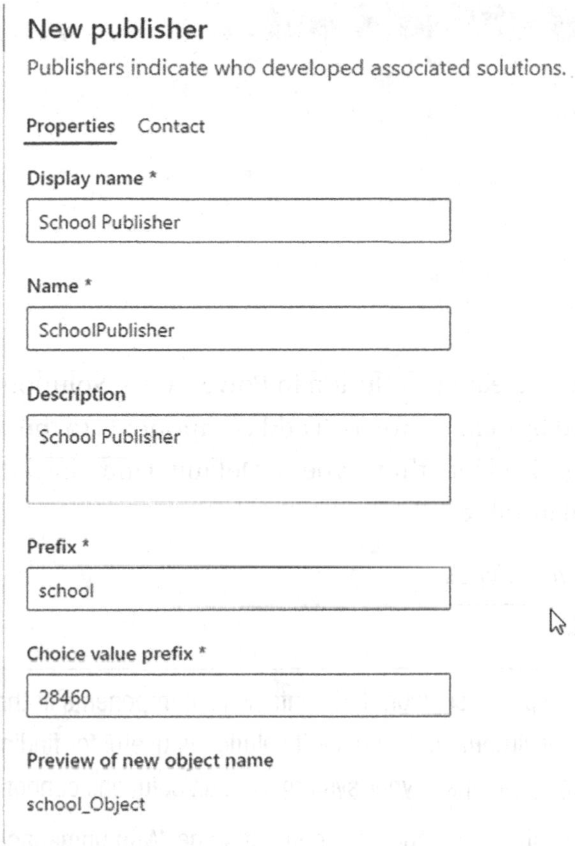

New publisher

Publishers indicate who developed associated solutions.

Properties   Contact

Display name *

> School Publisher

Name *

> SchoolPublisher

Description

> School Publisher

Prefix *

> school

Choice value prefix *

> 28460

Preview of new object name

school_Object

Figure 2-5. *The publisher creation panel*

In the Contact tab of the Publisher panel, you can add the contact information of the owner or developer. The prefix is useful to generate the component's unique name. For example, if you add a table called Student to the solution with this publisher, then the unique name of the component will be school_Student. Once the publisher is saved, you can choose the publisher from the Select a Publisher dropdown. Keep the initial version set to 1.0.0.0. Click Create. Now you will see that the new solution is created and is listed in the Solutions view, as shown in Figure 2-6.

Figure 2-6. *Solution in view*

You have successfully created a solution in Power Apps. Solutions that are freshly created are unmanaged by default. You can add components to the solution now.

Solutions are categorized into three types—Default, Unmanaged, and Managed solution—as explained in Table 2-1.

Table 2-1. *The Solution Types*

Solution Type	Details
Default	This is a special solution that contains all components in the system of the current environment. The default solution is useful for finding all the components and configurations in your system. Default solutions cannot be exported.
Unmanaged	Solutions that are in the development stage. With unmanaged solutions, you can add, remove, and delete components.
Managed	When an unmanaged solution is completed with the development activities and is ready for production or distribution, you can export the unmanaged solution as a managed solution by specifying the managed properties. You cannot edit components inside managed solutions unless the managed property is enabled. It is recommended that export solutions are always managed.

Managed Properties

Managed properties can be used to control which of your managed solution components are customizable in a managed solution. To set a managed property, open the unmanaged solution and, from the list of the components, click the three vertical dots next to the component and choose Managed Properties. Figure 2-7 shows the Managed Properties option.

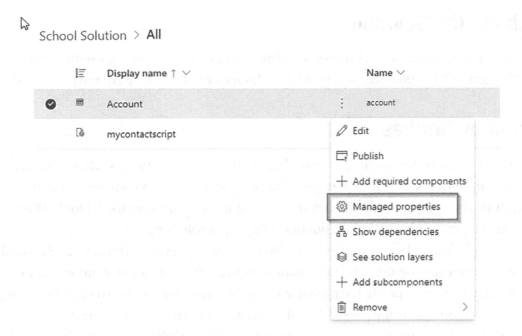

Figure 2-7. *The Managed Properties option*

The Managed Properties panel will open, where you can enable/disable the customization options. Remember that the properties will take effect only after the component is exported and imported as part of the managed solution. Figure 2-8 shows the Managed Properties option list.

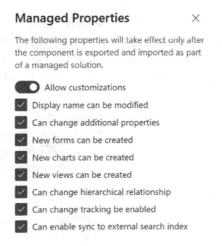

Figure 2-8. *The Managed Properties option lists*

Publish the Solution

Every time you update a solution component, you need to publish the solution so that the changes will be reflected; otherwise, the changes will be just saved, not published.

Solution Patches

A solution patch contains changes or updates to the parent solution, such as adding or editing components. You are not required to add parent solution components to the patch unless you want to edit the component. Solution patches are useful for hotfixes and small changes to existing components of a parent solution.

Solution patches let you choose a new build or release version. You cannot change the Major or Minor version of the parent solution. Figure 2-9 shows some solution patches.

When you clone a patch, the parent solution becomes read-only. You cannot change any components inside the parent directly; rather, you have to work on the patches. Once you are ready for a major upgrade, you can create a clone of the parent solution, which will roll up all patches and create a new major version of the previous parent solution with all the components.

You can use a patch when you want to move a small number of solution component changes from the source to the target environment that's part of the parent solution. Patches are also used when you want to delete a component from the target environment.

Parent Solution

Major	Minor	Build	Release
1	0	0	0

Patch - 1

Major	Minor	Build	Release
1	0	1	0

Patch - 2

Major	Minor	Build	Release
1	0	1	1

Patch - 3

Major	Minor	Build	Release
1	0	2	1

Figure 2-9. *Solution patches*

Cloning Solutions

When you clone an unmanaged solution, the original solution and all the patches of the solution are rolled up into a newly created version of the original solution. After you clone, the new solution version contains the original entities plus any components or tables that were added in the patch.

Solution cloning can be used to create a Major or Minor version of an existing solution. Figure 2-10 shows a solution that initially has three patches. When it was cloned, all the patches with the parent solution rolled up to create a new solution clone with a new Major version. After the clone, there is a patch for the newly created, cloned solution. This example also cloned the clone, which creates a new, cloned solution by rolling up all the previous patches and parent solutions.

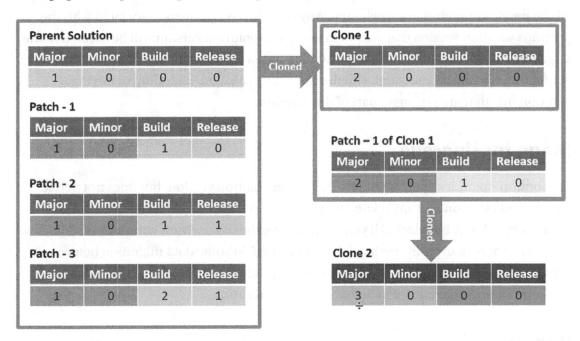

Figure 2-10. *Patch deployment diagram*

Export and Import Solutions

Solutions can be exported from a source environment as a managed or unmanaged solution and imported into a target environment. When you import a managed solution into a target environment where an older version of the same solution is imported, you have more options to choose when importing the managed solution.

As a best practice, you should export solutions as managed solutions so that when you import them, they can be rolled back. Unmanaged solutions cannot be rolled back.

Managed solutions are imported and stacked in multiple layers in the target environment. If you uninstall a managed solution, the changes will affect the solution below the uninstalled layer. Read more about solution layers at `https://docs.microsoft.com/en-us/power-apps/maker/data-platform/solution-layers`.

You can choose the Upgrade, Stage for Upgrade, and Update options when importing managed solutions.

Upgrade

Upgrade is the default option. It upgrades your solution to the latest version and rolls up all the previous patches in a single step. Any solution components associated with the previous solution version that are not in the newer solution version will be deleted in the target environment. This is the recommended option, as it will ensure that your resulting configuration state is consistent with the importing solution, including removing components that are no longer part of the solution.

Stage for Upgrade

This option upgrades your solution to the higher solution version, but does not delete the previous version and any related patches until you apply a solution upgrade. This option should only be selected if you want to have the old and new solutions installed in the system concurrently, perhaps so that you can do some data migration before you complete the solution upgrade. Applying the upgrade will delete the old solution and any components that are not included in the new solution.

Update

This option replaces your solution with the latest version. Components that are not in the newer solution won't be deleted and will remain in the system. This option is not recommended, as your destination environment will differ in configuration from your source environment, which could cause issues that are difficult to reproduce and diagnose. When updating, you can choose from these options:

- **Maintain customizations (recommended):** Selecting this option will maintain any unmanaged customizations performed on components but also implies that some of the updates included in this solution will not take effect.

- **Overwrite customizations:** Selecting this option overwrites any unmanaged customizations previously performed on components included in this solution. All updates included in this solution will take effect. Figure 2-11 shows the options while importing an existing managed solution.

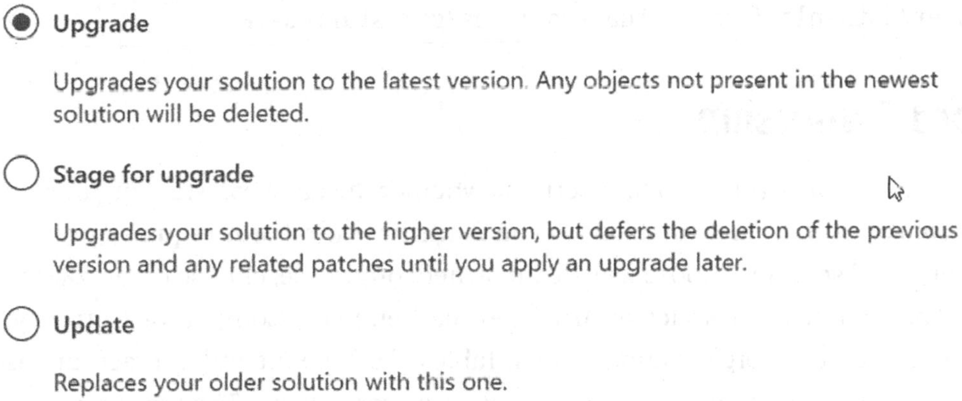

◉ Upgrade

Upgrades your solution to the latest version. Any objects not present in the newest solution will be deleted.

○ Stage for upgrade

Upgrades your solution to the higher version, but defers the deletion of the previous version and any related patches until you apply an upgrade later.

○ Update

Replaces your older solution with this one.

Figure 2-11. *Upgrading solution options*

Working with Table Configurations and Settings

In the previous section, you learned how to create solutions in Power Apps. In this section, you see how to configure tables in the Dataverse. In the Dataverse, tables are used to store data. For example, you can create a table to store student data.

Table Types

Tables are classified into three categories—Standard, Activity, and Virtual. Standard tables are best when you want to store transactional or master data. For example, Student, Professor, Time Sheet, Loans and so on, can be considered standard tables. Activity tables represent activities. For example, Letter, Email, Appointment, Booking, and so on. They require a timestamp to complete the activity. All activity type tables have date and time related columns, such as Due Date, Start Time, End Time, and so on.

Virtual tables are special tables that you can create for integration purposes. They are also known as virtual entities and they enable the integration of data residing in external systems by seamlessly representing that data as tables in the Microsoft Dataverse, without replicating the data and often without custom coding. Virtual tables replace previous client-side and server-side approaches to integrating external data. These old approaches required customized code and suffered from numerous limitations, including imperfect integration, data duplication, and extensive commitment of development resources. In addition, for administrators and system customizers, the use of virtual tables greatly simplifies administration and configuration. Read more about virtual tables from Microsoft at `https://docs.microsoft.com/en-us/power-apps/developer/data-platform/virtual-entities/get-started-ve`.

Record Ownership

While creating tables, you need to determine whether the table will store organization owned data or user/team owned data. If you think that the records require a proper user/team level security, choose user/team owned; otherwise, choose organization owned. For example, tables such as Article, Article Template, Competitor, Currency, and Web Resource are organization owned. Tables like Account and Contacts are user/team owned because these records are owned by a user or team. They're connected to a business unit and have specific security roles for the business unit. Therefore, these entities participate in role-based security.

Table Configurations

Tables are used to model and manage business data. When you develop an app, you can use standard tables, custom tables, or both. The Dataverse provides standard tables by default. These are designed, in accordance with best practices, to capture the most common concepts and scenarios in an organization. While configuring tables you can enable/disable many features, such as apply duplicate detection rules and enable them to create activity.

A table defines information that you want to track in the form of records, which typically include properties such as company name, location, products, email, and phone.

Types of Tables

Tables appear in Power Apps as one of three different types, which indicate how the table came into the environment, whether the table is managed or unmanaged, and whether it can be customized.

- **Standard**: Several standard tables, also known as out-of-box tables, are included with the Dataverse environment. Account, business unit, contact, task, and user tables are examples of standard tables in the Dataverse. Most of the standard tables included with the Dataverse can be customized. Tables that are imported as part of a managed solution and set as customizable also appear as standard tables. Any user with appropriate privileges can customize these tables, where the table property has customizable set to true.

- **Managed**: Tables that aren't customizable and have been imported into the environment as part of a managed solution.

- **Custom**: Unmanaged tables that are either imported from an unmanaged solution or are new tables created directly in the Dataverse environment. Any user with appropriate privileges can fully customize these tables.

Create a New Table

You can now create a new table to store student information. Open the solution you created in the previous section. Choose the +New option and then choose Table. Figure 2-12 shows how to add a table inside a solution.

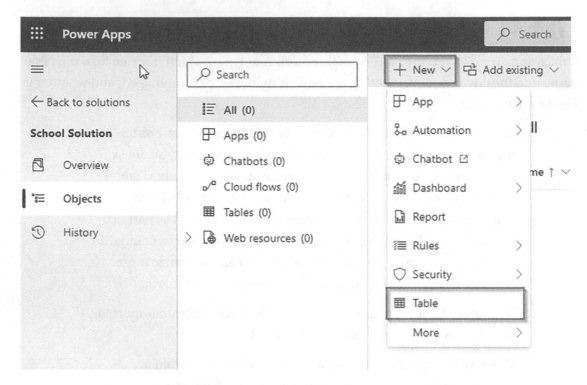

Figure 2-12. *Add a new table*

The new table creation side panel will open, where you can provide table information. This chapter builds a school management system, so you see how to design the tables based on these requirements.

Requirements

This school management system must allow users to enter student information such as roll number (auto-number), name, address, father's name, mobile, email, and qualification. The system should capture course information and the users should be able to record students joined for courses. The app must create payment information with term facility and payment details.

Add a new table with Display Name set to Student (the plural name is automatically populated as Students). Provide a description for the table, such as "Stores student information". If you want to enable features, click the Advanced options. Choose Type as Standard and Record Ownership as User/Team.

Every component has three names—Display Name (to display on the screen), Schema Name (used for web API calls client-side), and Logical Name (used in server-side code calls). Figure 2-13 shows the table configuration.

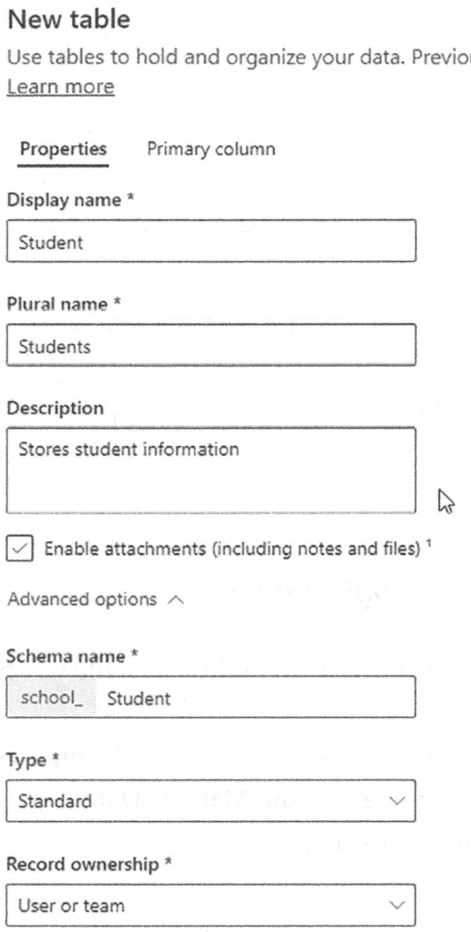

Figure 2-13. *Table configuration*

In this case, the Student table has three names—Display Name: Student, Schema Name: school_Student, and Logical Name: school_student.

In the Primary column section, define the Display Name, which will be treated as the default column to identify the record. For the Student table, the Name will identify the student name. Figure 2-14 shows the primary field configuration of this table.

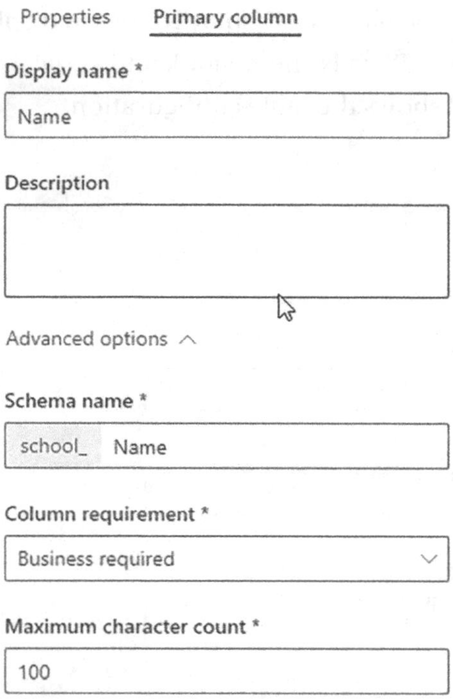

Figure 2-14. *Primary field of table configuration*

After providing these details, save the Student table. The table will be listed under the component list of the solution.

For any table, you can configure Columns, Relationships, Business Rules, Views, Forms, Dashboards, Charts, Keys, Commands, and Manage Data. You learn more about these options in upcoming sections of this chapter.

Working with Columns, Datatypes, Calculated Fields, and Rollup Fields

Click the table to open the table component to add or edit the columns. Columns are fields that store information about the student, such as roll number (auto-number), name, address, father's name, mobile, email, and qualifications.

System Columns vs. Custom Columns

Every time you create a new table, the system creates system columns that are used by the system, such as createdon, modifiedon, and so on. These field values are updated by the system. Figure 2-15 shows system columns that are automatically created when you create a standard table.

School Solution > Tables > **Student**

Columns   Relationships   Business rules   Views   Forms   Dashboards   Charts   Keys   Commands   Data

Display name ∨		Name ∨	Data type ∨	Type ↑ ∨	Custom...
Name Primary Name Column	···	school_name	🔤 Text	Custom	✓
Created By	···	createdby	🔍 Lookup	Standard	✓
Status Reason	···	statuscode	☰ Choice	Standard	✓
Status	···	statecode	☰ Choice	Standard	✓
Owning Team	···	owningteam	🔍 Lookup	Standard	✓
Modified By (Delegate)	···	modifiedonbehalfby	🔍 Lookup	Standard	✓
Created By (Delegate)	···	createdonbehalfby	🔍 Lookup	Standard	✓
Record Created On	···	overriddencreatedon	📅 Date Only	Standard	✓
Import Sequence Number	···	importsequencenumber	🔢 Whole Number	Standard	✓
Owner	···	ownerid	👤 Owner	Standard	✓
Time Zone Rule Version Number	···	timezoneruleversionnumber	🔢 Whole Number	Standard	
Student	···	school_studentid	⬚ Unique Identifier	Standard	✓
Modified On	···	modifiedon	📅 Date and Time	Standard	✓
Created On	···	createdon	📅 Date and Time	Standard	✓
Owning User	···	owninguser	🔍 Lookup	Standard	✓
Version Number	···	versionnumber	🔢 Big Integer	Standard	
Owning Business Unit	···	owningbusinessunit	🔍 Lookup	Standard	✓
Modified By	···	modifiedby	🔍 Lookup	Standard	✓
UTC Conversion Time Zone Code	···	utcconversiontimezonecode	🔢 Whole Number	Standard	

Figure 2-15. *System columns*

You can add custom columns as per your business needs. The custom fields can be identified by their Name, which is specified with the publisher prefix. The primary key is represented as `<prefix>_<tablename>id`, which is a 32-bit digit called a unique identifier. It behaves as a primary key of records.

Datatypes

Datatypes define the type of value the column will hold. For example, if you want to store the name of a person, you can use a single line of text as the datatype. Figure 2-16 shows the datatypes of columns in the Dataverse.

🔤 Text	
Text	Stores alphanumeric single line values
Text Area	Stores alphanumeric text area values
Email	Stores Email Address
URL	Stores Websites information
Ticker Symbol	Stores Ticker Symbol
Phone	Stores Phone Number value
Autonumber	Stores Auto Number value
🔢 Whole Number	
Whole Number	Stores Whole Number
Duration	Stores Durations as WHole Number
Timezone	Stores Timezone
Language	Stores Language Information
📅 Date Time	
Date and Time	Stores Date with time value
Date Only	Stores Date only
≡ Choice	Stores list of item selected one at a time
≡ Choices	Stores multi select item
💷 Currency	Stores monetary value
👤 Customer	Stores reference to Account, Contact
x_1 Decimal Number	Stores decimal number
📄 File	used for file upload
⬤ Floating Point Number	used for floating point number
🖼 Image	used for uploading image
🔳 Lookup	used to reference to another table
🗒 Multiline Text	used to store multiline text
≡ Yes/No	used to boolean value

Figure 2-16. *Column datatypes*

Calculated Fields

Calculated fields are the fields for which values can be automatically calculated using conditions and formula in design time. These values will be automatically assigned to the field once certain conditions are satisfied. For example, if you want to store the next renewal date of a student automatically after the student is created, you can use the Feature Calculated field to auto-calculate the renewal due date and store that value. You don't have to write any custom code,

Read more about calculated columns and their configurations at `https://docs.microsoft.com/en-us/power-apps/maker/data-platform/define-calculated-fields`.

Rollup Fields

A rollup field contains an aggregate value that's computed over the records related to a specific record, such as unpaid payments. You can also aggregate data from activities directly related to a record, such as emails and appointments, and activities indirectly related to a record via the Activity Party entity. In more complex scenarios, you can aggregate data over a hierarchy of records. As an administrator or customizer, you can define rollup fields by using the feature, all without needing a developer to write code.

Read more about rollup fields and their configuration at `https://docs.microsoft.com/en-us/power-apps/maker/data-platform/define-rollup-fields`.

Configure the following columns for the Student table with the corresponding datatypes listed in the table.

Column Name	Datatype
Address	Multiline text
Father Name	Text
Mobile	Phone
Email	Email
Gender	Choice (Male, Female, Other)
Qualification	Choices (MCA, MBA)

Click the +Add Column option to create these columns. Set the Required option to Optional, Required, or Business Recommended, as needed. If the business need is to require a mobile number, choose Required here. If a field value is not mandatory, it can be defined as Business Recommended. That way, a plus sign appears next to the field, indicating it's recommended. The system will not restrict record creation if you leave the field blank.

To add the Choice datatype field, you need to add items to choose the field by selecting the New Choice option. Every choice field has a Text value to display and a Value option to be used internally. You can change them if you want.

Read more about the Choice field configuration at `https://docs.microsoft.com/en-us/learn/modules/working-with-option-sets/3-exercise`.

Figure 2-17 shows how to add columns. Repeat this step to add all the new columns and finally save the table.

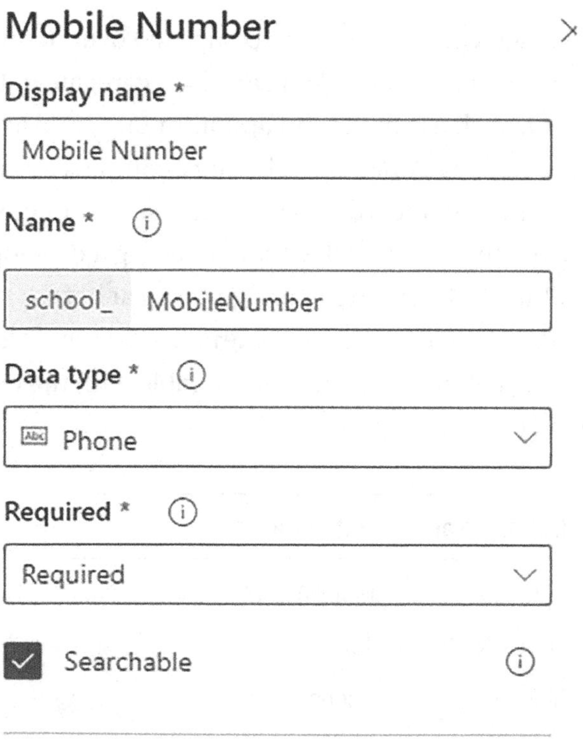

Mobile Number

Display name *

Mobile Number

Name * ⓘ

school_   MobileNumber

Data type * ⓘ

🔤 Phone ⌄

Required * ⓘ

Required ⌄

☑ Searchable   ⓘ

Figure 2-17. The Mobile Number column

After adding all the columns, they will be listed in the Columns section of the solution component. Figure 2-18 shows the custom columns in the Student table.

Student	...	school_studentid	Unique Identi...	Standard	✓	Required	✓
Qualification	...	school_qualification	Choices	Custom	✓	Optional	✓
Name Primary Name Column	...	school_name	Text	Custom	✓	Recommen...	
Mobile Number	...	school_mobilenumber	Phone	Custom	✓	Required	
Gender	...	school_gender	Choice	Custom	✓	Optional	
Email	...	school_email	Email	Custom	✓	Optional	✓
Address	...	school_address	Multiline Text	Custom	✓	Optional	✓

Figure 2-18. *Custom columns*

Auto-Number Columns in the Dataverse

The auto-number field is a special type of datatype that's very useful to generate sequential numbers without writing code. For example, you can generate a roll number for students in a sequential format, such as STD-0001, STD-0002, and so on. You can use a string prefixed number, a date prefixed number, or a custom prefix, depending on your needs. Add a new column with a datatype of Auto-Number and define the pattern as shown in Figure 2-19.

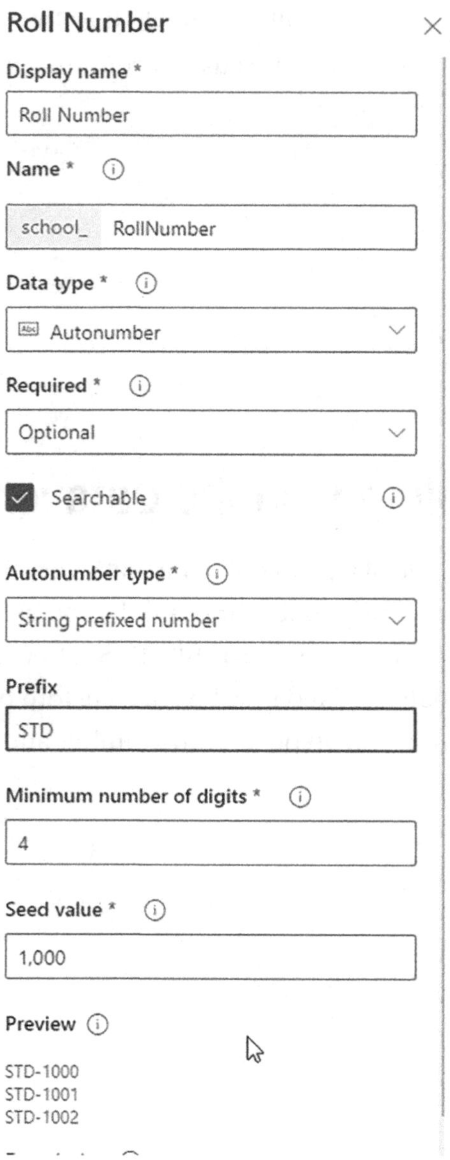

Roll Number   ✕

Display name *

| Roll Number |

Name *   ⓘ

| school_   RollNumber |

Data type *   ⓘ

| ▣ Autonumber   ∨ |

Required *   ⓘ

| Optional   ∨ |

| ✓ | Searchable   ⓘ

Autonumber type *   ⓘ

| String prefixed number   ∨ |

Prefix

| STD |

Minimum number of digits *   ⓘ

| 4 |

Seed value *   ⓘ

| 1,000 |

Preview ⓘ

STD-1000
STD-1001
STD-1002

Figure 2-19. *Roll Number column auto-number*

Set Prefix to STD, Minimum Digits to 4, and Seed Value to 1000. The preview will display as STD-1000, STD-10001, and so on.

Save the column after configuration and then save the table. Now, whenever you create a student record, the roll number will be automatically generated.

Configuring Relationships and Relationship Behaviors

Relationships in the Dataverse are between two tables. For example, a student might have multiple payments, and one student can register for multiple courses. So, for such scenarios, you can associate two tables with a relationship.

There are three types of relationships in Power Apps—one to many (1:N), many to one (N:1), and many to many (N:N). The 1 is the parent and the N is the child.

Configure a new table called Student Payment with Payment ID, Amount, and Terms columns and build a 1:N relationship between Student and Student Payment.

Navigate to the solution and add a new table as you created the Student table. Add the following columns.

Column Name	Datatype
Payment ID	Auto Number
Amount	Currency
Term	Choice (1, 2, 3)

After the columns are added, the solution component for the Payment table will look like Figure 2-20.

Amount	···	school_amount
Amount (Base)	···	school_amount_base
Name Primary Name Column	···	school_name
Student Payment	···	school_studentpaymentid
Term	···	school_term

Figure 2-20. *Payment table columns*

Now add a relationship to the Student Payment table. The following diagram defines the relationship between Student and Student Payment.

Students	
Roll Number	Auto-Number
Full Name	Single Line Text
Address	Multi Line Text
Father Name	Single Line Text
Mobile	Phone
Email	Email
Qualification	Choices
Gender	Choice

Student Payments	
Payment ID	Auto-Number
Student	Lookup
Amount	Money
Terms	Choice

1   N

Navigate to the solution, open the Student Payment table, and select Relationship. Choose many-to-one. Figure 2-21 shows how to add a many-to-one relationship.

Figure 2-21. *The many-to-one relationship*

The relationship configuration panel will open. Select the Student as Related (One) option. A new lookup field will be created in the Student Payment table because of this relationship. Figure 2-22 shows the setup of the many-to-one relationship.

Many-to-one   ✕

Choose the **Related table** to which to create your relationship lookup. Learn more

Current (Many)   **Related (One)**

Table *   Table *

| Student Payment | * — 1 | Student ⌄ |

Lookup column display name *

| Student |

Lookup column name *

| school_   Student |

Figure 2-22. *The many-to-one relationship setup*

For every many-to-one relationship, a new lookup field will be created in the table, which represents the many; the lookup points to the table record, which represents the 1.

In this case, Student Payment represents the many, so a new lookup column is created called school_Student in the Student Payment table, which holds the student record.

Relationship Behavior

Relationship behavior defines how the parent records behave when you perform an operation such as delete, assign, share, and so on, on their child records.

There are three types of relationship behavior, as explained in the following table.

Type of Behavior	Datatype
Referential	Referential behavior has two actions:
	Delete - Remove Link: You can delete a parent record and the related child records remain in the system. The lookup field that holds the parent record association will be blank.
	Delete - Restrict: Any related records can be navigated to. Actions taken on the parent record will not be applied to the child record, but the parent record cannot be deleted while the child record exists.

(continued)

Type of Behavior	Datatype
Parental	Any action taken on a record of the parent table is also taken on the related child table records.
Custom	Custom behavior for each possible action can be selected.
	You can define custom cascade behavior for operations such as Share, Assign, Un-share, Reparent, or Delete.
	Cascade All: Any action taken on a record of the parent table is also cascaded to the related child table records.
	Cascade Active: Any action taken on a record of the parent table is cascaded to the related active child table records.
	Cascade User-Owned: Any action taken on a record of the parent table is cascaded to the related child table records owned by the current, logged in user.
	Cascade None: Actions taken on a record of the parent table will not cascade to the related child table records.

For the current scenario, use the Referential relationship behavior and the Restrict Delete operation.

This way, you can configure the relationship behavior as one-to-many or many-to-one only. For a many-to-many relationship, this type of behavior is not applicable.

Design the other tables with the relationships shown in Figure 2-23, as per the datatype. You can keep the relationship behavior for other relationship set to Referential and the Delete operation set to Restrict Delete. Figure 2-23 shows the ER diagram overview.

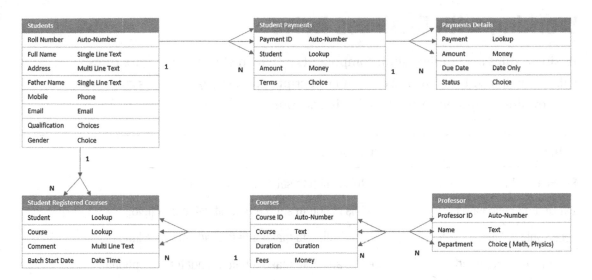

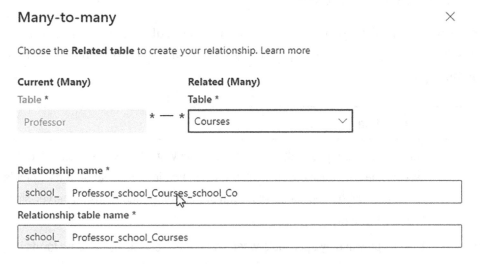

Figure 2-23. *ER diagram overview*

For Professor and Courses, the relationship is many-to-many. Every many-to-many relationship creates an intersect table in the background, which is hidden to the users. You can choose the relationship name and relationship table. Figure 2-24 shows the many-to-many relationship setup.

Figure 2-24. *The many-to-many relationship*

You have now created all the tables and relationships for the school management system.

Working with Business Rules

Business rules are configuration components by which you can configure rules to validate fields without writing custom JavaScript codes. Using business rules, you can use conditions and perform the following actions.

Action	Explanation
Set Field Value	Use this action to set a value of a field.
Set Default Field Value	Use this action to set the default value of a field.
Lock/ Unlock Field	Use this action to make a field read-only or editable.
Set Business Required	Use this action to make a field mandatory or optional.
Set Visible	Use this action to hide or show a form field.
Recommendations	Use this action to recommend some action to the user.
Show Error Message	Use this action to display an error message.

Scope of Business Rules

There are three levels of scope when setting up business rules in your Microsoft Dynamics 365/CRM system. The scope controls when or in which scenario the business rules will be triggered.

Scopes	Explanation
Entity	This scope ensures that the business rule will work on the client-side and the server-side. The business rule will run when you interact with data using table forms and will be applicable when you are creating records using server-side code, like plugins.
All Forms	This scope will only applicable when you create records using table forms i.e., only on the client-side.
Specific Form	This scope will only applicable when you create records using a specific table form, not all forms.

You cannot use datatype fields in business rules. Business rules are table specific. So, to add a business rule, you have to open a table and select the Business Rule option.

Create a Business Rule

Navigate to the Student table and select the Business Rule option. Click the Add Business Rule button, which will open the Business Rule Designer window. Figure 2-25 shows the Business Rule Designer window, with options like Name, Description, Rule Canvas, Conditions, Actions, and Scope.

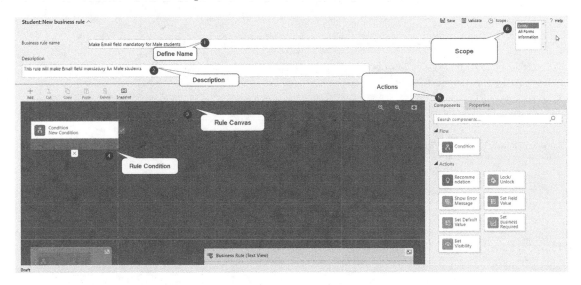

Figure 2-25. *The Business Rule Designer*

Business Requirement: Make the email field mandatory for all mail students.

Provide a Name, Description, and Scope as Entity and then click the condition box on the rule canvas to enable the property window.

In the property panel, choose Display Name for Condition and Entity as Student. In Rule 1, choose Source as Entity, Field as Gender, Operator as Equals, and Type as Value. In the Value field, select Male, as we will run the rule for male students only. Click Apply. Figure 2-26 shows the setup.

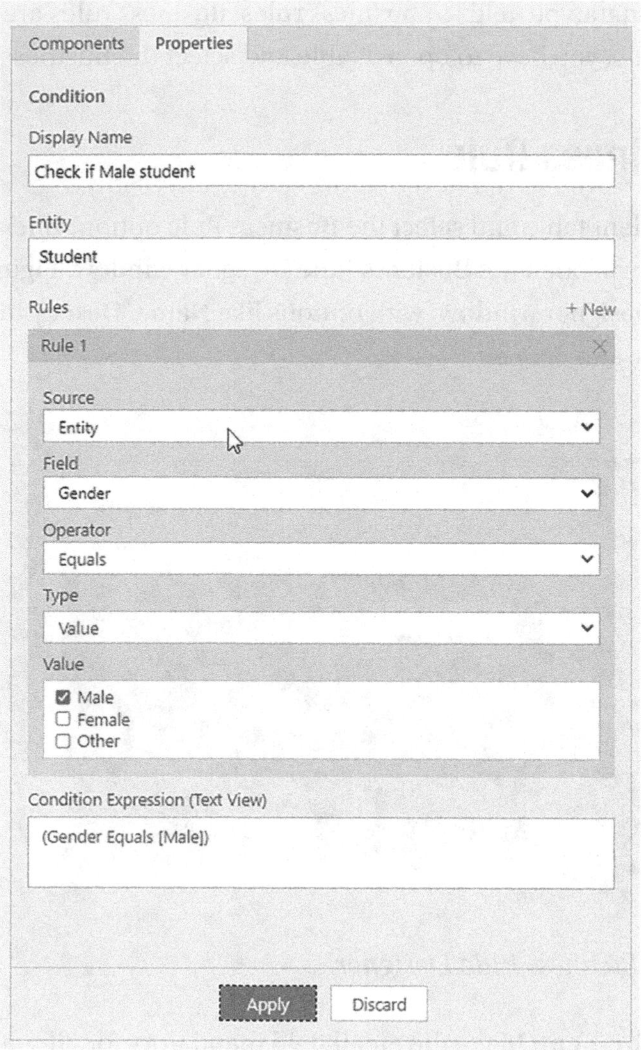

Figure 2-26. *The business rule condition setup*

Click the Components tab to drag the Set Business Required component and then tick part of the condition box. Configure the Display Name, Field as Email, and Status as Business Required properties. Apply these changes. Figure 2-27 shows the components attached to the condition.

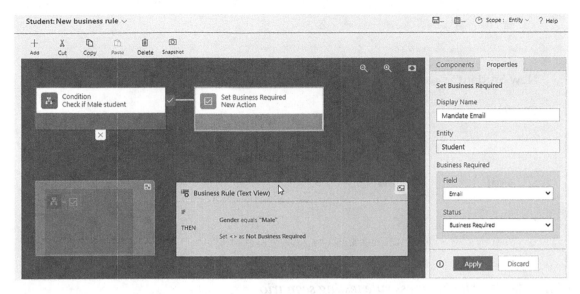

Figure 2-27. *The business rule components*

In the negation part, drag the same Set Business Required component and choose Not Business Required for the status. Click Apply. Figure 2-28 shows actions on the positive and negative conditions.

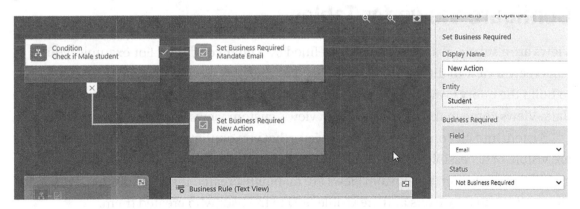

Figure 2-28. *The business rule components using the negation branch*

Validate, save, and then activate the business rule to test this in action. Navigate to the solution and open the Student table. Choose the Data tab and click Add Record. This will open a student main form, where you can test the rule. In the form, provide the name of the student and choose male for gender. The email field will show an asterisk symbol, meaning the field is mandatory. Figure 2-29 shows the business rule testing scenario.

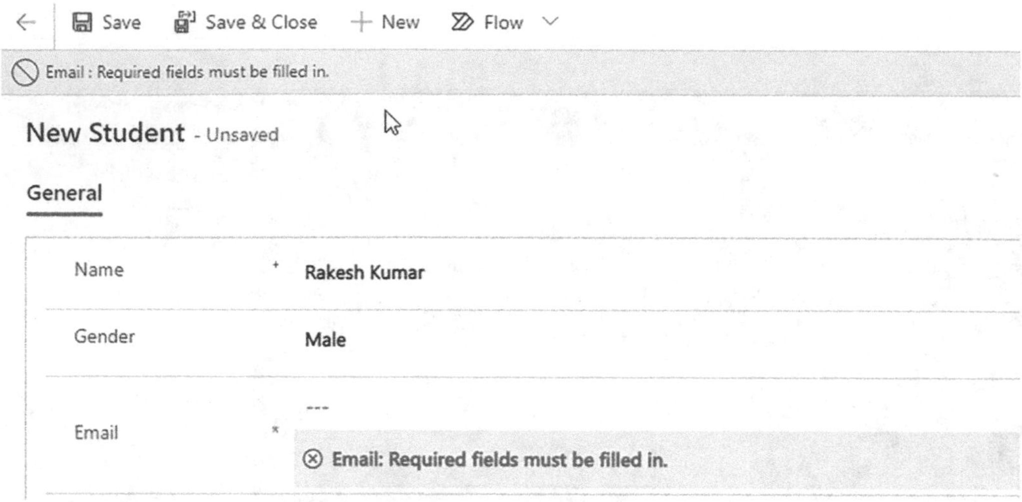

Figure 2-29. *The business rule testing scenario*

Now you can configure multiple business rules for tables, based on your business needs. Make sure to choose the correct scope for these business rules.

Configure Views for Tables

Views are a subset of a table's records, defined by a filter condition. For example, you can create a view to display students joined this year as a view so that you do not need to build the query every time to fetch data. Instead, you can select the view and get the data. Views come in three types—system views, custom views, and user/personal views.

System and custom views are those views that you configure inside a solution; they are visible or accessible to any user in the organization. System views are by default created by a solution, but custom views are manually created inside a solution. Personal views are created by users and are visible only to the user who created them.

System views cannot be shared because they are available to all users. Personal views can be shared by users, as they are created by specific users. You can use Advance Find to create personal or user views.

There are different types of system views available in the system for a table. You can also create your own custom view for a table. System views are explained in the following table.

System View	Explanation
Active View	This view displays active records.
Inactive View	This view displays inactive records.
Quick Find Active View	This view displays records in the search option.
Advanced View	When you search records in Advanced Find, this view is used.
Associated View	This view is responsible for displaying records in a related table view.
Lookup View	This view is used when you search records in a lookup control.

For the Student table, the views in Figure 2-30 are created. You can also create custom views for any table inside a solution, which will be available to any user. Figure 2-30 shows the different views available in the Dataverse tables.

Columns	Relationships	Business rules	Views	Forms	Dashboards	Charts	Keys	Commands

Name ↑ ∨		View type ∨	Status ∨	Type ∨
Active Students	···	Public View Default	Active	Standard
Inactive Students	···	Public View	Active	Standard
Quick Find Active Students	···	Quick Find View Default	Active	Standard
Student Advanced Find View	···	Advanced Find View Default	Active	Standard
Student Associated View	···	Associated View Default	Active	Standard
Student Lookup View	···	Lookup View Default	Active	Standard

Figure 2-30. *The views list*

Create a Custom View

Create a custom view to display only male students. For this requirement, you simply navigate to the solution and open the Student table, select Views, and then click Add View.

Provide a name for the view with a description. Then click Create. Figure 2-31 shows how to create a view.

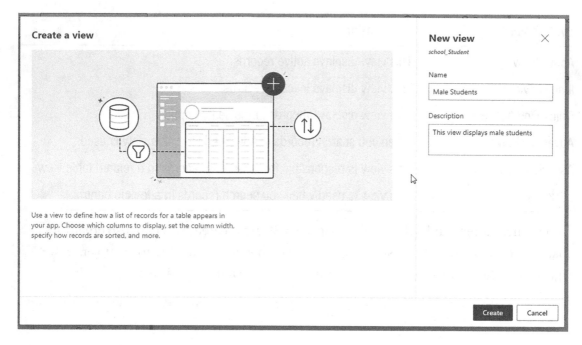

Figure 2-31. *The views list*

This will open the View Designer, where you can drag-and-drop columns and add filters. Add Roll Number, Name, and Email to the columns list. Figure 2-32 shows the columns to add to this view.

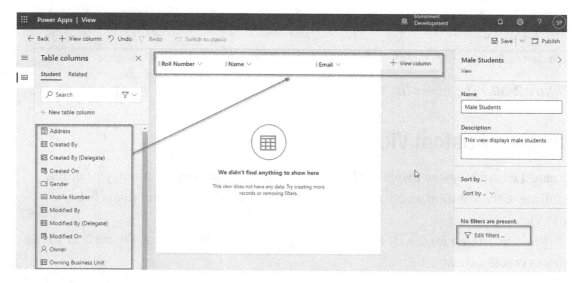

Figure 2-32. *The views columns*

Click the Edit Filters option on the bottom-right side to open the Filter Editor panel. Add a new row and choose male for the gender. Click OK. Figure 2-33 shows the filter condition of these views.

Edit filters

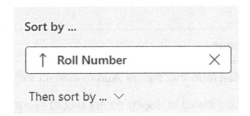

Figure 2-33. The views filter condition

You can also configure sorting on the view by clicking the Sort By option available on the right panel of the View Designer. Figure 2-34 shows how to sort columns to add a view as needed.

Sort by ...

↑ Roll Number   ✕

Then sort by ... ∨

Figure 2-34. Sorting views

Once you have completed these steps, save and publish the view. You have successfully created a custom view. Now you can test it.

Open the table, go to the Data tab, and click the top-right corner view selector. You will see that the Male Students view is available. The view will display all students whose gender is male, sorted by roll number. Figure 2-35 shows the view selector in the Dataverse.

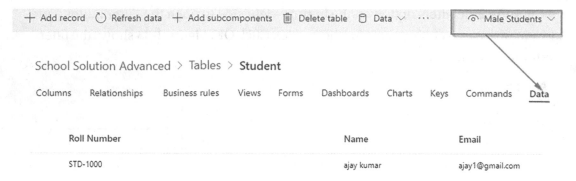

Figure 2-35. *View selector option*

Table Forms Design and Layouts

Forms are user interface elements by which users can interact with datasource. You can use forms to create new records and update existing records.

There are four types of forms in Power Apps. They are explained in the following table.

Form	Explanation
Main Form	The default form that can be used to interact with table records.
Quick View Form	Can be configured to display parent record information inside the child record form.
Quick Create Form	Used to quickly create records of a table type with fewer data items. This form can be created if you have enabled the table setting for Quick Create form.
Card Form	Used to display information in a card format.

You will find these forms by default and you can edit them, per your business needs. Figure 2-36 shows the forms created for the Student table.

Columns	Relationships	Business rules	Views	Forms	Dashboards	Charts	Keys	Commands	Data

Name ↑ ∨		Form type ∨		Status ∨	Type ∨
Information	···	QuickViewForm		Active	Custom
Information	···	Card		Active	Custom
Information	···	Main		Active	Custom
Student quick create form	···	QuickCreate		Active	Custom

Figure 2-36. *Form types*

You can edit the form layouts as needed. The main form consists of three parts—header, body, and footer. Inside the body, you can add tabs, and inside tabs, you can add one or multiple column sections. Section can be used to hold one or multiple fields.

Form Security

Every form in the Dataverse is security-role driven. You can select access forms by all users or select a specific security role. For example, if you apply an account manager security role to a specific main form, then only the users having account manager security role can access it unless the form is not a fallback form. You will learn more about security roles in Chapter 8. Figure 2-37 shows the form security option.

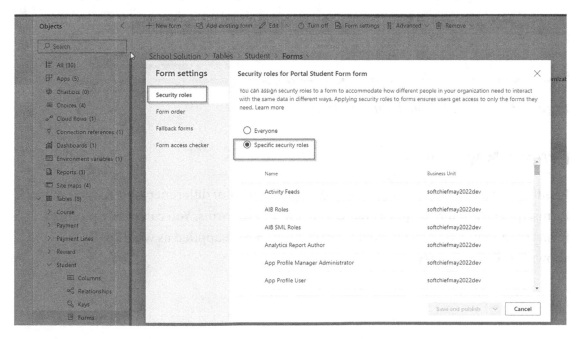

Figure 2-37. *Form security*

Enable Fallback Form

You can enable security roles so that only users with a specific security role can access certain forms. When a security role is not enabled for a form, the form that has been enabled as the fallback form will load for those users. Figure 2-38 shows the fallback option.

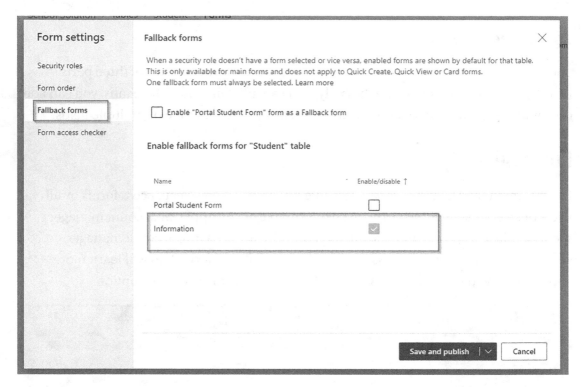

Figure 2-38. *The fallback form option*

Create New Forms

In addition to existing forms, you can create new forms of different types, such as main forms, quick view forms, quick create forms, and card forms. You can create multiple forms of the same type as needed. Form security can be applied as well. Figure 2-39 shows these new form types.

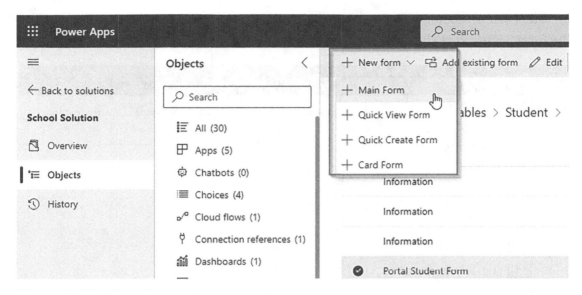

Figure 2-39. New form types

Edit Student Main Form

To edit the main form of the Student table, click the three dots next to the Information Main form and choose Edit Form in New Tab. Figure 2-40 shows this process.

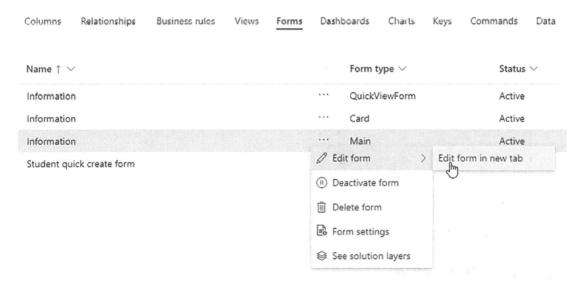

Figure 2-40. Edit existing form types

The Form Designer will open. You can use the Components panel on the left to edit the form. Figure 2-41 shows the layout components.

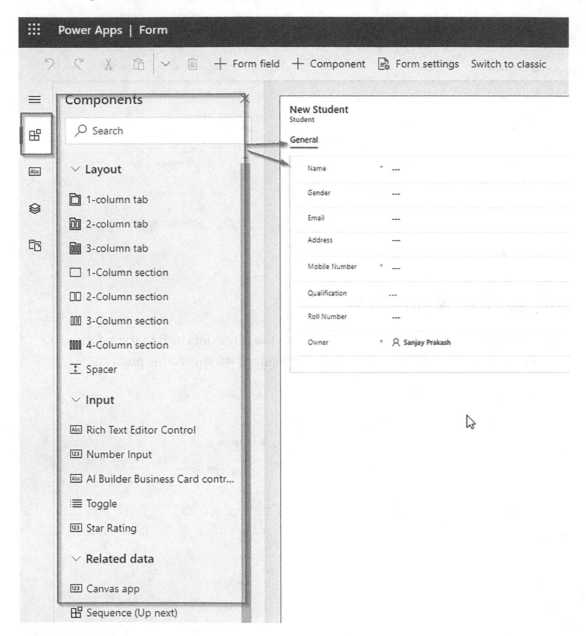

Figure 2-41. *Form layout*

By default, one tab and one column section are available on the form. You can drag-and-drop fields onto the section by using the Columns option. Figure 2-42 shows the form fields.

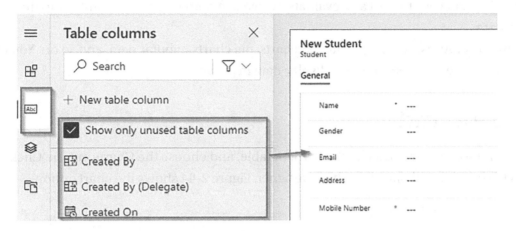

Figure 2-42.   *Form fields*

Once the fields are dropped onto the section, you can save and publish the form. Then users can use the form by providing field values. Figure 2-43 shows the New Student form.

New Student - Unsaved

General

Name	*	**Robert Hook**
Gender		**Male**
Email	*	**robert@gmail.com**
Address		**London**
Mobile Number	*	**6666666666**

Figure 2-43.   *The New Student form*

Chart Configuration and Dashboard Pinning

A chart is a graphical representation of table data. Charts can make data interesting, attractive, and easy to read and evaluate, which can help you analyze and compare your data.

In Power Apps, you can create bar charts, pie charts, tabular data, and so on. You can connect to the Dataverse table to display data in graphical images.

Create a Chart

Open the solution, navigate to the Student table, and choose the Charts option. Click Add Chart. This will open the Chart Designer. Figure 2-44 shows the chart option.

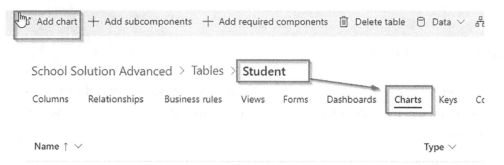

Figure 2-44. *Student table chart option*

Provide a name for your chart and choose the view to use for the chart. Choose Legend entries, which adds Series and Category as labels. Figure 2-45 shows the Chart Designer.

Figure 2-45. *Student table chart designer*

Choose Name with Aggregation, Count: All, and Gender for the horizontal axis. This scenario creates a chart to display students by gender. The preview of the chart will be displayed on the Designer Screen. Save the chart. The chart can be used in model-driven apps.

You can create multiple charts for a specific table with different scenarios, such as students by payment, top five students with highest payments, students by joined on date, and so on.

Dashboards

To display multiple charts on a single page, you can use dashboards. You can choose a layout like two-column or four-column dashboards. There are two types of dashboards—table-specific and global.

When you create a dashboard in a table, you can only use charts from the same table in the dashboard; these are called table-specific dashboards.

Create a Dashboard

Open the solution and navigate to the Student table to choose the Dashboard option. Click Add Dashboard and choose 2-Column Overview. This will open the Dashboard Designer. Figure 2-46 shows the Dashboard Designer.

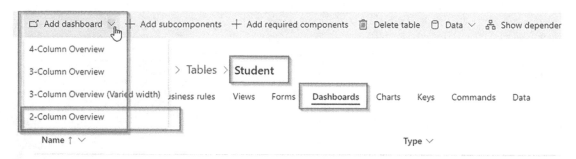

Figure 2-46. *Student table Dashboard Designer*

The dashboard has multiple tiles in two columns, so you will see two tiles on the dashboard. You have to select visual filters to add charts and stream to choose a view that will be used to render the visual filters. Figure 2-47 shows the table dashboard designer tiles.

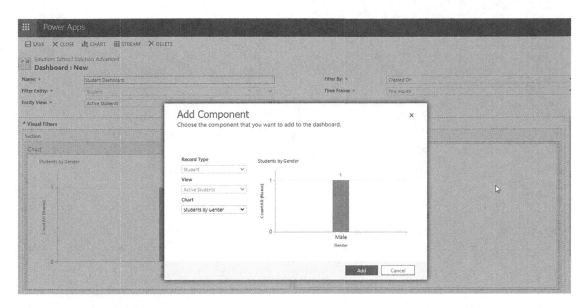

Figure 2-47. Student table dashboard designer tiles

Name the dashboard and then choose Entity View. You can choose any chart from the selected table by clicking the chart icon from the dashboard tile. After that, click the Stream to choose the view. Figure 2-48 shows the dashboard stream.

Figure 2-48. Student table dashboard stream

Save the dashboard. When designing model-driven apps, you can use this dashboard as an asset of the Student table. Figure 2-49 shows the final dashboard in action.

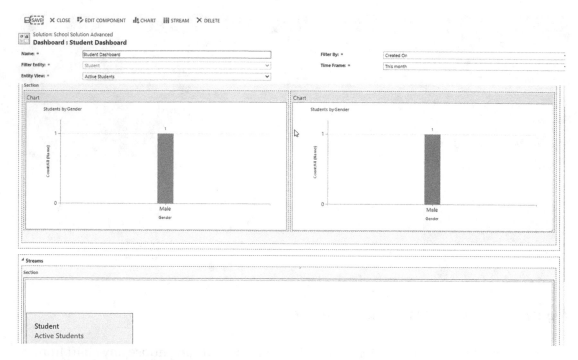

Figure 2-49. *The rendered Student table dashboard*

You can configure multiple dashboards for a single table to represent different strategic visual screens. Charts and dashboards can both be added in model-driven Power Apps as entity assets.

To configure global dashboards, you need to create model-driven Power Apps. Then you can add multiple charts, web resources, and insight tiles by connecting multiple tables on a single page.

Configure Table-Specific Dashboards

Dashboards configured inside a table are called table-specific dashboards. In these dashboards, you can only use the charts related to that table. You cannot use multiple tables in a table-specific dashboard.

For more information about dashboards, see the Microsoft site at https://docs.microsoft.com/en-us/power-apps/developer/model-driven-apps/create-dashboard.

Concepts of Alternate Keys

Alternate keys are useful for third-party system integrations. Power Apps store their primary keys in GUID format. However, third-party systems do not use GUID format, so for system integration, you have to configure an alternate key. This is done by combining multiple columns to uniquely represent a row or record. To add an alternate key, navigate to the table, choose Key, and click Add Key.

Name the key (for example, studentkey) and choose one or multiple columns to represent the unique key for third-party systems. When a third-party system tries to create a new record or update an existing one, this alternate key will be required. Figure 2-50 shows how to configure an alternate key.

studentkey   ✕

Display name *

studentkey

Name *

school_   studentkey

Columns *

☑ Email

☐ Gender

☐ Import Sequence Number

☑ Mobile Number

☐ Name

☐ Record Created On

☐ Roll Number

☐ Time Zone Rule Version Number

☐ UTC Conversion Time Zone Code

Done   Cancel

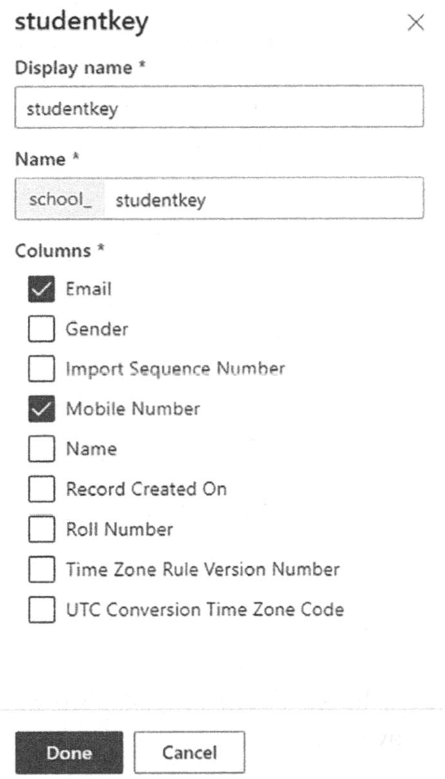

Figure 2-50. *Alternate key configuration*

The alternate key calls the UPSERT command in Power Apps. The UPSERT command will check the record to be inserted or updated, as per the key check.

Working with Data in the Dataverse

The Data option in tables can be used to import data or manually create records for that table. To create a new student, click the Data tab and then click Add Record, which will open the student main form. You then provide the student information and save the record. Figure 2-51 shows the main form of the Student table.

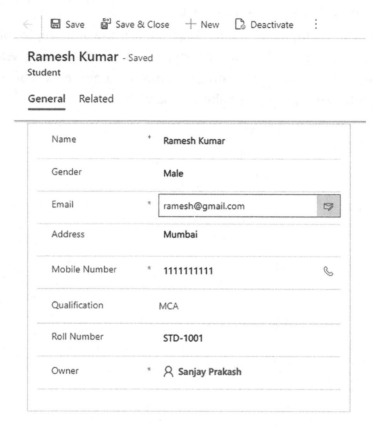

Figure 2-51. *Student main form*

After the data is saved, you can see the data in the view area. Figure 2-52 shows the student records inside the Dataverse.

School Solution Advanced > Tables > **Student**

Columns   Relationships   Business rules   Views   Forms   Dashboards   Charts   Keys   Commands   **Data**

Name	Address	Email	Gender	Mobile Number	Qualification	Roll Number
ajay kumar	Mumabi	ajay1@gmail.com	Male	222222		STD-1000
Ramesh Kumar	Mumbai	ramesh@gmail.com	Male	1111111111	MCA	STD-1001

Figure 2-52. *Student records*

Business Scenario, Use Cases, and Implementation

In this chapter, you learned how to configure Dataverse tables, columns, relationships, business rules, views, forms, charts, dashboards, keys, and data options. You can perform the following scenarios with the skills explained in this chapter.

1	Systems should be able to combine different configuration and customization components in a package so that they can be distributed to other environments.	Configure Power Apps Solution and add required components to it for packaging.
2	The school management system must allow users to enter student information such as roll number (auto-number), name, address, father's name, mobile, email, and qualifications. The system should capture course information and users should be able to record students joined. The app must create payment information with term facility and payment details.	Solution components include tables, fields, forms, views, and relationships.
3	The system should display student-level total amount to be paid by student and it should display the next renewal due date of the student after one year of joining.	The solution requires you to configure rollup fields and calculated fields.
4	Mobile number and email should be mandatory when creating students.	Use business rules to solve this business need.
5	The system should allow associate courses for students. One student can have multiple courses and one course can be chosen by multiple students.	Configure relationships and relationship behaviors.
6	The system should have a visualization to display courses by students joined and display students by joining date.	Configure charts for the solution.
7	The system should display a page of all visualizations for the Student table.	Create a table-specific dashboard.

In the next chapter, you see how to work with Power Apps to leverage these Dataverse concepts.

Summary

In this chapter, you learned about the following concepts:

- Understanding Power Apps solutions

- Working with table configurations and settings

- Working with columns, datatypes, calculated fields, and rollup fields

- Using auto-number columns in the Dataverse

- Configuring relationships and relationship behaviors

- Working with business rules

- Configuring table views

- Designing table forms and layouts

- Chart configuration and dashboard pinning

- Configuring a table-specific dashboard

- Understanding alternate keys

- Working with data in the Dataverse

- Business scenarios, use cases, and implementation

In the next chapter, you learn about the following:

- The concept of Power Apps and a no-code, less-code platform

- Working with Canvas apps in detail

- Using Power Fx for Power Apps

- Working with model-driven apps

- Power Portal concepts and designing with deployment

- Managing Power Apps

- Business scenarios and implementations

CHAPTER 3

Working with Microsoft Power Apps

Microsoft Power Apps is the no-code, less-code platform used to develop applications. Power Apps can be configured on top of the Dataverse as a database. Although you can connect with diversified cloud sources such as Salesforce, OneDrive, Dropbox, and many more, the Dataverse can also be used as an in-house database to build applications and connect with other datasources for integration through connectors.

There are three types of Power Apps—you can build model-driven apps, Canvas apps, and Power Portals. All apps have their own features. Figure 3-1 shows the types of Power Apps.

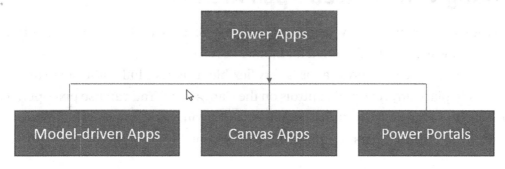

Figure 3-1. *Types of Power Apps*

Model-Driven Apps

Model-driven app design is an approach that focuses on adding components—such as forms, views, relationships, charts, and dashboards—to tables using an App Designer tool. Additionally, relationships connect tables in a way that permits navigation between them and ensures that data is not repeated unnecessarily. If you are building an app to

S. Prakash Pradhan, *Power Platform and Dynamics 365 CE for Absolute Beginners*,
https://doi.org/10.1007/978-1-4842-8600-5_3

manage a complex process, such as onboarding new students and employees, managing a sales process, or handling member relationships in an organization such as a bank, a model-driven app is a great choice.

Canvas Apps

Canvas apps are designed for a no-code, less-code platform with a drag-and-drop concept. You can create Excel-like expressions for specifying logic and working with data. The Canvas app can connect to diversified cloud datasources to pull data.

Power Portals

Power Portals are public-facing websites designed for external users to interact with customer data. These apps are often used for customer self-service and partner communications.

Working with Canvas Apps in Detail

Canvas apps are a convenient way to build, with the no-code and less-code platform. These apps are specifically designed for mobile devices.

The user interface in Canvas apps is very flexible. You have full authority to use the full screen to place any required controls on the Canvas app. You can use pixel-perfect controls on the screen, like buttons, textboxes, and so on. Canvas apps can also be included in your Power Apps solutions as a component.

Features of Canvas Apps

There are many features that come with Canvas apps. Some of them are given here:

- Can connect with the Dataverse and other cloud datasources

- Can be designed for mobile and tab devices

- Flexible UI to add components

- Can be packaged in Power Apps solutions

- Can be shared with other users

- Can call Power Automate for better integration power

Build Your First Canvas App

Before building your first Canvas app, you have to understand the fundamentals and basic theories about Canvas app design. Read more about Canvas app theories from Microsoft at https://docs.microsoft.com/en-us/power-apps/maker/canvas-apps/getting-started.

You can build a Canvas app by using a Power Apps solution. The scenario is to perform Create, Update, Read, and Delete (CRUD) operations by connecting the Student table of the Dataverse.

Open the solution and click Add New App to choose a Canvas app. Figure 3-2 displays how to add a Canvas app to the solution.

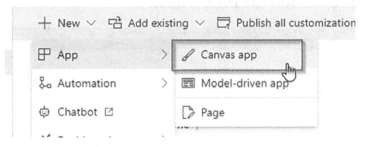

Figure 3-2. *Adding a Canvas app type to the solution*

This will open the Canvas App Creation dialog. Provide a name and choose the device type for which you want to make the app. Click Create. Figure 3-3 displays the screen where you provide the app name and format.

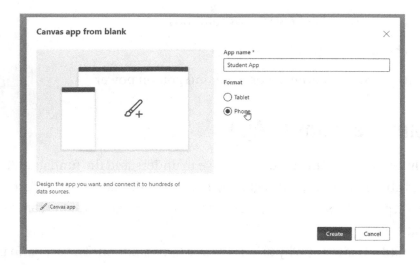

Figure 3-3. *Screen to provide the app name and format*

The Canvas App Designer Studio will open, where you can use screens, components, and set properties of components. There are many more options you can perform. Figure 3-4 displays the Canvas App Design Studio.

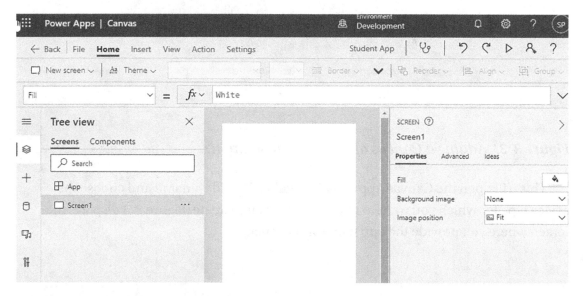

Figure 3-4. *Screen to provide the app name and format*

The left panel consists of multiple options. Table 3-1 explains the option panels available in the Canvas app Designer Studio.

Table 3-1. *Option Panels Available in the Canvas App Designer Studio*

Panel Option	Details
1. Tree view	This option displays screens and components used in Canvas apps in Power Apps. You can modify the properties of individual components.
2. Insert	This panel is used to insert screens and components, such as buttons, textboxes, etc., on the screens.
3. Data	This option lets you to connect datasources so that you can interact with the data.
4. Media	This option used to upload images and videos to a Canvas app.
5. Advanced Tools	This option is used for monitoring and testing the app.

Note By default, the datasource Dataverse tables are available in the datasource panel, but if you want to connect multiple datasources, you should choose connectors. Read more about connectors at `https://docs.microsoft.com/en-us/connectors/connector-reference/connector-reference-powerapps-connectors`.

Follow the numbers in Figure 3-5 to connect the Dataverse table with the gallery control.

Number	Details
1. Insert panel	Use the Insert panel to add a gallery control to the Canvas.
2. Gallery control	The gallery control display on the Canvas.
3. Data source	In the datasource property of the gallery search student.
4. Choose Table	Select the Student table to connect to the gallery.
5. Student Table Connected	After selection, the student records display on the gallery.

Figure 3-5 displays the gallery on the screen.

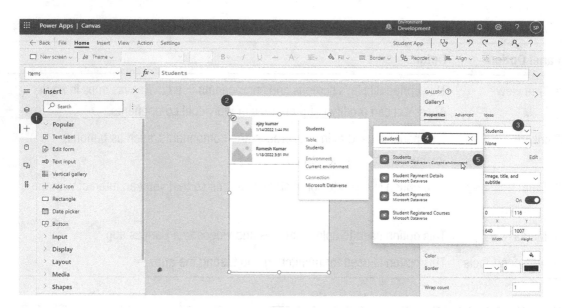

Figure 3-5. *Adding a vertical gallery to the Canvas screen*

You can change the layout data items you want to display in an item of the gallery. To change the layout, click Layout Property and select a layout of your choice from the right panel by selecting the gallery control. Figure 3-6 shows the gallery layouts.

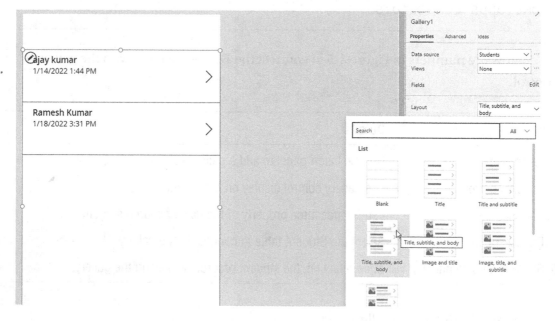

Figure 3-6. *Gallery layouts*

Inside a gallery item, you can decide which fields you want to display by configuring the field's properties. Figure 3-7 shows how to edit fields in a list item of the gallery.

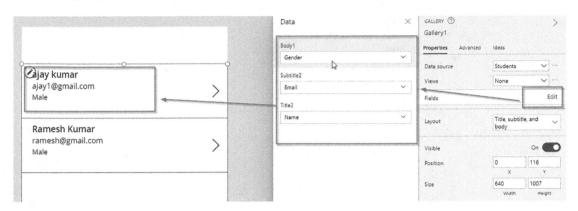

Figure 3-7. *Changing fields on an item*

Drag a rectangle control and resize it to show the header and add a text label with Text property set to Students. The screen will look like Figure 3-8.

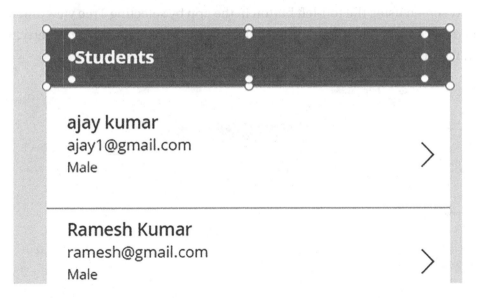

Figure 3-8. *The Text property is set to Students*

Now you can click the Run button at the top-right corner of the screen to see the app in action. Figure 3-9 shows the app in action.

Figure 3-9. *The app in action*

Create a New Dataverse Record from the Canvas App

Add a new screen using the top-left button in the app by selecting Tree view and insert an Edit Form control. Select the control and navigate to the datasource property. Select Student. Figure 3-10 shows the Edit Form control.

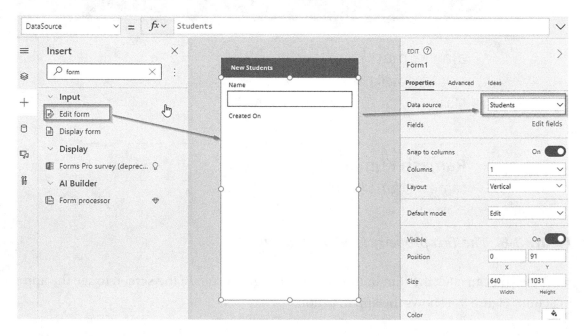

Figure 3-10. *Edit Form control*

Add any desired fields to the form control by selecting the Fields property and remove any unnecessary fields. Figure 3-11 shows the fields on the form.

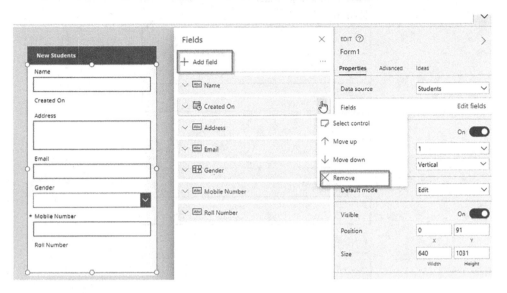

Figure 3-11. *Adding fields*

Set the Default Mode property to New, since you want to create a new record. Figure 3-12 shows the form mode.

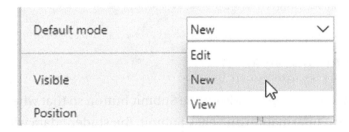

Figure 3-12. *Default form mode*

You can also sort fields by dragging and dropping. Drag a button control onto the screen and define the text as Submit. Figure 3-13 shows how the Create Student Form looks.

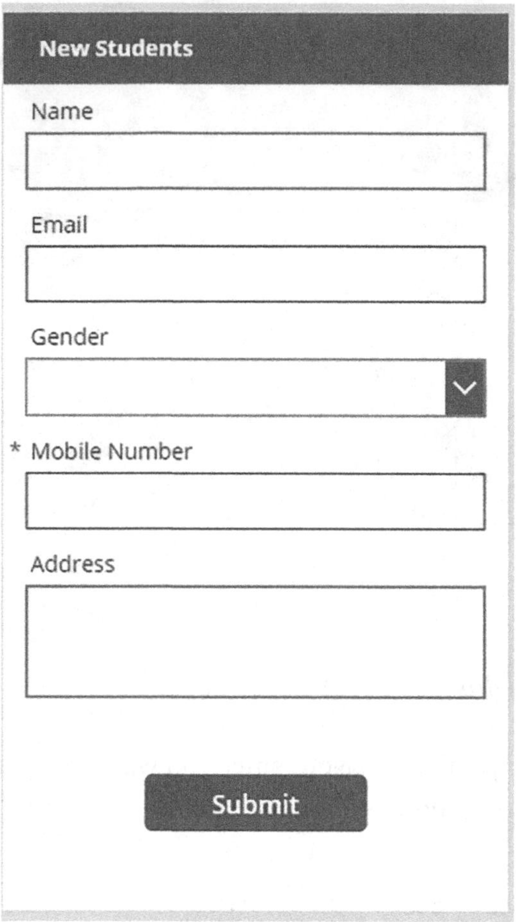

Figure 3-13. *Create new student form*

Now you have to write some code for the Submit button so that when the users provide their student information and click Submit, the student data will be submitted to the Dataverse server. Rename the form StudentCreateForm. Figure 3-14 shows how to rename a form.

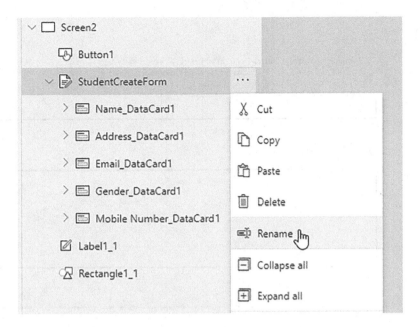

Figure 3-14. *Renaming a form*

Click the button control and select Action and then the On Select property. In the OnSelect event, add the formula `SubmitForm(StudentCreateform)`. Figure 3-15 shows how to connect Power Fx to the button control. Read more about Power Fx from Microsoft at `https://docs.microsoft.com/en-us/power-apps/maker/canvas-apps/working-with-formulas`.

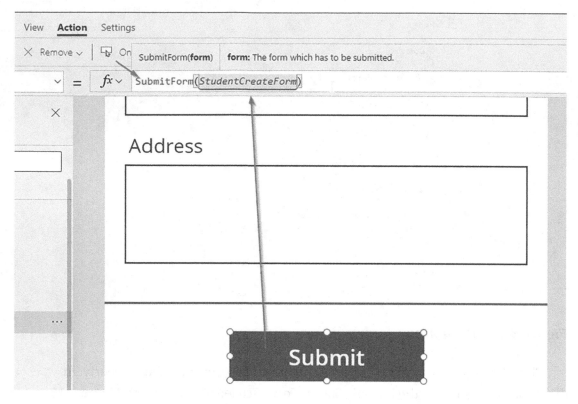

Figure 3-15.   *Adding a Submit form*

Now run the app and provide new student information. Then click Submit. The
record will be inserted into the Dataverse student database. Figure 3-16 shows how to
create a new record.

Figure 3-16. *Adding a new record*

Navigate to the first screen and run the app. You will see the new record in the gallery. Add an icon and mention the On Select property as RE. See Figure 3-17.

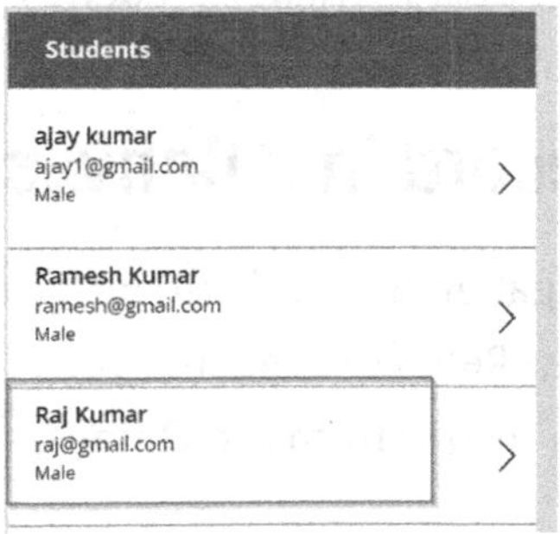

Figure 3-17. *Adding a new record*

Edit Existing Records in a Canvas App

You can edit existing student records from the Dataverse. Add a new screen and add a form control. Then rename the form formeditstudent. Change the datasource property to Students and the Items property to a Power Fx Gallery1.Selected. Make sure to use the gallery control ID and the Form Mode property as Edit. Figure 3-18 displays an existing record edit.

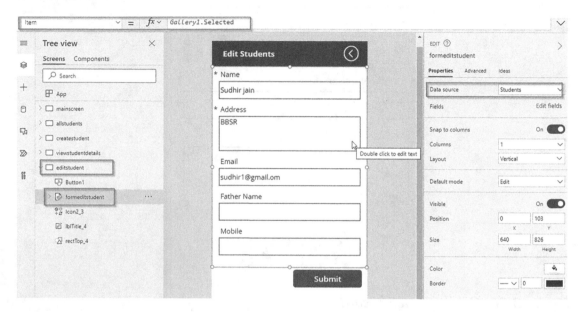

Figure 3-18.   *Edit an existing record*

For the Edit screen, you can take a Submit button to post the changed data of the record. Use the Power Fx SubmitForm(formeditstudent);.

Delete an Existing Record in a Canvas App

Open the screen containing the gallery control and add a trash icon to every row. In the Select property, write Power Fx as Remove(Students,Gallery1.Selected);. Figure 3-19 shows the process of removing a record from the Dataverse.

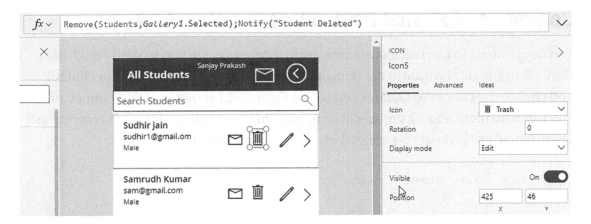

Figure 3-19. *Removing a record from the Dataverse*

View More Details about a Dataverse Record

Add a new screen and a form control. Rename the form viewstudentdetails. Change the datasource property to Students and the Items property to a Power Fx Gallery1.Selected. Make sure to use the gallery control ID and the Form Mode property as View. Figure 3-20 displays how to view more of an existing record.

Figure 3-20. *Displaying more of a record from the Dataverse*

This section explained how to perform CRUD operations in a Canvas app that's connected to the Dataverse data.

Connect an External Datasource in a Canvas App

You can connect to external datasources using connectors, such as to send email using Outlook or Gmail. Navigate to the Data option and click Add Data. Search for Outlook and choose the Office 365 Outlook connector. Figure 3-21 shows the O365 connector. You can read more about external datasources at `https://docs.microsoft.com/en-us/learn/modules/work-with-external-data/2-add-data-source`.

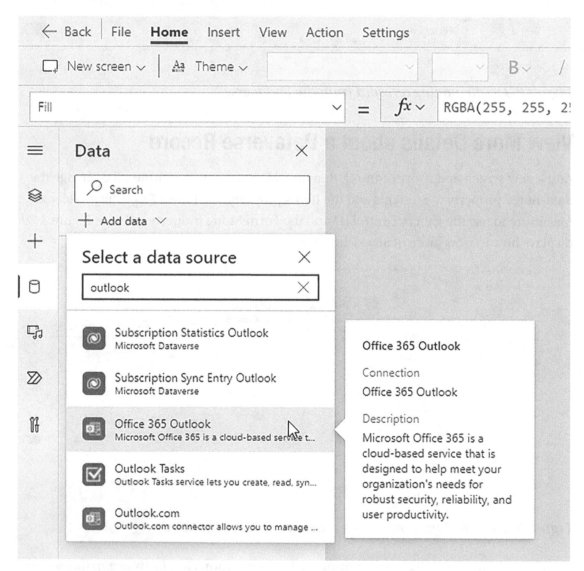

Figure 3-21. *Displaying the Office 365 connector*

In the next screen, click Connect, which will use your current Office 365 subscription credential to create a connector. Now the connector is available in the data area of the Canvas app. Navigate to the Student List screen and add an email icon to the first item, which will display this for every item.

In the OnSelect property, mention the Power Fx to send an email using an Office365 connector. Figure 3-22 displays the Power Fx for sending email.

Figure 3-22. *The send email Power Fx*

Variables in Canvas Apps

There are two types of variables available in a Canvas app—local and global. Local variables are available only on the screen where they are initialized, but global variables are available on every screen.

Local variables are initialized using the UpdateContext Power Fx and global variables use the Set Power Fx. Read more about variables from Microsoft at https://docs. microsoft.com/en-us/power-apps/maker/canvas-apps/working-with-variables.

Power Fx for Power Apps

Power Fx is the low-code language that's used across the Microsoft Power Platform. It's a general-purpose, strong-typed, declarative, and functional programming language.

Examples of Power Fx

Table 3-2 lists different examples of Power Fx and their use in the Canvas app context.

Table 3-2. *Power Fx Examples*

Panel Option	Details
Navigate one screen to another screen.	Navigate(targetScreen)
Display the previous screen.	Back()
Return a blank value that can be used to insert a NULL value in a datasource.	Blank()
Submit form data to the server.	SubmitForm(form1)
Return a filtered table based on one or more criteria.	Filter(IceCream, OnOrder > 0)
Return the first record from a table.	First(Employees)
Modify or create a record in a datasource, or merge records outside of a datasource.	Patch(Customers, First(Filter(Customers, Name = "Contoso")), { Phone: "1-212-555-1234" })

For detailed references, visit https://docs.microsoft.com/en-us/powerapps/ maker/canvas-apps/formula-reference.

Working with Model-Driven Apps

Model-driven apps are a Power Apps design that focus on adding components such as forms, views, charts, dashboards, keys, and relationships to tables using an App Designer tool. Model-driven apps are driven by their data model. There are many differences between Canvas apps and model-driven apps. Table 3-3 compares Canvas apps and model-driven apps.

Table 3-3. *Canvas Apps vs Model-Driven Apps*

Canvas Apps	Model-Driven Apps
Canvas apps enable users to design and develop task-specific apps while designing flexibility in the user interface.	Model-driven apps enable users to design and develop component-focused apps to implement an end-to-end business process.
Canvas apps can connect with over 300 connectors, empowering users to have more functionalities by connecting cloud apps.	Model-driven apps can connect and interact with only one data connector that is the Dataverse.
You can write Power Fx for complex operations.	You can configure business rules, workflows, actions, and plugins.
Changing the look and feel of a Canvas app is very flexible.	Look and feel and UI is restricted by the data model.

Model-driven apps use the Dataverse for application design. In Chapter 2, you learned about complete Dataverse configurations, such as tables, columns, relationships, charts, views, forms, and so on.

The Dataverse table assets are used to build model-driven apps and the solution you created to configure the Dataverse components can be used for model-driven apps.

Configure a Model-Driven App

Navigate to the Power Apps solution and open it. Add a new model-driven app to the solution. Name the app Student Hub. Figure 3-23 shows adding a model-driven app to the solution.

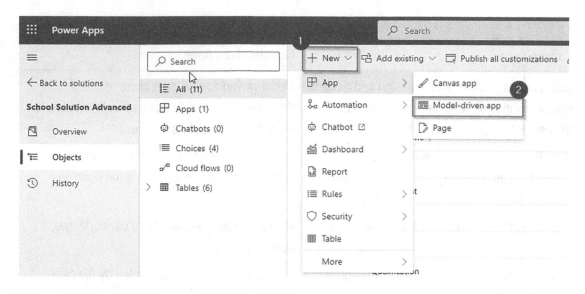

Figure 3-23. *Adding a model-driven app*

Choose the Classic App Designer and click Create. In the next screen, Name it School Hub; the Unique Name will be auto-populated based on the Name. Give a description and set the Icon as the Default icon. You are going to use your Power Apps solutions to build the model-driven app, so enable the Use Existing Solution to Create the App option. Now click Next. Figure 3-24 shows this process.

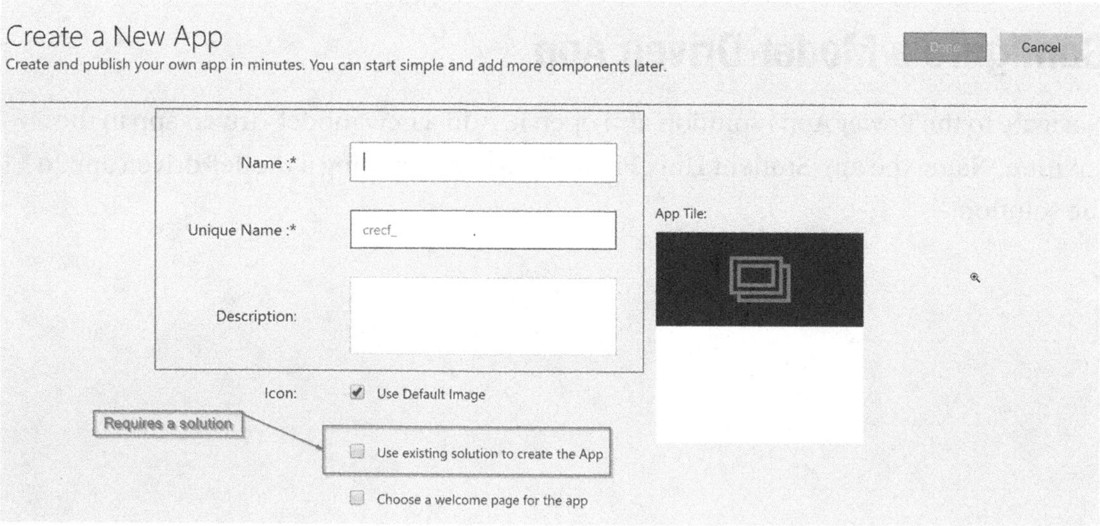

Figure 3-24. *Use the existing solution*

In the next screen, select the Power Apps solution you created from the dropdown list and click Done. This will open the App Designer window. Figure 3-24 displays areas of the model-driven app. You can add a sitemap, global dashboards, business process flows, and entity assets to the model-driven app. Figure 3-25 shows the App Designer.

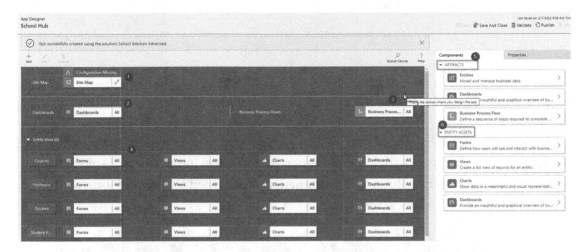

Figure 3-25. *The App Designer*

The first thing is to configure the sitemap. Click the Edit option of the Sitemap box. This will open the Sitemap Designer.

The sitemap consists of three parts—Area, Group, and Sub-Area. Area contains a large group of actions and Groups option groups multiple sub-areas together.

By default, one of each is available on the screen; you just need to rename them. Click the New Area and add a custom title (in this case, Student Area) using the right panel property window. Click the New Sub-Area and in the Property panel and choose Type as Entity. A sub-area can point to an entity, dashboard, web resource, or URL at one time. While selecting Type as Entity, choose the entity the link will point to, such as Student.

Drag another area to hold groups to point to student payment entities. The final sitemap will look like Figure 3-26.

Figure 3-26. *The final sitemap*

Now save and publish the sitemap. Click the App Designer breadcrumb in the top-left corner to navigate to the App Designer. Because you have chosen a solution, all tables that are part of the solution will automatically be added to the model-driven app. Figure 3-27 shows the entity assets.

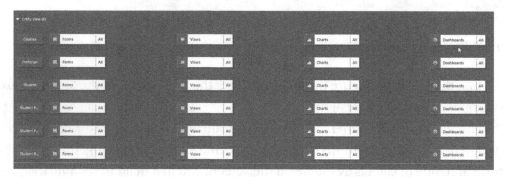

Figure 3-27. *Sitemap with entity assets*

Now Save and publish the app from the App Designer screen. Click the Play button to see the app in action. The model-driven app will open. Figure 3-28 shows the model-driven app in action.

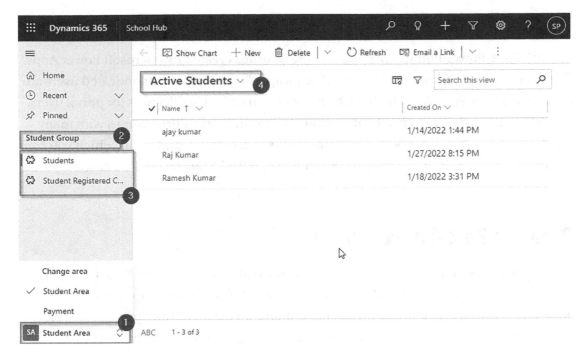

Figure 3-28. *Model-driven app*

You can restrict forms, views, charts, and entity-specific dashboards for tables specific to your app. Figure 3-29 shows how to restrict assets.

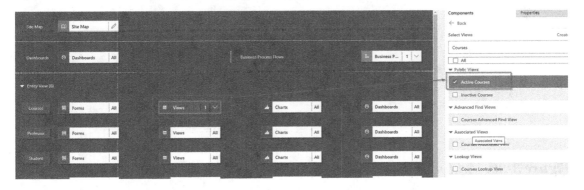

Figure 3-29. *Restricting views*

You can also configure the global dashboard in model-driven apps and business process flows. Read more about global dashboards at https://docs.microsoft.com/en-us/power-apps/maker/model-driven-apps/create-edit-dashboards. For business process flow, read https://docs.microsoft.com/en-us/power-apps/user/work-with-business-processes.

Power Portal Concepts and Design with Deployment

As explained, Power Portals are public-facing websites created by Microsoft Power Apps. Power Portal can only use the Dataverse for its app. Power Portal authenticated users are not stored in a user entity, which is why it does not require user licenses for portal users.

Portal users are stored in a contact table. Microsoft Power Portal comes with many templates, such as partner portal, customer self-service portal, and so on, which you can use for specific needs. If you need a custom Power Portal, you can create a custom portal from scratch.

Create a Portal in Power Apps

Power Portals cannot be added to a Power Apps solution, as the Power Portal components are stored as data. So, to create a Power Portal, navigate to make. powerapps.com and choose the correct environment. Then click the Apps option from the left sitemap. Click New App and choose Portal. Figure 3-30 shows how to add portals.

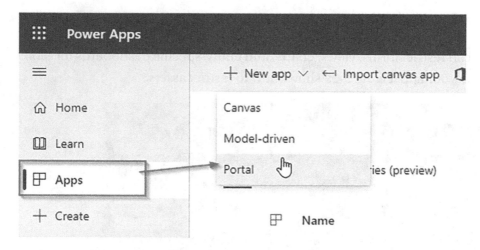

Figure 3-30. *Adding a portal*

Call the portal Softchief Portal, add an address of softchiefportalnew, and set the language to English. Click Create. Figure 3-31 shows the information about this new portal.

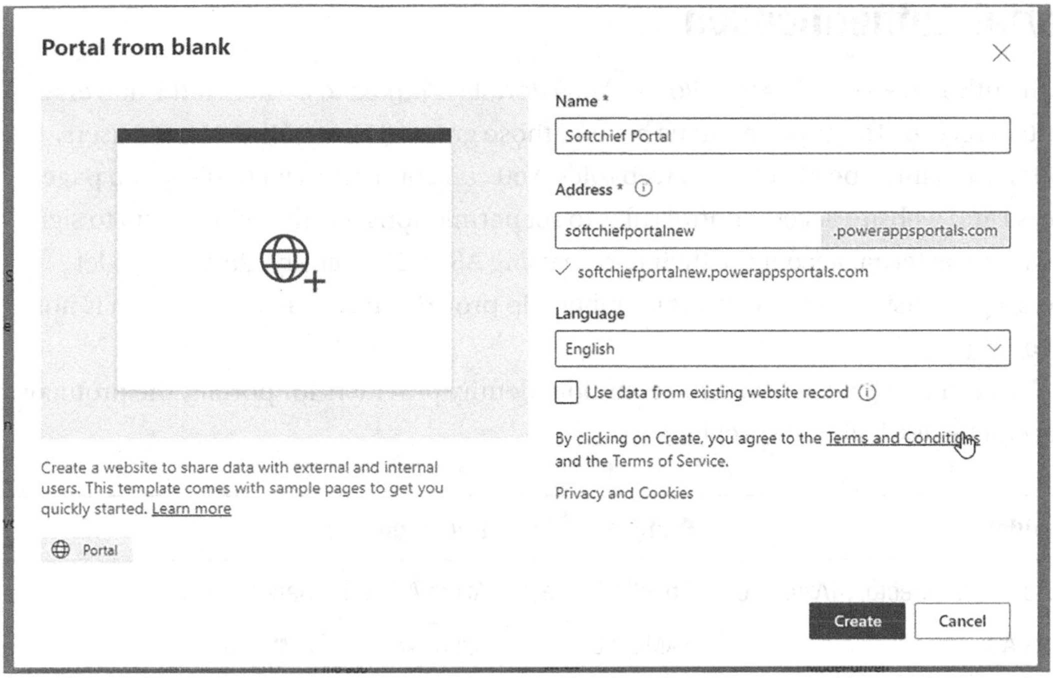

Portal from blank   ✕

Name *

Softchief Portal

Address * ⓘ

softchiefportalnew   .powerappsportals.com

✓ softchiefportalnew.powerappsportals.com

Language

English   ⌄

☐ Use data from existing website record ⓘ

By clicking on Create, you agree to the Terms and Conditions
and the Terms of Service.

Privacy and Cookies

Create a website to share data with external and internal
users. This template comes with sample pages to get you
quickly started. Learn more

⊕ Portal

                                    Create   Cancel

Figure 3-31. *Portal info*

The portal provision process will start in the background. This will take 20 to 30
minutes to complete.

After the provision process is complete, you will see two apps created. One is the
POWER PORTAL app and the other is the model-driven app called Portal Management.
The Portal Management model-driven app is used to configure Power Portals. Click the
Power Portal app to see the app. Figure 3-32 shows the portal in action.

Figure 3-32. *Portal in action*

Portal Authentication

Each authorized portal user in Power Apps Portals is linked to a Microsoft Dataverse contact record. To get permissions beyond those granted to unauthenticated users, portal users must be allocated to web roles. You can configure a web role's web page access and website access control rules to set permissions. Portals allow users to sign in with an external account of their choice using ASP.NET identity. Portals also let users sign in using a local contact membership provider-based account, which is not encouraged.

The following table lists some common identity providers for portals, the protocol that can be used with the provider.

Provider	Protocol	Documentation
Azure Active Directory (Azure AD)	OpenID Connect	Azure AD with OpenID Connect
Azure AD	SAML 2.0	Azure AD with SAML 2.0
Azure AD	WS-Federation	Azure AD with WS-Federation
Azure AD B2C	OpenID Connect	Azure AD B2C with OpenID Connect Azure AD B2C with OpenID Connect (manual configuration)
Azure Directory Federation Services (AD FS)	SAML 2.0	AD FS with SAML 2.0
AD FS	WS-Federation	AD FS with WS-Federation
Microsoft	OAuth 2.0	Microsoft
LinkedIn	OAuth 2.0	LinkedIn
Facebook	OAuth 2.0	Facebook
Google	OAuth 2.0	Google
Twitter	OAuth 2.0	Twitter **Note**: Twitter authentication for portals is temporarily unavailable because of compatibility issues.
Local authentication(not recommended)	Not applicable	Local authentication

104

Read more about Power Portal authentication at `https://docs.microsoft.com/en-us/power-apps/maker/portals/configure/configure-portal-authentication`.

The Local Authentication Process (Not Recommended)

Open the portal in action and click Sign In. Choose Register to provide user information. If you're already registered, use the Login button. Figure 3-33 displays the portal registration page.

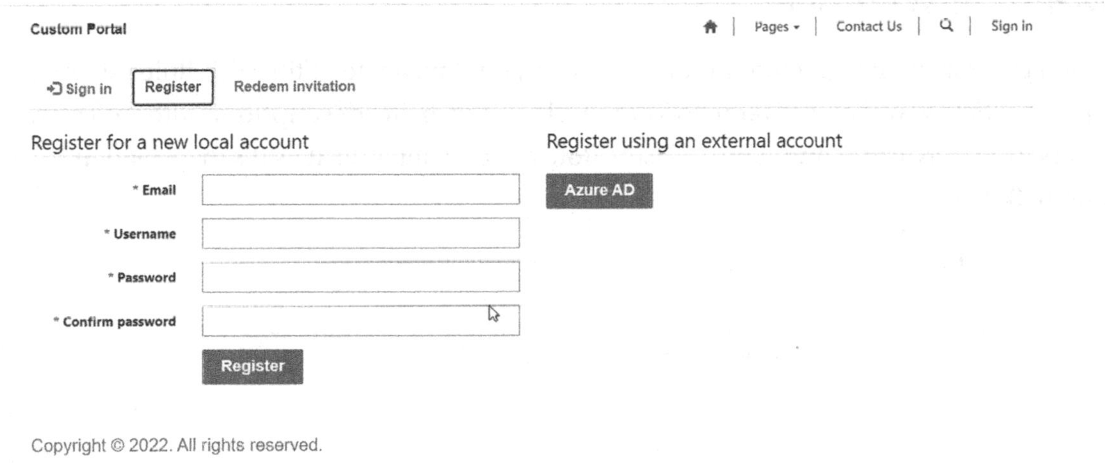

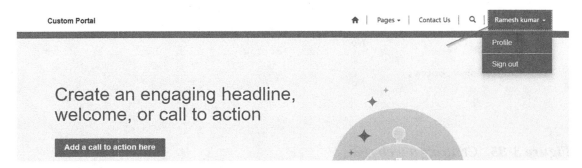

Figure 3-33. *Portal authentication process*

Click Sign In and provide your username and password to log in. It will take you to the home page. Now you are authenticated. Figure 3-34 shows the authenticated screen.

Figure 3-34. *Authenticated screen*

Portal Authorization

After the portal has been authenticated, you need to provide authorization to the user by defining the table permissions and web roles. Authorization is given using three related entities—contact, web roles, and table permissions.

You can define a student web role and allow create, read, update, and delete permissions for the Timesheet entity in the Dataverse for a portal user.

Create a Web Role

Open the Portal Management model-driven app and navigate to the Web Roles sitemap option. Click New. Set the Name to Vendor, choose website, description, Authenticated Users Role as No, and Anonymous Users Role as No. Then save it as it's displayed in Figure 3-35.

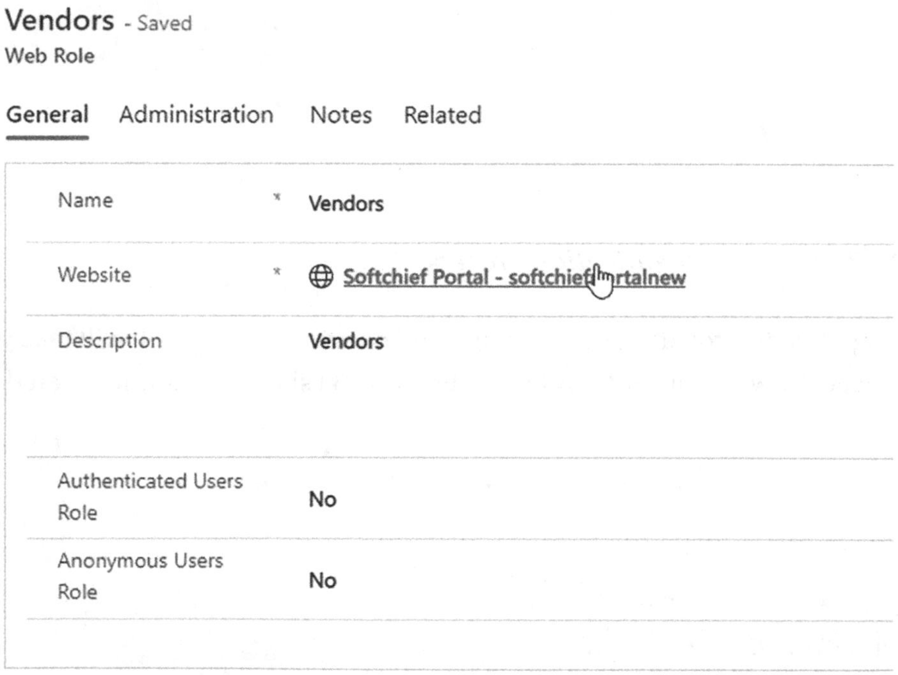

Figure 3-35.   *Creating a web role*

If you select Yes for Authenticated Users Role for a web role, then the web role will be atomically assigned to all authenticated users. If you select Yes for Anonymous Users Role, then anyone who lands on your portal has the power of the web role.

Create a Table Permission

Open the Portal Management model-driven app and navigate to the table permissions sitemap option. Click New. On the page, name it Vendor Student Permission, set the table name to Student, set the website as the portal name, and set the Access Type to Global. In the Privileges area, enable Read, Create, and Write permission. You can enable other permissions also, like Delete, Append, and Append To.

Now save the record. Figure 3-36 shows the table permission record.

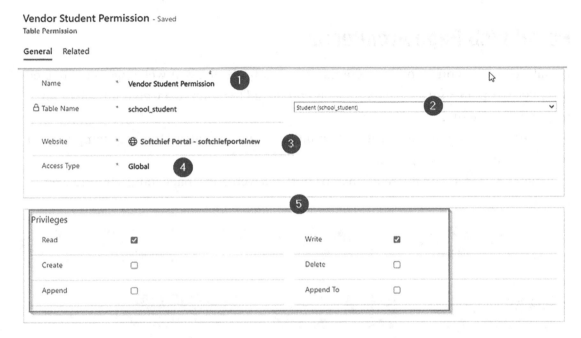

Figure 3-36. *Table permission creation*

Associate the web role with Table permission using the web roles sub-grid on the Table Permission record. Click Add Existing Web Role and choose Vendor and then click OK. The vendor web roles now have the privileges defined in the Table permission. Vendors can now create, read, and update student records. Figure 3-37 shows the table permission associated with the web role.

Web Roles

🗐 Add Existing Web Role

✓	Name ↑ ∨	Website ∨
	Vendors	Softchief Portal - softchiefportalnew

Figure 3-37. *Table permission with the web role*

Portal Web Page Architecture

Portal web pages consist of page templates and web templates. A web page is connected
to a page template and a page template is connected to either to a web template or an
external link rewrite.

One web template can be called by multiple page templates. One page template can
be used by multiple web pages.

Figure 3-38 displays the relationship chart of a web page, page template, and web
templates.

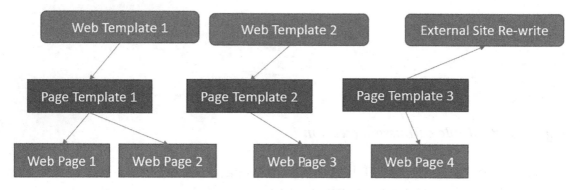

Figure 3-38. *Web page, page template, and web template relationship diagram*

Create a Web Template

A web template will generally contain Liquid code for dynamic content rendering and
is the central table used to integrate Liquid templates with the rest of the Power Apps
portals system. (Liquid is an open-source template language that integrates natively
into Microsoft Power Apps portals.) Web templates can be included in other content or

combined with other templates by using template tags, and are referenced in these tags by their Name attribute. They can also be used to create custom page templates, custom headers, and custom footers for your portal's website. Navigate to Portal Management model-driven app and click Web Templates and then choose New. Call this Student Web Template. Choose Website as the portal. In the source, provide some HTML code. Figure 3-39 displays the web template.

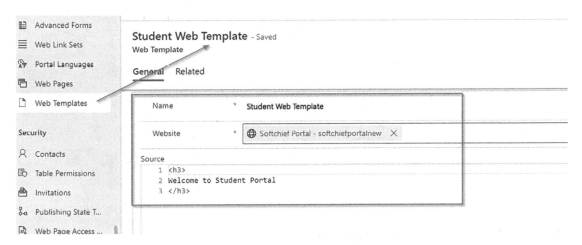

Figure 3-39. *Creating web templates*

Now this web template can be called by a page template.

Create a Page Template

Navigate to Page Template and create a new page template. Associate the web template you created with this new page template. Figure 3-40 displays the page template.

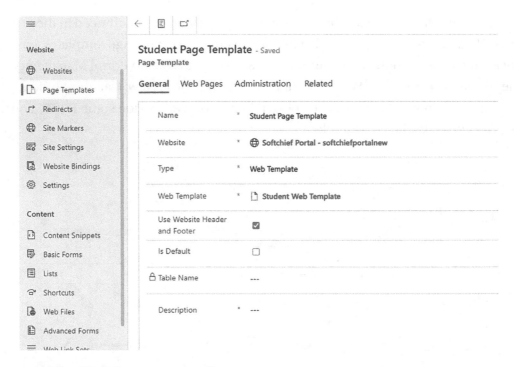

Figure 3-40.   *Creating page templates*

Once the association is complete, you can create a new web page and choose the page template for the web page.

Create a Web Page

Navigate to Web Pages and click New. Provide a name, choose Website for the Portal, Parent Page for the Home Page, and set the partial URL to studentwebpage. For the Page Template, choose Student Page Template. For the Publishing State, select Published. Now choose Save. Figure 3-41 shows the Web Page record.

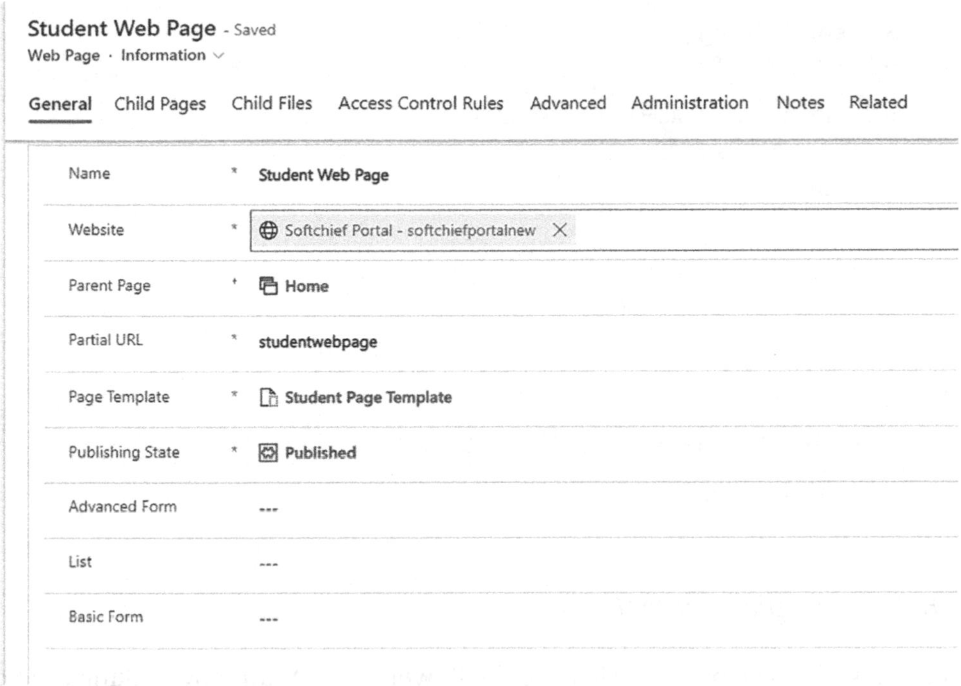

Student Web Page - Saved
Web Page · Information ˅

General   Child Pages   Child Files   Access Control Rules   Advanced   Administration   Notes   Related

Name	*	**Student Web Page**
Website	*	🌐 Softchief Portal - softchiefportalnew ✕
Parent Page	*	🗐 **Home**
Partial URL	*	**studentwebpage**
Page Template	*	🗋 **Student Page Template**
Publishing State	*	🔲 **Published**
Advanced Form		---
List		---
Basic Form		---

Figure 3-41. *The Web Page record*

You can use the localized content section to add content for different languages. As Power Portal supports multiple languages, you can configure multiple localized content for the same web page. Now go to the Localized Content section of the web page and double-click the English record to open it. Scroll down to the content section and add some text. Figure 3-42 shows the web page content. Now click Save.

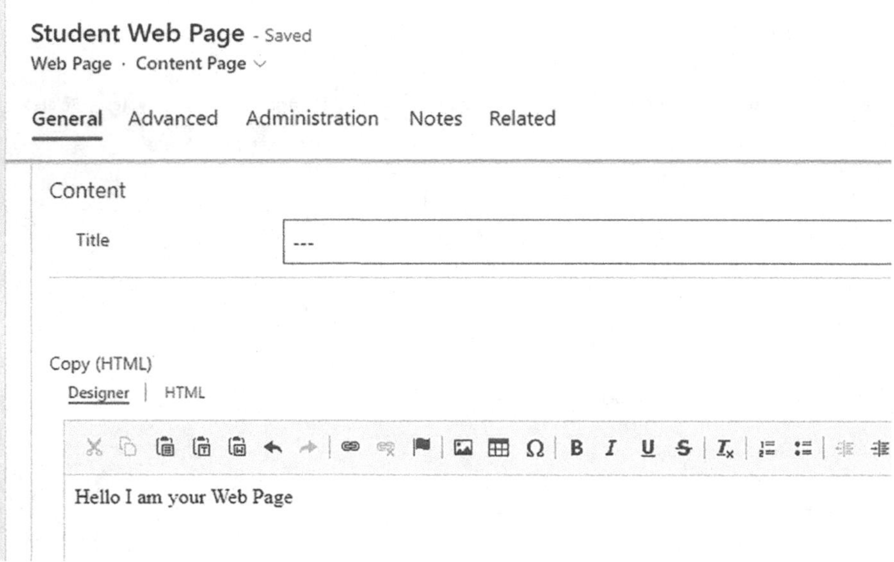

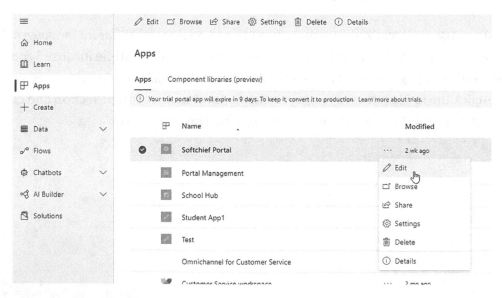

Figure 3-42. *Web page content*

You can test the web page. Navigate to the Power Portal Studio by clicking the Edit option in the portal app you created. Figure 3-43 shows the Portal Edit option.

Figure 3-43. *Portal edits*

In the Portal Studio, click the Sync Configuration option and in the Pages option, choose Students Web Page. Click Browse. Now the page will render with the web template and page template mentioned previously. Figure 3-44 shows the portal page in action.

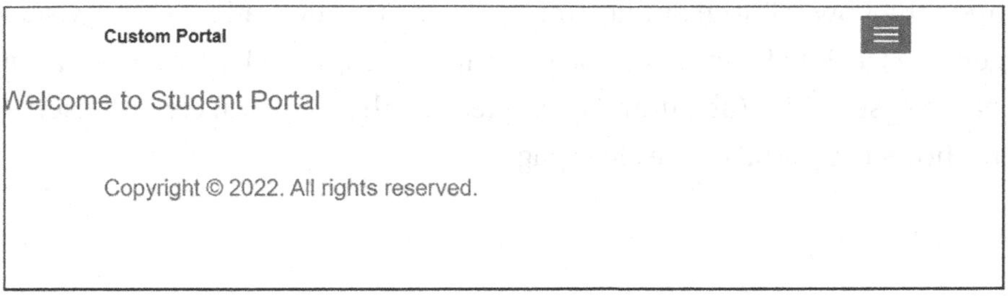

Figure 3-44. *Page is live*

Portal Menu

You can add a menu item to load the web page created in the last step. Open the Portal Management App. In the sitemap, navigate to Web Links sets. Open the Primary Navigation. You can also create your own web link set. But by default, when you create a portal, the primary navigation gets associated with the portal.

On the Web Link Set record, click the Links tab. In the list, click the New Web link. In the new screen, add a name and a web link set, set the publishing state to published, and set the page to the web page created in the last step. Figure 3-45 shows the web link creation. Click Save and close.

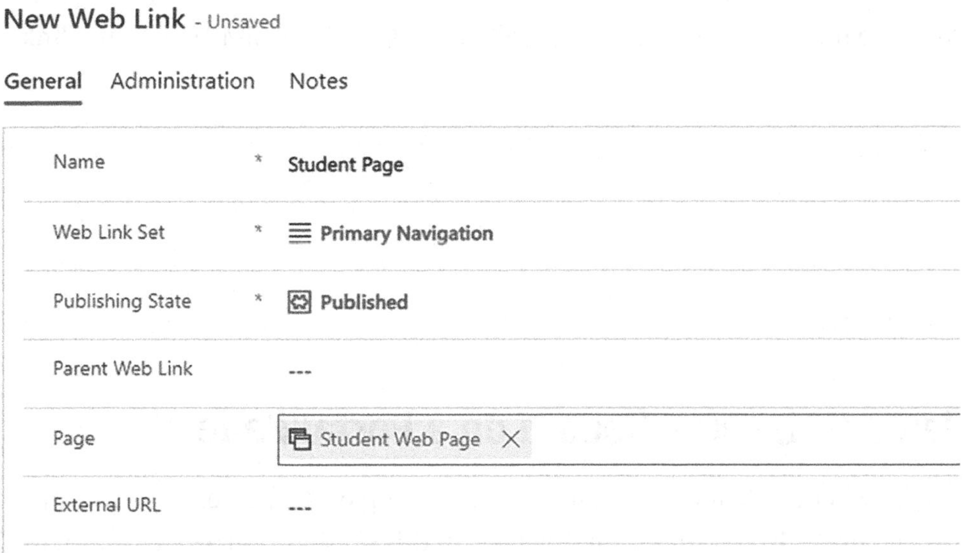

Figure 3-45. *Web link creation*

Now open the Power Portal Studio and click Sync Configuration. Otherwise, if you logged in as a global administrator, you can use a special URL as given here `<portal_path>/_services/about` and click Clear Cache. This will clear the server cache. Figure 3-46 shows the portal cache clear page.

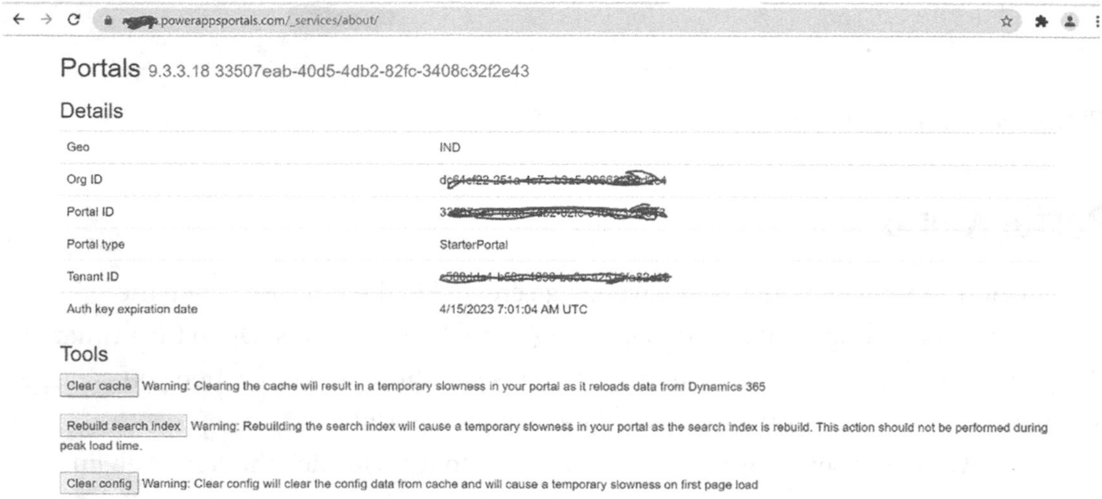

Figure 3-46. *The portal cache clear page*

After clearing the cache, browse the portal. You will see a new menu item at the top. By clicking the menu item, the web page will be loaded. Figure 3-47 shows the link with the page.

Custom Portal

Student Page | 🏠 | Pages ▾ | Contact Us | Q | Sign in

Welcome to Student Portal

Copyright © 2022. All rights reserved.

Figure 3-47. *Web link and page*

Display a Dataverse Record on a Portal Page

You can use the Portal Management model-driven app or the Power Portal Studio to configure or customize Power Portal websites. In this section, you learn how to display Dataverse table records on a portal page. You have already created a web page in the last step, so you can display the Dataverse table records on the portal page. To do this, go to

114

the Dataverse and open the table inside the solution. Navigate to views and create a new view. Call it Portal Student View for Vendors and choose Save. Add four fields to the view (Name, Mobile, Email, and Address). Figure 3-48 shows this view.

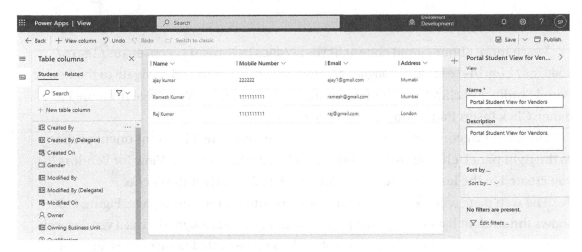

Figure 3-48. *Student view for the portal*

Save and publish the view. Navigate to the Portal Management model-driven app. In the Portal Management app sitemap, choose List and Create a New List. Provide a name for the list, then choose table as Student and website as Portal Record.

Now choose Add View and select the Portal Student View for Vendors view. Save the list. Figure 3-49 shows the list record.

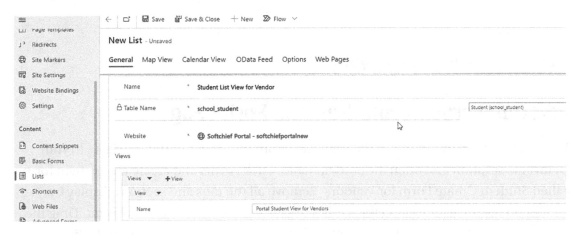

Figure 3-49. *Student list form*

Scroll down the record and make sure the Enable Table Permission is enabled. Go to Web Template and select Student Web Template. In the source code, add the following Liquid code.

```
{% include 'Page Copy' %}
```

Learn more about Liquid code at `https://docs.microsoft.com/en-us/learn/modules/liquid-template-language/`. Now save the record and navigate to the Power Portal Studio and click Sync Configuration. Click the Student Web Page from the Page panel. Click Insert Panel and choose a List component.

Once the List component has been added, configure the List Component property. In the right panel, choose Use Existing and select the Student List View for Vendors list you created in the last step. Now click Browse Website to clear the cache.

The web page will display the students list record on the portal page. Figure 3-50 shows the student list on the portal page. Make sure you are signed in as a vendor web role; otherwise, the data will not be displayed, as you enabled table permissions for the table student list.

Custom Portal				Student Page ■ Pages ▾ Contact Us Q ABC ABC ▾
Hello I am your Web Page				
Name		Mobile Number	Email	Address
ajay kumar		222222	ajay1@gmail.com	Mumabi
Ramesh Kumar		1111111111	ramesh@gmail.com	Mumbai
Raj Kumar		1111111111	raj@gmail.com	London

Figure 3-50. *Student list is displayed*

Edit Dataverse Record from the Portal Page

You can edit existing records in the Dataverse from the Power Portal. Navigate to your Dataverse solution and open the Student table. Click Forms and create a new main form called Student Create Form for Vendors. Remove all the tabs and sections display by default on the form. Only drag the fields that you want to allow vendors to edit. Drag the fields and save the form. Figure 3-51 shows the new main form for the portal edit.

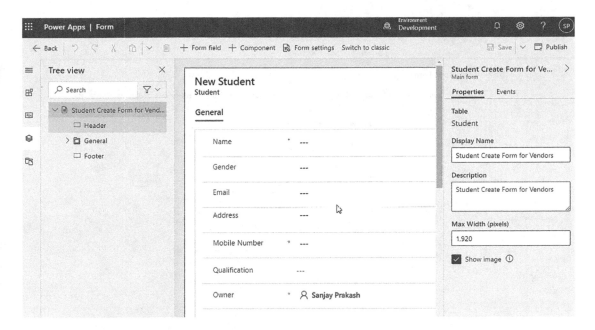

Figure 3-51. *Student Dataverse form*

Once the form is created in the Dataverse, use the following steps to create a basic form in the portal:

1. Go to the Portal Management model-driven app and select the Basic Forms option from the sitemap.

2. Create a new basic form called Student Basic Form Edit for Vendor. Set the Table to Student, the Form Name to Student Create Form for Vendor, and the Mode to Edit. The record source type should be set to Query String and the Record Id Parameter should be ID. Set the website as your portal app. Make sure the Enable Table Permission flag is enabled. Now save the form.

Note   You can set the mode to Insert, Edit, or Read-Only. When you want to create a new record, choose Insert. When you want to update an existing record, choose Edit. To display data, choose Read-Only.

Figure 3-52 shows the basic form for a student.

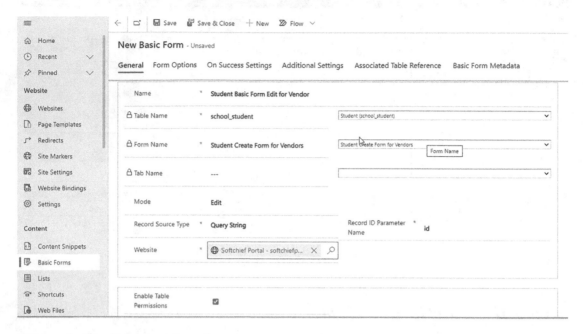

Figure 3-52. *Basic student form*

Once the Basic form has been created, navigate to the Power Portal Studio and click the Sync Configuration button to synchronize configurations from the Portal Management app to the Studio. Then open the Student Web page inside the Portal Studio and click the List component created in the last step. Go to the right side panel and enable the Edit Record option. In the Target type, choose Form and in the second dropdown, choose Student Basic Form Edit for Vendor. After that, click Browse Website. The Browse Website button will clear the server portal cache and load a fresh page. Figure 3-53 shows the Enable Edit option for record.

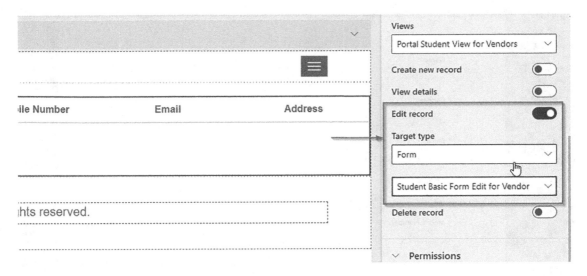

Figure 3-53. *Enable Edit option*

Once the page is loaded, the list will display a dropdown option. Figure 3-54 shows the list with the Edit dropdown.

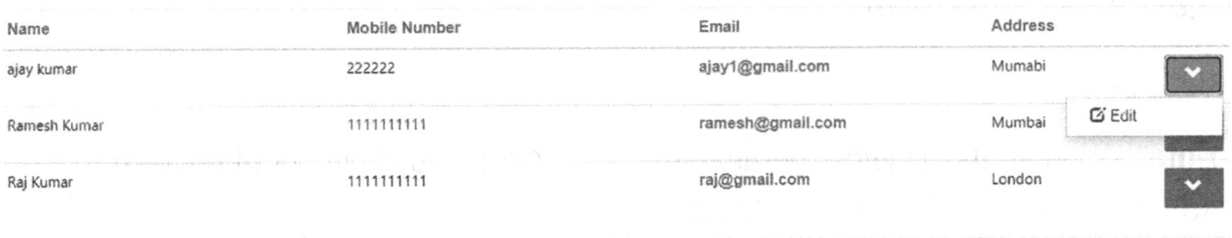

Name	Mobile Number	Email	Address	
ajay kumar	222222	ajay1@gmail.com	Mumabi	⌄
Ramesh Kumar	1111111111	ramesh@gmail.com	Mumbai	☑ Edit
Raj Kumar	1111111111	raj@gmail.com	London	⌄

Figure 3-54. *List with Edit dropdown*

Upon clicking the Edit option, the Edit Form dialog will open, where you can edit student data and click Submit. Figure 3-55 shows the Edit Form for students.

119

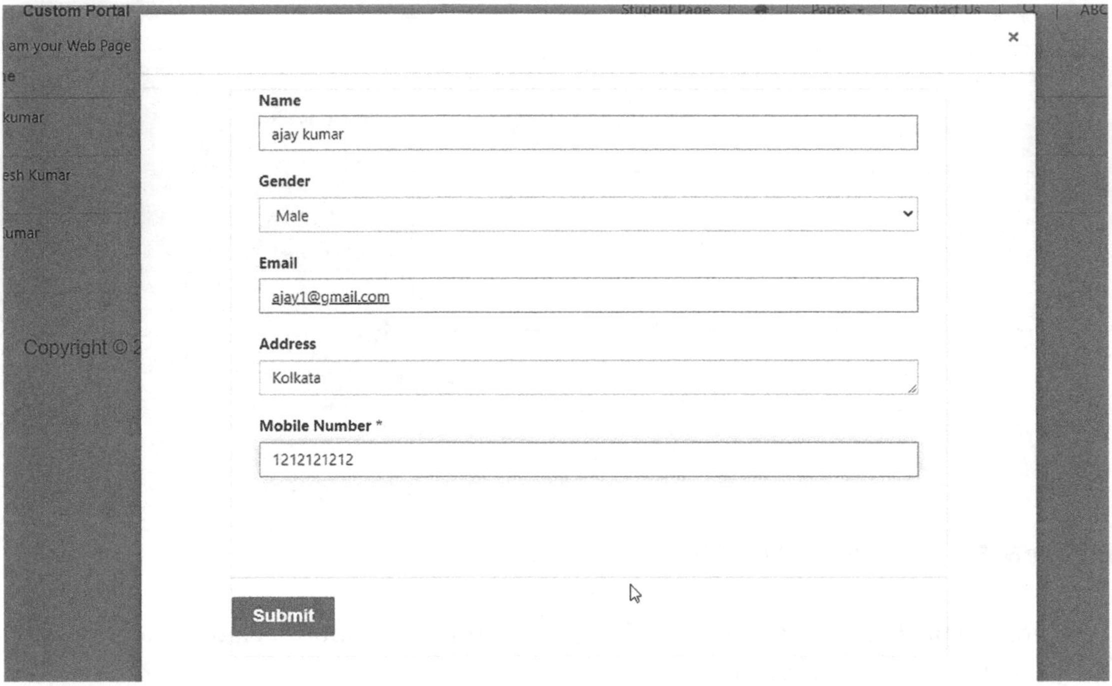

Figure 3-55. *Edit popup*

Note   You can use Liquid programming, JavaScript, and client scripting such as jQuery for dynamic logic in the Power Portal.

View More about Record

To learn more about a list record, you can create a new Dataverse form with the needed fields or you can use the same Edit form. This time, create a new basic form and set the Mode to Read-Only.

Figure 3-56 shows a new basic form with read-only mode set.

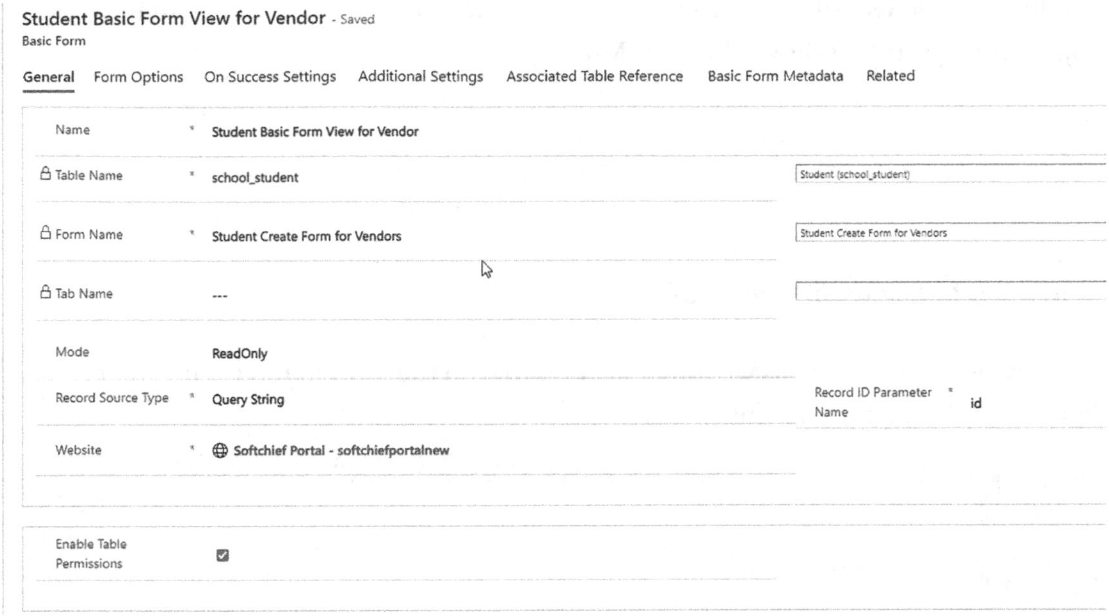

Student Basic Form View for Vendor - Saved
Basic Form

General   Form Options   On Success Settings   Additional Settings   Associated Table Reference   Basic Form Metadata   Related

Name	* Student Basic Form View for Vendor	
🔒 Table Name	* school_student	Student (school_student)
🔒 Form Name	* Student Create Form for Vendors	Student Create Form for Vendors
🔒 Tab Name	---	
Mode	ReadOnly	
Record Source Type	* Query String	Record ID Parameter * id
		Name
Website	* 🌐 Softchief Portal - softchiefportalnew	

Enable Table Permissions	☑

Figure 3-56. *View only form*

Now navigate to the Portal Studio and click Sync Configuration. Select the List component and, in the Property, enable the View details option. Set the Target type to Form and, in the second dropdown, choose the new basic form created with read-only mode. Figure 3-57 shows the view details enabled.

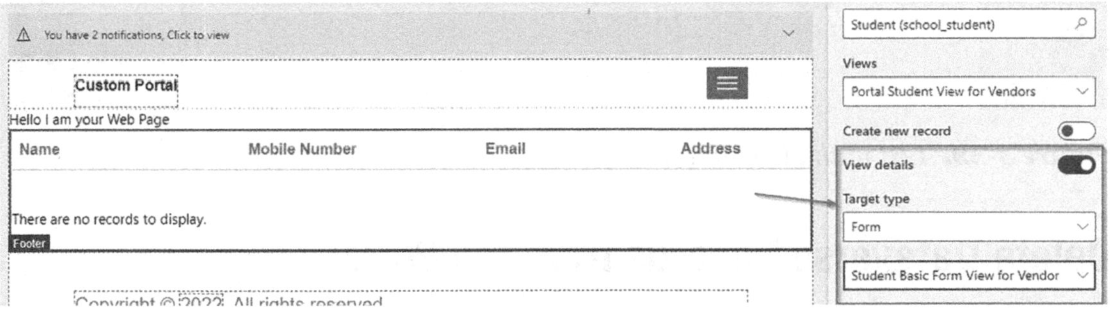

Figure 3-57. *View only form*

Click Browse Website. Now you will see the View More option for the item inside the dropdown. Figure 3-58 shows the View More option.

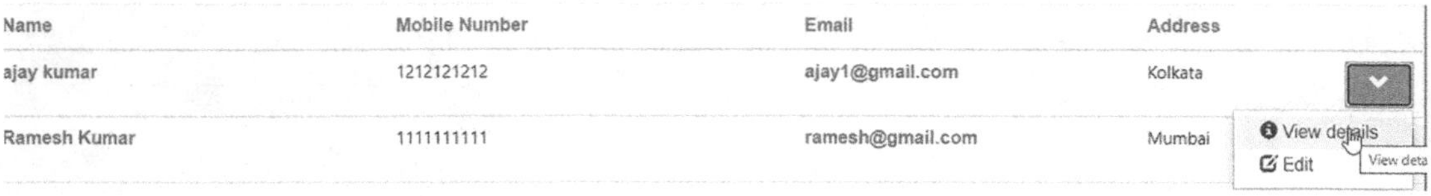

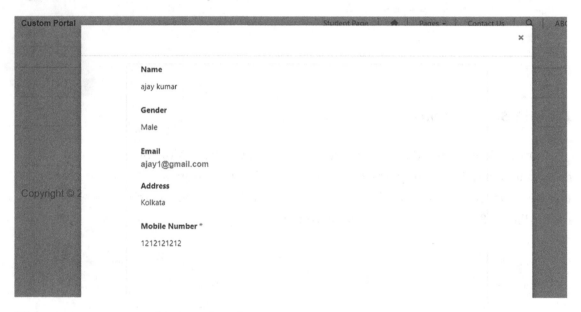

Figure 3-58. *List with view details*

Clicking the View details will open the popup with the form in read-only mode. Figure 3-59 shows the read-only form.

Figure 3-59. *List with view details*

Delete Dataverse Records from the Portal

You can delete records from the Dataverse using the portal. Enable the Delete option for the list in Power Portal and browse the website. Figure 3-60 shows the Delete option enabled.

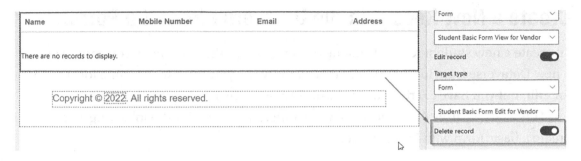

Figure 3-60. *The Delete Record option*

Now browse the website and you will see the Delete option in the dropdown for each item in the list. Make sure to enable Delete Table Permission for Vendor in the student entity.

Figure 3-61 shows the delete table permission for the vendor.

Figure 3-61. *Delete table permission*

In the Portal Studio, sync the configuration and browse the website. The list will show the Delete option. Figure 3-62 shows the Delete option for the list.

Mobile Number	Email	Address	
1212121212	ajay1@gmail.com	Kolkata	⌄
1111111111	ramesh@gmail.com	Mumbai	❶ View details
1111111111	raj@gmail.com	London	☑ Edit
			🗑 Delete

Figure 3-62. *Delete operation in the list*

If you click Delete, the specific item will be deleted from the Dataverse.

Create a New Record in the Dataverse from the Portal

To create a new student record from the Power Portal in the Dataverse, you should create a new Dataverse form for the student table; otherwise, you can use the same form used for edit, but you have to create a new basic form with the mode set to Insert.

This example uses the same form with a different mode. Use the following steps to create a basic form with Insert mode:

1. Go to the Portal Management model-driven app and, in the sitemap, select Basic Forms. Create a new basic form with the Insert mode and save it.

2. Go to the Power Portal Studio and click Sync Configuration. Select the List and enable the Create New Record property with the Form as the target type. In the second dropdown, choose the new basic form created with Insert mode.

3. Click Browse Website from the portal. You will see a Create New button at the top of the list.

Figure 3-63 shows the basic form with the Insert mode.

New Basic Form - Unsaved

| General | Form Options | On Success Settings | Additional Settings | Associated Table Reference | Basic Form Metadata |

Name	*	Student Basic Form Create for Vendor	
🔒 Table Name	*	school_student	Student (school_student)
🔒 Form Name	*	Student Create Form for Vendors	Student Create Form for Vendors
🔒 Tab Name	---	
Mode	Insert	
Website	*	🌐 Softchief Portal - softchiefportalnew	
Enable Table Permissions	☑	

Figure 3-63. *Creating a basic form*

Make sure you enabled Create Permission for the Vendor Table permission. Figure 3-64 shows the Create option enabled for the list.

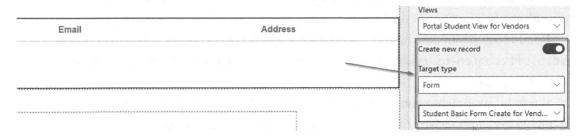

Figure 3-64. *Create basic form property*

When you browse the website, the Create New button appears. By clicking the button, the form will load as a popup. By providing data and pressing Submit, you can create a new record. You can also choose target type as Webpage or URL. If you choose Webpage, when you click the Create button, it will redirect to another web page. For URL target type, you can specify a URL to load upon a button click. For a small number of fields, the Form target type is best, but for more complex forms with more fields, you can use Webpage as the target type. Figure 3-65 shows a form list with the Create New button.

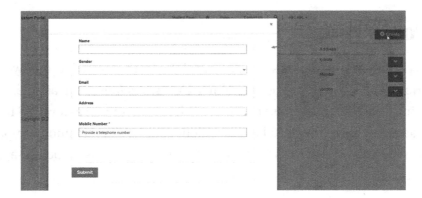

Figure 3-65. *Create new button for the list*

This way you can achieve CRUD operations for Dataverse tables from Power Portals without writing any code.

Form Validations and Client Scripts in Power Portal

You can validate form fields using Form metadata configurations. For complex validations, use JavaScript or jQuery.

Read more about adding form validation using form metadata at `https://docs.microsoft.com/en-us/power-apps/maker/portals/configure/configure-basic-form-metadata`.

For validation using JavaScript or jQuery, read `https://docs.microsoft.com/en-us/power-apps/maker/portals/configure/add-custom-javascript`.

Liquid Codes in Power Portal

Recall that Liquid is an open-source template language that is integrated natively into Microsoft Power Apps portals. It acts as a bridge between the Dataverse and the HTML or text output that is sent to the browser. Liquid can be used to add dynamic content to pages and to create a variety of custom templates. Additionally, Liquid provides access only to the data and operations that are explicitly allowed by the portals.

You can read more about Liquid codes for Power Portals at `https://docs.microsoft.com/en-us/learn/modules/liquid-template-language/`.

CSS in Power Portal

Cascading Style Sheets (CSS) allows you to control the formatting of your Power Portal website. By default, the `bootstrap.min.css` and `theme.css` files are available. You can edit the existing CSS files and upload new ones. When you upload a new CSS file, it will be available as a web file in the Portal Management app. Read more about uploading custom CSS in Power Portal at `https://docs.microsoft.com/en-us/power-apps/maker/portals/edit-css`.

Manage Power Apps

You can manage Power Apps inside the environment. As an administrator, you can do the following activities with Power Apps.

- Add or remove user permissions for the app

- Delete apps not in use

Navigate to the Power Admin Center at `https://admin.powerplatform.microsoft.com/`. In the top-right navigation bar, choose the correct environment. Then select the Power Apps resource. Figure 3-66 shows the Power Apps settings screen.

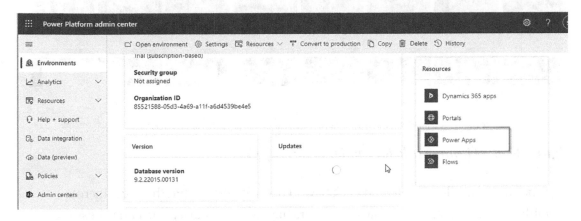

Figure 3-66. *Create a new button for the list*

It will display a list of Power Apps created in the current environment. Select the app you want to manage by clicking the three dots. You can choose Delete or Share. The Delete action will remove the app from the environment. Figure 3-67 shows actions that can manage the app.

✓	🖻	Sales Hub	⋯	1 wk ago	⋯ ⋯	Model-driven
	🖻	Resource Scheduling	🖻 Share		⋯ ⋯	Model-driven
	🖻	Project Service	🗑 Delete		⋯ ⋯	Model-driven
	🖻	Project Resource Hub	⋯	1 wk ago	⋯ ⋯	Model-driven

Figure 3-67. *Actions of app manage*

When you share the app, it will open the sharing screen, where you can choose which user you want to share with. If it is model-driven app, the sharing will use the app area. Navigate to **App Dashboard.** and click the three dots. Then click Manage Role. Figure 3-68 shows the Manage Role option for a model-driven app.

Figure 3-68. *Manage role for model-driven apps*

From the list, select a role and click Save. This will ensure that the security role is enabled for this app. That means that users having the security role can access the model-driven app. Figure 3-69 shows the access list.

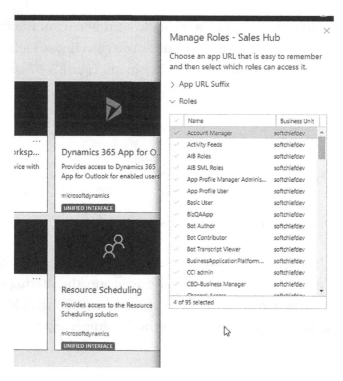

Figure 3-69. *Role list for access to the model-driven app*

If it is Canvas app, click Share and then find the user you want to share with. Once that's done, click Share. The app can now be accessed by the user. If you want to make the user a co-owner, check the Co-Owner checkbox and then click Share. Co-owners can edit the app. Figure 3-70 shows the sharing option for the Canvas app.

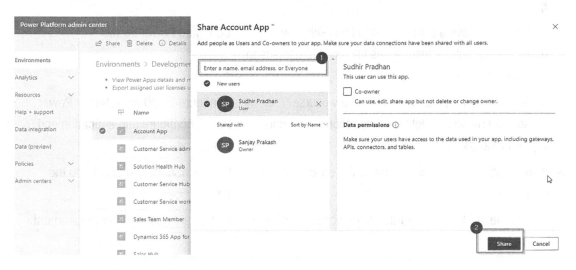

Figure 3-70. *Sharing the Canvas app popup*

Business Scenarios and Implementations

In this chapter, you learned how to configure model-driven apps, Canvas apps, and Power Portal options. You can now perform the following scenarios from Chapter 1 with the skills explained in this chapter.

8	System should provide a portable application of the student management system with dashboards, tables, forms, etc.	Configure a model-driven app and customize a sitemap.
9	The app should be accessible only by sales person security roles.	Manage roles for model-driven apps.
10	Configure a mobile device to enter student information by salesperson. Users should be able to create, update, read, and delete students from the app.	Configure a Canvas app for student entry.

11	Users can search students and send email to them from the mobile app.	Configure Canvas apps with an Outlook connector.
12	Display login user information in all screens of the mobile app.	Use global and local variables.
13	System must have a public website by which new students can register themselves and choose courses to join from the portal.	Configure Power Portal.
14	Students from the portal can create new course registration records, delete existing records, and update existing records.	Configure CRUD operation in Power Portal, configure authentication and authorization.
15	Hide the student's father's name while registering from the portal.	Use JavaScript and CSS to do the task.
16	Display the student's full name on the portal after logging in.	Use Liquid code for this requirement.

In the next chapter, you learn about Power Automate concepts and its use in various cloud applications to automate processes.

Summary

What you learned in this chapter:

- Understanding Power Apps solutions

- Working with table configurations and settings

- Working with columns, datatypes, calculated fields, and rollup fields

- Creating auto-number columns in the Dataverse

- Configuring relationships and relationship behaviors

- Working with business rules

- Configuring views for tables

- Designing table forms and layouts

- Chart configuration and dashboard pinning

- Configuring table-specific dashboards

- Concept of alternate keys

- Working with data in the Dataverse

- Business scenario, use cases, and implementation

- Concept of Power Apps and no-code, less-code platform

- Working with Canvas Apps in details

- PowerFX for Power Apps

- Working with Model-driven apps

- Power Portal Concepts and Design with Deployment

- Manage Power Apps

- Business Scenarios and Implementations

What you will learn in the next chapter:

- Concept of Power Automate

- Connectors in Power Automate

- Types of flows and uses

- Dynamic values and expressions in flows

- Using variables, loops, and conditions

- Working with approvals in Power Automate

- Business scenarios, use cases, and implementations

Working with Power Automate

Microsoft Power Automate (previously known as *Flow*) helps you create automated workflows between your favorite cloud and on-premise apps. It provides services to synchronize files, get notifications, collect data, and more.

Power Automate is an important pillar of Microsoft Power Platform ecosystem that builds robust automation over cloud apps.

These days, most apps are available in the cloud, although some are still available from on-premise environments. Integrating these cloud systems is tricky, and using a no-code, less-code platform to do this is a real benefit. Power Automate solves these integration automation needs, regardless of the datasource's location. Using connectors, you can connect practically any datasource to automate your business needs.

Power Automate's Building Blocks

Power Automate has three building blocks. These are triggers, connectors, and actions. Every Flow must have a trigger and one or more connectors and actions.

Table 4-1 explains the concepts of triggers, connectors, and actions.

© Sanjaya Prakash Pradhan 2022
S. Prakash Pradhan, *Power Platform and Dynamics 365 CE for Absolute Beginners*,
https://doi.org/10.1007/978-1-4842-8600-5_4

Table 4-1. *Triggers, Connectors, and Actions*

Building Block	Description
Triggers	Events that initiate a flow instance. For example, running a flow on-demand from a button click, or running a flow when a file is uploaded to SharePoint.
Connectors	Adaptors that communicate with other products or services. For example, if you want to create a file in OneDrive, you need a OneDrive Connector. If you want to read data from Dynamics 365, you can create a connector to the Dataverse. Connectors require authentication. You must have a subscription to the service you want to connect from Power Automate.
Actions	Operations that you define so that the Flow will perform them. For example, creating a file in SharePoint, deleting a record from the Dataverse, sending an email, etc.

Features of Power Automate

Automate quickly and more securely

With Power Automate, anyone can create automated processes using flows. You can automate repetitive, monotonous operations with ease, using low-code, drag-and-drop tools and hundreds of pre-built connectors.

Boost efficiency

With process adviser, you can record and visualize your end-to-end processes while getting guided advice for developing flows and detailed insights that take the guesswork out of deciding what to automate.

Enhance workflows with AI

With AI Builder, you can make your automation even smarter. Use document automation to quickly process forms, handle approvals, identify photos and text, and generate with pre-built models.

Connectors in Power Automate

A *connector* is a wrapper or proxy that allows an underlying service to communicate with Microsoft Power Automate, Microsoft Power Apps, and Azure Logic Apps. It allows users to link their accounts and use a library of pre-built actions and triggers to create apps and processes.

Microsoft has 200+ connectors you can use to automate business process and flows, but if a specific connector is not available, you can create your own custom connector. Figure 4-1 displays a list of connectors.

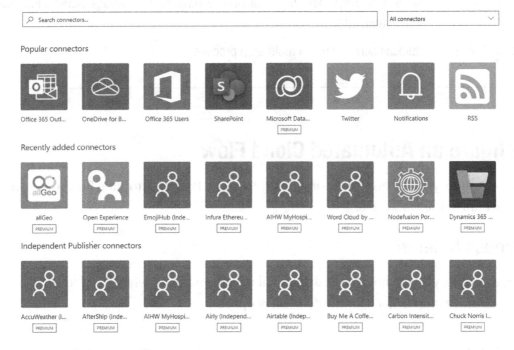

Figure 4-1. *Connector list*

Types of Flows and Uses

There are five types of flow you can create. The type of trigger decides the type of flow. These are explained in Table 4-2.

Table 4-2. Types of Flows

Type	Description
Automated Cloud Flow	Triggered by designated events.
Instant Cloud Flow	Triggered manually as needed.
Scheduled Cloud Flow	You can choose when and how often it runs.
Desktop Flow	Automated processes on your desktop environment. Leverage Robotic Process Automation (RPA).
Business Process Flow	Guides users through a multi-step process.

Configure an Automated Cloud Flow

In this example, you see how to automatically trigger a Power Automate flow when an event occurs in the Dataverse.

Business Scenario

In this example, you see how to send an email to your manager when Lead annual revenue is more than $5,000 for notification purposes.

Solution

This solution requires a Power Automate configuration with an event trigger. The following steps show how to configure the flow.

Step 1: Use the Solution to Create a Flow

Open the solution and click the Add New option. Choose Automation then the Cloud Flow with Automated option. Figure 4-2 shows this process.

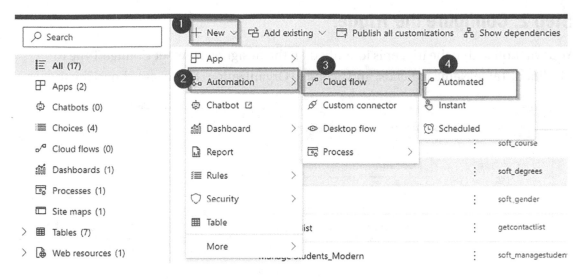

Figure 4-2. *Adding an automated flow to the solution*

Now specify a name and a trigger. Call it Send Email to Manager for Lead more than 5000 USD revenue. Call the trigger Dataverse and, in the list, choose When a row is added, modified, or deleted trigger. You can learn more about the Dataverse connectors from Microsoft at `https://docs.microsoft.com/en-us/connectors/commondataserviceforapps/`. Click Create. Figure 4-3 shows the trigger and the name of the flow.

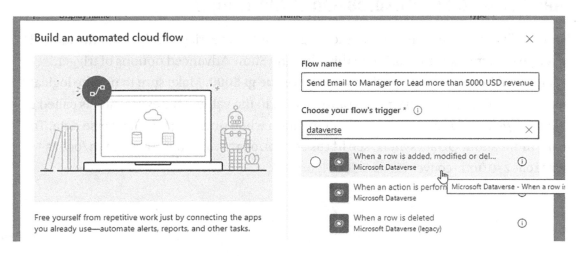

Figure 4-3. *Adding an automated flow to the solution*

Step 2: Configure the Trigger

You will notice that the trigger is identified on the designer. Now set Change Type to Modified, Table Name to Leads, and Scope to Organization. Figure 4-4 shows the trigger.

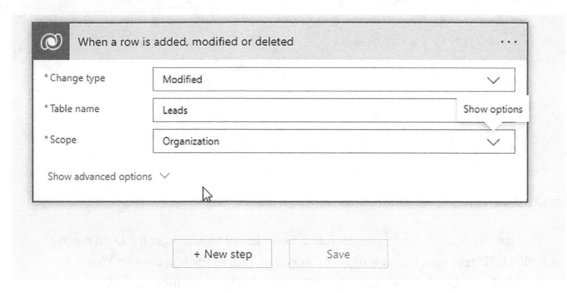

Figure 4-4. *The Dataverse trigger*

Step 3: Add a Filter Expression to the Trigger

Now you'll add a filter condition to the trigger to filter and trigger only when the annual revenue is more than $5,000. To do this, click the Show Advanced options of trigger.

In the Filter Rows box, specify **annualrevenue gt 5000**. Make sure to use the logical name of the field you are trying to compare with to the value. This expression is called an *OData expression* and it defines a filter condition while querying the Dataverse data. To learn more about OData syntax, see https://www.odata.org/documentation/odata-version-2-0/uri-conventions/. See Figure 4-5.

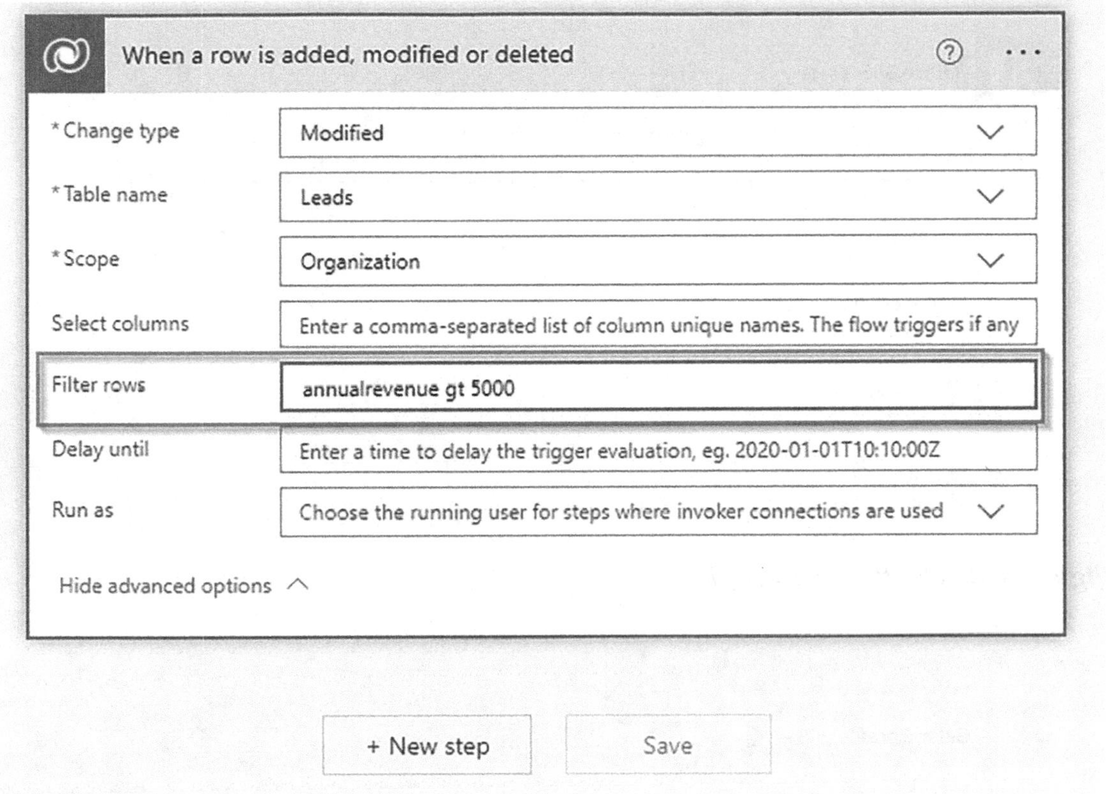

Figure 4-5. *Adding a filter condition*

Step 4: Get the Current User Manager

Click +New Step and search Get My Profile. This creates a connection to Office 365 Users so that you can use Get My Profile. See Figures 4-6 and 4-7.

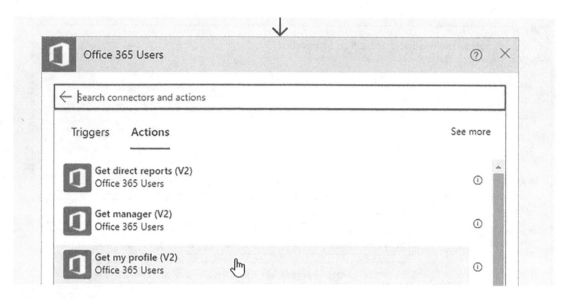

Figure 4-6. *Get the user profile*

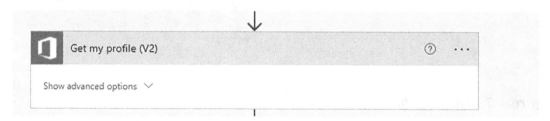

Figure 4-7. *The get user profile step*

Click +New Step and search for the Get Manager trigger. Once you type **get manager,** it will display related triggers and actions that you can use. Figure 4-8 shows the Get Manager trigger.

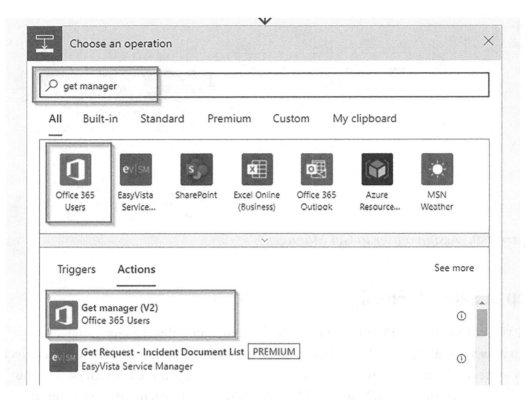

Figure 4-8. *The Get Manager trigger and action*

Select the Get Manager action. This will sign in automatically and create a background connector with the Office 365 Users application using the current login user credential.

This Get Manager action requires a user email so that it can get the manager information.

In the User box, assign the Mail attribute from the Dynamics content so that it will pass the current user profile mail into the Get Manager action for which it will read manager information. This Mail attribute will be available in the Dynamic panel because of the Office 365 Users connector. To learn more about the Office 365 Users connector, see `https://docs.microsoft.com/en-us/connectors/office365users/`. See Figure 4-9.

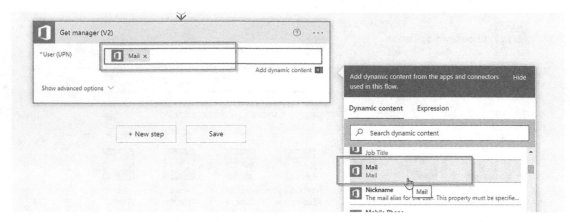

Figure 4-9. *Assign a user to Get Manager*

Step 5: Send an Email

Now you can send a well formatted email to the manager. After the Get Manager step, add a new step called Send Email Using Gmail connector. Assign features to the subject body as needed using the Dynamic content panel. If the Dynamic content panel is not visible, click the blue icon labeled Add Dynamic Content. It will open the Dynamic panel. The Dynamic content panel displays the dynamic values that are part of the previous steps associated with different connectors. Figure 4-10 shows the process of assigning dynamic contents to the email send step.

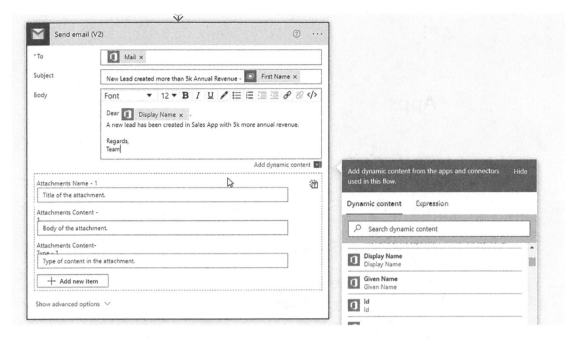

Figure 4-10. *Send an email and adding dynamic content*

Now if you create a lead in the Dataverse and update the annual revenue with more than $5,000, the system will send an email to your manager from your Gmail Account. You can use the Outlook connector to send email as well.

Configure an Instant Cloud Flow

Instant flow creates a mobile button to click on demand and the actions will be performed as per the flow design. Say you want to send an email with an attachment to a person on demand via a button click.

Create an Instant Flow by Navigating to Power Automate

Open office.com, click All Apps, and choose Power Automate. You can also create the instant flow inside a solution, but it will not display the button on mobile devices. Figure 4-11 shows the Power Automate link.

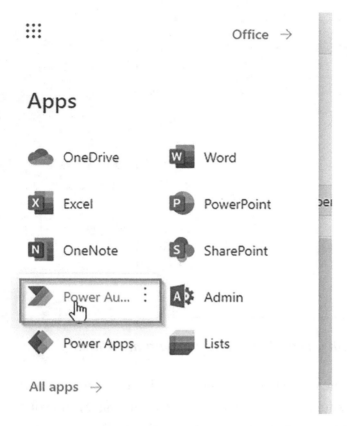

Figure 4-11. *Power Automate link*

On the Power Automate screen, click Environment and choose the correct environment. Figure 4-12 shows the environment change option.

Figure 4-12. *Power Automate environment change*

Click + Create and choose Instant Cloud Flow. Figure 4-13 shows the instant flow option.

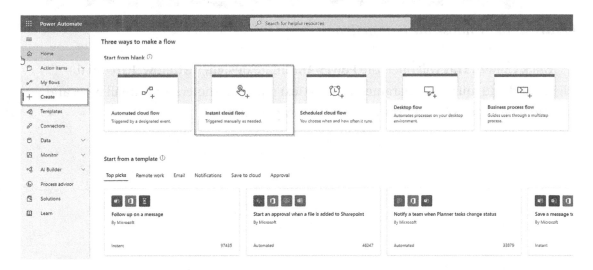

Figure 4-13. *Instant flow option*

Call this Send Email with File and, from the connector list, choose Manually Trigger a Flow. Figure 4-14 shows the button flow option.

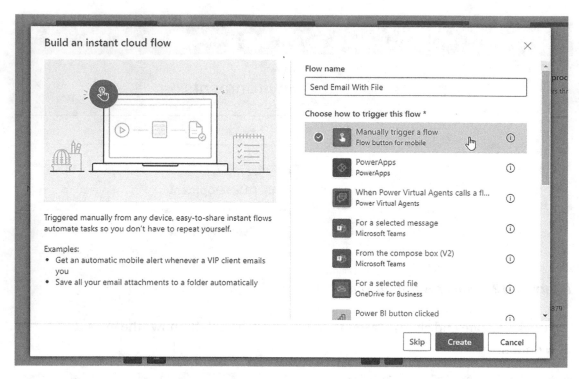

Figure 4-14. *Choose the button flow*

Click Create. This will open the Power Automate designer window. Expand the trigger and add four input parameters—two text type parameters, one email type, and one file type. Figure 4-15 shows the instant flow parameters.

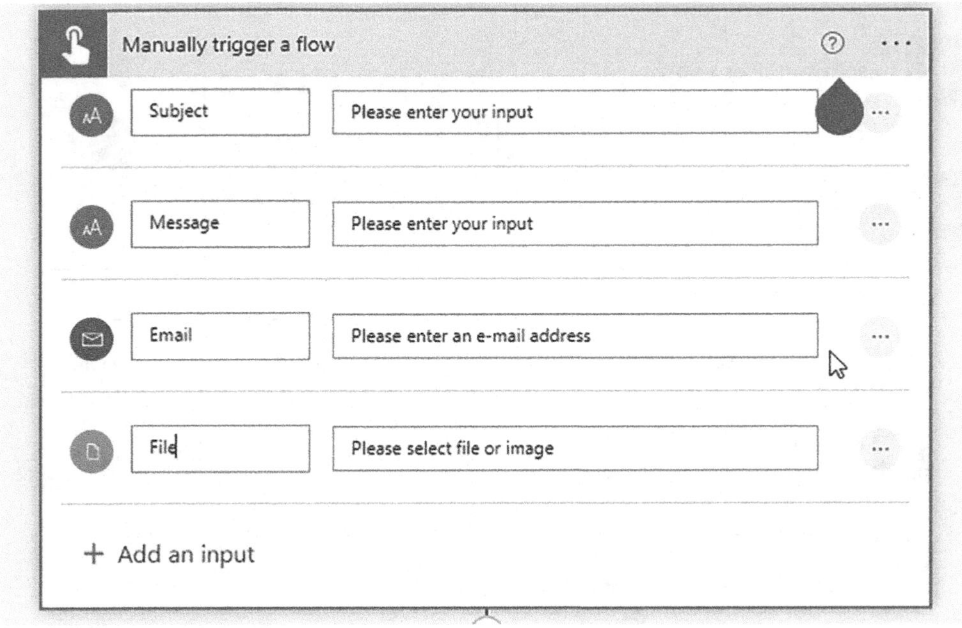

Figure 4-15. Parameters

Click + New Step and search for the Gmail connector. Choose the Send Email action. To learn more about Gmail connector, see `https://docs.microsoft.com/en-us/connectors/gmail/`. Figure 4-16 shows the Gmail connector.

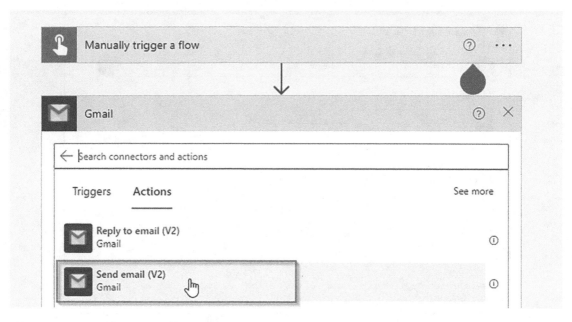

Figure 4-16. *The Gmail connector*

Click the Connect button, which will open the Gmail Login screen for authentication. Provide authentication and click OK. Using the Dynamic content panel, assign the To, Subject, and Body of the Gmail Send steps from the Parameter list. Figure 4-17 shows the process of assigning values to fields.

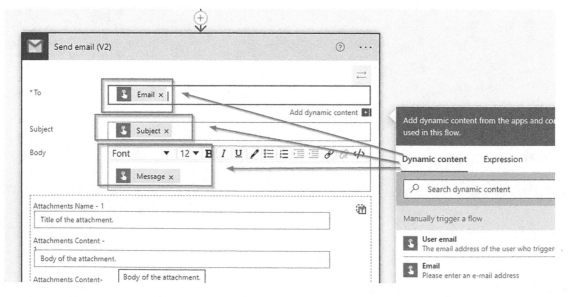

Figure 4-17. *Assigning values from the Dynamic panel*

148

For the File option, provide document.pdf for the Attachment Name and File for the dynamic content panel. For Content-Type, specify pdf. Figure 4-18 shows the file field assignment.

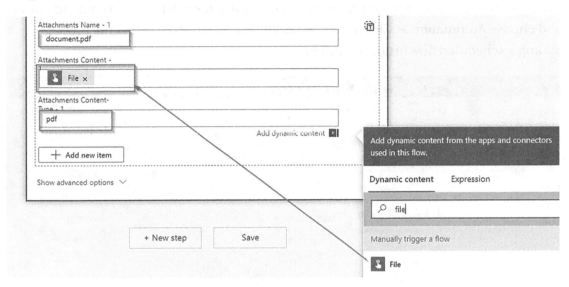

Figure 4-18. *File assignment*

Now save Power Automate. Open your mobile device and install the Power Automate app from Google Play Store or Apple App Store. Once it's installed, open the app and log in using your credentials. Follow the site at `https://us.flow.microsoft.com/en-us/mobile/download/` to download the app and then install it. Select the correct environment. Now if you click the link at the bottom-center of the app, you will see the flow. Clicking the Send Email with File button will prompt you to provide a subject, message, email address, and a file to upload. Once you click Done, the email will be sent to the respective email account.

Configure a Scheduled Cloud Flow

Scheduled cloud flows can be used to run business logic repeatedly in a specific time interval. For example, if you want to run a flow everyday 10AM, you can configure scheduled cloud flow.

Let's consider a business scenario. You want to send an attendance email every day at 10AM to all the students at your school. Follow these steps to configure Power Automate to do this.

Step 1: Create a Scheduled Flow by Navigating to Power Automate

Navigate to your Power Apps solution and open it. Click the + Add New command button and choose Automation ➤ Cloud Flow ➤ Scheduled. Figure 4-19 shows the process of adding a scheduled flow inside a solution.

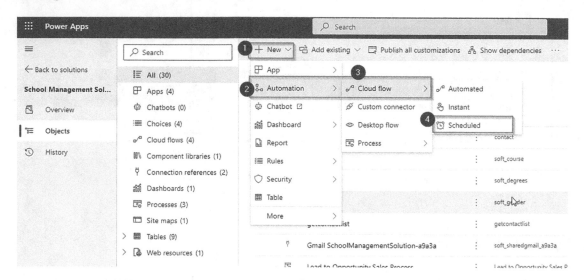

Figure 4-19. *Adding a scheduled flow*

Call this Send Reminder for Attendance Fillup. Select a starting date and time. Configure the Repeat Every option in the next screen. Figure 4-20 shows the recurrence configuration.

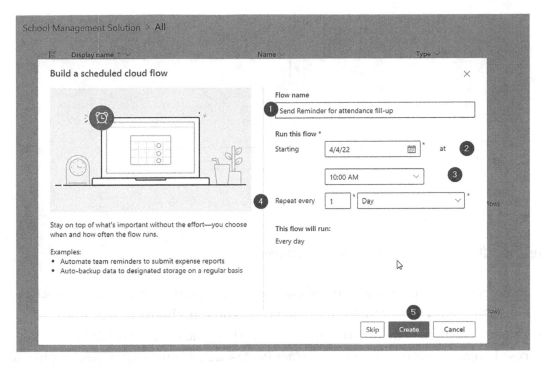

Figure 4-20. *Configuring recurrence*

Click Create. This will open the Flow Designer, where you can add actions.

Step 2: Connect to the Dataverse to Get Students

Click +New Step. Because you want to send the email to all students from the Dataverse, you need the Dataverse connector. You must also choose the List Row action to read all student records from the Dataverse. Figure 4-21 shows the List Row action of the Dataverse. You can learn more about List Row action from the Dataverse connector topic at `https://docs.microsoft.com/en-us/connectors/commondataserviceforapps/`.

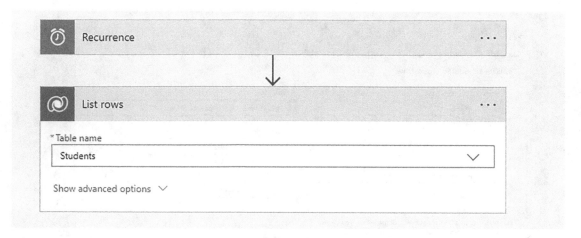

Figure 4-21. *List Row action of the Dataverse*

In the next step, add a new step and choose Control Connector ➤ Apply to Each Action. In the Select an Output from Previous Steps option, choose a value from the Dynamic content panel. Learn more about the loops action at `https://docs.microsoft.com/en-us/power-automate/apply-to-each`. Figure 4-22 shows how to add a value object to a loop step.

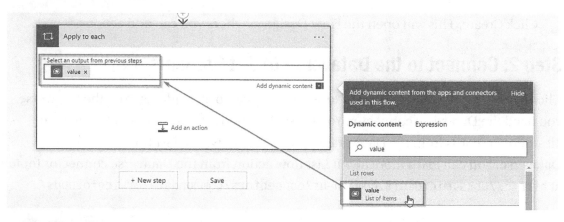

Figure 4-22. *Adding a value object to a loop*

Inside Apply to Each Action, add a new step. Choose the Gmail connector and select the Send Email action. Specify Email in the To field using the Dynamic content panel. In the Subject field, specify the Reminder – Attendance Filling for the Day static value.

In the Email body, specify some content as you wish. For example, "Dear Student, please fill in the attendance now." Figure 4-23 shows how to assign email fields.

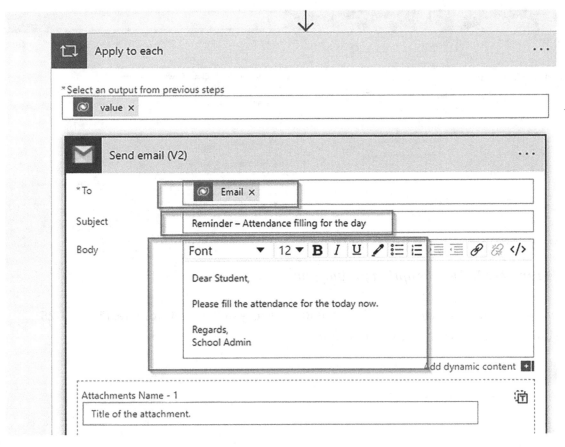

Figure 4-23. *Assigning email fields*

Save the flow. Now the scheduled flow is ready. It will run every day at 10AM, as scheduled. You can check the run status using Details page of the Flow. Figure 4-24 shows the details option for flow.

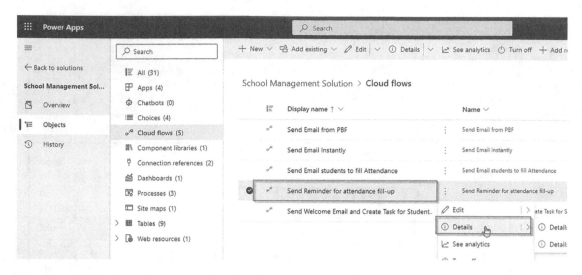

Figure 4-24. *Details option for the flow*

In the Details page, you will see the Run History of Power Automate. Figure 4-25 shows the details run history of the flow.

Figure 4-25. *Details option for the flow*

This is how you create a scheduled flow for your business needs.

Configure a Business Process Flow

Business Process Flows (BPF) guide users to follow a predefined process with multiple stages in order to complete a specific task. For example, for a process called Student On-Boarding, your business might follow specific stages so that all users follow the same steps to complete the process. For more about BPF, visit https://docs.microsoft.com/en-us/power-automate/business-process-flows-overview.

A typical business process flow could be student on-boarding. Figure 4-26 shows details for this flow. The stages may include the following:

1. Capture personal details

2. Capture communication details

3. Capture enrolled courses

4. Record payment details

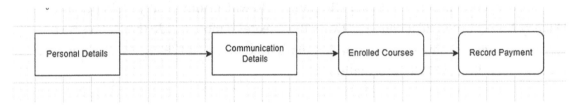

Figure 4-26. *Details option for this flow*

To configure a Business Process Flow (BPF), use the following steps.

Step 1: Use the Solution to Create a BPF

Open the Power Apps solution and choose + New ➤ Automation ➤ Process ➤ Business Process Flow. Figure 4-27 shows how to add a BPF inside a solution.

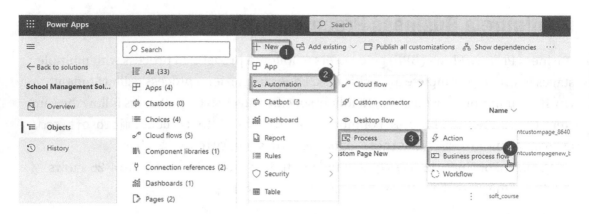

Figure 4-27. *Adding a BPF inside a solution*

Once you click the option, it will open a side panel where you can specify a display name and table for which you are going to create the BPF. For example, the "student on-boarding" BPF is connected to the Student table.

Choose Student from the table. The Name field will automatically fill in per the Display Name, but in all lowercase. Every BPF creates a table inside the Dataverse to store the stage and data step information that's used in the BPF. Figure 4-28 shows the process of adding the BPF information.

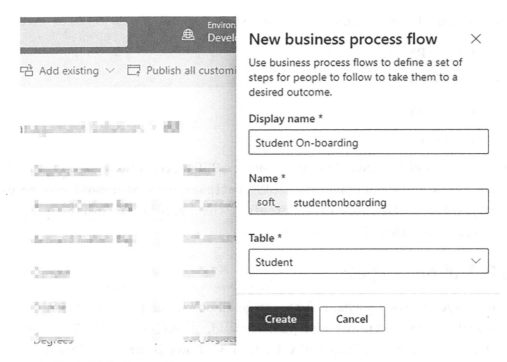

Figure 4-28. BPF information

Click Create. The BPF Designer will open in a new window. Use the right side component panel and drag four stages to the designer canvas. Four stages are required. Every stage contains one or more data steps, which point to the column of the specific table to which the stage is connected. Figure 4-29 shows the BPF designer.

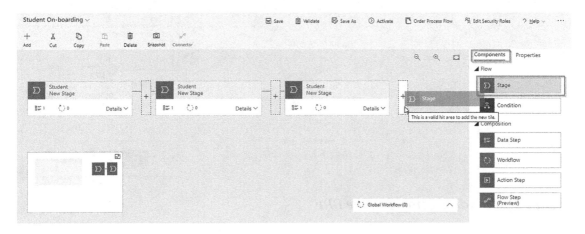

Figure 4-29. The BPF designer

You can add different components inside a stage, including:

- Data steps

- Workflows

- Action steps

- Flow steps

You can also add conditional branches inside a BPF for complex business processes. Read more about branching in BPF at https://docs.microsoft.com/en-us/dynamics365/customerengagement/on-premises/customize/enhance-business-process-flows-branching?view=op-9-1.

Step 2: Edit the Stages

Click First Stage and specify a name for the stage. Choose a category and click Apply. Notice that the first stage Entity option points to Student and is read-only. That means you cannot change this First Stage entity. Figure 4-30 shows the process of adding stages to the BPF.

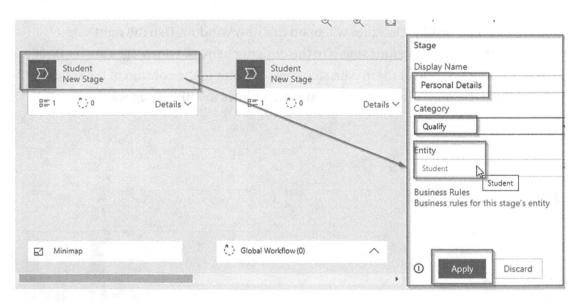

Figure 4-30. *Adding stages to the BPF*

Click the Details option in the First Stage and choose Data Steps #1. From the Properties panel, specify a data step name and select Data Field for the Name. You can select the Required flag if you want the data step to be mandatory. Users cannot move to the next stage until any mandatory data steps are complete. Click Apply. Figure 4-31 shows the process of adding a data step inside a stage.

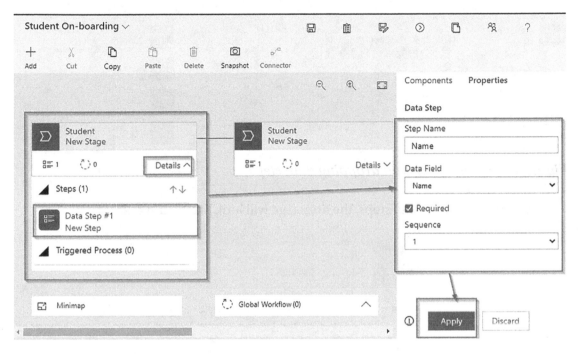

Figure 4-31. *Adding a data step inside a stage*

Repeat this step to add multiple data steps. Use the Component panel and the drag-and-drop operation. Figure 4-32 shows the drag-and-drop process.

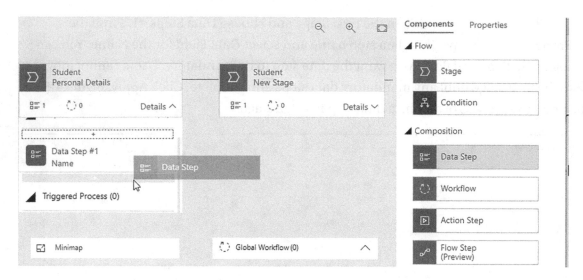

Figure 4-32. *Dragging and dropping data steps*

After you add more data steps, the first stage will look like Figure 4-33.

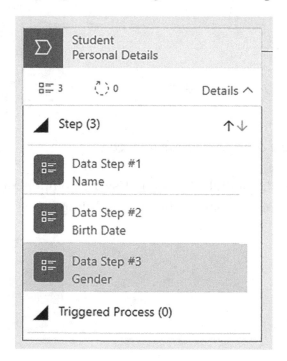

Figure 4-33. *The final look of the first stage*

Click the second stage and give it a name and a category and then set Entity to Student. Click Apply. Note that you can modify the Entity dropdown from the second stage onward. You are capturing communication details for the student, so choose Student as the Entity in this stage also. Figure 4-34 shows the process of adding a new stage.

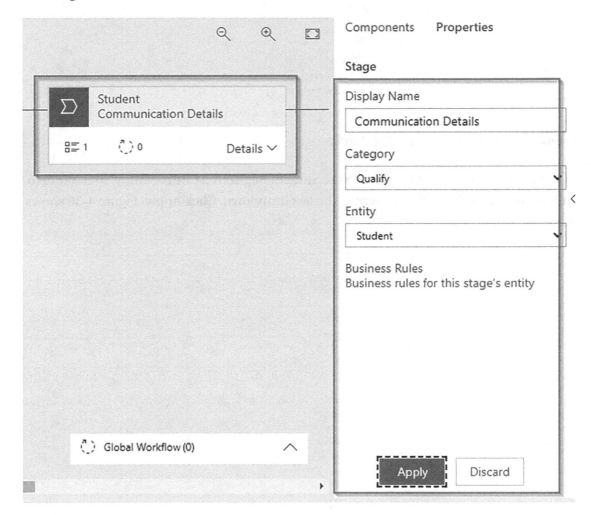

Figure 4-34. *Adding a new stage*

Keep adding data steps inside the second stage. The completed second stage will look like Figure 4-35.

Figure 4-35. *Second stage, final look*

The third stage should connect to the Student Registered Course entity. Make sure to choose Relationship for the Student in the last dropdown. Click Apply. Figure 4-36 shows the stage properties.

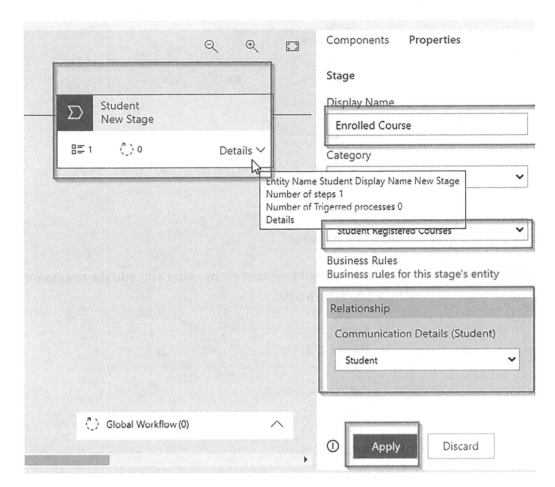

Figure 4-36. *Stage properties*

The final version of the third stage will look like Figure 4-37.

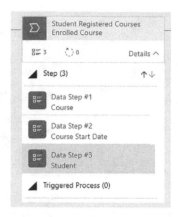

Figure 4-37. *Final look of the third stage*

The fourth stage points to the Student Payment entity. After you add the necessary data steps, this stage will look like Figure 4-38.

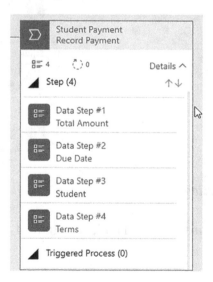

Figure 4-38. *Final look of the fourth stage*

After adding all these stages and their data steps, validate and save the BPF. Now activate the BPF by clicking the Activate button. Figure 4-39 shows the final look of this BPF.

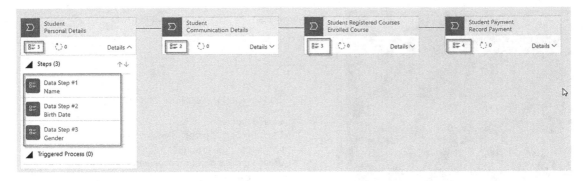

Figure 4-39. *Final look of the BPF*

To test this BPF, navigate to Power Apps and open the Apps area. Choose the model-driven app of your choice, where the Student table is added to the sitemap. For this example, it's Student App. Click School Management and choose Edit. Figure 4-40 shows the Edit the Model-Driven App option.

Figure 4-40. *Edit the model-driven app option*

This will open the Model App Designer window. Click Business Process Flow Area and select the BPF from the list. Unselect the other BPF. Figure 4-41 shows the BPF added to the model-driven app.

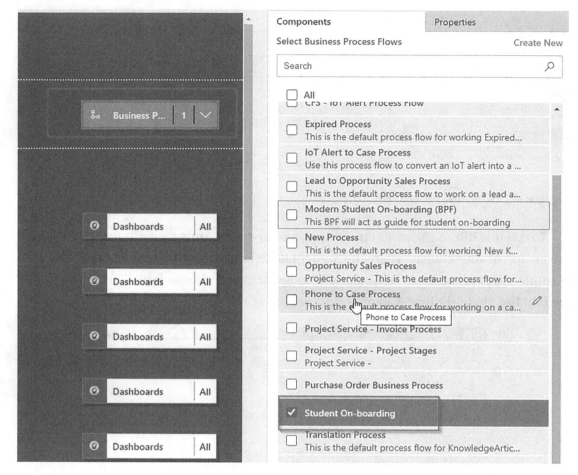

Figure 4-41. *Adding the BPF to the model-driven app*

Now save and publish the model-driven app. Click the Play button on the top-right corner.

The Student App will open. Click the Students sub-area and click the +New command to open a new form for the student.

Now you will see that the BPF is available on the top of the form. The BPF will display with all stages you designed. All these stages remain inactive until you visit and take action on every required data step.

To start the BPF, you need to first save the student record by providing the mandatory values; then you can work with the BPF.

Provide the student's mandatory fields and click Save. If you then click the First Stage, you will see the data steps and you can specify data step values and click the Next Stage button. Figure 4-42 shows the BPF in stage 1.

Figure 4-42. *The BPF in stage 1*

Once you click Next Stage, the first stage will be complete. You'll navigate to the second stage. Figure 4-43 shows the BPF in stage 2.

Figure 4-43. *BPF in stage 2*

Complete the second stage and click Next Stage. This will show you a message that no records are found, as the student enrolled course record has not been created. Click +Create. This will open a new form to capture the course information for the student. Figure 4-44 shows the BPF in stage 2, notification.

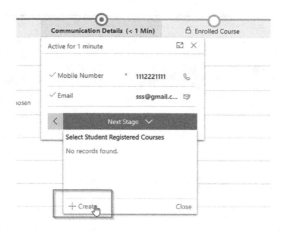

Figure 4-44. *BPF in stage 2. notification*

From the new course enroll form, provide the mandatory values and click Save. Now you will find Next Stage button. Figure 4-45 shows the BPF in stage 3.

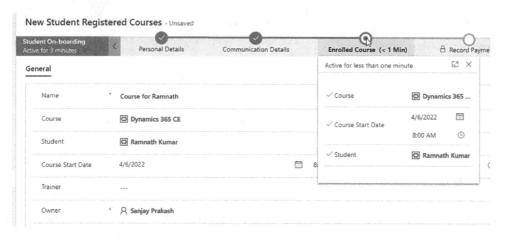

Figure 4-45. *BPF in stage 3*

Now click the + Create option to create a new payment record for the student. Figure 4-46 shows the BPF in stage 4.

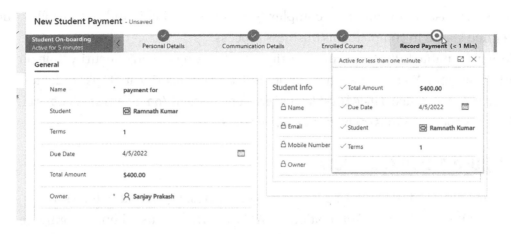

Figure 4-46. *BPF in stage 4*

Click Save. The Finish button appears for the last stage. Click Finish to complete the student on-boarding process. Figure 4-47 shows the BPF in the final stage.

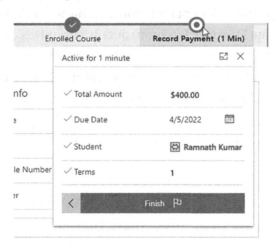

Figure 4-47. *The BPF in the final stage*

Now the BPF is complete. Figure 4-48 shows the completed BPF.

Figure 4-48. *The completed BPF*

This way, users can ignore the complexity of tables and fields and simply follow the predefined stages to complete this business process.

You can enable BPF for specific security roles by using the Edit Security Role on the BPF Designer. You can read more about BPF and its security at `https://docs.` `microsoft.com/en-us/dynamics365/customerengagement/on-premises/customize/` `business-process-flows-overview?view=op-9-1`.

Configure a Desktop Flow

Desktop Flows are designed using Power Automate Desktop. Desktop Flows are also called Robotic Process Automation (RPA) flows. You can use them to configure automation for desktop and web application tasks.

For example, if you want to download an Excel sheet from a website, extract data from the Excel sheet, and put it in a file, you can use the Desktop Flow. Or if you want to back up certain folders on a regular basis, you can use the Desktop Flow.

You can use Desktop Flow in lots of real-world scenarios. To create Desktop Flows, download Power Automate Desktop. For more details about Desktop Flow, visit `https://docs.microsoft.com/en-us/power-automate/desktop-flows/create-flow`.

Log in to `flow.microsoft.com` using your credentials. Choose the correct environment. Figure 4-49 shows how to change the environment.

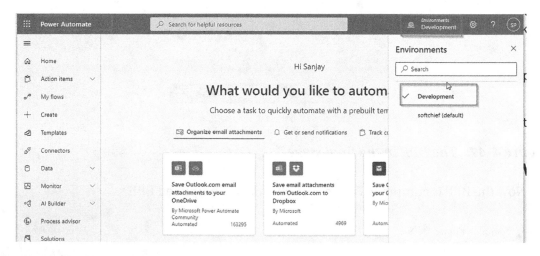

Figure 4-49.   *Changing the environment*

Click + Create and choose Desktop Flow. Figure 4-50 shows the Desktop Flow option.

Figure 4-50. *Select the Desktop Flow option*

A new popup will open; click the Download app. If you already downloaded it, click the Launch app. It will download an .EXE file. Double-click the setup file and install it in your desktop. After installation, click the Launch app from the popup. Figure 4-51 shows the launch Desktop Flow app option.

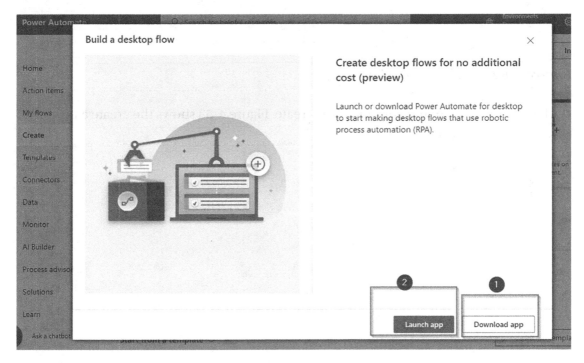

Figure 4-51. *Launch Desktop Flow app option*

The Launch app will open the Power Automate Desktop app. From the desktop app, click login and choose the correct environment. Click + New Flow. Figure 4-52 shows the Desktop Flow home screen.

Figure 4-52. *Desktop Flow home screen*

Provide a name for the flow and click Create. Figure 4-53 shows the create a new Desktop Flow process.

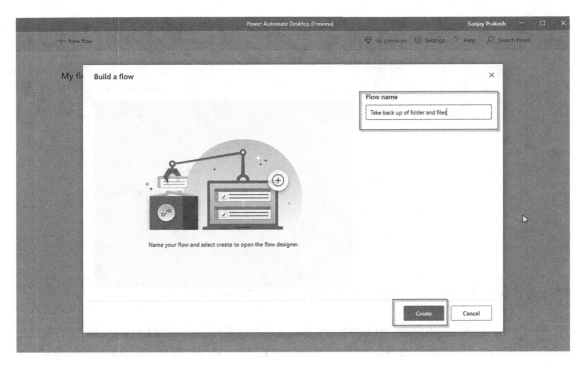

Figure 4-53. *Creating a new Desktop Flow*

This will open the Desktop Flow designer, where you can drag-and-drop actions to the main screen. The following example shows how to copy a folder with files from one location to another.

Use the Search Folder action and drag the Copy Folder step from the action pane to the main screen. Figure 4-54 shows the home screen of the Desktop Flow editor.

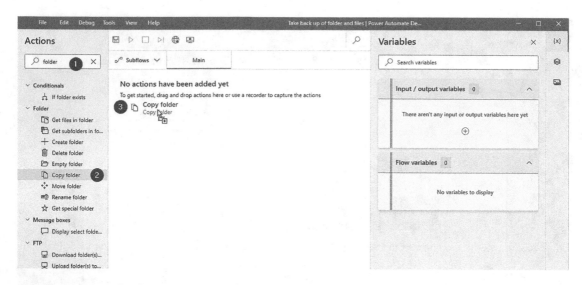

Figure 4-54. *The home screen of the Desktop Flow editor*

You now have to provide information about the folder you want to copy. Select the Folder to Copy, Destination Folder, and If Folder Exist options. If you want to override the folder, choose the Overwrite option and click Save. Figure 4-55 shows the Copy Folder action.

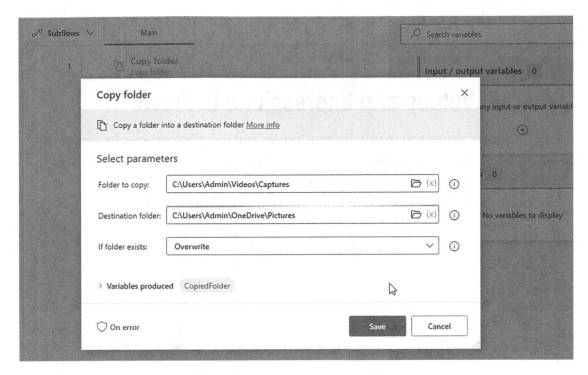

Figure 4-55. The Copy Folder action

Now click the Run button to play the flow. After the flow run, you will see the folders copied from the source folder to the destination. Figure 4-56 shows the copy folder result.

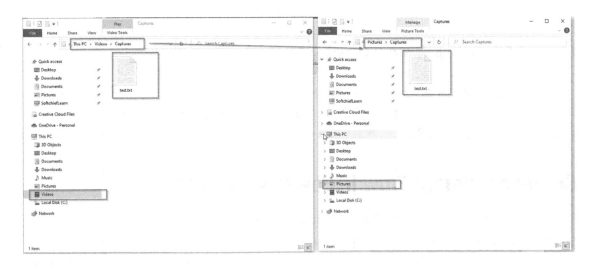

Figure 4-56. The copy folder result

You can create a Desktop Flow for web and desktop automation using actions and running it as needed.

Dynamic Values and Expressions in Flows

Power Automate allows you to use dynamic values and write expressions for more complex data operations. To any field value, you can assign a static field or use the Dynamic panel to choose dynamic data from the previous steps.

Figure 4-57 shows the process of adding dynamic values to a field.

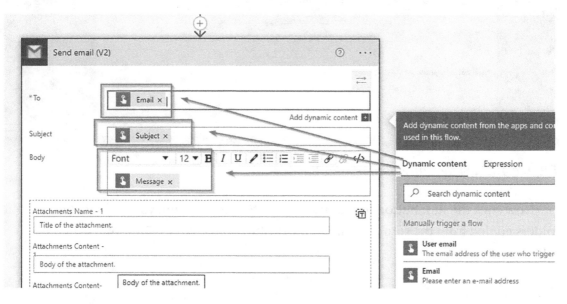

Figure 4-57. *Adding dynamic values*

Using expressions, you can do string operations, date operations, and so on, in Power Automate. Let's consider an example here. You want to send renewal due date email to a student using an instant flow.

Create an Instant Flow in Power Automate

Open flow.microsoft.com and log in using your credentials. Choose the correct environment. Choose the +Create option and then choose Instant Cloud Flow. In the Manual Trigger area, add a Text parameter for the email field. In the next step, add a new action to send an email using the Gmail connector.

In the Email To, assign the Email parameter from the Dynamic content panel, which is part of the Manually Trigger a Button step. Specify the email subject as "Reminder – Student Renewal Pending" and, in the Email body, add "Dear Student, your renewal due date is". After "is," you'll want to display the current date plus one year. So, for these types of scenarios, you need expressions.

Click the location where you want to add the expression and then click the Add Dynamic Content link, which will open the Dynamic panel.

Select the Expression tab from the Dynamic panel. You can type in expressions, as shown in Figure 4-58, which uses the addDays expression. The first parameter is the current date, so we used utcNow(). The second parameter is how many days you want to add to the current date. After these steps, click Update.

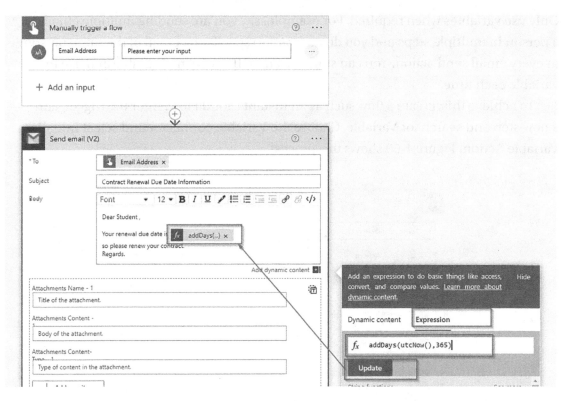

Figure 4-58. *Adding an expression*

When you run the flow, the expression is evaluated in real-time and updated in the email body.

There are hundreds of expressions available. You can refer to all such expressions using the Microsoft knowledge base at `https://docs.microsoft.com/en-us/azure/logic-apps/workflow-definition-language-functions-reference`.

Using Variables, Loops, and Conditions

You can use variables, loops, and conditions inside Power Automate as needed. Variables are a good way to store data temporarily in a placeholder.

Working with Variables and Conditions

Only use variables when required. For example, say you are sending multiple emails to a person in multiple steps and you do not want to specify the email of the same person in every email send action. You can store the email ID once in a variable and use the variable each time.

To achieve this, create a flow such as an Instant Cloud Flow. After the trigger, add a new step and search for Variable. Choose the Variable connector and select Initialize Variable Action. Figure 4-59 shows this process.

Figure 4-59. *Choosing a variable*

Specify a name for the variable and set the Type to String. You can choose a variable type of Boolean, Integer, Float, String, Object, or Array. Figure 4-60 shows the process of choosing the variable data type.

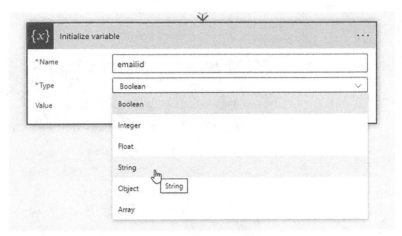

Figure 4-60. *Choose a variable data type*

In the Value field, provide the email ID that you want to use in further steps. Figure 4-61 shows the process of assigning a value to a variable.

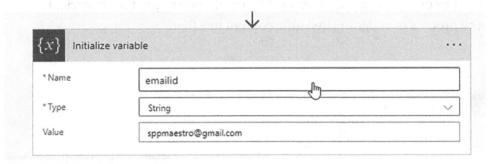

Figure 4-61. *Assigning a value to a variable*

You can add new steps to perform your additional actions, such as if Today Day is Monday, send email body "You have to work on consulting"; otherwise, send email body "Work on Training".

Use a Condition Connector step and, to the Condition value, add the dayOfWeek expression. Inside that expression, pass utcNow. This will return the day of the week as an integer. If the current day is Monday, it will return 1. Figure 4-62 shows the assign expressions to condition process.

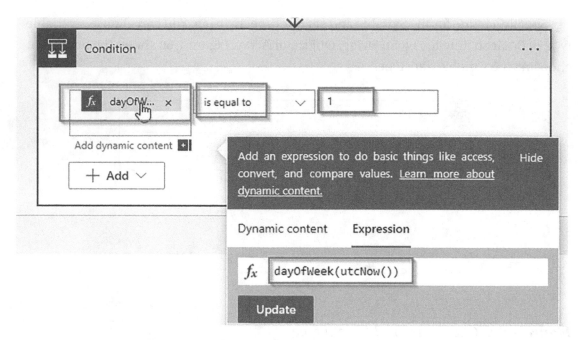

Figure 4-62. *Assigning expressions to conditions*

In the Yes condition, add a Send Email step. In the To field, choose a variable from the Dynamic content panel. Choose a subject and body as per the scenario. Figure 4-63 shows the process of assigning dynamic content to a field.

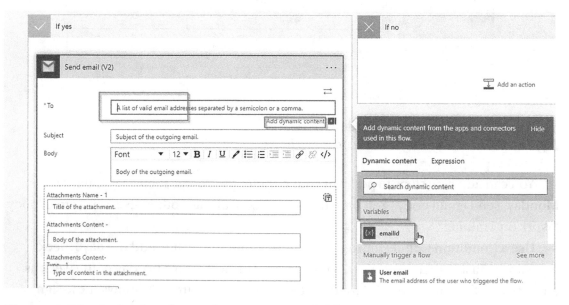

Figure 4-63. *Assigning dynamic content to a field*

180

Now add another Send Email action inside the No section. If the condition is not met, the step will execute. Figure 4-64 shows this condition branch.

Figure 4-64. *The condition branch*

You used the same variable in both steps. If you test this, you will get an email based on the current day of the week.

Working with Loops

You can use loops to read values from a list of items using iteration. For example, you can use loops to read all rows from an Excel sheet, you can use loops to insert data into the Dataverse from an Excel sheet, and so on.

Say you want to send an email to all the students of your schools stored in the Dataverse. For this scenario, you have to use a loop that will run every student record and send the emails.

Create an Instant flow and add two input parameters—Subject and Body—using the Text type. Add a new step and search the Dataverse. Choose the Students table and the List Row action to read all the students. Figure 4-65 shows the List Row action for the Dataverse.

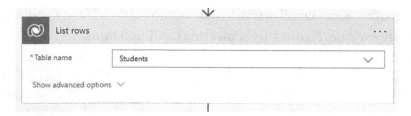

Figure 4-65. *List Row action for the Dataverse*

Now add a new step and choose Control ➤ Apply to Each. Figure 4-66 shows the process of assigning a value list to a loop.

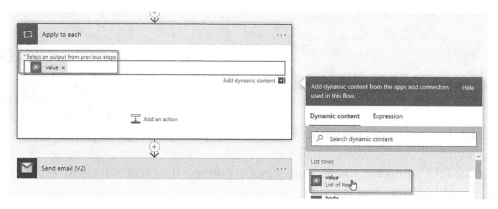

Figure 4-66. *Assigning a value list to a loop*

Inside the loop, add a Send Email action and assign the email from the List Row step to the To value. Figure 4-67 shows this process.

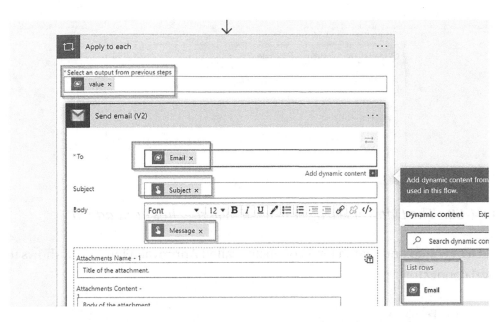

Figure 4-67. *Assigning an email field value using dynamic content*

This is how you use loops in Power Automate.

Working with Approvals in Power Automate

Approvals are important scenarios in every business. Say you want to send an approval to one or more people to approve an amount of student joining fees when the amount is less than $200.

To achieve this business scenario, previously you had to write lots of code. Now you can achieve this with no-code. Use the following steps to do this.

Make sure you have an Office 365 Outlook license for your employees to use approvals.

Step 1: Add an Automated Cloud Flow

In your Power Apps solution, add an automated cloud flow named Send Approval for Student Payment Less Than 200 USD. Choose Connector for the Dataverse and the When A New Row Added trigger. Set the Scope to Organization. Set the Table name to Student Payments. Figure 4-68 shows the Dataverse trigger after a new row has been added.

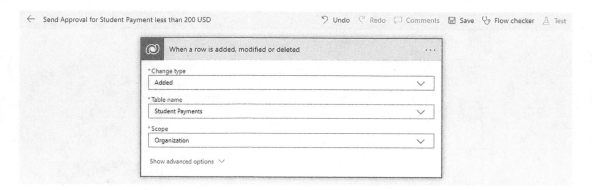

Figure 4-68. *The Dataverse trigger when a new row has been added*

Add a new step and search for a connector called Approval. Figure 4-69 shows the Approval connector.

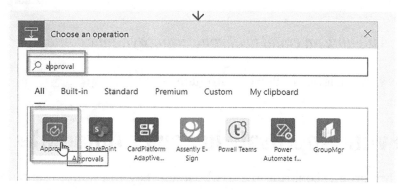

Figure 4-69. *The Approval connector*

From the list of actions, select Start and Wait for an Approval. You can choose Create an Approval or Wait for an Approval also, depending on your needs. The approval will raise and wait until the approver takes action so that the payment record will be updated. Figure 4-70 shows the Approval action type.

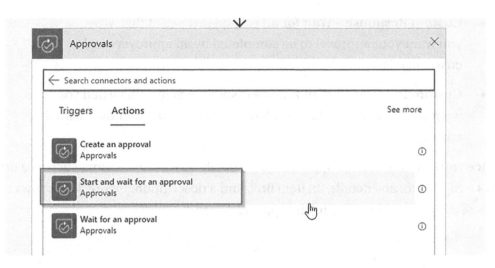

Figure 4-70. *Approval action type*

It will automatically create a connection for the Approval connector. Set the Approval Type to Approve/Reject – First to Respond. Figure 4-71 shows the approval types.

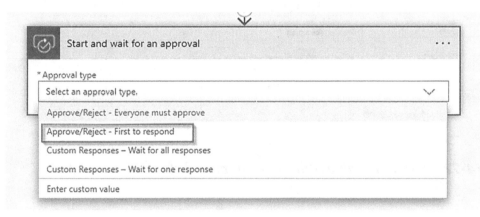

Figure 4-71. *Approval types*

Approval Types

- **Approve/Reject – Everyone must approve:** Select this when you want all approvers to have to approve this action.

- **Approve/Reject – First to respond:** Select this when you want your approval to be completed by the first approver to take action.

- **Custom Response – Wait for all responses:** Select this when you want your approval to be completed by all approvers with a custom action.

- **Custom Response – Wait for one response:** Select this when you want your approval to be completed by at least one approver with a custom action.

Once you have chosen the approval type, specify other information, such as a title, who it's assigned to, any details, an item link, and a description. Figure 4-72 shows the process of assigning values during the approval stage.

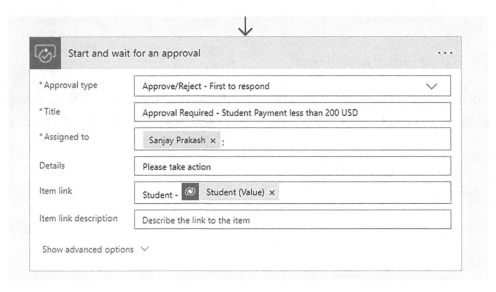

Figure 4-72. *Assigning values during the approval stage*

Step 2: Check the Approval Status

Add a new step to check if the approver has taken action—either approved or rejected the approval. In the Condition value, choose the Responses Approver response. It will create a loop automatically, as the Responses field contains multiple responses from approvers. Figure 4-73 shows the Read Approval response.

Figure 4-73. *Read Approval response*

Expand the Condition Inside loop and, in the Condition value, specify Approve. If the Response is Approve, then send an email as approved. Otherwise, the email will be rejected. Figure 4-74 shows the conditional approval branch.

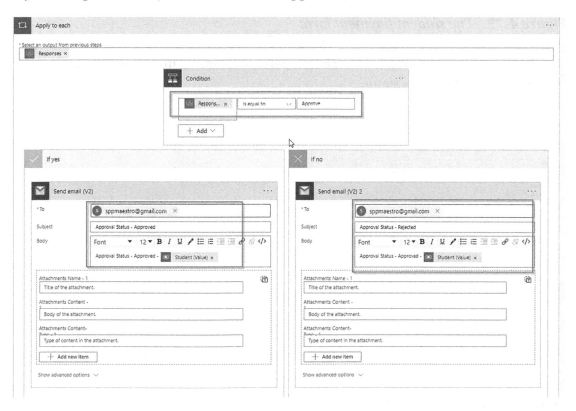

Figure 4-74. *The conditional approval branch*

187

Now save the flow and create a student payment record with less than $200. The flow will trigger. Figure 4-75 shows the student payment form.

payment for Rahul - Saved
Student Payment

General   Related

Name	*	payment for Rahul
Student		🎴 Rahul Sharma
Terms		1
Due Date		4/11/2022
Total Amount		$188.00
Owner	*	👤 Sanjay Prakash

Figure 4-75. *The student payment form*

Check the flow status in the Flow Details page. It's showing in running status. Figure 4-76 shows the flow status.

Development > Cloud flows > Send Approval for Student Payment less than 200 USD

Details		Edit

Flow
Send Approval for Student Payment less than 200 USD

Owner
Sanjay Prakash

Status
On

Created
Apr 11, 12:32 PM

Modified
Apr 11, 12:42 PM

Type
Automated

Plan
This flow runs on owner's plan

28-day run history ⓘ   ○ All runs

Start	Duration	Status
Apr 11, 12:44 PM (20 sec ago)	00:00:20	Running

Figure 4-76. *The flow status*

If you click the item, it will display in run mode and that you can check where it is waiting. Figure 4-77 shows the flow status in progress.

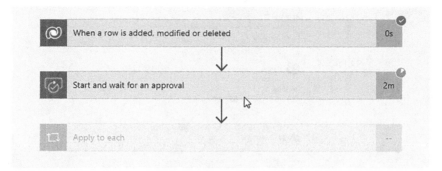

Figure 4-77. *The flow status in progress*

Now it's waiting for the approver's response. The approver will open their Outlook to see the approval email. Figure 4-78 shows the approval email received.

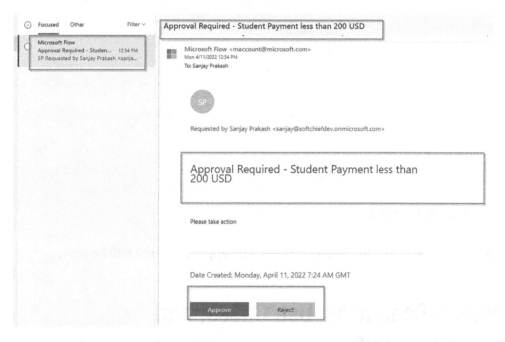

Figure 4-78. *The approval email was received*

If the approver clicks Approve, it will resume the flow. It will open a confirmation page, where the approver can click Confirm. Figure 4-79 shows the approval taking action.

Figure 4-79. *Taking action*

Now the flow will resume and complete. The approval email will be sent.

Business Scenarios, Use Cases, and Implementations

You can work on the following business scenarios for practice.

1	The system must provide a process to streamline the student on-boarding process and capture general information, communication information, and course information.	Configure Business Process Flow using Power Automate.
2	As soon as a student is created, the system should send a welcome email to the student and create a task to collect payment from the student after three days.	Use Automated Cloud Flow using Power Automate.
3	Automatically send a timesheet fillup email and link the Power Portal to students to fill in the timesheet daily.	Use Scheduled Flow in Power Automate.
4	Fetch the latest currency exchange rates from a third-party WEB API currency layer and display them on a Canvas app.	Use Power Apps Trigger Flow.
5	Whenever a lead is created in the Dataverse with more than $50,000 annual revenue, send approval for the manager and wait for approval. After approval, update the lead for qualification process.	Approvals in Power Automate

Summary

In this chapter, you learned about the following concepts:

- Power Automate building blocks

- Connectors in Power Automate

- Types and uses of flows

- Dynamic values and expressions in flows

- Using Variables, loops, and conditions

- Working with approvals in Power Automate

- Business scenarios, use cases, and implementations

In the next chapter, you will learn about the following:

- Concept of Power Virtual Agent

- Building blocks of Power Virtual Agents

- Configuring a sample Power Virtual Agent

- Deploying a Power Virtual Agent in public websites/portals

- Business scenarios, use cases, and implementations

Working with Power Virtual Agent

Microsoft Power Virtual Agent (PVA) is another important pillar of the Power Platform, no-code, less-code echo system. Using PVA, you can create digital chatbots that can interact with real end users like a human. Using chatbots, you can respond rapidly to your customers' and employees' needs. No coding is required. You can call Power Automate from chatbots for complex operational conversations.

The Power Virtual Agent

Power Virtual Agents are chatbots that are designed to interact with live users without a real agent. The features of PVA are explained in the following sections.

Build Bots Quickly and Easily

You can make, test, and publish powerful bots faster than ever using automation, AI, and a collaborative, low-code graphical interface. No training is required.

Deploy Across Channels and Languages

You can engage with customers and employees in multiple languages across websites, mobile apps, Facebook, Microsoft Teams, and any channel supported by the Azure Bot Framework tool.

© Sanjaya Prakash Pradhan 2022
S. Prakash Pradhan, *Power Platform and Dynamics 365 CE for Absolute Beginners*,
https://doi.org/10.1007/978-1-4842-8600-5_5

Scale Securely with Centralized Management

You can deploy bots securely using central administration, built-in security roles, and simple management across environments to maintain compliance and governance.

Improve Your Bots Over Time

You can automatically track critical KPIs and identify future bot topics, as well as enable self-learning AI with natural language processing that continuously improves your bots.

Building Blocks of Power Virtual Agents

Power Virtual Agents have three building blocks:

- Topics

- Entities

- Actions

Topics are points of discussion between the chatbot and the end user. For example, Account Management, Case Management, Greetings, Escalation, and End of Conversation are all different topics.

Trigger phrases are an important concept in chatbots. Trigger phrases are English phrases that users can enter into a chatbox to identify a topic to which the phrase belongs. Trigger phrases are configured inside topics. You can create multiple trigger phrases for a specific topic so that, for a specific phrase, the chatbot will respond as per the actions defined in the topic. Learn more about this concept from Microsoft at https://docs.microsoft.com/en-us/power-virtual-agents/fundamentals-what-is-power-virtual-agents.

Figure 5-1 shows a topic and its trigger phrases.

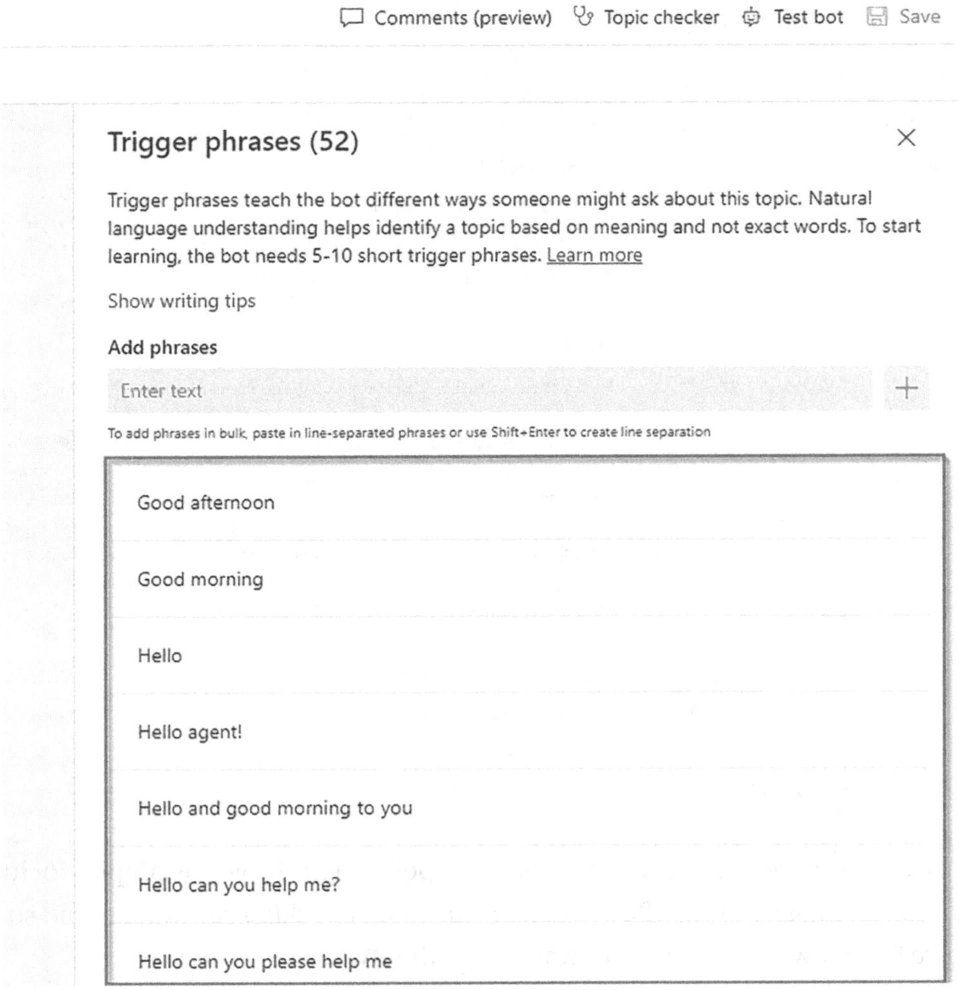

☐ Comments (preview)   ✂️ Topic checker   ⚕️ Test bot   💾 Save

Figure 5-1. *Trigger phrases for the Greetings topic*

Entities are predefined datatypes that store values, such as email addresses, a person's name, and so on. Figure 5-2 displays some sample entities used in PVA. You can create custom datatype entities.

Entities ⓘ

Name	Description	Method
Usage Type	Lesson 4 Usage Type Entity	ClosedList
Age	Age of a person, place, or thing, extracted as a number	Prebuilt
Boolean	Positive or negative responses, extracted as a Boolean	Prebuilt
City	City names, extracted as a string	Prebuilt
Color	Primary colors and hues on the color spectrum, extracted as a string	Prebuilt
Continent	Continent names, extracted as a string	Prebuilt
Country or region	Country and region names, extracted as a string	Prebuilt
Date and time	Dates, times, days of the week, and months relative to a point in time, extrac	Prebuilt
Duration	Lengths of time, extracted as a string, in standard TimeSpan format	Prebuilt
Email	Email addresses, extracted as a string	Prebuilt
Event	Event names, extracted as a string	Prebuilt

Figure 5-2. *Pre-built entities*

Actions are the steps that a chatbot performs per design. Typical examples include displaying a message, calling a flow, asking a question, checking conditions, and so on.

Figure 5-3 shows a list of actions available in the PVA.

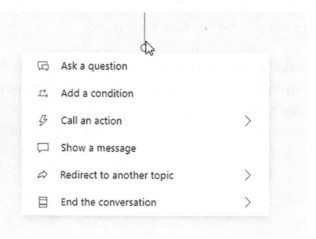

Figure 5-3. *List of actions*

Configure a Sample Power Virtual Agent

With the basic information behind you, you can now create a sample chatbot. Use the steps in this section to do so.

Step 1: Create a Chatbot from Power Apps

Open the Power Apps solution and then open the solution you want to use to store the chatbot. Click the Add New Chatbot option. This will open the Chatbot Editor in a new window. Figure 5-4 shows how to add a chatbot inside a solution.

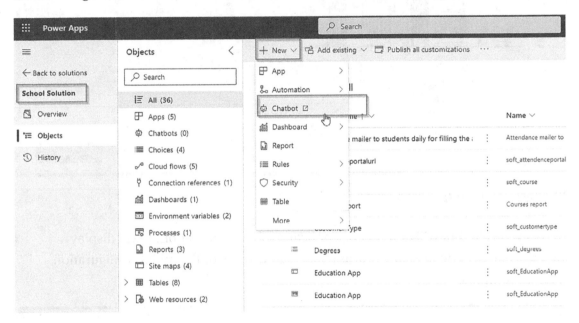

Figure 5-4. *Adding a chatbot inside a solution*

Provide the name of the chatbot and then choose the language and the environment to store it. Click Create. Figure 5-5 shows the process for creating a chatbot.

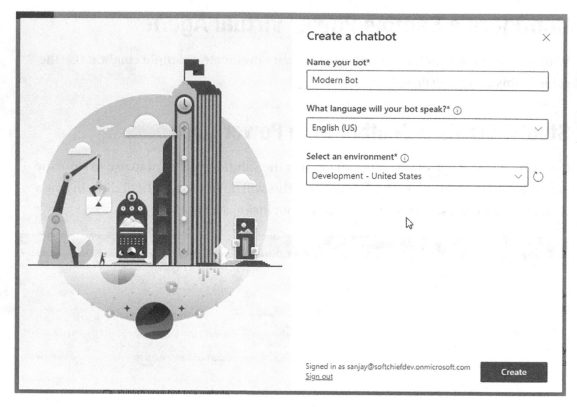

Figure 5-5. *Creating a chatbot*

Now the chatbot will prepare the application for configuration. It will display a message like the one in Figure 5-6, as it takes some time for the initial configuration setup to complete.

ⓘ **Creating your bot**   When it's ready, you can save your work, see analytics, and deploy your bot.

Figure 5-6. *An alert of bot creation*

Wait for the system to complete. The screen will refresh automatically after some time, when it's ready for your configuration.

The screen will look like Figure 5-7. The left panel shows links to Topics, Entities, and other options. Besides that, you will find the Test bot option, which allows you to test any changes you make.

Most chatbots start with a Greeting topic and some generic phrase like Hi, Hello, and so on. If you type **Hi** in the Test bot and press Enter or click the Send button, it will display a default message. Figure 5-7 shows the test bot.

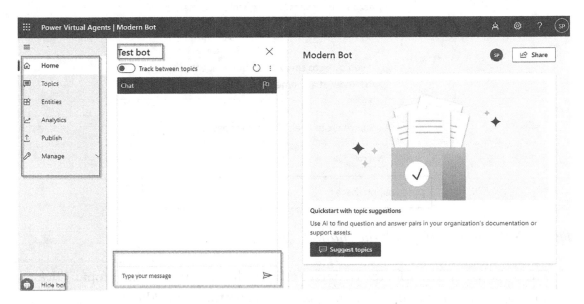

Figure 5-7. *A test bot*

The messages are preconfigured. You can edit them. Figure 5-8 shows interacting with the chatbot.

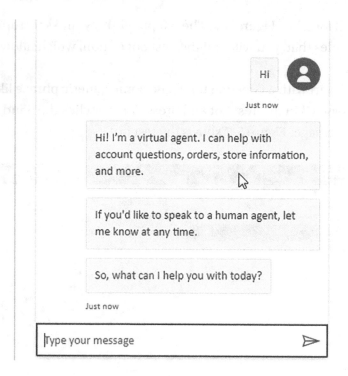

Figure 5-8. *Interacting with the chatbot*

The response returned for the Hi phrase can be edited in the Greetings topic. Click any message to reach the Topic Editor. Figure 5-9 shows the Topic Editor.

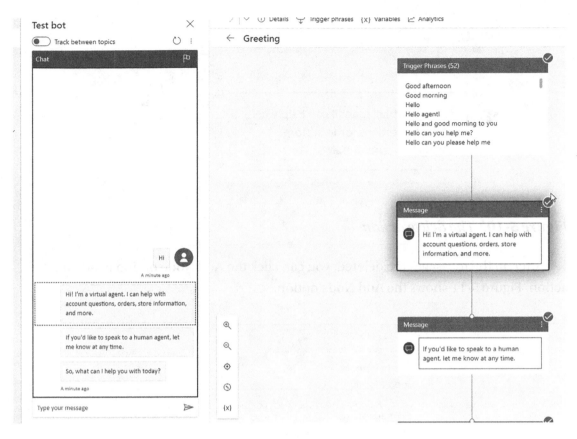

Figure 5-9. *The Topic Editor*

From there, you can remove and add actions as needed.

Step 2: Edit Actions in the Greetings Topic

You can edit your custom steps using the options available. Click the dots in the message boxes and select Delete to remove the steps. Figure 5-10 shows the delete action.

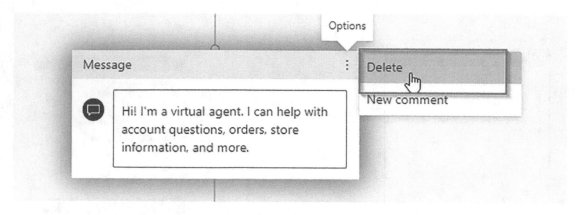

Figure 5-10. *The delete action*

After all the messages are deleted, you can click the Add Node option to add an action. Figure 5-11 shows the Add Node option.

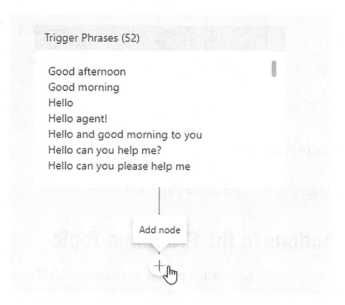

Figure 5-11. *The Add Node option*

Click the Add Node option and select Show a Message. Using this action, your chatbot can display a message to the users. Figure 5-12 shows how to add the Show a Message option.

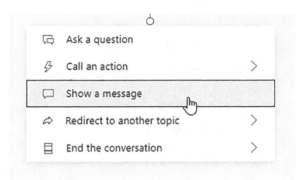

Figure 5-12. *Add the Show a Message option*

Specify the message in the message box. Figure 5-13 shows how to display the message.

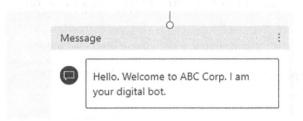

Figure 5-13. *Displaying a message*

Now when you test the bot by clicking Hi, the chatbot will respond with the new message you configured.

Step 3: Configure the Ask a Question Action in the Chatbot

You can configure questions that your chatbot can ask to users and collect their responses. The responses can be stored using an entity datatype and you can use variables to store the responses.

Variables can be of local topic scope or of global bot scope. Local scope means you can use the variable in the same topic only, not in other topics. Bot specific or global variables can be used in any topics within that bot.

To configure the Ask a Question option, click the Add Node option and select Ask a Question. Figure 5-14 shows this process.

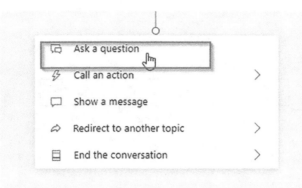

Figure 5-14. *Asking a question*

In the Question configuration panel, provide the question and select the datatype. The variable will be automatically defined. Figure 5-15 shows this process.

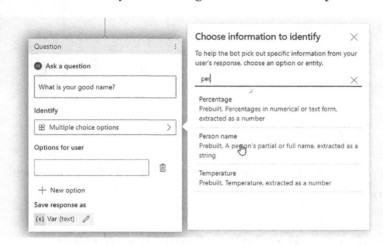

Figure 5-15. *Choosing an entity*

You can now rename the variable per your needs. Select the Usage scope as local or bot specific to make it a global variable. Figure 5-16 shows the variable declaration process.

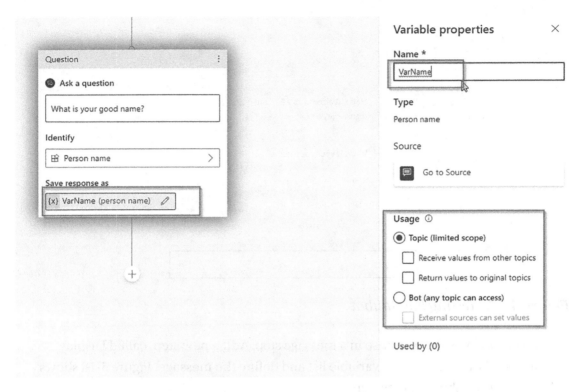

Figure 5-16. *Variable declaration process*

Now save the bot and test it. Type **Hi**. It should show the message and ask the question. Next, you will see how to provide a response. Figure 5-17 shows the testing process.

Figure 5-17. *Testing the chatbot*

You can display the response in a message step. Add a new step, called Display Message, and then choose the variable list and define the message. Figure 5-18 shows how to add a variable to a message.

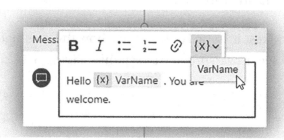

Figure 5-18. *Adding a variable to a message*

The message will display the name of user in the next step if you test the bot after saving. Figure 5-19 shows the testing chatbot process.

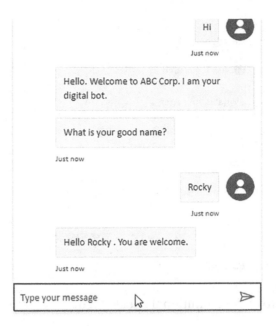

Figure 5-19. *Testing the chatbot*

Step 4: Add a Conditional Check to the Chatbot

You can add a conditional check to the users' responses and do different actions based on the conditions. Consider a scenario where you want to determine if the user is under 15 years old.

Click the Add New Node option and select Ask a Question to capture their age. Store the age in a variable with local scope. Figure 5-20 shows this step.

Figure 5-20. *Asking a question*

Add another node to add a conditional check. Figure 5-21 shows the process of adding a condition.

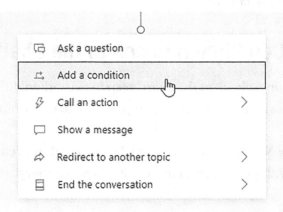

Figure 5-21. *Adding a condition*

In the condition property, specify the conditions you need. It will automatically show two branches—one for the main condition and another for the else condition.

You can set the age to be less than 15 as a condition in the Condition check branch. Figure 5-22 shows these branches.

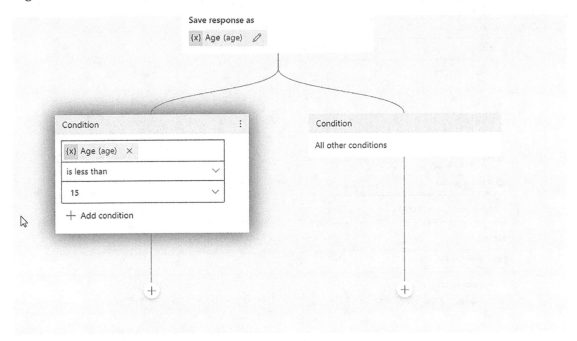

Figure 5-22. *Adding conditional branches*

If the age is less than 15, you can add another node to ask another question to collect the person's father's name. Figure 5-23 shows this step.

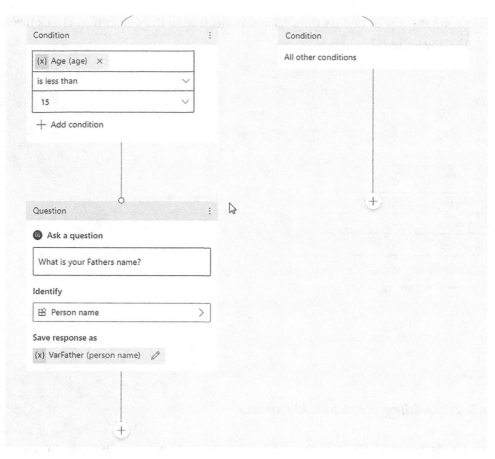

Figure 5-23. *Adding an Ask a Question step*

Save the bot. If you now test it, it will ask for the user's father's name when you supply an age that's under 15; otherwise, it will not ask any more questions. Figure 5-24 shows this testing process.

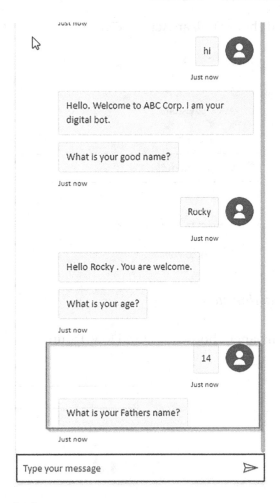

Figure 5-24. *Testing the bot*

This is how you add conditional checks to the chatbot.

Step 5: Call the Power Automate Flow from the Chatbot

For complex requirements, you can call a flow from a chatbot. Chatbots can call a flow and send data to the flow. After the flow completes the actions, it will return data to the chatbot.

Let's consider a scenario. Say you want to create a new customer record by getting information from users. The chatbot will ask for the first name, the last name, and an email address, and then send this information to Power Automate. Power Automate will create a contact record with the information and return the status to the PVA.

Add a new node and choose Call an Action. Figure 5-25 shows the Call an Action step.

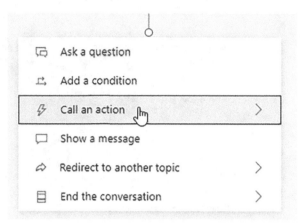

Figure 5-25. *Call an action step*

In the Call an Action panel, choose Create a Flow. Figure 5-26 shows the Create a Flow option inside PVA.

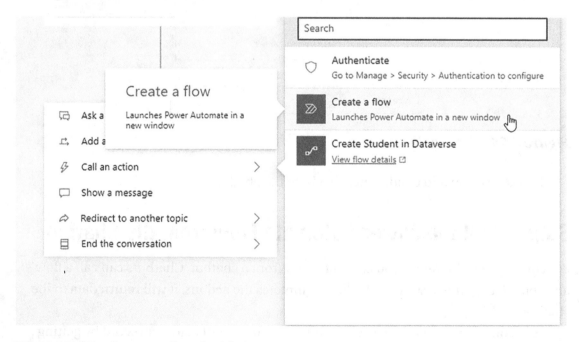

Figure 5-26. *Create a flow inside PVA*

PVA will open the Flow Designer with the preselected trigger and return a message step. Figure 5-27 shows the flow with the PVA triggers.

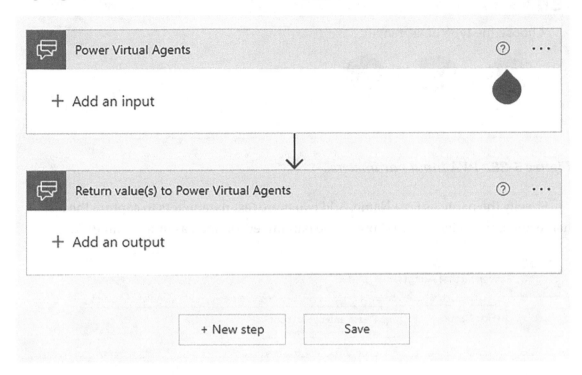

Figure 5-27. *Flow with PVA triggers*

Now you can define the required input parameters to accept the user's first name, last name, and email. That way, you can add a new step to connect to the Dataverse and create a contact record.

Click + Add an Input. Select the Text parameter. Figure 5-28 shows the PVA input parameters.

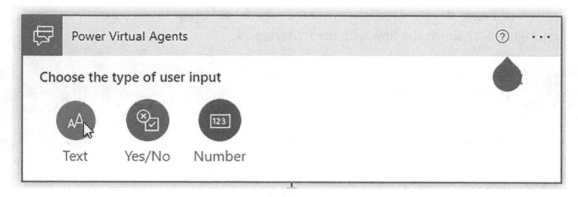

Figure 5-28. *PVA input parameters*

Specify the name as First Name. Add two more text parameters to capture the last name and email. Figure 5-29 shows these parameters defined as input from PVA.

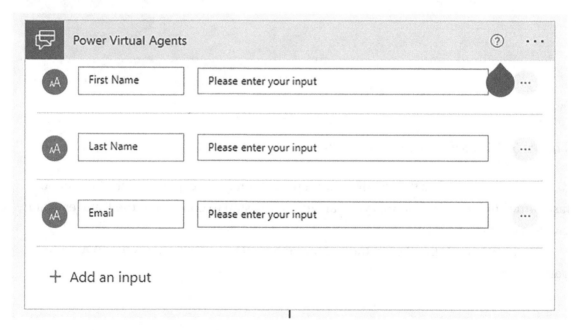

Figure 5-29. *Parameters defined as input from PVA*

Now add a new action to connect to the Dataverse. Select Add a New Row, and then Contact Entity. Map the first name, last name, and email from the Dynamic Content panel. Figure 5-30 shows how to assign dynamic content to these fields.

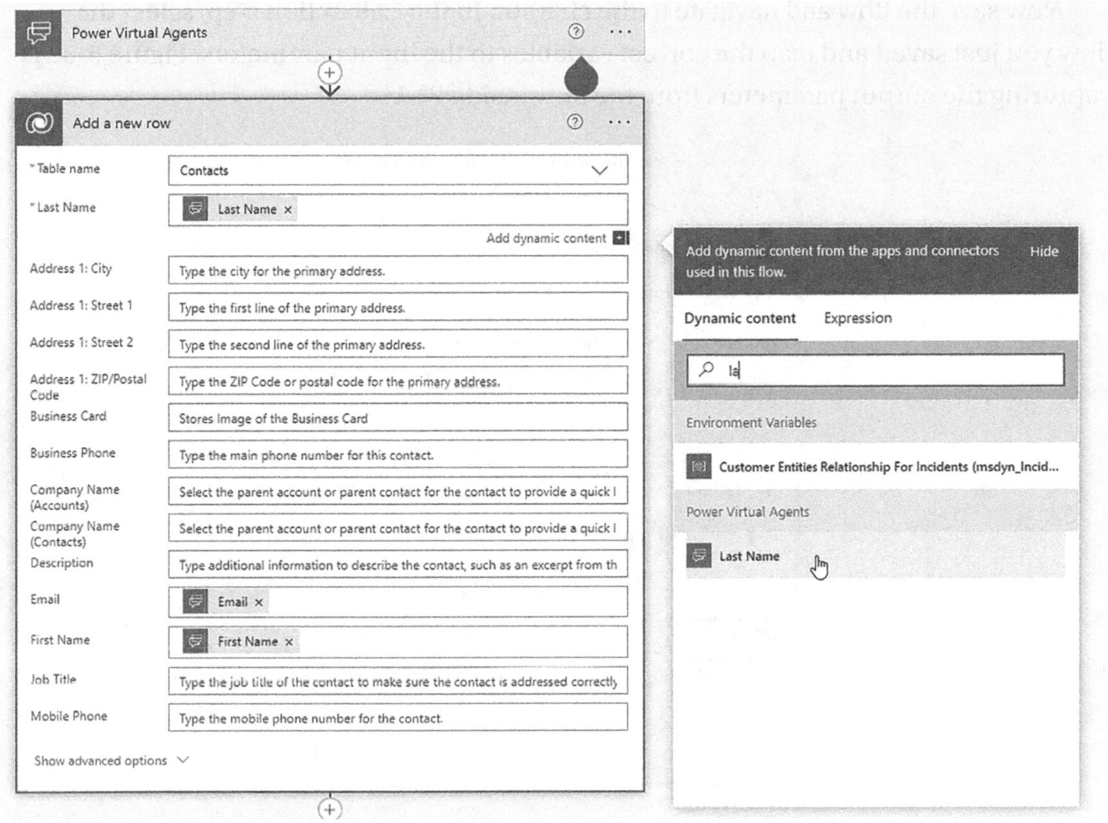

Figure 5-30. *Assigning dynamic content to fields*

Now you can specify the return type to the chatbot. Click the +Add an Output parameter and select Text. Figure 5-31 shows the return parameter to PVA.

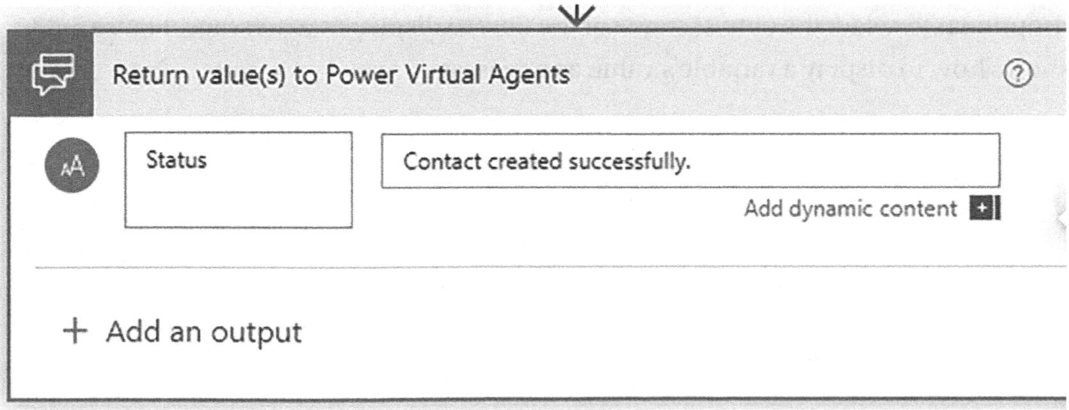

Figure 5-31. *The return parameter to PVA*

Now save the flow and navigate to the chatbot. In the Call Action step, select the flow you just saved and map the correct variables to the input parameters. Figure 5-32 is capturing the output parameters from the flow inside PVA.

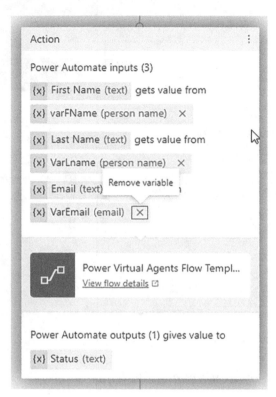

Figure 5-32. *Capture the output parameters from the flow inside PVA*

Add another node to show a message that returned from the flow. Use the Variable dropdown to select the output status of the flow to display as a message. Figure 5-33 shows how to display a variable's value as a message.

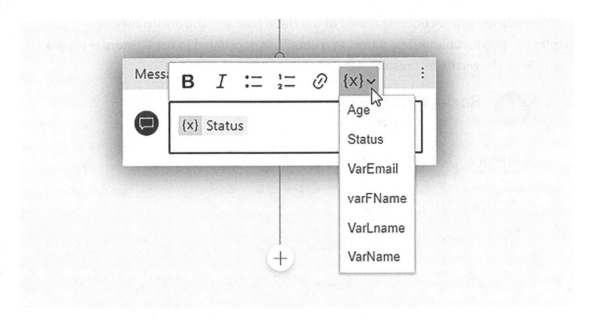

Figure 5-33. *Display the variable's value as a message*

Now save the bot and test it. Figure 5-34 shows the final test bot.

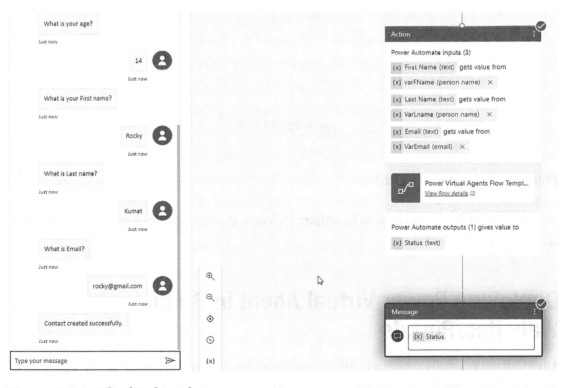

Figure 5-34. *The final test bot*

You will see a new contact created in the Dataverse and the return message displayed. The first name, last name, and email are populated in the Customer record. Figure 5-35 shows the test result.

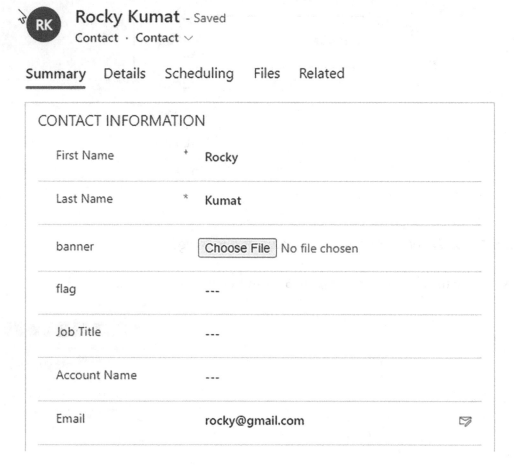

Figure 5-35. *The test result*

Now you understand how to configure PVA or a chatbot and for a complex scenario and how to call a flow.

Deploying Power Virtual Agent in Public Websites/Portals

After you successfully create a chatbot, you'll want to publish the chatbot to your websites. To publish it, click the Publish link and press the Publish button.

This will publish the chatbot so that you can use it in other websites. Figure 5-36 shows the PVA deployment options.

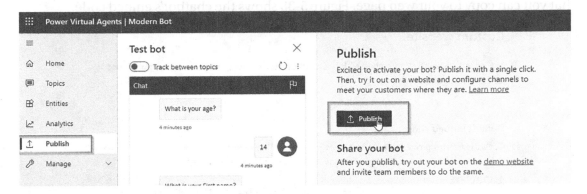

Figure 5-36. *PVA deployment options*

Once it's been published, click Go to Channels. Figure 5-37 shows the available channels for deployment.

Figure 5-37. *Available channels for deployment*

You can choose a channel where you want the chatbot to be published. If you want to embed the chatbot in the custom website, select Custom Website. It will display a script that you can copy to your web page. Figure 5-38 shows the chatbot's embed code.

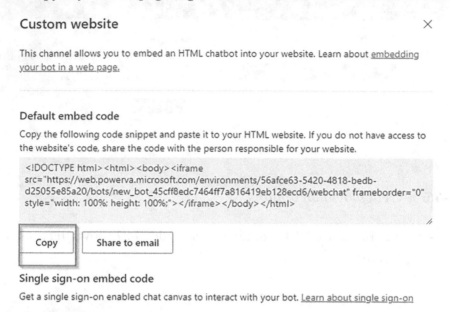

Custom website   ×

This channel allows you to embed an HTML chatbot into your website. Learn about embedding your bot in a web page.

Default embed code

Copy the following code snippet and paste it to your HTML website. If you do not have access to the website's code, share the code with the person responsible for your website.

```
<!DOCTYPE html><html><body><iframe
src="https://web.powerva.microsoft.com/environments/56afce63-5420-4818-bedb-
d25055e85a20/bots/new_bot_45cff8edc7464ff7a816419eb128ecd6/webchat" frameborder="0"
style="width: 100%; height: 100%;"></iframe></body></html>
```

Copy   Share to email

Single sign-on embed code

Get a single sign-on enabled chat canvas to interact with your bot. Learn about single sign-on

Figure 5-38. *The chatbot's embed code*

Now add a custom page. You can use the w3schools Try It window to test this process. Open the Try It window and copy the code to the HTML page editor. Figure 5-39 shows the chatbot in action externally.

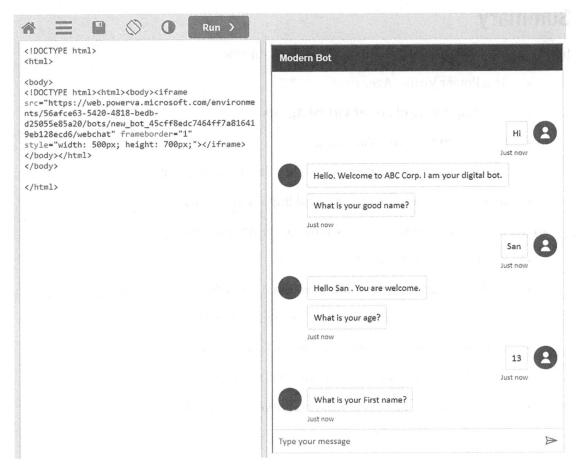

Figure 5-39. *The chatbot in action externally*

Business Scenarios, Use Cases, and Implementations

You can now implement the following scenario for your practice:

1	Configure a Power Virtual Agent for public users so that the chatbot can capture user information and validate it against the Dataverse. If the user is not valid, it will create a contact in the Dataverse. Display the Power Virtual Agent in an external website like Power Portal or other websites.	Use Power Virtual Agent and use call action.

Summary

In this chapter, you learned about the following concepts:

- The Power Virtual Agent
- Building blocks of Power Virtual Agents
- Configuring a Power Virtual Agent
- Deploying Power Virtual Agent in public websites/portals
- Business scenarios, use cases, and implementations

In the next chapter, you learn about the following concepts:

- The concept of Power BI
- Building blocks of Power BI, datasource, reports, and dashboards
- Connecting online datasources to use in Power BI
- Connecting on-premise datasources to use in Power BI
- Integrating Power BI with Dynamic 365 CE apps
- Business scenarios, use cases, and implementations

CHAPTER 6

Working with Power BI and Dynamics 365 Apps

Microsoft Power BI is used to identify insights in an organization's data. Power BI can help connect multiple diversified datasets, transform and clean the data into a data model, and create charts or graphs to provide data visualization.

Power BI can connect diversified cloud datasources and on-premise datasources to build visualizations, reports, and dashboards using the no-code, less code concept.

You can use Power Apps Canvas apps inside Power BI for complex dashboard designs. AI features can be integrated out-of-the-box. You can read more about Power BI from Microsoft at `https://docs.microsoft.com/en-us/power-bi/`.

You can access Power BI by visiting `https://powerbi.microsoft.com/`. You can also create Power BI reports and dashboards using its desktop application, called Power BI Desktop. You have to download Power BI Desktop from the Microsoft App Store at `https://aka.ms/pbidesktopstore`.

You can use the same Power Apps login credentials to subscribe to the Power BI 30-day trial version. To access the trial version, navigate to `https://powerbi.microsoft.com` and click Sign In. It will ask you to provide your credentials and will create a Power BI trial for you.

After signing into the Power BI screen, you will see the home page shown in Figure 6-1.

© Sanjaya Prakash Pradhan 2022
S. Prakash Pradhan, *Power Platform and Dynamics 365 CE for Absolute Beginners*,
https://doi.org/10.1007/978-1-4842-8600-5_6

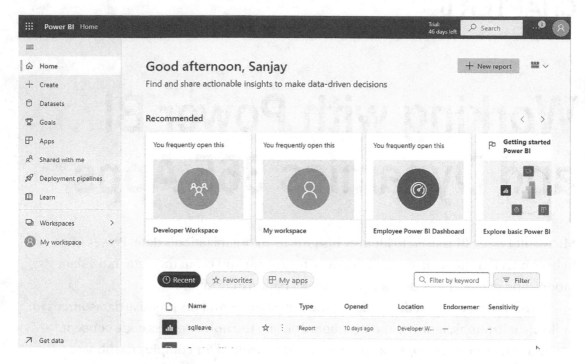

Figure 6-1. Power BI Online

Building Blocks of Power BI, Datasources, Reports, and Dashboards

There are seven building blocks available in Power BI. They are mentioned here:

- **Datasources** – Source of the data, such as like Excel, SQL Server, or the Dataverse

- **Dataset** – Subset of a datasource, like tables from the datasource

- **Visualizations** – Visual representation of datasets, like charts

- **Reports** –Multiple visualizations on one page

- **Dashboards** –Multiple reports on one page

- **Publishing** – Making the dashboard or report live for internal or external users

- **Workspaces** – Storing reports, datasets, and dashboards for team collaboration

After configuring Power BI dashboard, you can integrate it with Dynamics 365 model-driven Power Apps using embedded reports.

You can also create reports in the Power BI Desktop app and synchronize or publish them in Power BI Online. Every report and dashboard visualization is linked to a dataset, which is internally connected to a datasource. To get data real-time from the datasource, you need to configure data refresh techniques. You can schedule data refresh as per your needs, using time intervals. In Power BI, you can prepare the data model before designing visuals. Data modeling is the process of analyzing and defining all the data your business collects and produces, as well as the relationships between those bits of data. To read more about data modeling, see `https://powerbi.microsoft.com/en-us/what-is-data-modeling/`.

For cloud datasources, you just need to authenticate for scheduled data refresh. For on-premise data refreshes, you need to install an on-premise data gateway on your desktop using `https://go.microsoft.com/fwlink/?LinkId=2116849&clcid=0x409`.

Connect Online Datasources to Use in Power BI

Let's create a Power BI dashboard by connecting a cloud datasource. Say you have an Excel sheet with employee data stored in the OneDrive business app. You want to create a Power BI dashboard by connecting to this Excel datasource. The steps in the following sections explain how to do this.

Step 1: Create a Workspace

Power BI workspace is a place where you can work with your team creating dashboards and reports.

First you need to connect to the datasource. Open Power BI Online using `https://powerbi.microsoft.com/`.

By default, My Workspace is used for the current user to store reports in Power BI. If you are working on a team and collaborating in a shared workspace, you need to create a workspace.

To create a shared workspace, you need to click the Workspaces link in the left panel of Power BI Online screen. Click Create a Workspace to start new workspace. Figure 6-2 shows how to create a workspace.

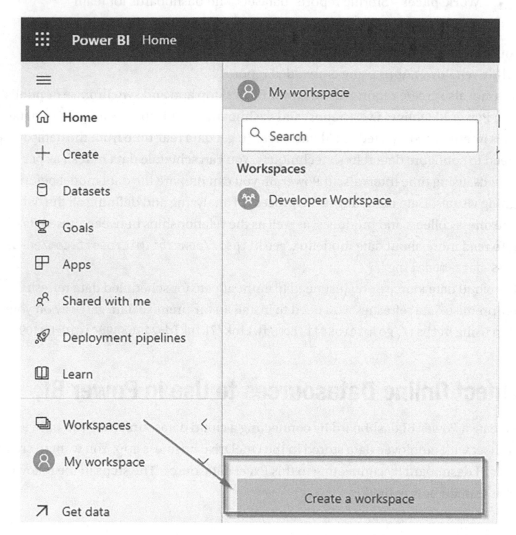

Figure 6-2. *Creating a workspace*

Provide a name for the workspace and a description. In the Advanced options, you can choose users to have access to this workspace. Click Save when you're done. Figure 6-3 shows the process of configuring a workspace.

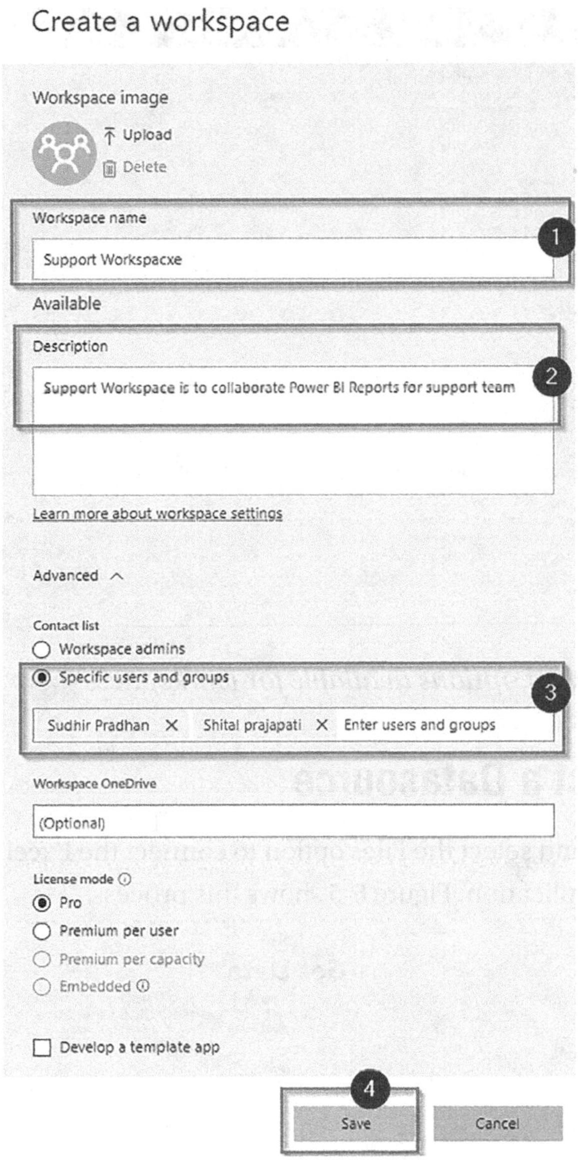

Create a workspace

Figure 6-3. *Configuring a workspace*

The new workspace will be created and you can add Power BI components to it. Figure 6-4 shows the component options available for workspaces.

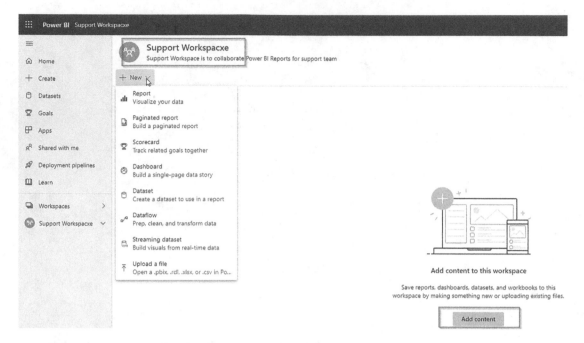

Figure 6-4. *Component options available for workspaces*

Step 2: Connect a Datasource

Choose Add Content and select the Files option to connect the Excel sheet stored in the OneDrive Business application. Figure 6-5 shows this process.

Figure 6-5. *Connect to a datasource*

Select OneDrive – Business Datasource from the Options panel. It will display all the files present in the OneDrive Business app. Figure 6-6 shows the OneDrive Business datasource option.

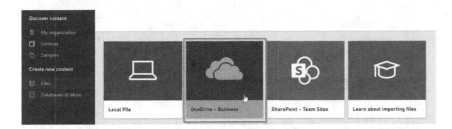

Figure 6-6. *Choosing the OneDrive Business datasource*

Select the Excel sheet containing your data. Figure 6-7 shows the process of selecting a file from OneDrive.

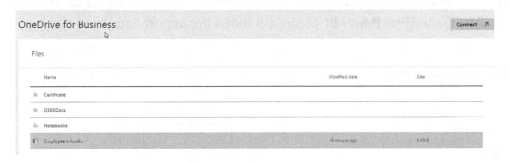

Figure 6-7. *Selecting a file from OneDrive*

Now click Connect. The Excel sheet contains a table that is available in OneDrive Business. Figure 6-8 shows how to check the records in the Excel sheet.

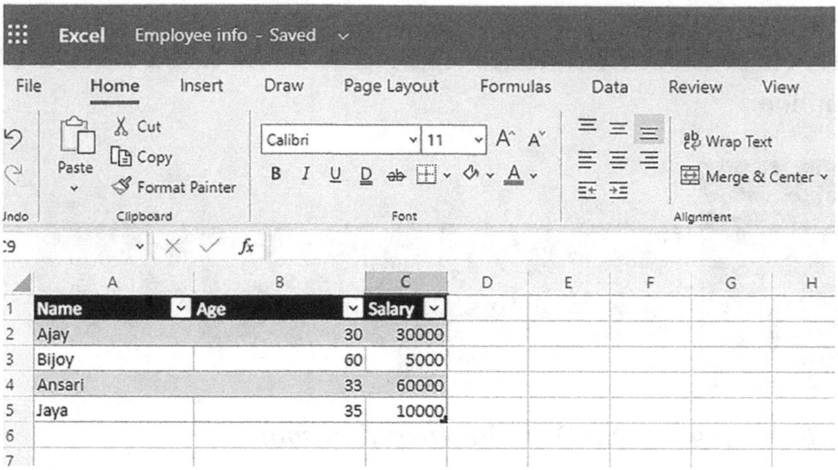

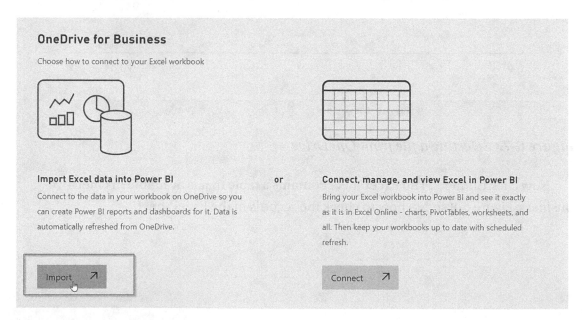

Figure 6-8. *Checking records in an Excel sheet*

Upon selection, click Connect. Now click Import Excel Data in Power BI. The data items will be loaded into Power BI. Figure 6-9 shows the import data process.

Figure 6-9. *Importing data*

It will take a couple of seconds and will load the data into Power BI. It will create a dataset with the same name as the Excel file and a dashboard with the same datasource name. Figure 6-10 shows the dataset and dashboard inside the workspace.

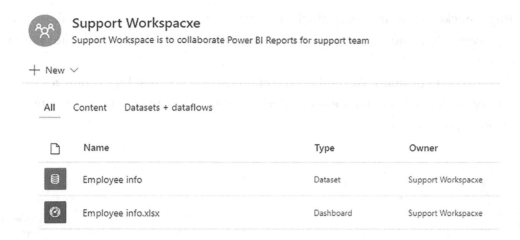

Figure 6-10. *The dataset and dashboard inside the workspace*

The Employee info dataset can be now used to create reports and you can add visualizations inside the reports. Select the dataset and click the three dots, then choose Create Report. Figure 6-11 shows how to create a report from the dataset.

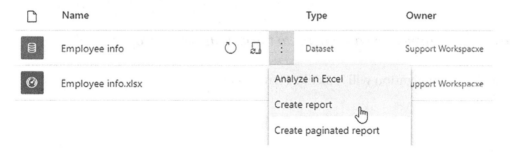

Figure 6-11. *Creating a report from the dataset*

Step 3: Create a Report from the Dataset

The Create Report option of the dataset will open a Report Designer, where you can drag-and-drop visualizations from the right visualization panel. The extreme right-side panel shows tables and fields, where that you can connect fields to visualizations.

Drag a stacked column chart onto the report canvas and select the Name field from the Employee Info Table Drop on Axis option. Drag the Salary field to the Values option of the chart.

After this configuration, you will see the chart rendered to display Employees by their salary, as displayed in Figure 6-12, which shows connecting data items to the visualization property.

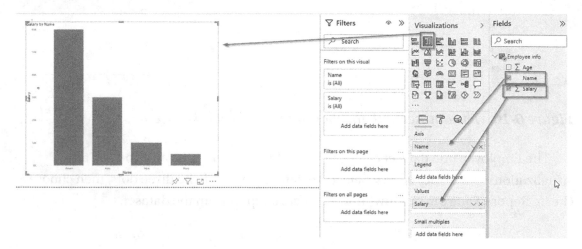

Figure 6-12. *Connecting data items to the visualization property*

The final visualization will look like Figure 6-13.

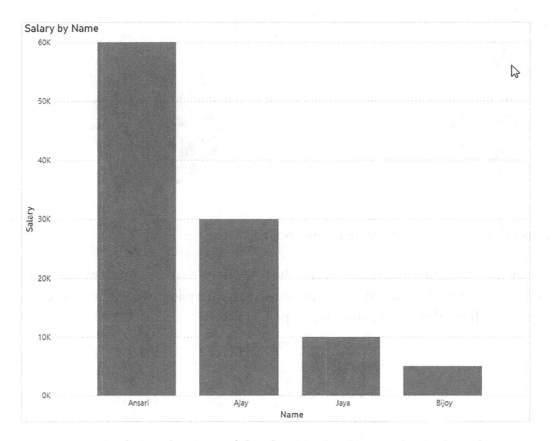

Figure 6-13. *Final visualization of the chart to display employees by salary*

You can now add more visual charts onto the report canvas and design your desired charts as needed. You can drag the edges of visual tiles to make them smaller or bigger as needed.

After adding two charts, the report looks like Figure 6-14.

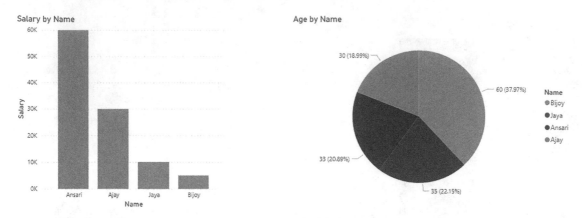

Figure 6-14. *Two visualization on one report*

Now you are ready to pin this report to the dashboard. Save the report with a name by clicking the Save button and choosing the correct workspace to store the report. Figure 6-15 shows the process of saving a report.

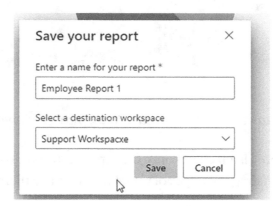

Figure 6-15. *Saving the report*

Step 4: Pin Reports to a Dashboard

Now the saved report can be pinned to a dashboard. Click on the three dots and choose Pin to a Dashboard. Figure 6-16 shows the Pin Report to Dashboard option.

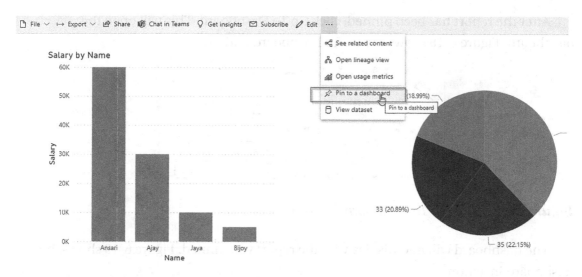

Figure 6-16. *The pin report to dashboard option*

Choose the dashboard you want to pin the report to. Click on Pin Live. Figure 6-17 shows the process of selecting the dashboard to pin the report.

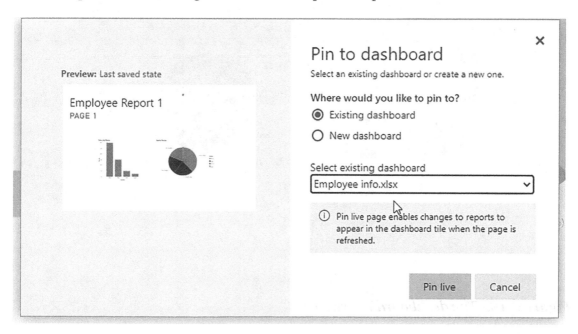

Figure 6-17. *Selecting a dashboard to pin the report*

After the report has been pinned, click Go To Dashboard. This will open the dashboard. Figure 6-18 shows the Go To Dashboard option.

Figure 6-18. *The Go To Dashboard option*

The dashboard will now display with the report you pinned. Figure 6-19 shows the dashboard in action.

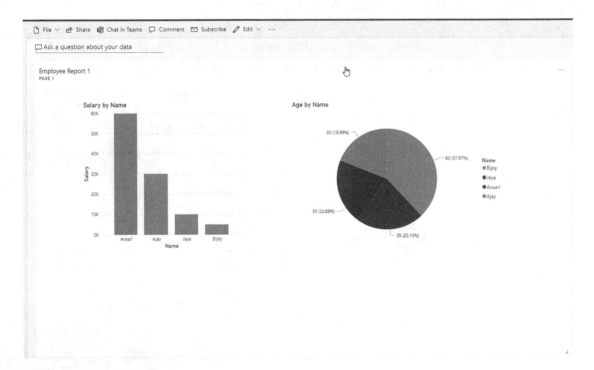

Figure 6-19. *The dashboard in action*

This way you can create multiple reports with multiple visualizations and pin reports in the dashboards as well as store them in workspaces of your choice.

Step 5: Connect to Dataverse Tables in Power BI

You can also connect to Dataverse tables inside Power BI. To do this, install Power BI desktop and Open Power BI after installation.

Click the Get Data menu item and select Dataverse. Figure 6-20 shows the process of connecting Dataverse from the Power BI Desktop.

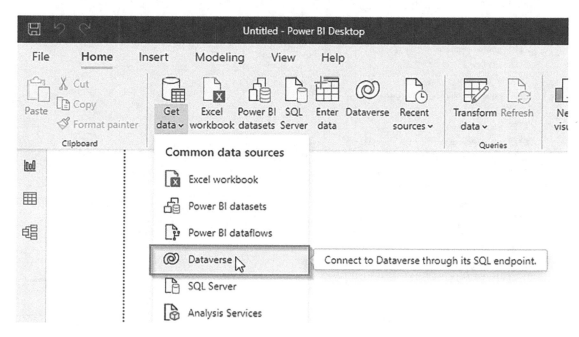

Figure 6-20. *Connect to the Dataverse from the Power BI Desktop*

It will automatically connect to the Dataverse and display the list of environments you created in your tenant.

Choose the correct environment you want to connect to and select tables. You can directly click the Load option or the Transform Data option. If you want to transform your table data, click Transform Data; otherwise, you can click Load to load the raw or unchanged data into Power BI Desktop.

Using Transform Data, you can remove unrequired columns, change column types, and enhance many more features available with respect to transforming data. Note that data transformation is not in the scope of this book.

Click Load to load the raw data items inside Power BI. Figure 6-21 shows the process of choosing the environment and the tables.

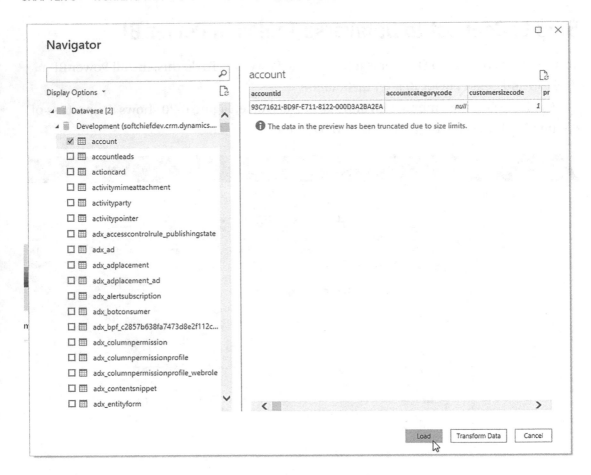

Figure 6-21. *Choosing the environment and the tables*

After clicking Load, you can choose whether you want to use Direct Query or Import. Click Import to load the data into Power BI. Figure 6-22 shows the Import Data from Dataverse process.

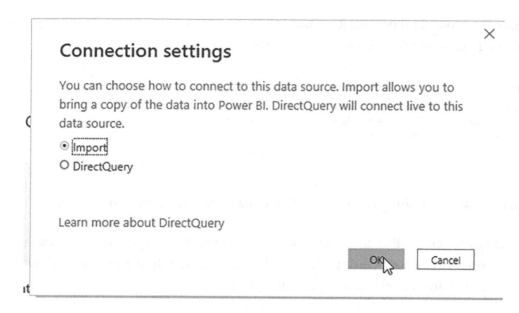

Figure 6-22. *Importing data from the Dataverse*

You can add visualizations by dragging and dropping and connecting fields with visualizations. Figure 6-23 shows the process of preparing visualizations using Dataverse tables.

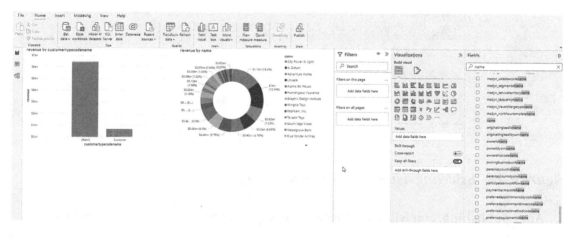

Figure 6-23. *Preparing visualizations using Dataverse tables*

Save the report and publish it to Power BI Online. Figure 6-24 shows the process of publishing the Power BI Desktop reports to Power BI Online.

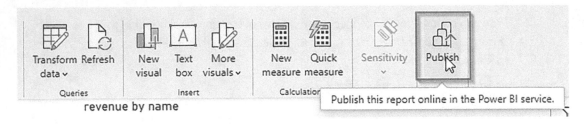

Figure 6-24. Publishing the Power BI Desktop reports to Power BI Online

Once you click Publish, if you have not yet saved the report, it will ask you to save. Next it will ask to choose a workspace to publish the report online. Figure 6-25 shows the process of selecting a workspace to publish reports.

Publish to Power BI

Select a destination

Search

My workspace

Developer Workspace

Support Workspacxe

Select   Cancel

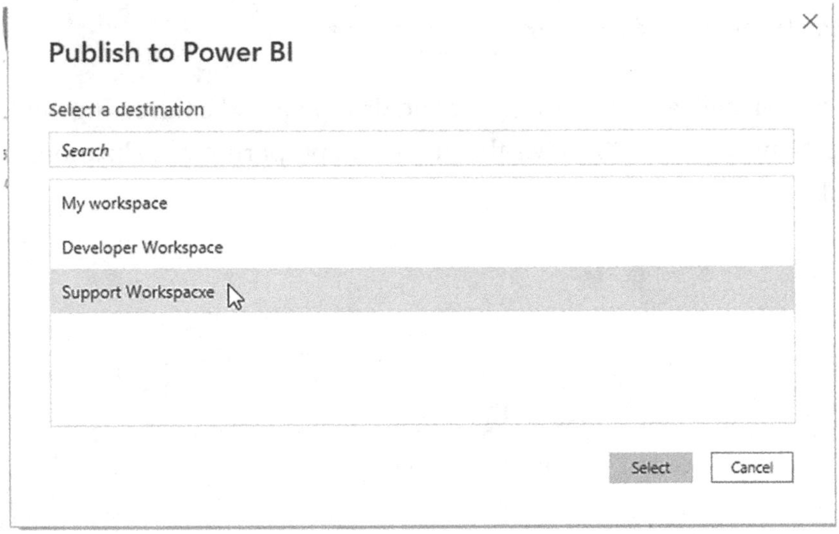

Figure 6-25. Selecting a workspace to publish reports

After publishing, you will see a success message. Figure 6-26 shows the publish success screen.

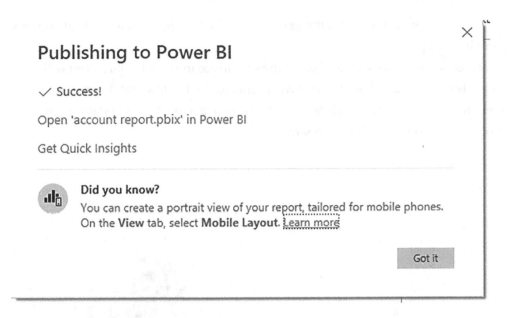

Figure 6-26. *Publish success screen*

Now navigate to Power BI Online and select the support workspace. You will see the report available in the workspace. You will also see that a dataset has been created. Figure 6-27 shows the published reports and the dataset in the Power BI Online workspace.

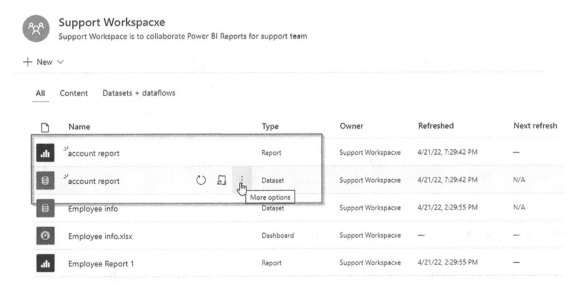

Figure 6-27. *Viewing published reports and dataset in the Power BI Online workspace*

Click the report and pin it to the existing employee info dashboard that you created in a previous step.

Now go to the workspace and open the employee info dashboard. You will see two reports on the same dashboard. One points to the Excel sheet datasource from the OneDrive and the other points to the Dataverse account table. Figure 6-28 shows multiple reports on a single dashboard.

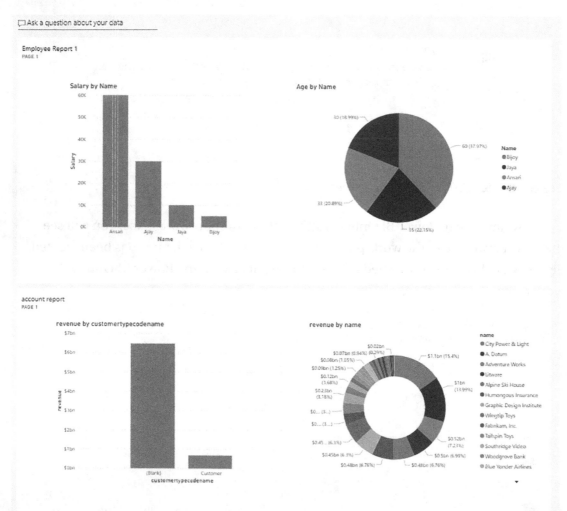

Figure 6-28. *Multiple reports on a single dashboard*

You have successfully created a dashboard that points to multiple online datasources.

Connect an On-Premise Datasource to Use in Power BI

You can also connect on-premise datasources to configure dashboards. Open the Power BI Desktop and choose Get Data. Then choose SQL Server.

You are now going to connect a local SQL Server table installed on the desktop. Click Get Data and choose SQL Server. If your business stores student information in a local database and wants to create Power BI visuals, you can do this using on-premise gateways. This example scenario shows how to create a sample table and connect it to Power BI. Read more about on-premise data gateways at `https://docs.microsoft. com/en-us/power-bi/connect-data/service-gateway-onprem`. Figure 6-29 shows the process of connecting the local SQL Server.

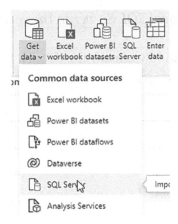

Figure 6-29. *Connecting the local SQL Server*

Now provide the SQL Server and database details. You have to specify the details about your local SQL Server. You can get these details from your local SQL Server screen. Figure 6-30 shows the process of connecting the local SQL Server to the server name and window.

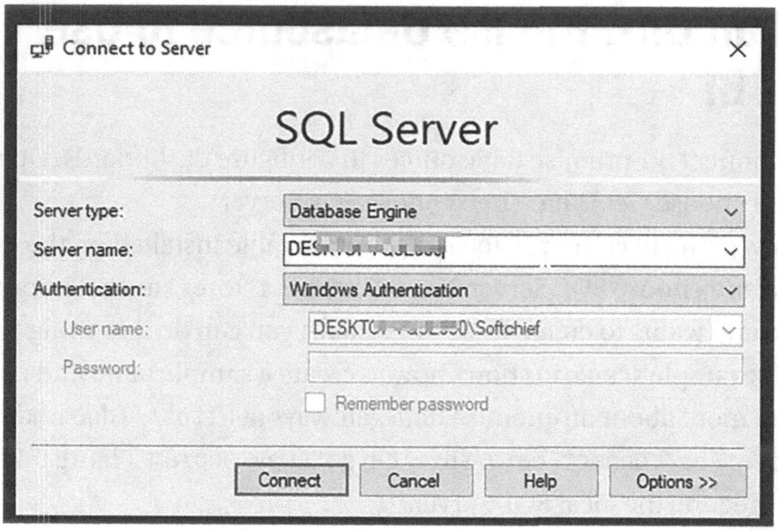

Figure 6-30. *Connecting a local SQL Server to the server name and window*

In the Power BI Desktop window, specify the details. Figure 6-31 shows the use of SQL Server in the Power BI Desktop for connection.

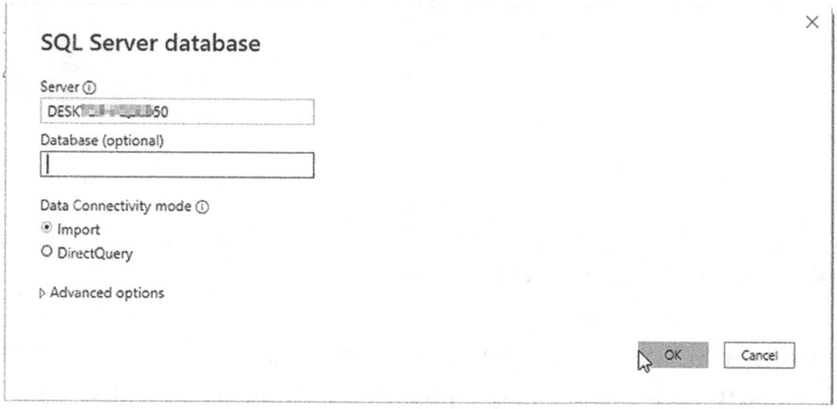

Figure 6-31. *Use SQL Server in the Power BI Desktop for connection*

Click OK. It will list all the databases of your local SQL Server. Select the table you want to connect to and click Load. Figure 6-32 shows the process of choosing a table from SQL Server for Power BI.

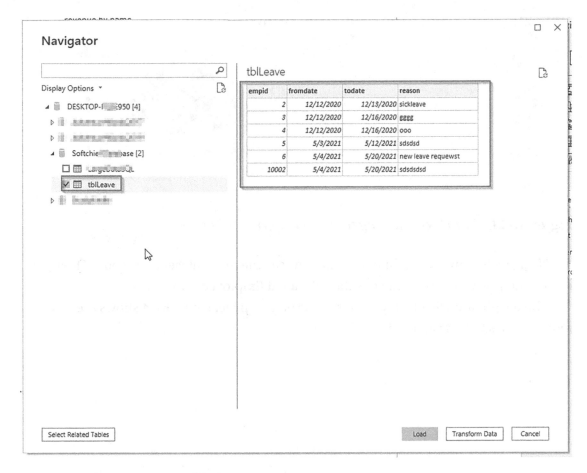

Figure 6-32. *Choose a table for Power BI*

Now the data will be loaded into Power BI. Create a new report by connecting the new table, as you did in the previous steps. Add visualization and connect to the table. Once the report is created, publish it online by selecting the workspace. The report looks like Figure 6-33.

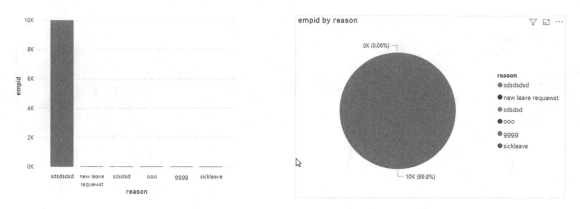

Figure 6-33. *Charts connecting to the SQL Server table*

Navigate to Power BI Online. You can now see the new dataset and report. Open the report and pin it to the existing dashboard, called Employee Info.

The dashboard will display three reports on one page. Figure 6-34 shows the three reports on a single dashboard.

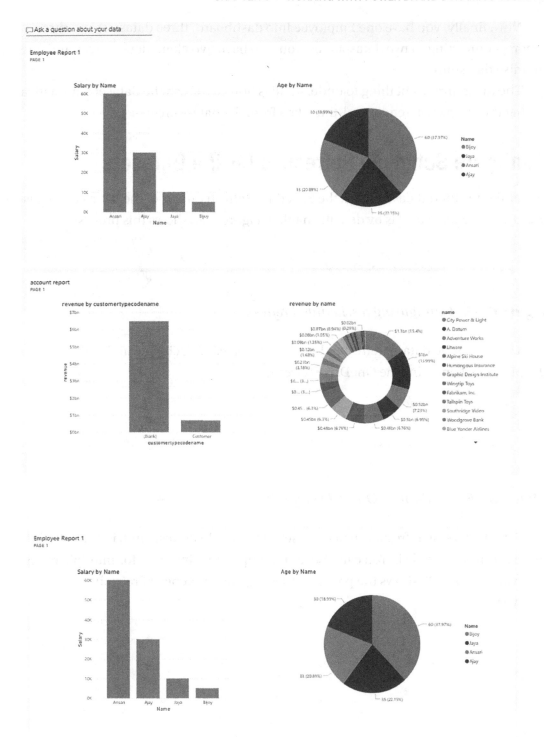

Figure 6-34. *Three reports on a single dashboard*

Now, finally, you have one Employee Info dashboard, three datasets, and three reports connecting to two datasources. You also have two cloud datasources and one on-premise datasource.

The most important thing to understand is how to refresh the dataset automatically so that the charts will render real-time data from the datasource.

Configure Schedule Refreshes for the Datasets

To configure cloud datasets, click the Schedule Refresh button of the dataset. Because it is a OneDrive dataset, it is by default enabled. Figure 6-35 shows this process.

***Figure 6-35.** Configuring a scheduled refresh*

The OneDrive dataset refreshes hourly and you cannot change it. Figure 6-36 shows the process of enabling the OneDrive refresh.

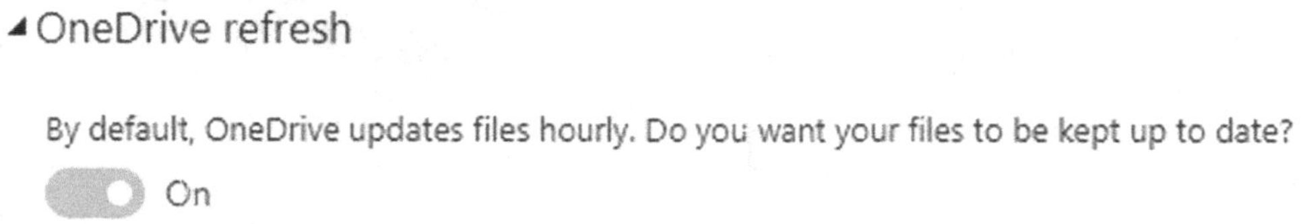

◢ OneDrive refresh

By default, OneDrive updates files hourly. Do you want your files to be kept up to date?

⬤○ On

***Figure 6-36.** Enabling a OneDrive refresh*

For a Dataverse refresh, you need to select Schedule Refresh and, in the Scheduled Refresh option, enable it. You can also add multiple time intervals for multiple refresh interval. Figure 6-37 shows the process of setting the frequency of refreshes for the Dataverse.

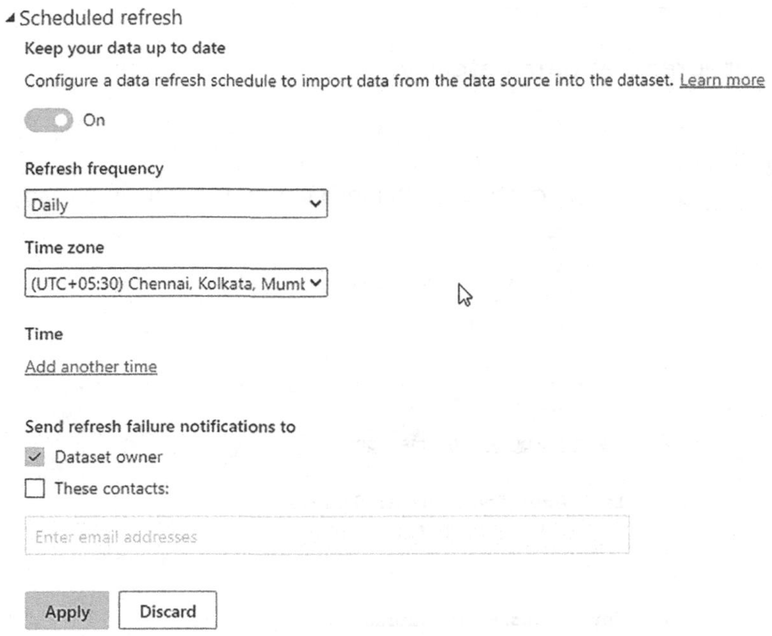

◢ Scheduled refresh

Keep your data up to date

Configure a data refresh schedule to import data from the data source into the dataset. Learn more

⬤▢ On

Refresh frequency

| Daily ⌄ |

Time zone

| (UTC+05:30) Chennai, Kolkata, Mumt ⌄ |

Time

Add another time

Send refresh failure notifications to

☑ Dataset owner

▢ These contacts:

| Enter email addresses |

[Apply] [Discard]

Figure 6-37. *Setting the frequency of refreshes for the Dataverse*

To refresh the local dataset, you need to set up and install an on-premise gateway. After installation, run the app and configure it by using your current credentials. Figure 6-38 shows an on-premise data gateway configuration process.

Figure 6-38. *On-premise data gateway configuration process*

Now create a gateway in Power BI Online. In the Gateway, add the current windows authentication and the username and password with the server and database. Figure 6-39 shows this process.

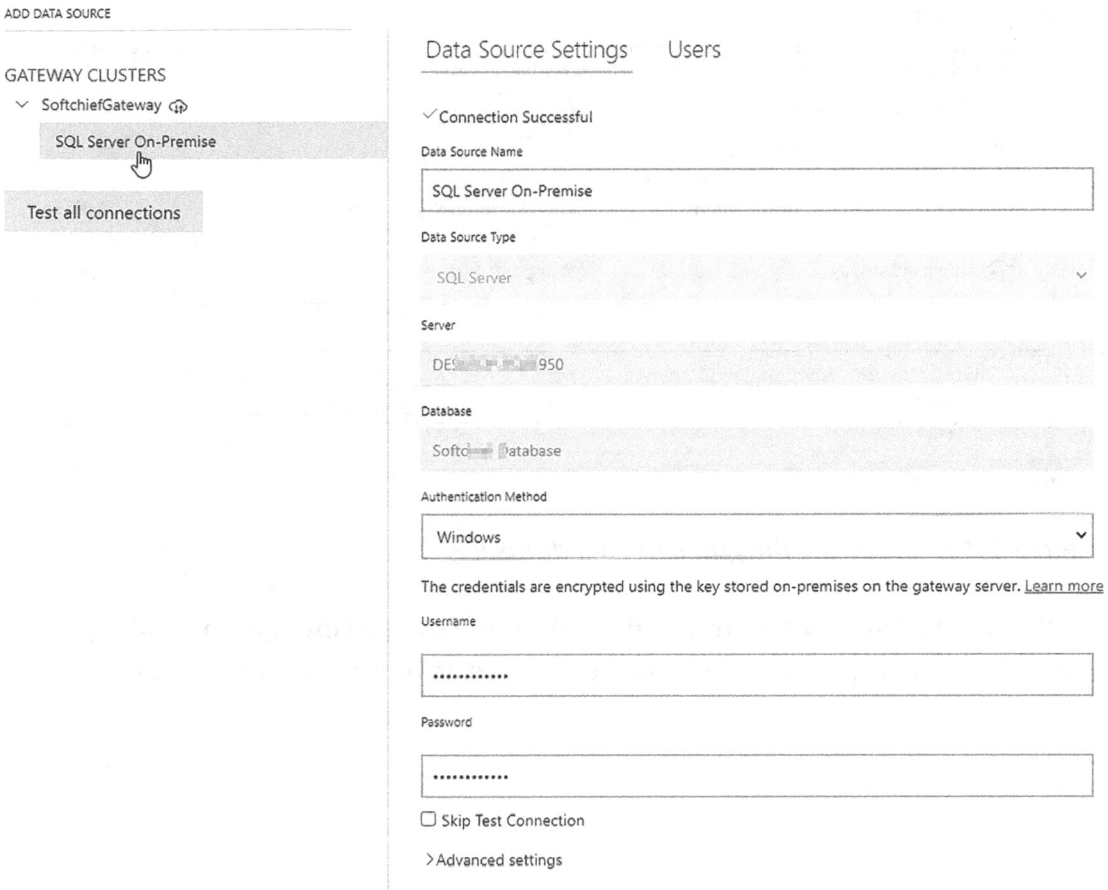

ADD DATA SOURCE

GATEWAY CLUSTERS
⌄ SoftchiefGateway ⛅
    SQL Server On-Premise

Test all connections

Data Source Settings   Users

✓ Connection Successful

Data Source Name

SQL Server On-Premise

Data Source Type

SQL Server   ⌄

Server

DE   950

Database

Softc   Database

Authentication Method

Windows   ⌄

The credentials are encrypted using the key stored on-premises on the gateway server. Learn more

Username

••••••••••••

Password

••••••••••••

☐ Skip Test Connection

> Advanced settings

Figure 6-39. Adding a dataset to an on-premise data gateway

In the Gateway Connection map, the gateway is shown with a local configured gateway. Figure 6-40 shows the mapping.

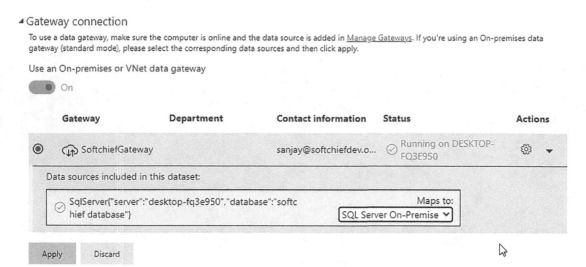

Figure 6-40. *Mapping the gateway to a dataset*

Navigate to Scheduled Refresh and enable it. You can add multiple intervals for refresh. Figure 6-41 shows the process of enabling data refresh for a local dataset.

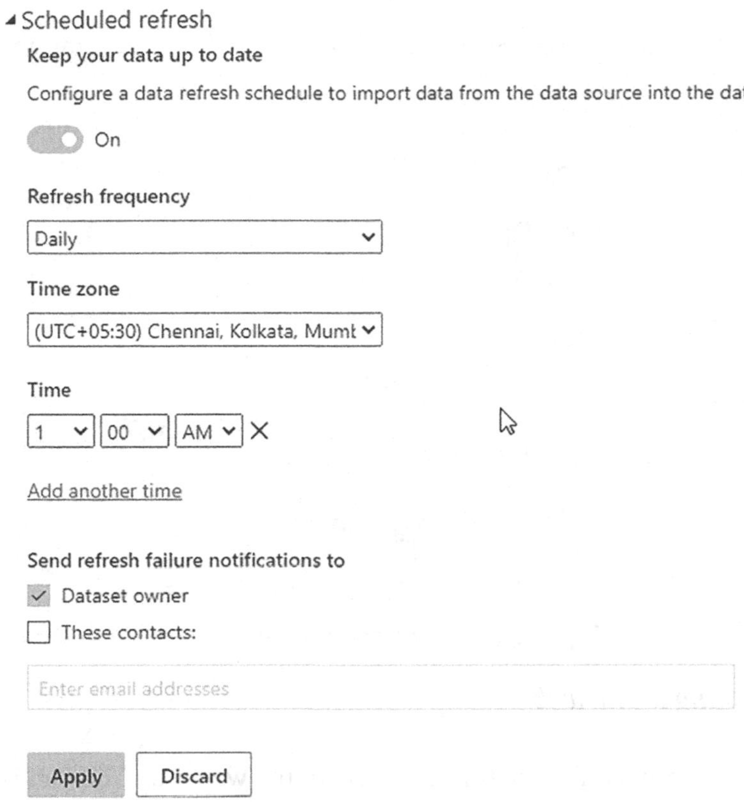

◢ Scheduled refresh

Keep your data up to date

Configure a data refresh schedule to import data from the data source into the dataset. Learn more

⬤⚪ On

Refresh frequency

| Daily ∨ |

Time zone

| (UTC+05:30) Chennai, Kolkata, Mumb ∨ |

Time

| 1 ∨ | 00 ∨ | AM ∨ | ✕

Add another time

Send refresh failure notifications to

☑ Dataset owner

☐ These contacts:

| Enter email addresses |

| Apply | | Discard |

Figure 6-41. Enabling a data refresh for a local dataset

This is how you schedule refresh for different datasources.

Integrate Power BI with Dynamics 365 CE Apps

Once your Power BI dashboards are configured, you can publish or embed them into published websites or into Dynamics 365 Model-driven Power Apps.

To display reports externally, open a report and click the File option. Then select Embedded Report. Select Publish to Website or Portal. Figure 6-42 shows the process of publishing to the web.

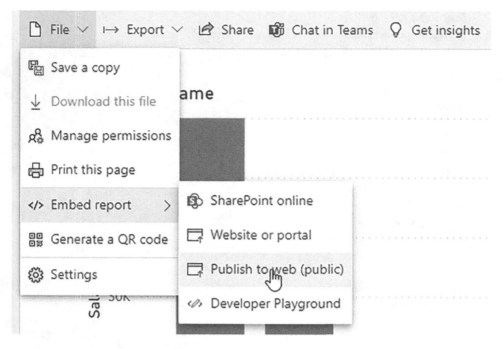

Figure 6-42. *Publishing to the web*

This process will give you a link and iframes to use in the websites. You can copy the code and insert it into the web pages you want to display. Figure 6-43 shows the URL for this report.

Figure 6-43. *URL for your report*

To display Power BI reports and dashboards inside Dynamics 365 model-driven apps, you need to add an embedded Power BI report component and connect to a specific report. Use the following steps to embed Power BI reports inside Dynamics 365 CE.

Step 1: Add an embedded Power BI component and connect to the report. Open the solution and add a new component. Choose an embedded Power BI component. Figure 6-44 shows the process of adding a Power BI dashboard inside a model-driven app using the solution.

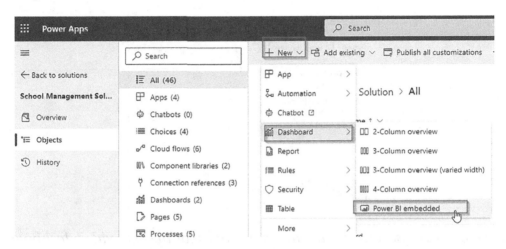

Figure 6-44. *Adding the Power BI dashboard inside a model-driven app using the solution*

In the Properties panel, provide a name, choose Dashboard for the Type, and select Power BI Workspace and Dashboard from the list. Save the settings. Figure 6-45 shows the process of choosing a workspace and dashboard for the embedded dashboard component.

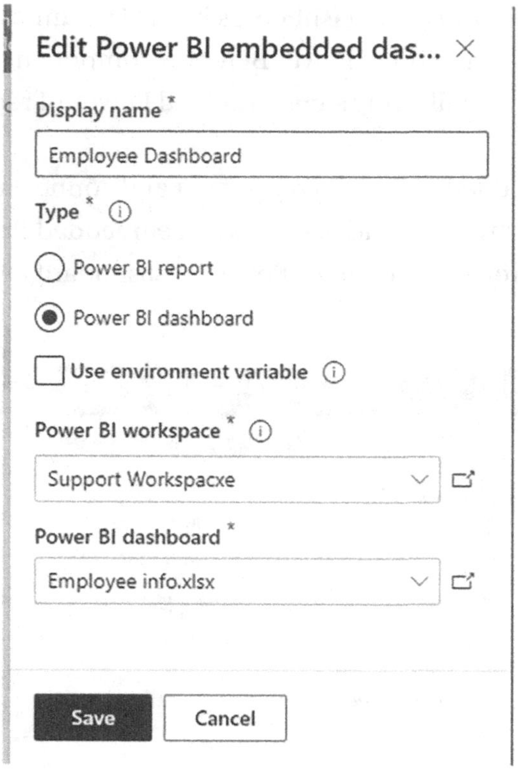

Edit Power BI embedded das... ✕

Display name *

Employee Dashboard

Type * ⓘ

○ Power BI report

⦿ Power BI dashboard

☐ Use environment variable ⓘ

Power BI workspace * ⓘ

Support Workspacxe ∨ ⌁

Power BI dashboard *

Employee info.xlsx ∨ ⌁

Save   Cancel

Figure 6-45. *Choose a workspace and dashboard for the embedded dashboard component*

Step 2: Open the model-driven app of your choice and, in the dashboard section, select the embedded dashboard you just created. Save and publish the app. Figure 6-46 shows the model-driven app once it's published.

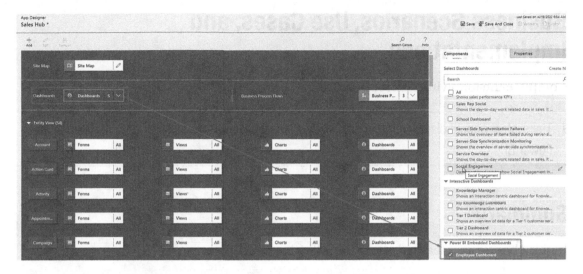

Figure 6-46. *The model-driven app*

If you run the app, you will see the dashboard in the Dashboard View Selector. Figure 6-47 shows the Power BI dashboard inside the model-driven app.

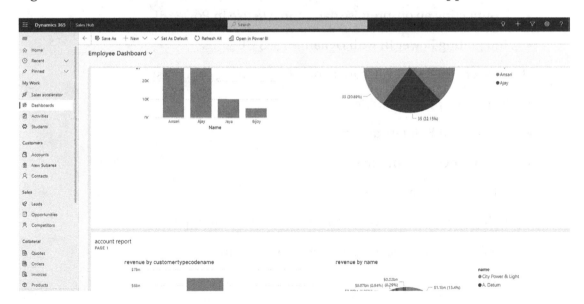

Figure 6-47. *The Power BI dashboard inside a model-driven app*

Business Scenarios, Use Cases, and Implementations

Complete the following task for practice:

1	The system should display student and course visualization dashboards in Power BI.	Configure Power BI.

Summary

In this chapter, you learned about the following concepts:

- The concept of Power BI

- Building blocks of Power BI, datasources, reports, and dashboards

- Connecting an online datasource to use in Power BI

- Connecting an on-premise datasource to use in Power BI

- Integrating Power BI with Dynamics 365 CE Apps

In the next chapter, you will learn about the following concepts:

- The concept of AI Builder

- Types of AI Builders and models

- Form processing models

- Object detection models

- Using AI Builder in Power Automate and Canvas apps

- Business scenarios, use cases, and implementations

Working with AI Builder

AI Builder is a Microsoft Power Platform capability that provides AI models that are designed to optimize your business processes. For example, you can configure a model to extract information from a PDF, detect an object, classify feedbacks, and more. With the no-code concept, you can configure and train models and use them in flows and Canvas Power Apps.

The Concept of the AI Builder

AI Builder models can be configured by non-developers, as they do not require coding knowledge. To configure AI models, you need to subscribe to the trial version of AI Builder or purchase it. To learn more about AI Builder licensing, visit `https://docs.microsoft.com/en-us/learn/modules/get-started-with-ai-builder-licensing/`.

Types of AI Builder Models

There are multiple AI models available. Some are listed here:

- Invoice Processing
- Receipt Processing
- Business Card Reader
- Detect Image

© Sanjaya Prakash Pradhan 2022
S. Prakash Pradhan, *Power Platform and Dynamics 365 CE for Absolute Beginners*,
https://doi.org/10.1007/978-1-4842-8600-5_7

Figure 7-1 shows several types of AI Builders.

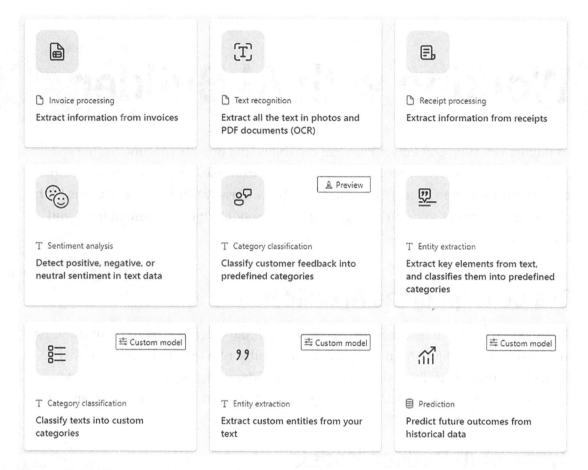

Figure 7-1. *Types of AI Builders*

Form Processing Models

In this section, you learn how to configure a Form Processing model so that you can extract information from a PDF receipt. Use the following steps to complete this task.

Step 1: Create a Custom Model

Navigate to make.powerapps.com and click the AI Builder link. Choose Explore.
Figure 7-2 the shows AI Builder called Explore.

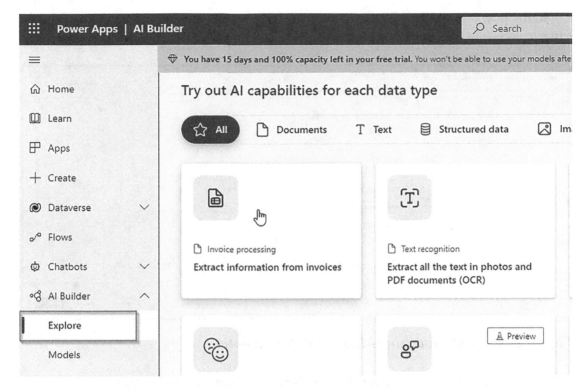

Figure 7-2. *The Explore AI Builder*

Click Custom Model for the Form Processing model. Figure 7-3 shows the Form Processing AI Builder.

Figure 7-3. *Form Processing AI Builder*

In the new popup, click Custom Model to start your custom Form Processing model. Click Get Started. Figure 7-4 shows the Form Processing Model Get Started option.

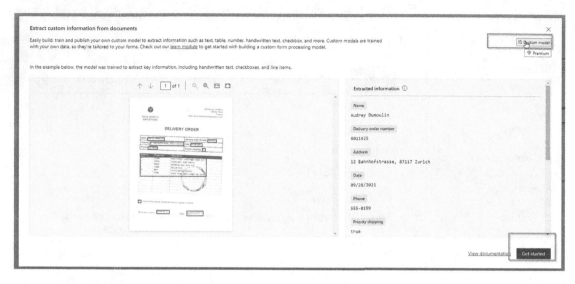

Figure 7-4. *Form Processing Model Get Started option*

Choose information to extract. Add fields and tables as needed. Figure 7-5 shows how to choose information to extract.

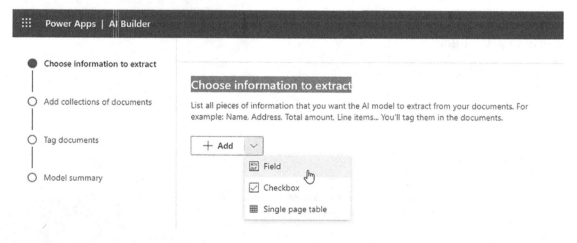

Figure 7-5. *Choosing information to extract*

After defining all the fields and tables, you will see something like Figure 7-6, which shows the final list of the data extract fields.

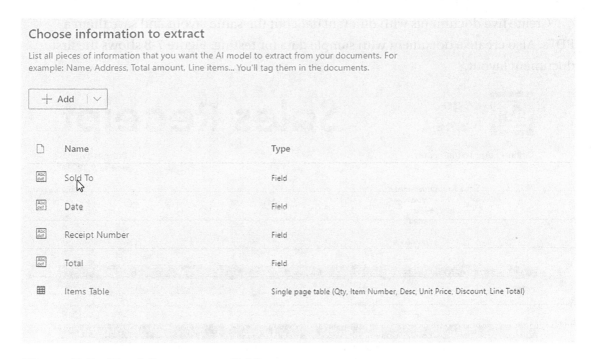

Figure 7-6. *Final data extract fields*

Once all the items are identified, click Next. In the next step, you need to create collections. Click New Collection and upload your PDF documents. You must have at least five documents with the same layout and different data items. You can create a template if you choose.

You can use the template in Figure 7-7 to design your receipt document layout. Open Microsoft Word and search for a receipt template. Figure 7-7 shows how to prepare layouts in Microsoft Word.

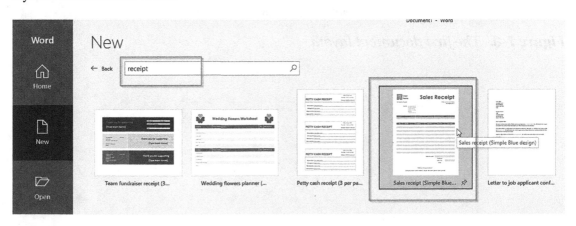

Figure 7-7. *Preparing layouts*

Create five documents with different data but the same layout and save them as PDFs. Also create a document with sample data for testing. Figure 7-8 shows the first document layout.

 **Logo Name**

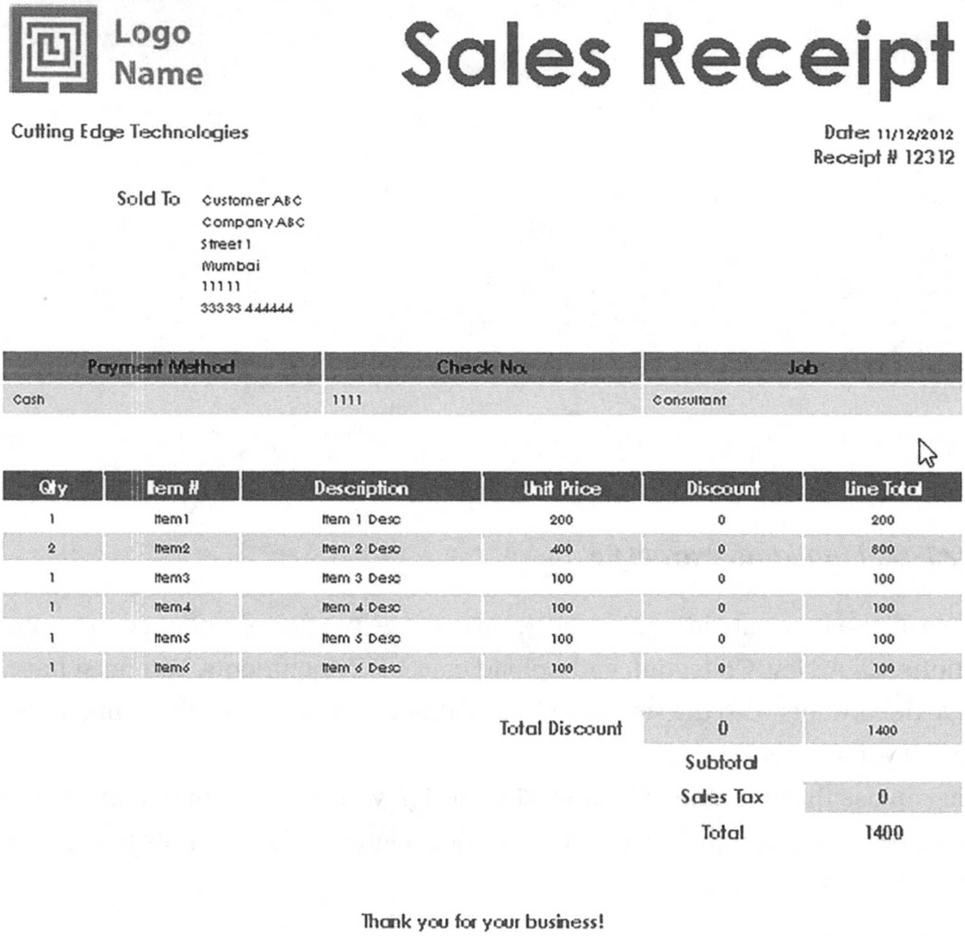

Sales Receipt

Cutting Edge Technologies

Date: 11/12/2012
Receipt # 12312

Sold To   Customer ABC
           Company ABC
           Street 1
           Mumbai
           11111
           33333 444444

Payment Method	Check No.	Job
Cash	1111	Consultant

Qty	Item #	Description	Unit Price	Discount	Line Total
1	Item1	Item 1 Desc	200	0	200
2	Item2	Item 2 Desc	400	0	800
1	Item3	Item 3 Desc	100	0	100
1	Item4	Item 4 Desc	100	0	100
1	Item5	Item 5 Desc	100	0	100
1	Item6	Item 6 Desc	100	0	100

Total Discount	0	1400
Subtotal	
Sales Tax	0
Total	1400

Thank you for your business!

Figure 7-8. *The first document layout*

Figure 7-9 shows the second document layout.

 **Logo Name**

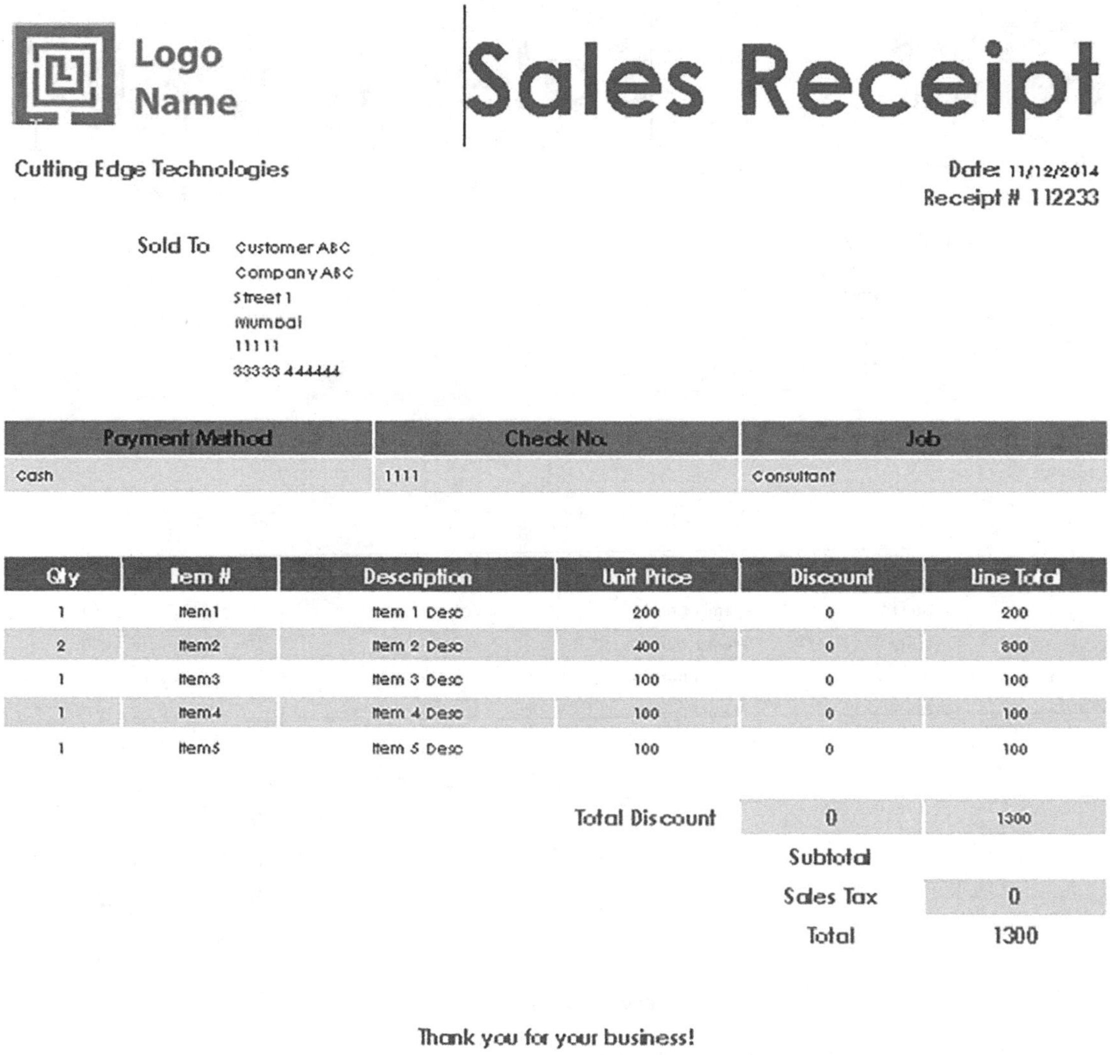

Sales Receipt

Cutting Edge Technologies

Date: 11/12/2014
Receipt # 112233

Sold To   Customer ABC
           Company ABC
           Street 1
           Mumbai
           11111
           33333 444444

Payment Method	Check No.	Job
Cash	1111	Consultant

Qty	Item #	Description	Unit Price	Discount	Line Total
1	Item1	Item 1 Desc	200	0	200
2	Item2	Item 2 Desc	400	0	800
1	Item3	Item 3 Desc	100	0	100
1	Item4	Item 4 Desc	100	0	100
1	Item5	Item 5 Desc	100	0	100

	Total Discount	0	1300
	Subtotal		
	Sales Tax	0	
	Total	1300	

Thank you for your business!

Figure 7-9. *The second document layout*

Figure 7-10 shows the third document layout.

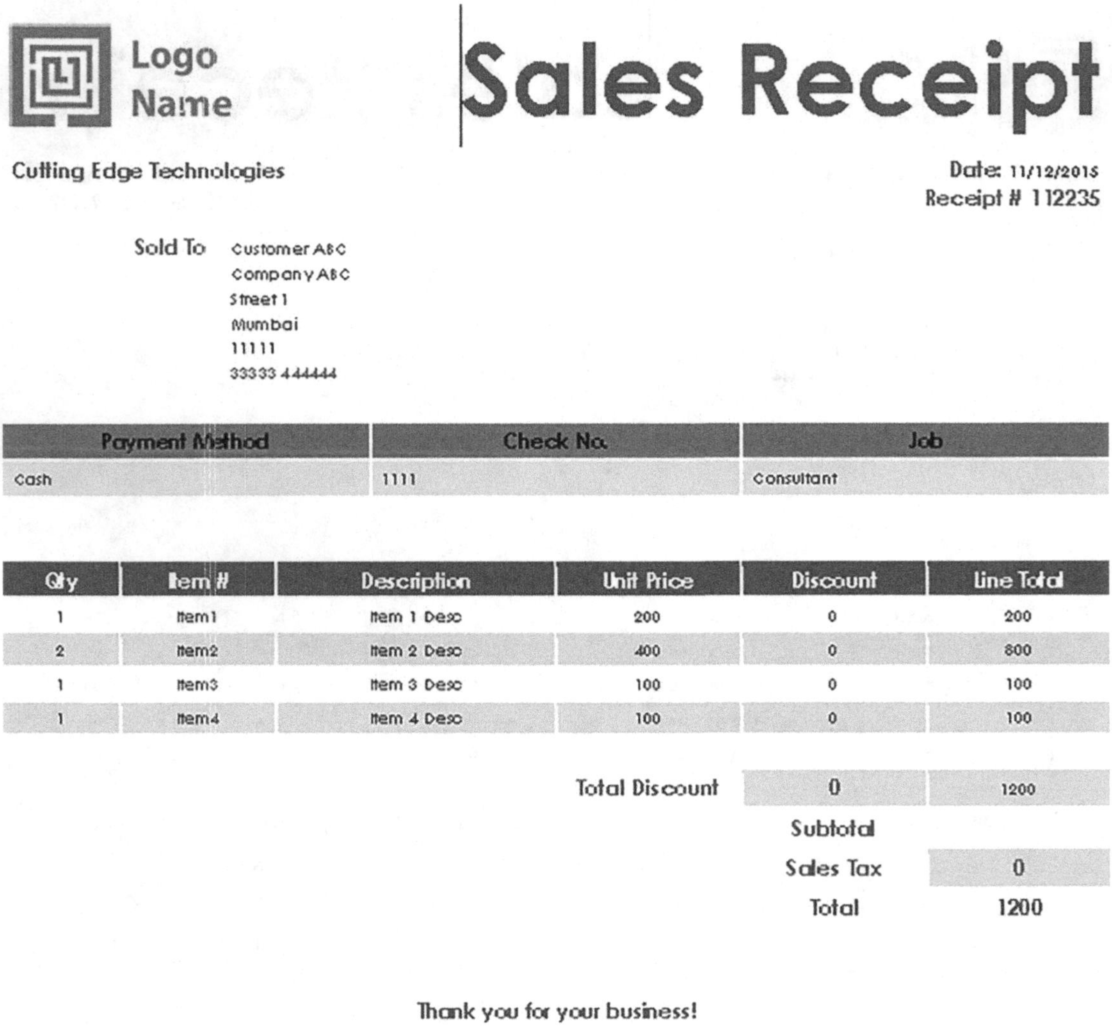

Sales Receipt

Cutting Edge Technologies

Date: 11/12/2015
Receipt # 112235

Sold To   Customer ABC
Company ABC
Street 1
Mumbai
11111
33333 444444

Payment Method	Check No.	Job
Cash	1111	Consultant

Qty	Item #	Description	Unit Price	Discount	Line Total
1	Item1	Item 1 Desc	200	0	200
2	Item2	Item 2 Desc	400	0	800
1	Item3	Item 3 Desc	100	0	100
1	Item4	Item 4 Desc	100	0	100

Total Discount	0	1200
Subtotal		
Sales Tax	0	
Total	1200	

Thank you for your business!

Figure 7-10. *The third document layout*

Figure 7-11 shows the fourth document layout.

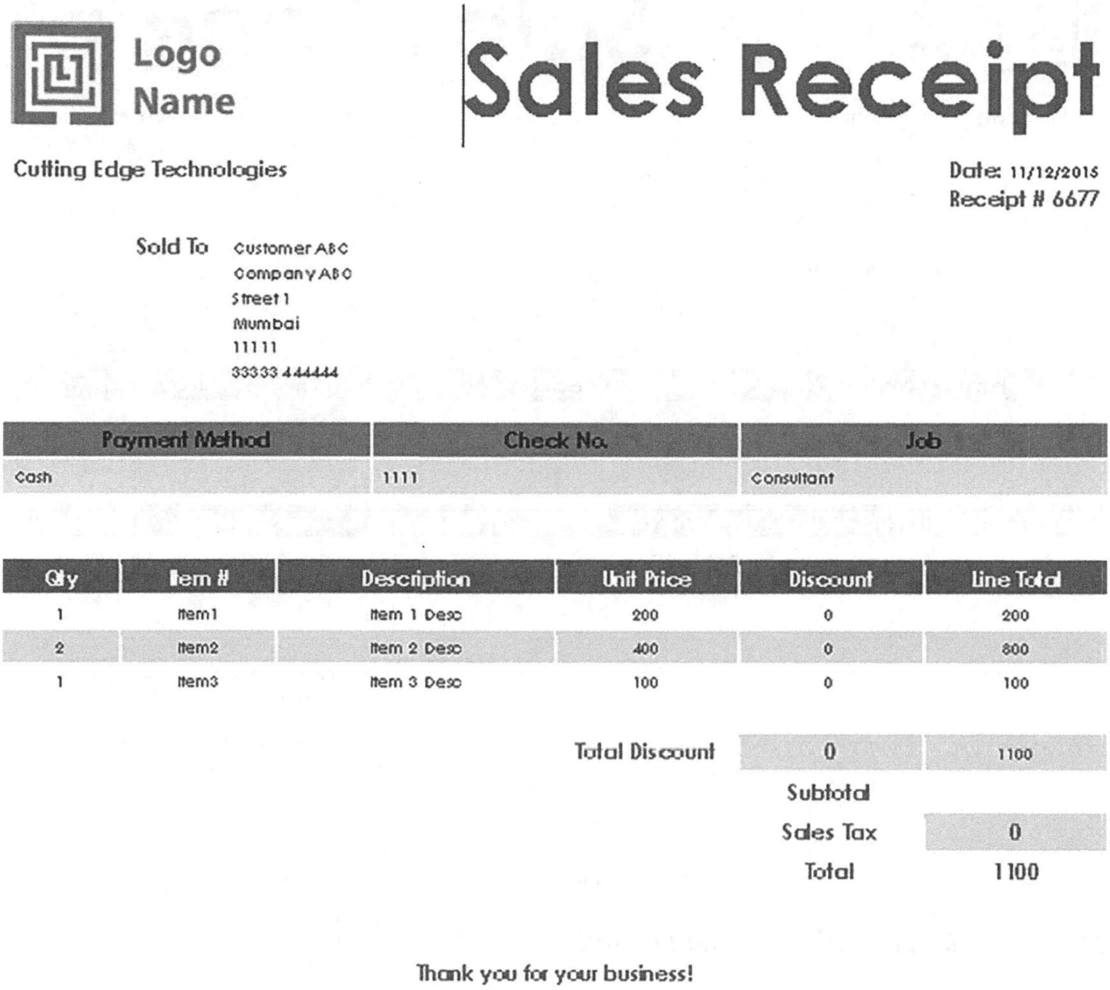

Cutting Edge Technologies

Sales Receipt

Date: 11/12/2015
Receipt # 6677

Sold To   Customer ABC
Company ABC
Street 1
Mumbai
11111
33333 444444

Payment Method	Check No.	Job
Cash	1111	Consultant

Qty	Item #	Description	Unit Price	Discount	Line Total
1	Item1	Item 1 Desc	200	0	200
2	Item2	Item 2 Desc	400	0	800
1	Item3	Item 3 Desc	100	0	100

	Total Discount	0	1100
	Subtotal		
	Sales Tax	0	
	Total	1100	

Thank you for your business!

Figure 7-11. *The fourth document layout*

Figure 7-12 shows the fifth document layout for AI Builder.

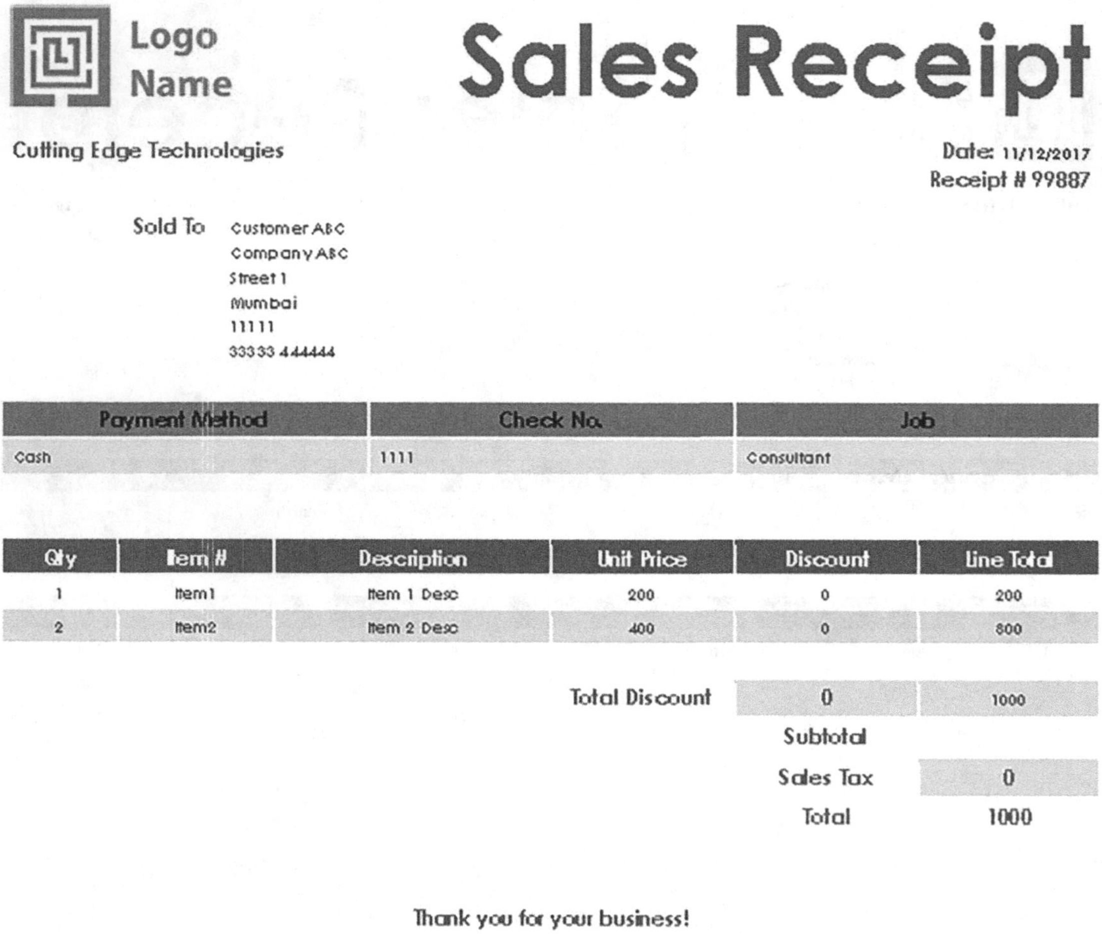

Sales Receipt

Logo Name

Cutting Edge Technologies

Date: 11/12/2017
Receipt # 99887

Sold To   Customer ABC
Company ABC
Street 1
Mumbai
11111
33333 444444

Payment Method	Check No.	Job
Cash	1111	Consultant

Qty	Item #	Description	Unit Price	Discount	Line Total
1	Item1	Item 1 Desc	200	0	200
2	Item2	Item 2 Desc	400	0	800

Total Discount	0	1000
Subtotal		
Sales Tax	0	
Total	1000	

Thank you for your business!

Figure 7-12. *The fifth document layout*

All these documents have the same layout but have different data items, such as items, price, and so on. Now create a test document with different data, which you will test after the model is created.

Navigate to the AI Builder model screen and upload all the documents except the test document in the collection. Figure 7-13 shows how to upload documents.

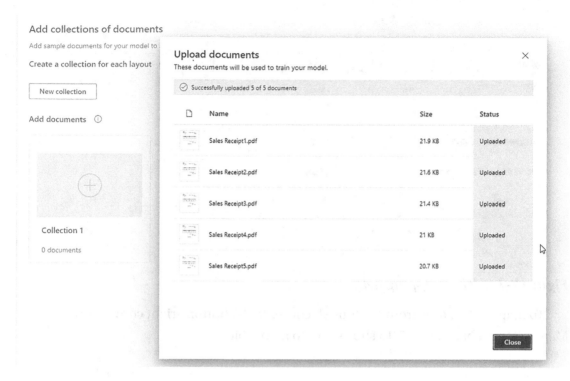

Figure 7-13. *Uploading documents*

After the upload is complete, click Next to map the fields.

Step 2: Map Fields in the PDF for All Five Documents

In the next screen, click each document and map the correct fields with the PDF
sections.

Click the first document and drag-and-drop the sections you want to map with the
fields you want to extract. Do this for all field types. Figure 7-14 shows the mapping field.

Figure 7-14. *The mapping field*

To map a table, drag from the top-left corner to the bottom-right corner and choose Map to Item Table. Figure 7-15 shows how to map tables.

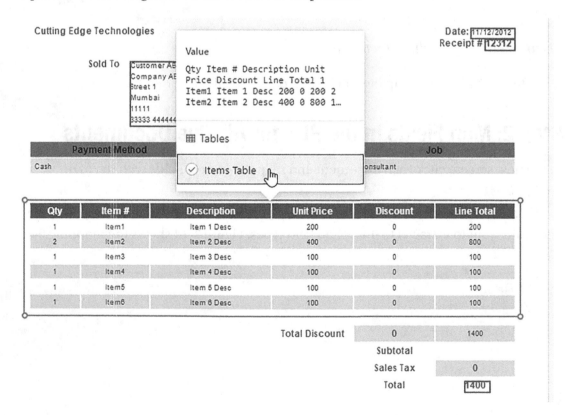

Figure 7-15. *Mapping tables*

Now specify columns and rows with header rows. Figure 7-16 shows this mapping process.

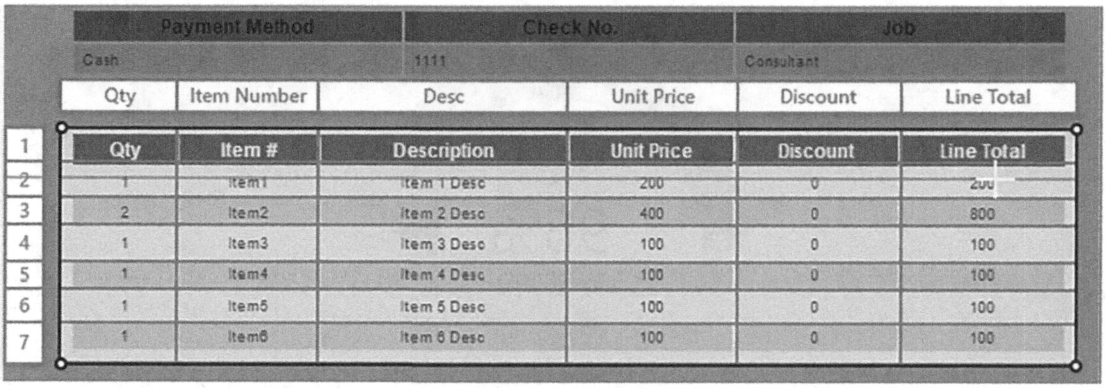

Payment Method		Check No.		Job	
Cash		1111		Consultant	
Qty	Item Number	Desc	Unit Price	Discount	Line Total

	Qty	Item #	Description	Unit Price	Discount	Line Total
1						
2	1	Item1	Item 1 Desc	200	0	200
3	2	Item2	Item 2 Desc	400	0	800
4	1	Item3	Item 3 Desc	100	0	100
5	1	Item4	Item 4 Desc	100	0	100
6	1	Item5	Item 5 Desc	100	0	100
7	1	Item6	Item 6 Desc	100	0	100

Figure 7-16. Mapping columns and rows

Click OK. Repeat these steps for all documents. Figure 7-17 shows the document mapping success.

Collection 1

< Document 5 of 5 >

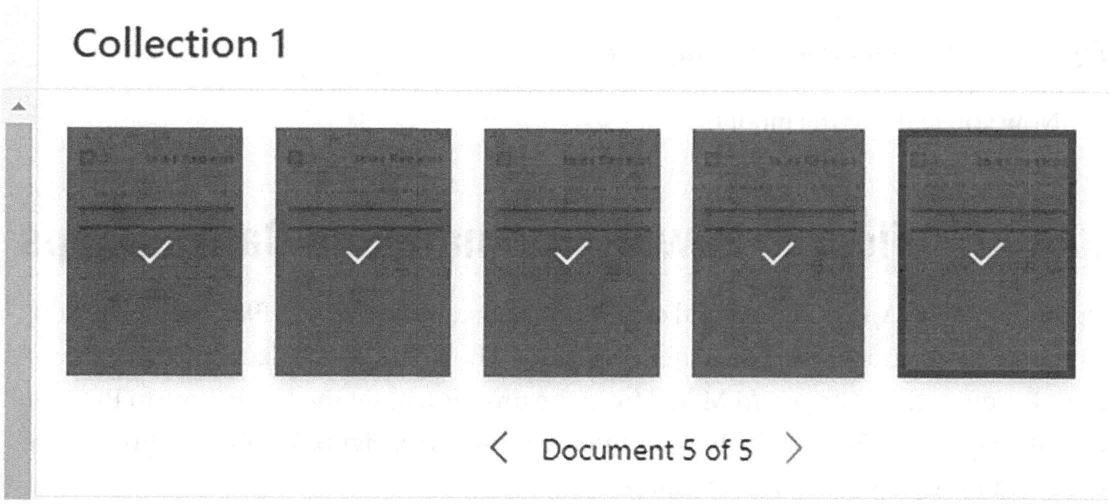

Figure 7-17. All document mapping success

You have successfully mapped all fields. Click Next and then Train. It will take a couple of seconds to train; after that, you can use the mapping in flow or Canvas apps.

Click Go to Model. Once the status changes to Trained, open the model and publish it. Figure 7-18 shows the AI model's accuracy score.

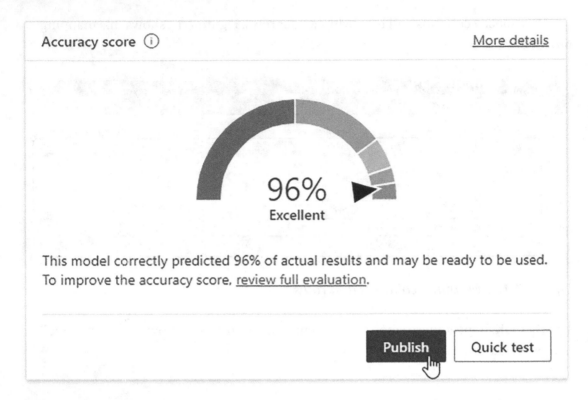

Figure 7-18. *AI model's accuracy score*

Now you can test the model.

Use AI Builder in Power Automate and Canvas Apps

Open the Power Apps solution and create a new instant flow with a file parameter. Add a new step and choose the AI Builder connector. Then choose the Extract Information from Forms action. Choose AI Model from the dropdown, set the Form Type to PDF, and assign a Dynamic Value to the File parameter in the form. Figure 7-19 shows how to use the Form Processor in Power Automate.

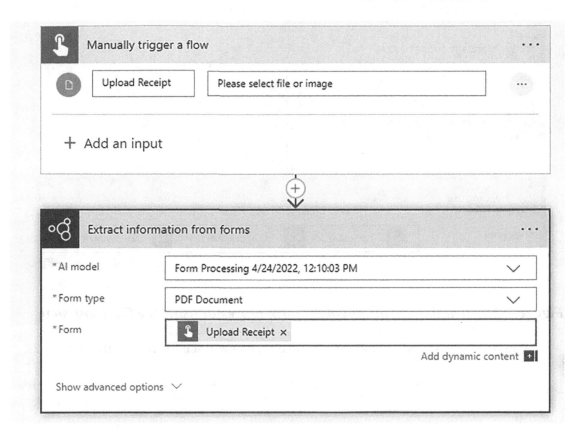

Figure 7-19. *Using Form Processor in Power Automate*

The extract step will extract information and you can assign values to compose steps or send emails as you wish.

In this example, the Compose step used to assign the AI model step output receipt number and total amount and date. Figure 7-20 is reading the output of the Form Processor using the Compose step.

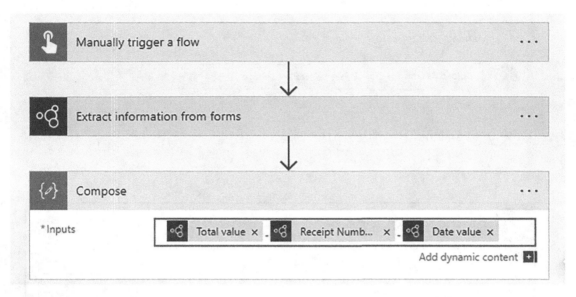

Figure 7-20. *Reading the output of the form processor using the Compose step*

If you run the test and upload the test receipt, you will see the results in Figure 7-21.

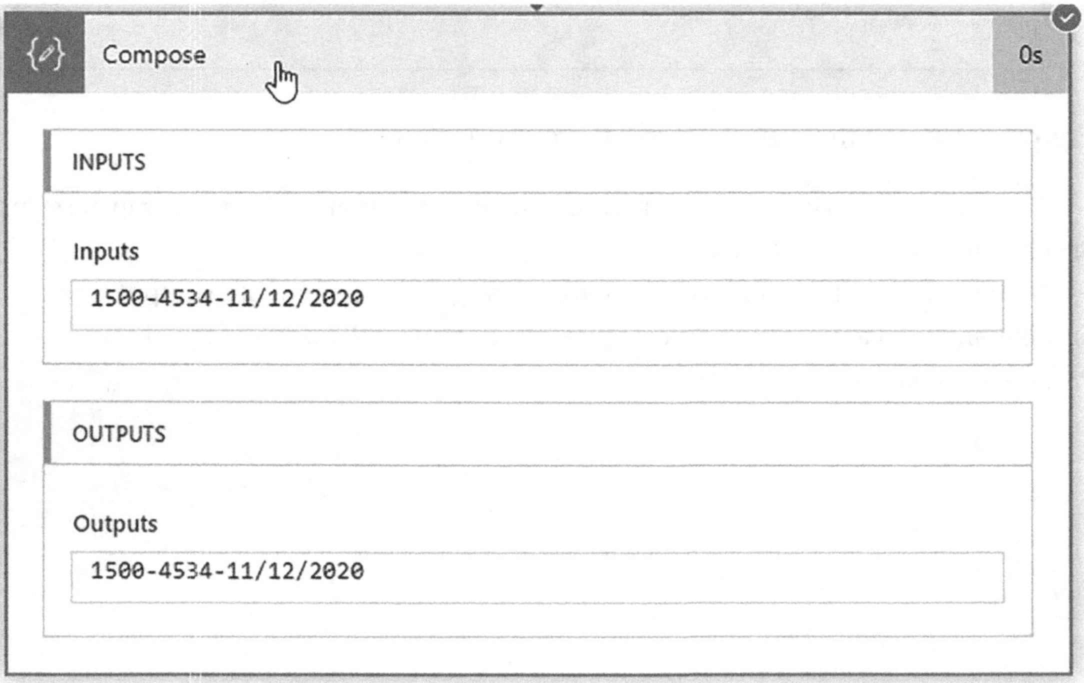

INPUTS

Inputs

1500-4534-11/12/2020

OUTPUTS

Outputs

1500-4534-11/12/2020

Figure 7-21. *Checking the Compose result*

Object Detection Models

You can use the Object Detection model to detect an object. Figure 7-22 shows how to create the Object Detection AI Builder.

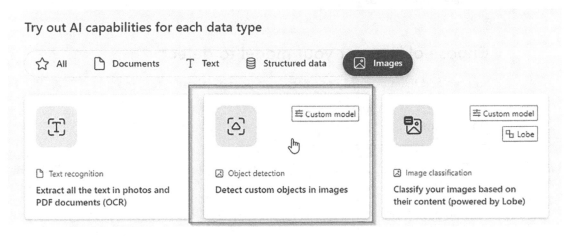

Figure 7-22. *Creating the Object Detection AI Builder*

Click Get Started. Click Common Objects and then click Next. Figure 7-23 shows how to choose objects for AI Builder.

Figure 7-23. *Choose objects*

In the next screen, add the objects you want to detect. Figure 7-24 shows the Define Object Names screen.

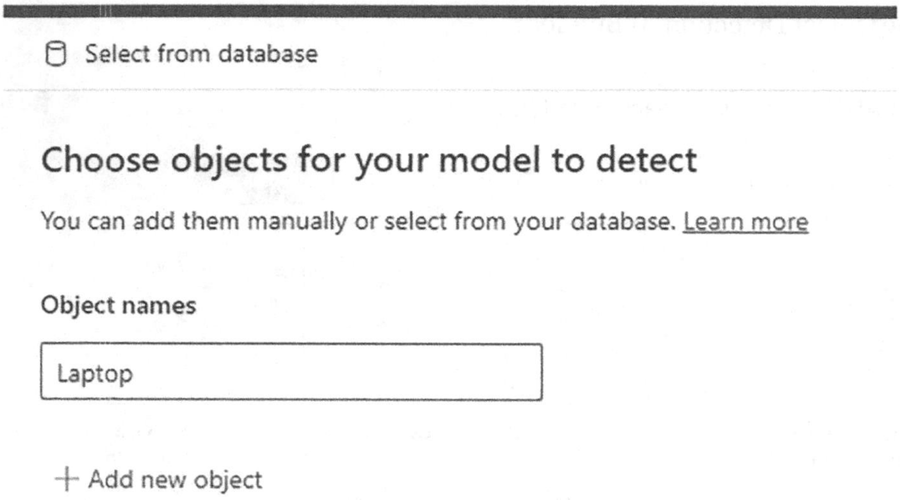

🗄 Select from database

Choose objects for your model to detect

You can add them manually or select from your database. <u>Learn more</u>

Object names

> Laptop

+ Add new object

Figure 7-24. *Defining object names*

Click Next. In the next screen, upload the images you want to detect. For this example, you can use the images shown in Figure 7-25 to detect laptops. You need at least 15 images for tagging.

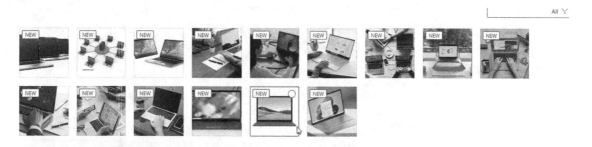

Figure 7-25. *List of objects are displayed*

Now tag the objects with the name defined by the drag-and-drop sections on the image. Figure 7-26 identifies the object from the image and map.

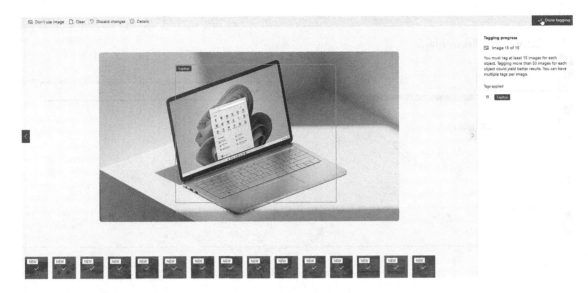

Figure 7-26. *Identify the object from the image and map*

After tagging is completed, click Done Tagging. Then click Next and Train.

Click Go to Model. After the status changes to Trained, click Publish. Now test the results.

Use the Object Detect AI Builder in Canvas Apps

Open the Power Apps solution and create a new Canvas app. Insert an AI Builder and use the object detect model. Figure 7-27 shows the use of object detection in a Canvas app.

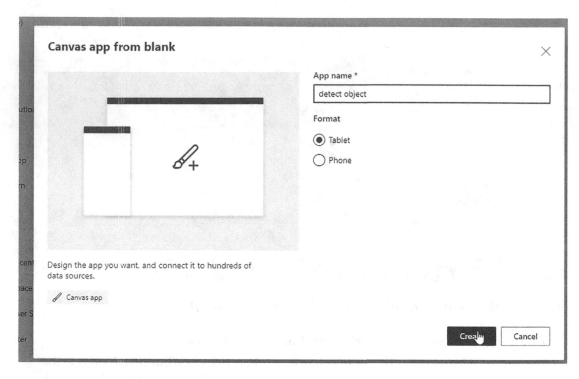

Figure 7-27. *Using object detection in a Canvas app*

In the new screen, go to the Insert menu and choose AI Builder. Select the Object Detector. Figure 7-28 shows how to add an Object Detector to a Canvas app.

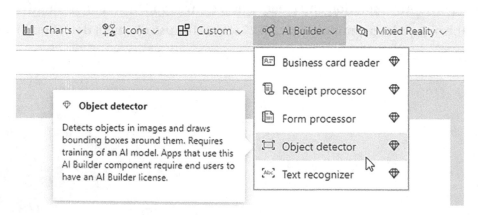

Figure 7-28. *Add an object detector to a Canvas app*

Figure 7-29 shows the process of uploading an image to analyze.

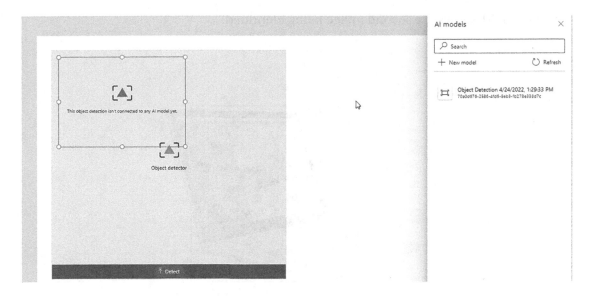

Figure 7-29. *Uploading an image to analyze*

Now run the app and detect and upload an image containing a laptop. You can see that it automatically detects laptop objects. Figure 7-30 shows the identified objects.

Figure 7-30. *Identified objects*

Figure 7-31 shows the second image being identified.

Figure 7-31. *Second image being identified*

Likewise, you can configure other AI models and use them in flows and in Canvas apps as needed. You can find your AI models in the AI Models list. Figure 7-32 shows a list of AI models.

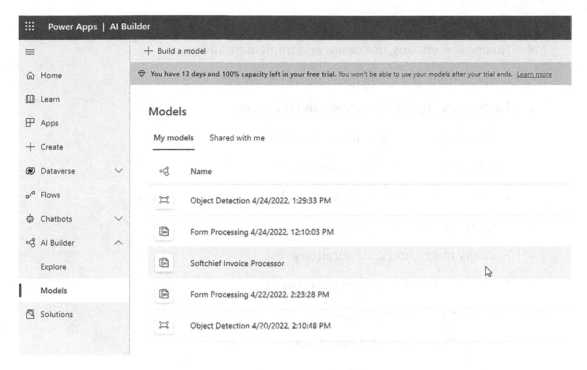

Figure 7-32. *List of AI models*

Business Scenarios, Use Cases, and Implementations

You can complete the following scenario for practice:

| 1 | Configure an AI Builder to process invoices to fetch data and push it to the Dataverse.   AI Builder |

Summary

You learned the following concepts in this chapter:

- The concept of the AI Builder

- Types of AI Builders and models

- Form processing models

- Object detection models

- Using AI Builder in Power Automate and Canvas apps

- Business scenarios, use cases, and implementations

You will learn about the following concepts in the next chapter:

- Understanding admin centers and their uses

- Performing data import in Power Apps

- Configuring duplicate detection rules

- Configuring the Auditing feature in Power Apps

- Adding users to environments

- Security matrix and configurations

- Configuring workflows and concepts

- Configuring custom actions

- Configuring reports in Power Apps

- Working with email templates and signatures

- Installing multiple languages in environments

- Working with translation

- Working with document templates

CHAPTER 8

Working with Power App Configurations

Power Apps provides many configurable components that you can configure based on your business needs. Its model-driven apps have personalization and advanced settings.

Using the personalization settings, you can set your personal preferences, which are applicable to you only. Using the advanced settings, you can configure settings that are applicable to all users.

Admin Centers and Their Uses

Table 8-1 lists the important links to various admin centers in Power Apps.

Table 8-1. *Admin Center Links*

Microsoft 365 Admin Center: Use this Admin Center to add/modify users and products and to add licenses to users.	`https://admin.microsoft.com/`
Power Platform Admin Center: Use this to manage environments and add users to the environment and other settings.	`https://admin.powerplatform. microsoft.com/environments`
Power Apps Admin Center: Points to the same Power Platform Admin Center.	`https://admin.powerapps.com/`
Dynamics 365 Advanced Settings: Use this to manage the advanced settings.	`https://[orgname].[region]. dynamics.com/main. aspx?settingsonly=true`

(continued)

© Sanjaya Prakash Pradhan 2022
S. Prakash Pradhan, *Power Platform and Dynamics 365 CE for Absolute Beginners*,
https://doi.org/10.1007/978-1-4842-8600-5_8

Table 8-1. (*continued*)

Power Apps Maker Portal: Use this to create and manage Power Apps.	`https://make.powerapps.com/`
Azure Active Directory: Use this to manage the Azure app registration and the Azure settings.	`https://aad.portal.azure.com`
Power BI Admin Center: Use this to define the Power BI settings.	`https://app.powerbi.com/admin-portal/tenantSettings`
Preview App Maker: Use this to see the preview features.	`https://make.preview.powerapps.com/`
Office Home Page: Use this for all apps on the Office dashboard.	`https://www.office.com/`

Personalization Settings

To configure personal settings, click the gear icon on any model-driven app from the top bar and choose Personalization Settings. Figure 8-1 shows this process.

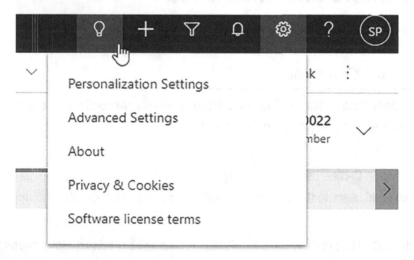

Figure 8-1. *Settings in Power Apps*

In the Personalization Settings, you will see many options, such as General, Synchronization, Activities, Formats, Email Templates, Email Signatures, Email, Privacy, Language, and so on.

Set the Default Pane Option

You can set a default pane so that when you log in, your default pane automatically loads.

In the Personalization Settings, General tab, change the Default pane and Default Tab. Click OK after you do the update. Figure 8-2 shows the General Personalization Settings options.

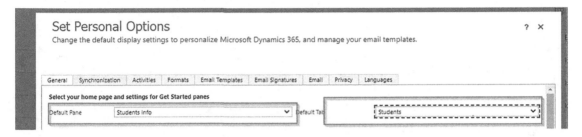

Figure 8-2. *General personalization settings*

Now when you open the app, the Student Info area and Students tab will load as the home page by default.

Change Record Count Per Page in Views

When you load an entity view, it displays 50 records of that entity per page by default. You can increase the records count per page using the settings in Figure 8-3.

Figure 8-3. *Changing the per page record count*

The result will now show 100 records per page, as shown in Figure 8-4.

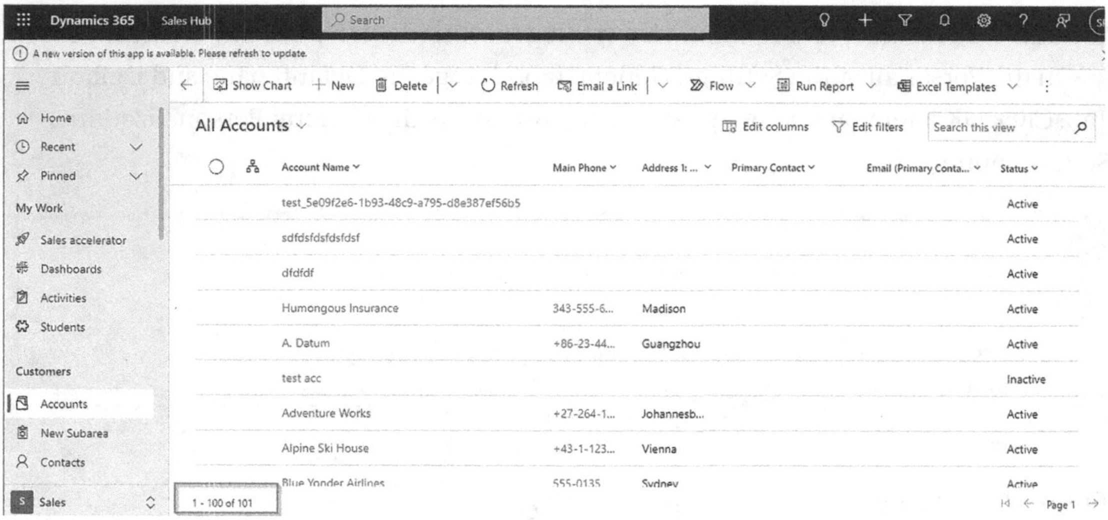

Figure 8-4. *Per page record count has been changed to 100*

Time Zone and Default Currency Setup

You can configure the default currency of your customers and the time zone you are in. This way, records that use the time zone and currency will be set properly. Figure 8-5 shows the time zone and currency options.

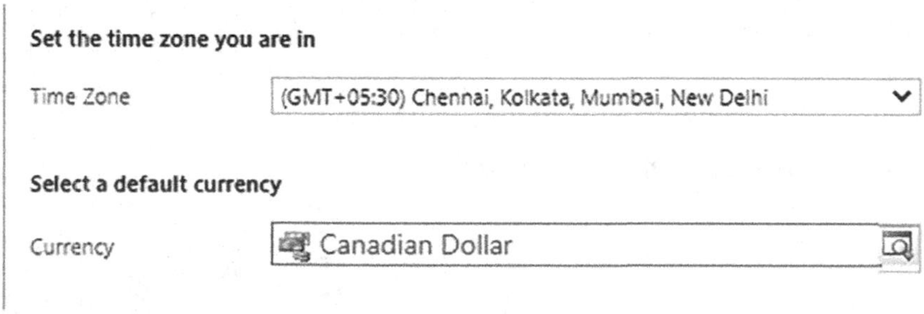

Figure 8-5. *Time zone and currency options*

Email Templates and Signatures

You may find that you often send very similar emails to customers, with some dynamic values being the exception. For example, when you send a welcome email to customers, the content might be the same except for the salutation and the customer's name. For these types of scenarios, you don't want to have to re-type the same content every time. Instead, you can configure email templates that contain reusable content in the email body with dynamic values. You simply need to click Send. This is a time-saving tool you can use in your day-to-day business dealings when sending emails.

To create a new email template, click the New option. Figure 8-6 shows the process of creating a new email template.

Figure 8-6. *Creating a new email template*

You can select a global template or an entity-specific template. Figure 8-7 shows the process of creating a global template.

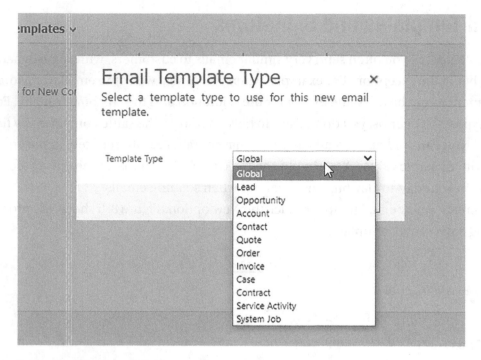

Figure 8-7. *Creating a global template*

For the global type, you can use dynamic field values from the User entity only. For the entity-specific type, you can use user entities and targeted entity-specific field information in the template. This example sets the Type to Contact and shows how to configure the template.

Give the template a name and set the Permission level to Individual. If you set Permission level to Organization, anyone from your organization can use the template.

Choose English for the Language and provide a description. In the subject, specify a common subject of the email. In the body, add the content. To insert dynamic content, click the Insert Dynamic Text button and select the corresponding field so that when the template is used, the value will render dynamically. Figure 8-8 shows the process of inserting dynamic content inside a template.

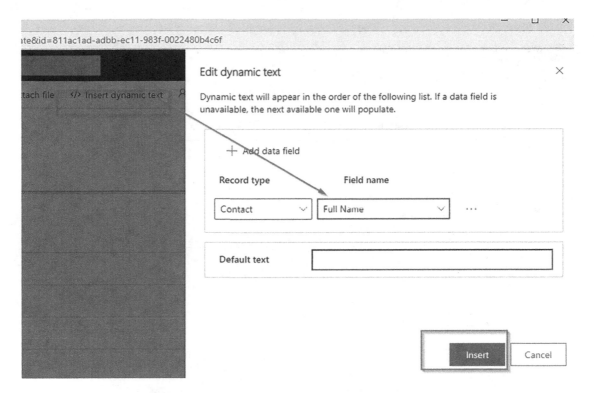

Figure 8-8. *Inserting dynamic content inside a template*

After the data is filled in, click the Save button. The final template will look like Figure 8-9.

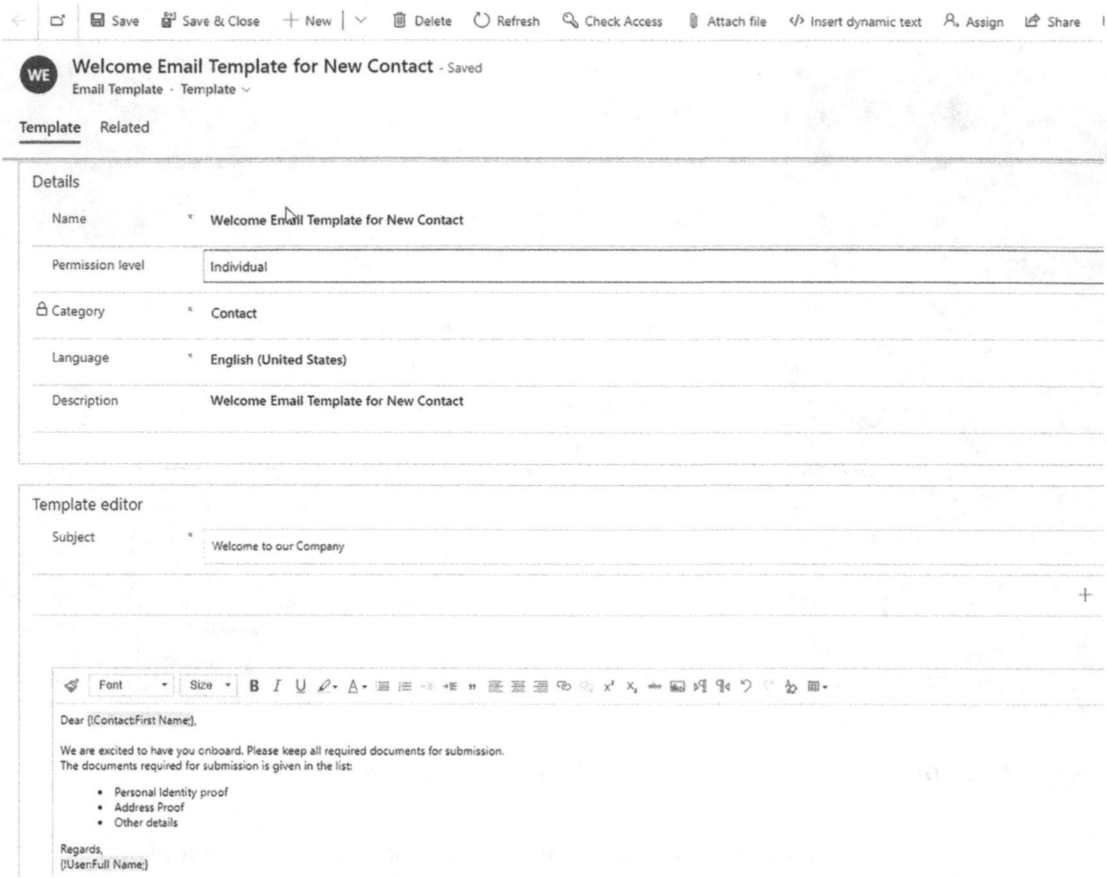

Figure 8-9. *Individual scope template*

After you successfully create an email template, it's time to create an email signature. Click the Email Signature tab and choose the New option. Figure 8-10 shows the Email Signature configuration page.

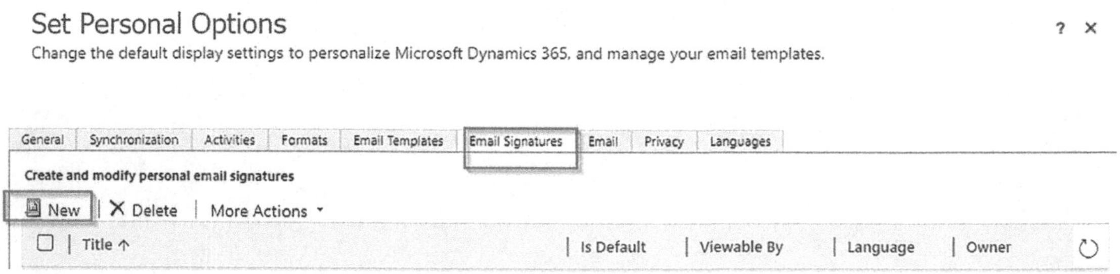

Figure 8-10. *Email signature configuration options*

In the Signature screen, provide a signature and save it. You can mark a signature as the default so that the signature will be copied into the email body. Figure 8-11 shows the process of saving a template record with the Default option set to Yes.

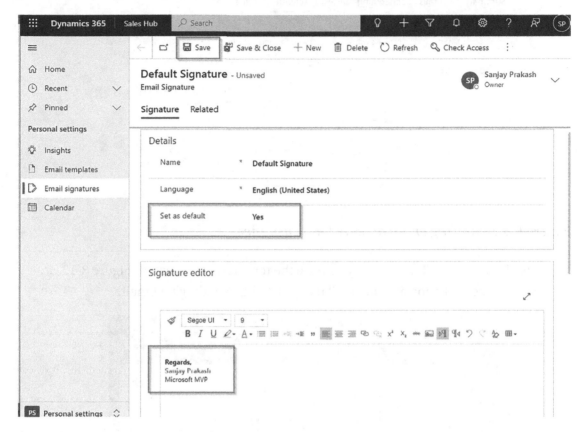

Figure 8-11. *Saving a template record with the Default option set to Yes*

You can use the email template to send an email to a contact. Open a contact and click Related Activities. Choose New Email. Figure 8-12 shows the process of adding an email activity for a customer.

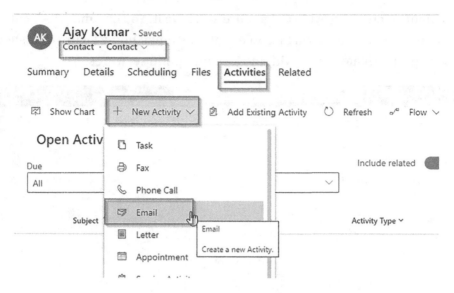

Figure 8-12. *Adding email activity for a customer*

Now choose Insert Template and choose the template you created. Figure 8-13 shows the process of choosing an email template while sending an email.

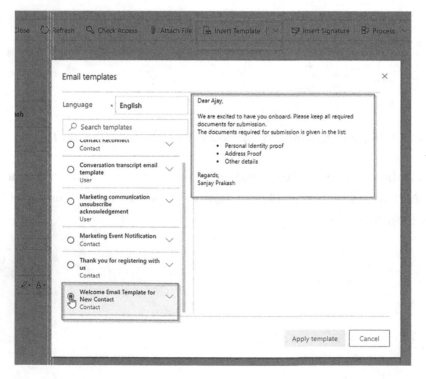

Figure 8-13. *Choosing an email template while sending an email*

Advanced Settings

Advanced settings are applicable organization-wide. To navigate to the advanced settings, go to make.powerapps.com and choose the correct environment. Click the gear icon to select Advanced Settings. Figure 8-14 shows the Advanced Find option.

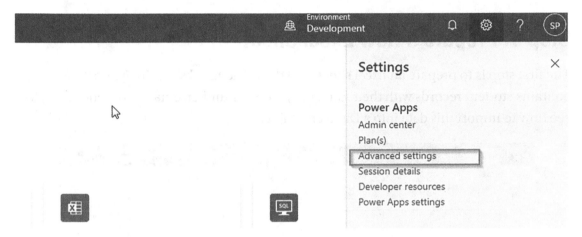

Figure 8-14. *Advanced find option*

This will open the Advanced Settings screen. In this screen, you will find many options that you can configure, including Business settings, Customization settings, System settings, Process Center settings, and so on. Figure 8-15 shows the Advanced Find screen with links.

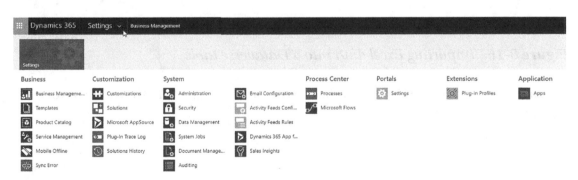

Figure 8-15. *Advanced find screen with links*

In this chapter, you will learn about some of the important settings for model-driven Power Apps.

Data Import in Power Apps

Using the Data Import feature, you can import data from Excel files into Dataverse entities. Say you store student records in an Excel sheet and want to import them to the Dataverse. You can use the import feature to do this. Use the following steps to do this.

Step 1: Prepare a Raw Excel Sheet

The first step is to prepare an Excel sheet with data. The Excel sheet in Figure 8-16 contains student records with their full name, mobile number, email, and gender. You'll see how to import this data into a Dataverse table.

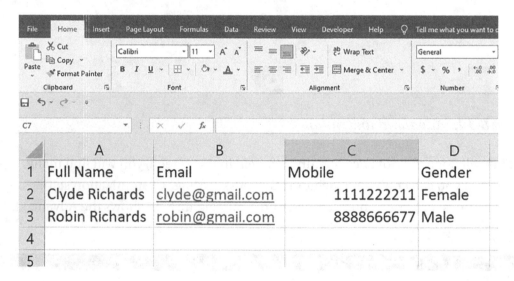

Figure 8-16. *Importing Excel data into a Dataverse table*

Save the file in the .CSV (comma-delimited) format. Figure 8-17 shows the Save As option.

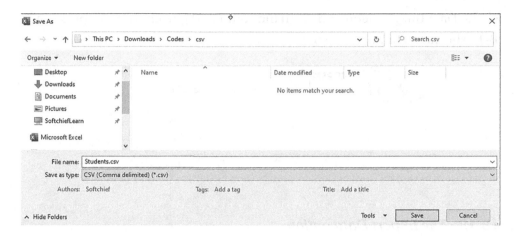

Figure 8-17.   *Saving a file as a .CSV file*

Step 2: Upload a CSV File

Once the CSV file saved, navigate to the Advanced Settings screen in Power Apps and click the Data Management option. Figure 8-18 shows the Data Management option.

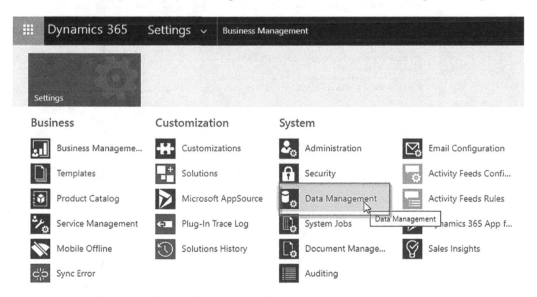

Figure 8-18.   *The Data Management option*

Click the Data Imports icon and, from the command bar, choose Import Data. Figure 8-19 shows the Import Data option.

Figure 8-19. *The Import Data option*

The Import Data option will open a window where you can browse the CSV file for processing.

Click the Browse link and select the CSV file. Then click Next. Figure 8-20 shows how to choose the .CSV file to import.

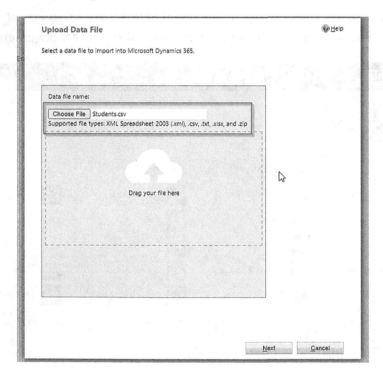

Figure 8-20. *Choosing the .CSV file to import*

On the next screen, you can review the file upload and click Next. On the next screen, choose Default Mapping and click Next. Figure 8-21 shows the default mapping option.

Figure 8-21. *Default mapping option*

Step 3: Map an Entity and its Fields

In the next step, you need to map a correct entity and field. Figure 8-22 shows the mapping table.

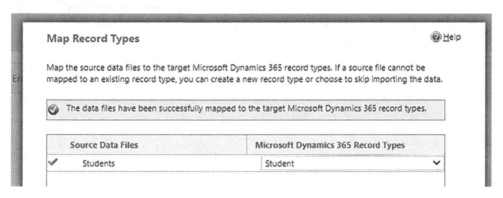

Figure 8-22. *Mapping table*

After your entity has been mapped, click Next for Field Mapping. Figure 8-23 shows the mapping columns.

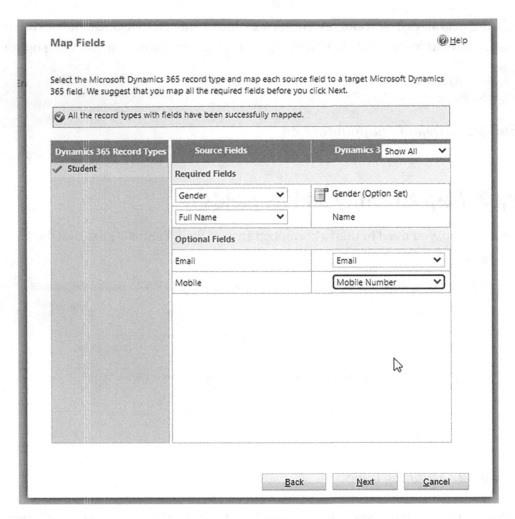

Figure 8-23.   *Mapping columns*

Once the fields have been correctly mapped with the Dynamics 365 entity, click Next to review. Then click Submit to finish the steps.

Now a new background import process instance that will run in the background to import data. Figure 8-24 shows the import result.

Dynamics 365
Settings
Data Management
Web client experience for security settings is being deprecated
Please use the Power Platform admin center to leverage the latest experience and manage security settings
Learn More
DELETE
EMAIL A LINK
EXCEL TEMPLATES
EXPORT TO EXCEL
IMPORT DATA
My Imports
Import Name
Status Reaso...
Successe...
Partial Failure...
Errors
Total Pr...
Created On
Created By
Students.csv
Submitted
0
0
0
0
4/26/2022 1:...
Sanjay Prakash

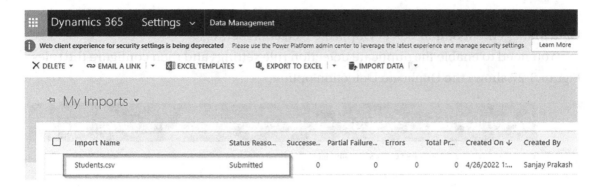

Figure 8-24. *Import result*

After some time, if you refresh the data import operation, you can check its status. Figure 8-25 shows the import success.

Import Name
Status Reaso...
Successe...
Partial Failure...
Errors
Total Pr...
Created On
Created By
Students.csv
Completed
2
0
0
2
4/26/2022 1:...
Sanjay Prakash

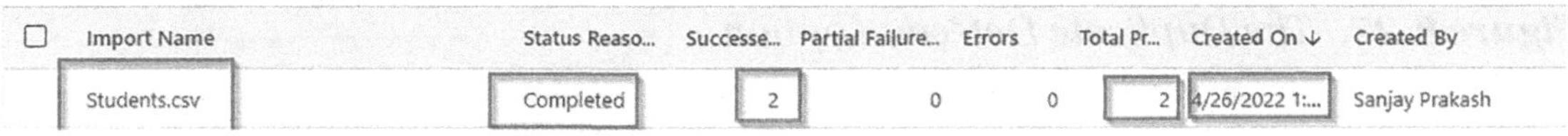

Figure 8-25. *Import success*

Now you can navigate to the Students view and see if all the records have been imported successfully. Figure 8-26 shows the import success records.

Active Students*
Edit columns
Edit filters
Search this view
Name
Created On
Birth Date
Email
Mobile Number
Clyde Richards
4/26/2022 1:18 PM
clyde@gmail.com
1111222211
Richi Sharma
4/26/2022 10:07 AM
Robin Richards
4/26/2022 1:18 PM
robin@gmail.com
8888666677

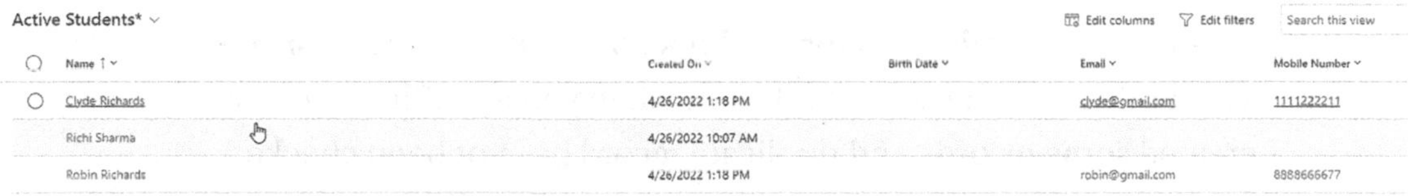

Figure 8-26. *Import success records*

This shows that you have successfully imported the student records into the Dataverse.

Configure Duplicate Detection Rules

Duplicate detection rules can be configured to determine if a record is a duplicate of another record by configuring matching fields. Duplicate detection checks are enforced while creating new records and updating existing ones. You can also enable duplicate detection rules when importing data.

To enable duplicate detection rules, navigate to the advanced settings and, from the Data Management option, select Duplicate Detection Settings.

You need to enable the duplicate detection rule settings and then configure the rules. Figure 8-27 shows the Duplicate Detection option.

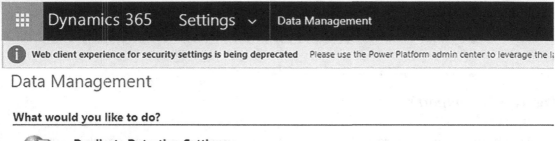

Figure 8-27. *The Duplicate Detection option*

In the Settings screen, enable the Enable Duplicate Detection checkbox and, in the Detect Duplicate options, enable the following options:

- **When a record is created or updated**: This option will check for duplicate records when creating new records or updating existing ones.

- **When MS Dynamics 365 for Outlook goes from offline to online**: This option will check for duplicates when you are offline and you created some records and duplicate record has not been checked. Once you are back online, the duplicate checks will run.

- **During data import**: This option will check for duplicates during the Data Import operation.

Figure 8-28 shows the Duplicate Detection settings.

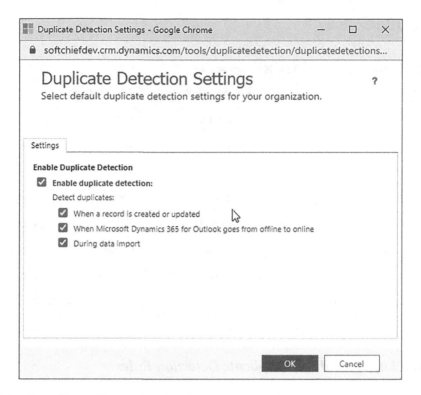

Figure 8-28. *Duplicate Detection settings*

Click OK after enabling these settings. Now you need to configure the rules. Click the Duplicate Detection Rules option, which is shown in Figure 8-29.

Figure 8-29. *Duplicate Detection Rules option*

This will open all the duplicate detection rules configured in the system. You can create your own rules. Click the New option to do so. Figure 8-30 shows the list of available Duplicate Detection Rules.

Duplicate Detection Rules

Entity Type:	All			View:	All Duplicate Detection Rules	

New | 🖨 📇 | ⊙ Publish ⊙ Unpublish | 👥 ✕ | More Actions ▾

☐	Rule Name ↑	Status Reason	Base Record Type	Matching Record Typ
	Accounts with the same Account Name	Published	Account	Account
	Accounts with the same e-mail address	Published	Account	Account
	Accounts with the same phone number	Published	Account	Account
	Accounts with the same website	Published	Account	Account
☐	Contacts with the same business phone number	Published	Contact	Contact
		Published		
	Contacts with the same e-mail address	Published	Contact	Contact
	Contacts with the same first name and last name	Published	Contact	Contact
	Leads with the same e-mail address	Published	Lead	Lead
	Social profiles with same full name and social ch...	Published	Social Profile	Social Profile

Figure 8-30. *List of available Duplicate Detection Rules*

In the New Rule screen, specify the name for the rule. Say you want to create a duplicate rule for the Students entity. If two students have the same email ID, those are duplicate records.

In the New Rule screen, set Base Record Type to Student and Matching Record Type to Student.

In the Rule Criteria, select the Email field. For Criteria, choose Exact Match. Save the rule and publish it.

If you don't publish the rule, it will not work. Every time you create a duplicate detection rule, you need to publish it. Figure 8-31 shows the configuration screen for the Student Duplicate Email rule.

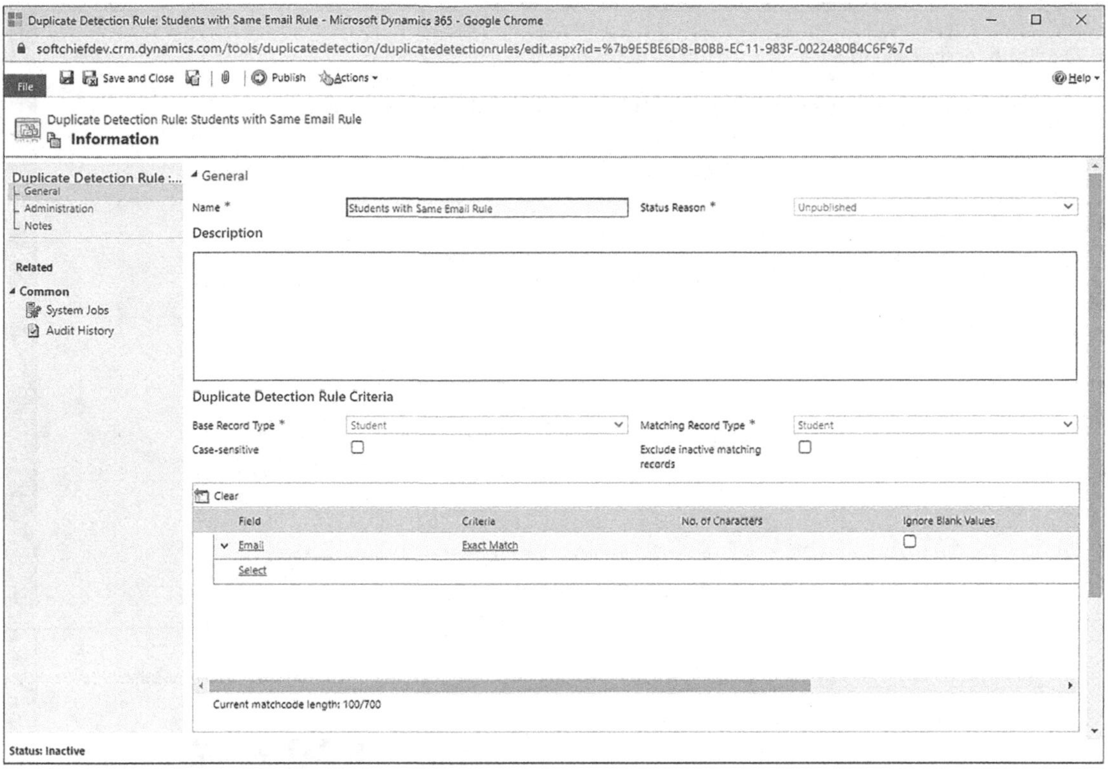

Figure 8-31. *Configuration screen for the Student Duplicate Email rule*

Once the rule is published, you can test it. Create a new student with an email ID and save it. Now create another student with the same email ID. You will see the Duplicate Records screen shown in Figure 8-32.

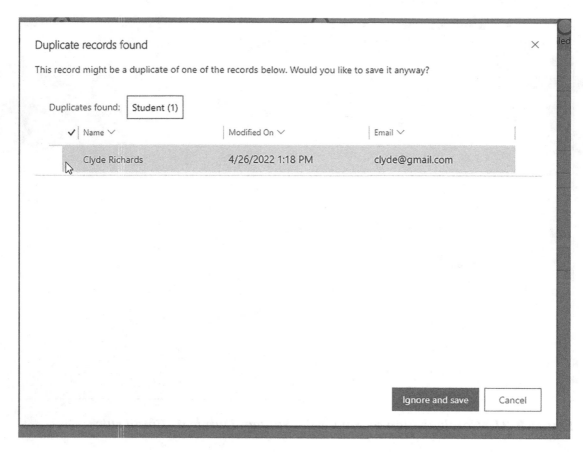

Figure 8-32. Duplicate record detected

You can either ignore the warning and save this field with duplicate data or you can cancel the save operation.

You can merge new record information with duplicate records and configure multiple duplicate detection rules for a single entity.

Configure the Auditing Feature in Power Apps

The Auditing feature logs changes that are made to customer records and user access so you can review this activity later. The Auditing feature is designed to meet the auditing, compliance, security, and governance policies of many regulated enterprises.

To enable the Auditing feature, navigate to advanced settings and select the Auditing option. Figure 8-33 shows the Auditing feature.

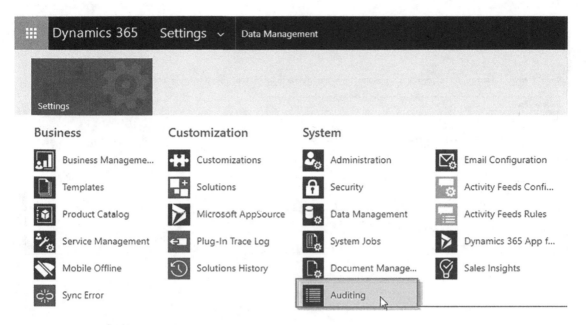

Figure 8-33. *The Auditing feature*

Follow below sections to enable auditing in Power Apps.

Enable the Global Audit Settings

From the Auditing option screen, click Global Audit Settings. Figure 8-34 shows the Global Audit Settings option.

Figure 8-34. *Auditing global settings*

Enable the Start Auditing option and other required options based on your business needs. You can enable User Access Audit, Read Access Audit, and common entities including custom entity audits. Figure 8-35 shows how to enable the Global Audit.

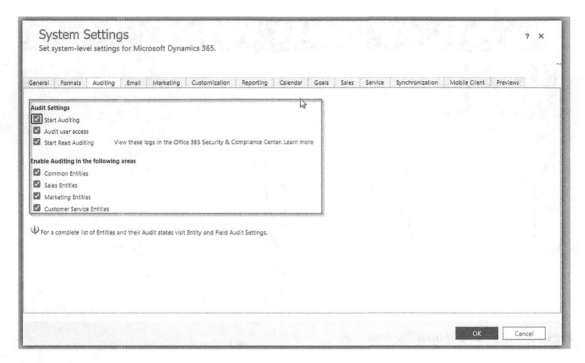

Figure 8-35. *Enabling Global Audit*

Enable an Audit at the Entity Level

The next step is to navigate to the corresponding entity and enable the Audit option. Say you want to enable auditing for contact entity mobile number. You have to click the Entity and Field Audit Settings, shown in Figure 8-36.

Entity and Field Audit Settings
Enable audit tracking on selected entities and fields.

Figure 8-36. *Entity and Field Audit settings*

When the screen open, expand the entity node and select the contact entity. In the Contact Entity Settings screen, enable the Audit flag.

After that, navigate to the Fields node and select the field you want to audit. In the Fields settings, enable the Auditing flag. Figure 8-37 shows this process.

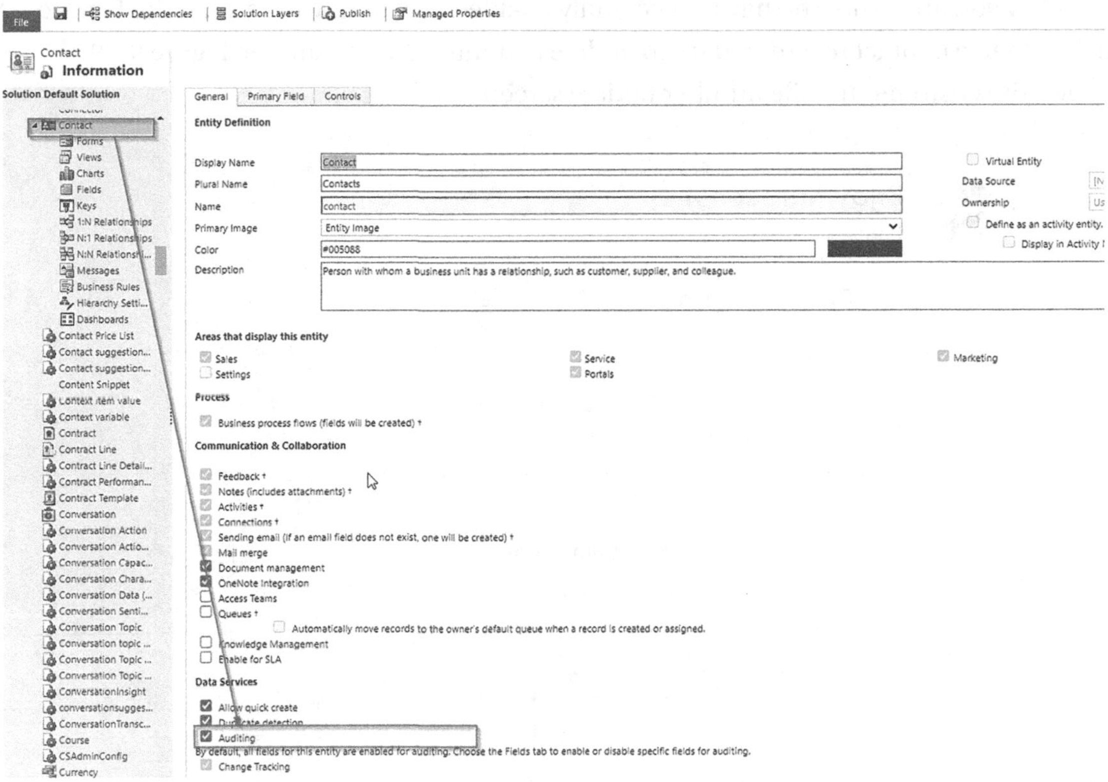

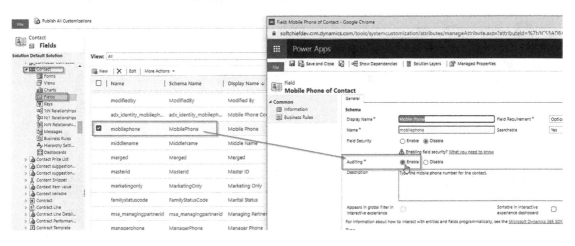

Figure 8-37. *Selecting an entity for auditing*

Enable field-level auditing. Figure 8-38 shows the select columns for auditing.

Figure 8-38. *Selecting columns for auditing*

Now you are done. You have successfully enabled auditing. You can test the feature now. Open a contact record and try to update a mobile phone number. Figure 8-39 shows the customer mobile number update screen.

Figure 8-39. *Customer mobile number update screen*

Click the Related tab and choose Audit History. You will now see the old mobile phone and the new value with the Changed By value. Figure 8-40 shows this process.

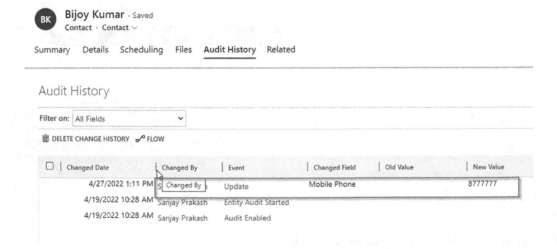

Figure 8-40. *Verify the audit data using the Audit History option*

Add Users to Environments

You can add new users to an environment using Office 365 Admin Center. After you add new users, you can assign a license to them so that they can access correct apps and tables with security roles.

Use the following steps to add new users to your environment.

Step 1: Open the Admin Center and Add a User

Navigate to office.com and log in. Click the All Apps icon and choose the Admin icon. Figure 8-41 shows the Admin option of the Office home page.

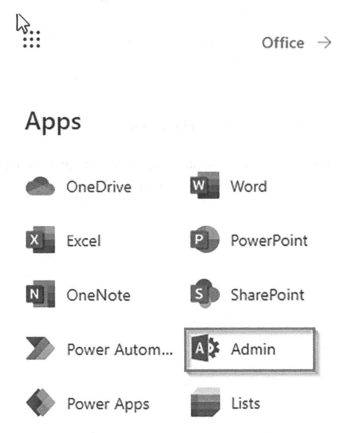

Figure 8-41. *Admin option of the Office home page*

From the User option, choose Active Users and click Add a User. Figure 8-42 shows how to add a new user to the Dataverse.

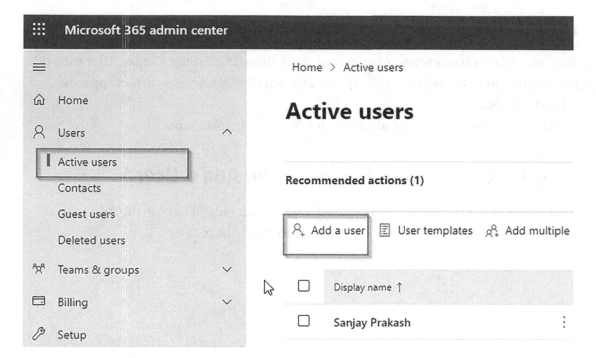

Figure 8-42. *Adding a new user to the Dataverse*

In the Add User panel, provide a first name, last name, display name, and username and then click Next. Figure 8-43 shows basic info about the user.

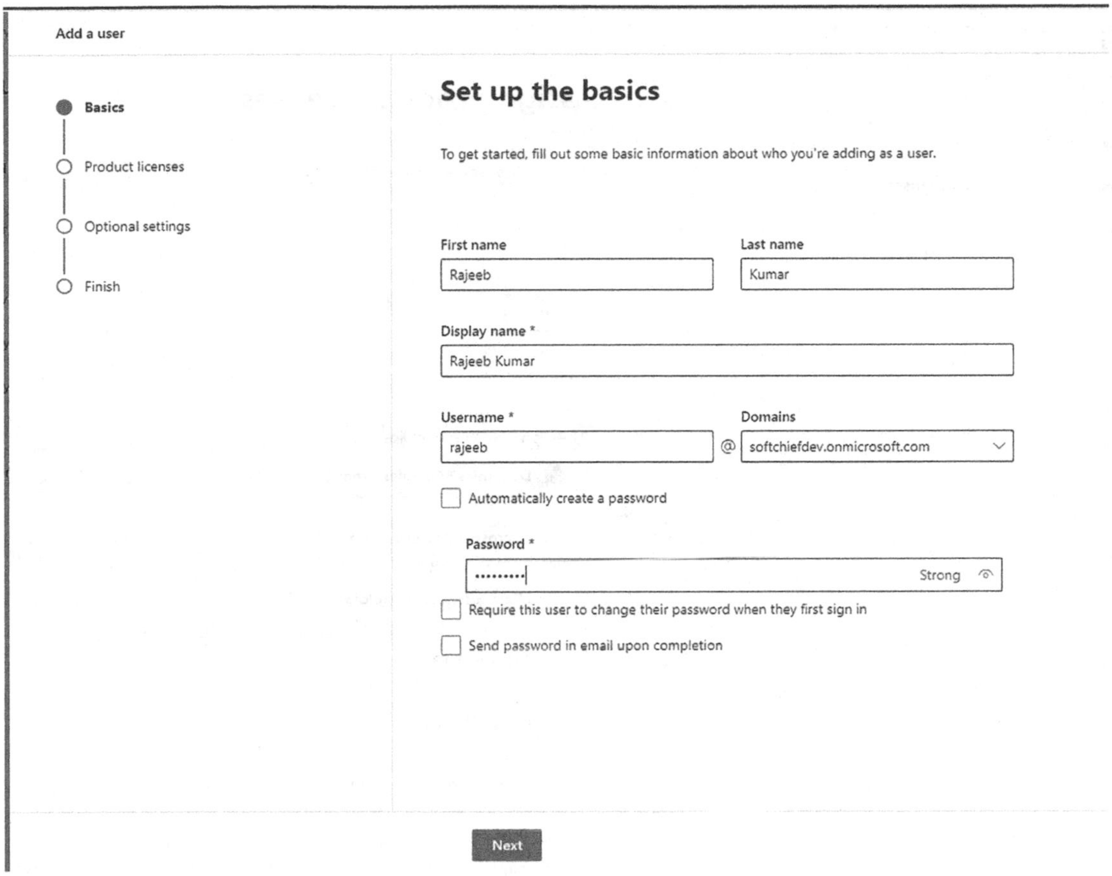

Add a user

● **Basics**

○ Product licenses

○ Optional settings

○ Finish

Set up the basics

To get started, fill out some basic information about who you're adding as a user.

First name

Rajeeb

Last name

Kumar

Display name *

Rajeeb Kumar

Username *

rajeeb

Domains

@ softchiefdev.onmicrosoft.com ⌄

☐ Automatically create a password

Password *

········| Strong 👁

☐ Require this user to change their password when they first sign in

☐ Send password in email upon completion

[Next]

Figure 8-43. *Basic info about the user*

In the next screen, select a license for the user and click Next. Figure 8-44 shows the process of assigning a product license to a user.

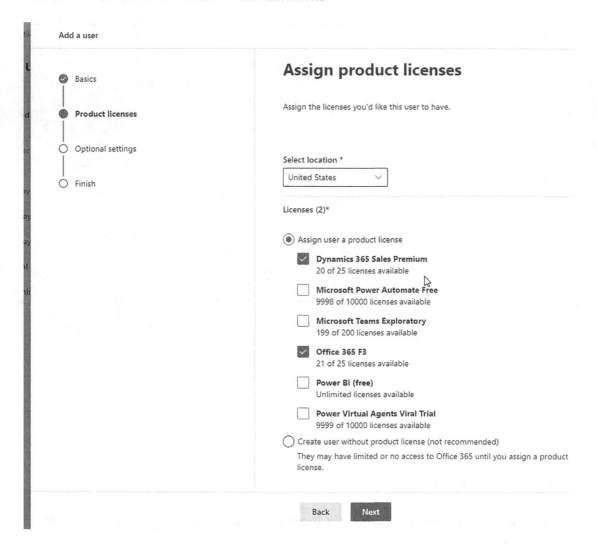

Figure 8-44. *Assigning a product license to a user*

In the next screen, you can add more information about the user profile or you can skip that for now and click Next. In the last screen, you can review and finish. Figure 8-45 shows this process.

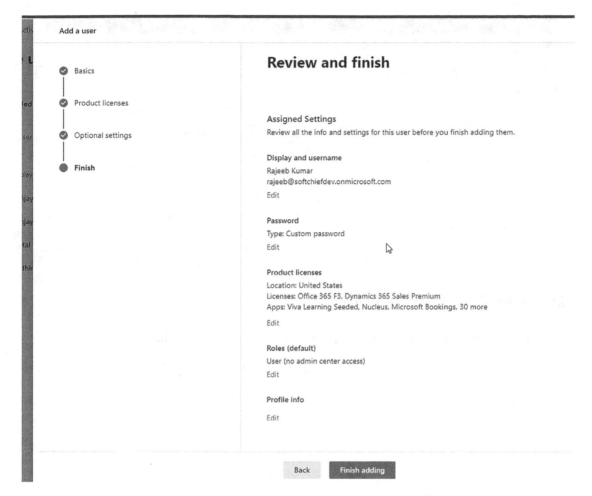

Figure 8-45. Finish adding a user

Now you have successfully added a user to your Office 365 system. You can now assign a security role to that user. You will learn more about security roles later in this chapter.

Go to `https://admin.powerplatform.microsoft.com/` and select the correct environment. Click the Settings option. Figure 8-46 shows the process of selecting the environment settings.

Power Platform admin center
Deselect
Open
Settings
Resources
Convert to production
Copy
Delete
Home
Environments
Analytics
Resources
Help + support
Data integration
Data (preview)
Policies
Admin centers
Environments
Environment
Type
State
Development
Trial (subscription-based)
Ready
softchief (default)
Default
Ready

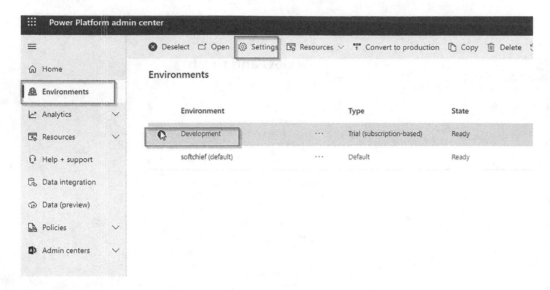

Figure 8-46. *Selecting environment settings*

Click the Users option and then click User. Figure 8-47 shows this process.

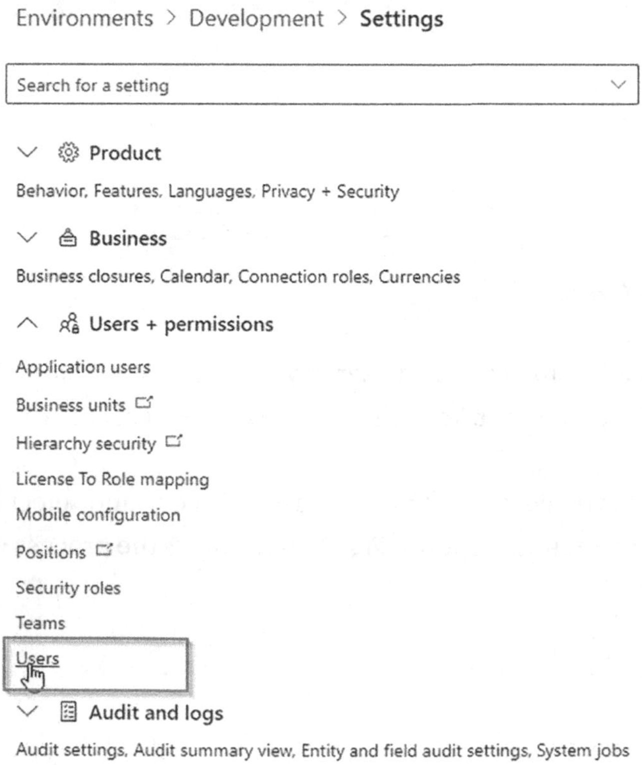

Environments > Development > Settings
Search for a setting
Product
Behavior, Features, Languages, Privacy + Security
Business
Business closures, Calendar, Connection roles, Currencies
Users + permissions
Application users
Business units
Hierarchy security
License To Role mapping
Mobile configuration
Positions
Security roles
Teams
Users
Audit and logs
Audit settings, Audit summary view, Entity and field audit settings, System jobs

Figure 8-47. *Choosing the Users option*

Figure 8-48 shows how to add a user to the environment option.

Figure 8-48. *Adding a user to the environment*

Search for the user and click the Add option. Figure 8-49 shows the search process.

Figure 8-49. *Searching for a user*

This will add the user to the current environment. In the next step, you can select a security role that you want to assign to the user.

Figure 8-50 shows the process of adding a security role to the user.

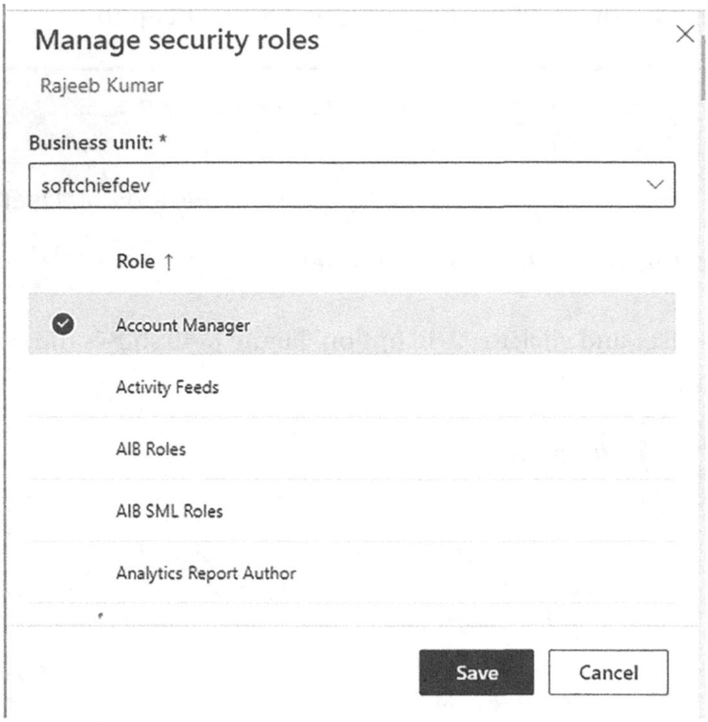

Figure 8-50. *Adding a security role to the user*

Select a security role and click Save. You have successfully created a user and assigned a product license with a security role. The user can log in to Dynamics 365 using their credentials.

If you want to enable some model-driven apps for the security role, you can go to the app and click Manage Roles. Watch this video to learn about giving security access to model-driven apps for users: `https://www.youtube.com/watch?v=StsyOdUo6s4`.

Security Matrix and Configurations

The *security matrix* is an important concept in Power Apps. You can configure different security matrixes for the following purposes:

- Securing records from unauthorized users

- Securing fields from unauthorized users

The security matrix combines access levels and privileges for entities to define a security role. On the top ladder of this security concept is the business unit.

Business Unit (BU)

A *business unit* is a logical grouping of related business activities. It is the foundation of the security structure in Microsoft Dynamics 365. Each user has to be part of a business unit. A default business unit is created when Dynamics 365 is installed.

Business units are hierarchical. One BU can be a child of another BU. In Figure 8-51, TATA is the root business unit. TCS and Tata Motor are immediate children BUs of TATA. Under TCS, there are two immediate children BUs—TCS India and TCS UK. Under TCS India, there are two children BUs—TCS East India and TCS South India.

So TCS India, TCS UK, TCS East India, and TCS South India, are child of TCS business unit. One user can be tagged with one Business Unit only. Multiple users can be tagged with the same business unit. One user cannot be tagged with multiple BUs. You can add multiple security roles to a business unit. All security roles of the parent BU are inherited by the children BU. Figure 8-51 shows the BU structure of this TATA example.

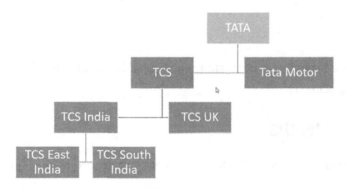

Figure 8-51. *BU structure of the TATA example*

If you take the example of the School Management system, you can configure multiple business units per the organizational structure. You might want to manage your schools by geography, for example. In that case, the business unit structure could look like Figure 8-52.

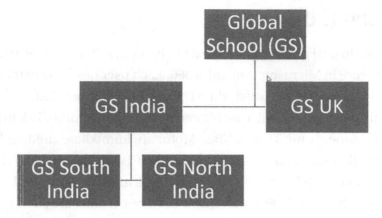

Figure 8-52. *BU structure of the Global School example*

As per a new enhancement, you can add multiple security roles to a user from one BU or multiple BUs.

Privileges

Privileges are actions that users perform on a record. For example, they can create, read, update, and delete records.

Access Levels/Depths

An access level defines the level or depth of access to a record item. There are five types of access level:

- **None**: No record access.

- **User**: Only access to records owned by the user who's logged in.

- **Business Unit**: Access to records owned by the user plus access to records created by other users belonging to the same business unit as the initial user.

- **Parent Child BU**: Access to records owned by the user plus access to records created by other users belonging to the same business unit as the initial user belongs, plus access to records created by users from the child business unit of the initial BU.

- **Organization**: Access to records belonging to the organization regardless of the business unit.

Security Role

A *security role* defines how different users, such as salespeople, access different types of records. To control access to data, you can modify existing security roles, create new security roles, or change which security roles are assigned to each user. Each user can have multiple security roles. You can create a new security role or modify existing ones.

It is always a best practice to open an existing security role and copy it to create a new security role instead of creating a brand new role from scratch.

To check security roles for a specific BU, click the Settings option from Power Platform Admin Center. Figure 8-53 shows the Security Roles option.

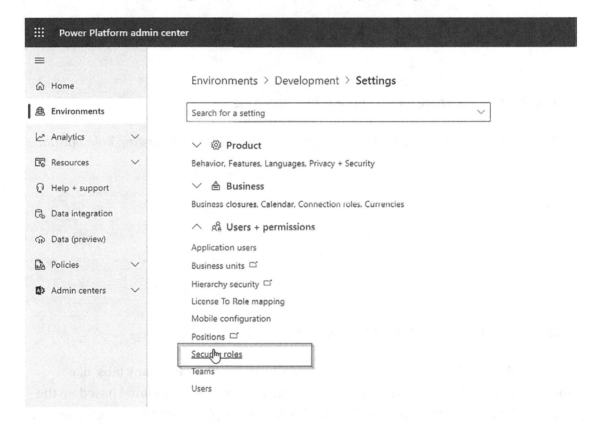

Figure 8-53. *The Security Roles option*

Here you will see a list of security roles specific to a business unit. Figure 8-54 shows the security roles of the parent business unit.

☐ New role   ☐ Go to legacy

Environments > Development > Settings > **Security roles**

Manage security roles within this environment so that people can access their data. <u>Learn more</u>

Business unit

| softchiefdev ⌄ |

Role ↑   More actions

Account Manager   ...

Activity Feeds   ...

AIB Roles   ...

AIB SML Roles   ...

Analytics Report Author   ...

Figure 8-54. *Security roles of a parent business unit*

Select a security role and click Edit. Figure 8-55 shows the Edit Existing Role option.

Figure 8-55. *The Edit Existing Role option*

This will open the security role in Edit mode. Here you'll notice many tabs, like Core Records, Marketing, Custom Entities, and so on. The tabs are defined based on the nature of the entities, such as Core Records. These are simply out-of-the-box entities and are gathered inside the Core tab. If you want to configure security access to an existing core or an out-of-the-box entity, you can click the Core Records tab and do the configuration. Click the Core Records tab. You will observe the privileges on the top row, the entities on the left panel, and the access levels at the bottom. In the middle portion, you define the matrix. To provide access to custom entities, you need to click the Custom Entities tab and search the entity from the list. Then you update the access level and privilege. Figure 8-56 shows the Access Levels and Privileges with Entity matrix.

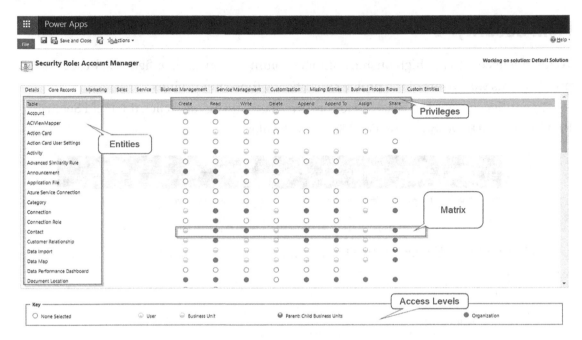

Figure 8-56. *The Access Levels and Privileges with Entity matrix*

Let's look at the matrix for the Account Manager Role. The matrix is denoted by circles in Figure 8-57. An empty circle means no access; a quarter-full circle indicates user-level access; a half-full circle indicates business unit-level access; a three quarters-full circle indicates a parent/child business unit-level access; and a filled circle indicates organization-level access.

Table	Create	Read	Write	Delete	Append	Append To	Assign	Share
Account	◒	●	●	◒	●	●	◒	●

Figure 8-57. *Access level*

This matrix shows that the Account Manager role has organization read access to the Account entity, which means account managers can read all account records available in the organization, regardless of business unit and owners.

The Account Manager role also has business unit-level delete permission to account records, which means account managers can delete account records that they created or that were created by other users in the same business unit.

The create, read, delete, write, append, append to, assign, and share privileges honor this security matrix. To copy an existing security role to a new security role, you can use the Copy Role option.

Field Security

To restrict access to the high business impact columns, you can configure field security profiles. This way, users of the profile cannot view those field values.

To configure a field security, go to the advanced settings and click the Field Security Profiles. Figure 8-58 shows the Field Security Profiles.

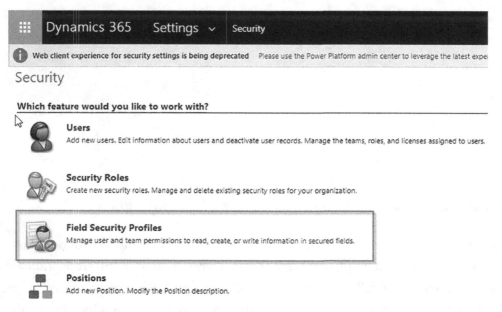

Figure 8-58. *Field Security Profiles*

In the next screen, click the New option to create a new field security profile and give it a name. Say you want to hide the actual revenue field from a user named Rajeeb.

For this, you need to add the user using the Add User option. Figure 8-59 shows the process of adding a user to the field security profile.

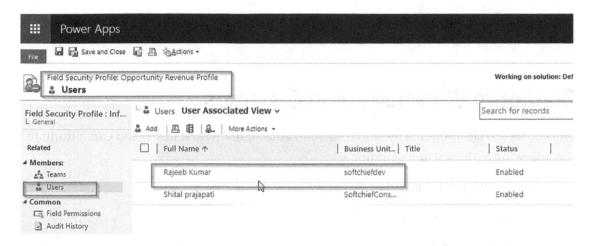

Figure 8-59.   Adding a user to the field security profile

You can also add a team. After adding the user or team, you need to define the field permission. Click the Field Permission link. You will see only the columns with the Column Security flag enabled in its field settings. If you don't see any columns, go to a table and choose the Column setting and then enable Column Security.

In the field list, double-click the column. In the small popup, define the permissions. Select No for all the options. Figure 8-60 shows the process of choosing permissions for the field.

Figure 8-60.   Choosing permissions for the field

Now click OK and save and close. When Rajeeb opens an opportunity record, he will not be able to see the value of the actual revenue.

Configure Workflows and Concepts

Workflows are components by which you can automate manual tasks. You can automate the following actions using workflows:

- Creating new records

- Updating existing records

- Sending email

- Calling custom workflows

- Calling custom actions

- Using conditions

These workflows are classic CRM workflows that can be used to automate Dynamics 365 CE business needs. You can replace the classic workflows with Power Automate modern flows, which gives you more scope in automating diversified cloud apps, including Dynamics 365 CE. Since many businesses are still using the classic workflow, you should have knowledge about this classic approach.

You can configure real-time or background workflows as needed. Real-time workflows are executed in the same transaction with the core operation. For example, if you want to run a real-time workflow when creating an account, the process of Create Account will not be completed until the real-time workflow execution is complete.

If the workflow runs in the background, the account will be created successfully. After a period of time, when the server is free, the background workflow or asynchronous workflow instance will start execution, without depending on the account creation process.

In real-time workflows, you can choose to run it before or after a value change, but in the background workflow, there is no before option. It will take only the updated value.

You can first define a trigger that will initiate the workflow. The trigger can be event based or on-demand by the user to manually run. Choose the scope as needed. The organization scope will ensure that the workflow will run on all records of the entity type.

Create a Background Workflow

Use the following section to create a background workflow.

Define Basic Info About the Workflow

Open the Power Apps solution. Click Add New Component and choose Automation ➤ Process ➤ Workflow. Figure 8-61 shows the process of adding a classic workflow inside a Power Apps solution.

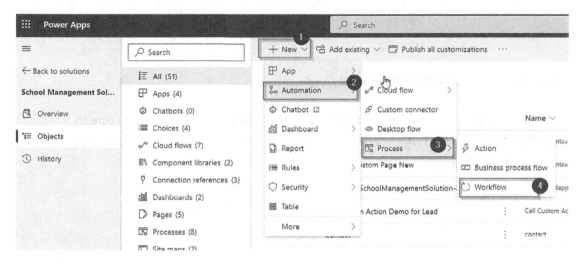

Figure 8-61. *Adding a classic workflow inside the Power Apps solution*

Provide a display name and choose a table for which you are configuring the workflow. Enable the Background Run checkbox if you want to run it in the background. For this example, the background is enabled. Say you want to create a task record that's due three days after the account is created to follow up with the account. Figure 8-62 shows the configuring workflow.

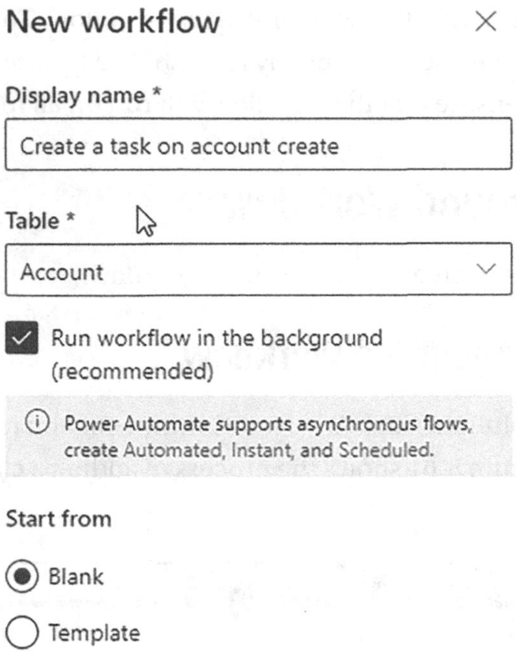

New workflow   ×

Display name *

Create a task on account create

Table *

Account   ∨

☑ Run workflow in the background
   (recommended)

ⓘ Power Automate supports asynchronous flows,
   create Automated, Instant, and Scheduled.

Start from

◉ Blank

◯ Template

Figure 8-62. Configuring the workflow

Click Create. This will open the Workflow Designer. You can set the Scope to
Organization, and the Trigger to Record. Figure 8-63 shows the process of adding steps
and selecting triggers.

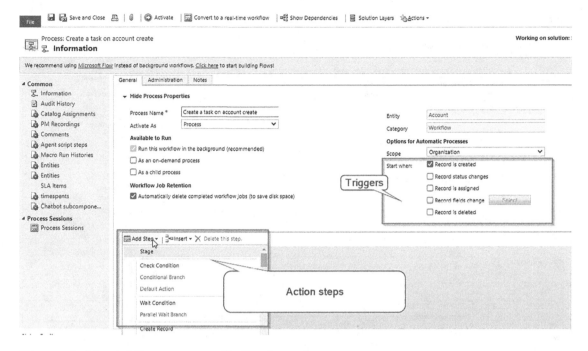

Figure 8-63. *Adding steps and selecting triggers*

Click Add Step and choose the Create Record step. In the Create Record step, set the Record Type to Task. Figure 8-64 shows adding the Create New Record step and properties.

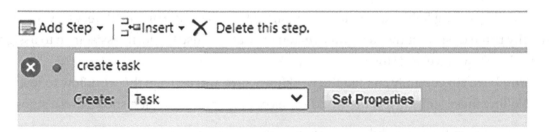

Figure 8-64. *Adding the create new record step and properties*

Click Set Properties to specify the task record field values such as Task Subject, Description, and so on. You can specify static values or use the Form Assistance panel to use dynamic values related to the entity for which the workflow was defined. Figure 8-65 shows this process.

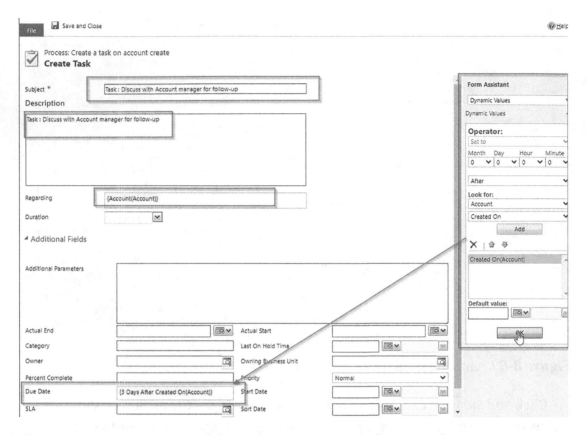

Figure 8-65. *Set property of the Create New Record of Type Task*

The Regarding field is automatically assigned to Account. For Due date, you want to specify three days after the Account Created On date, so use the form assistance to assign the value. Now save and close.

You have successfully created the workflow. Save and activate the workflow to test it. Follow these steps to test the workflow as per Figure 8-66, which shows these steps.

1. Open the Sales Hub app and create an account record.

2. Navigate to the Activities tab.

3. Click Open Activity Associated View.

4. You will see the task record.

Figure 8-66. *Testing the workflow*

If you want to check the status of a background workflow, you can go to advanced settings in the System Jobs area. Filter workflows by entity and you will see the workflow instance status. Figure 8-67 shows the process of checking the workflow instance in a system job.

Figure 8-67. *Checking the workflow instance in a system job*

You can also create real-time workflows using this same process. In later chapters, you learn how to call custom workflow activities from background and real-time workflows.

Configure Custom Actions

You can extend the functionality of Dynamics 365 Customer Engagement by creating custom messages, known as *actions*. These actions will have associated request/ response classes and a Web API action will be generated. Actions are typically used to add new domain-specific functionality to the organization's web service or to combine multiple organization web service message requests into a single request. For example, in a support call center, you may want to combine the Create, Assign, and Setstate messages into a single new message, called Escalate.

The business logic of a custom action is implemented using a workflow. When you create a custom action, the associated real-time workflow is automatically registered to execute in stage 30 (core operation) of the execution pipeline. In the next chapter, you learn more about the execution pipeline.

You can create custom actions that are specific to an entity or that are global (not specific to any entity). You can call plugins against the custom action in the pre-operation or post-operation stage. You learn more about these stages in later chapters. You can also define input and output parameters inside custom actions.

Create a Custom Action

Let's consider a business scenario in this section. This example invokes a custom action to request the manager's approval when a discount for a particular opportunity exceeds 50%.

Open the Power Apps solution and add a new component called Action by selecting Automation ➤ Process ➤ Action. Figure 8-68 shows this process.

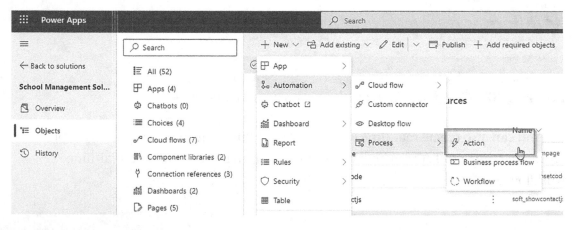

Figure 8-68. *Adding an action to the solution*

Specify a name and select the Opportunity table. Click Create. Figure 8-69 shows this configuring action.

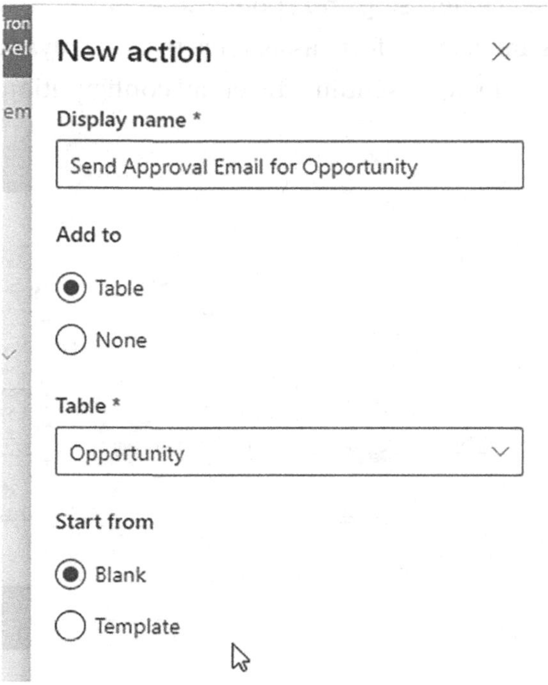

New action   ✕

Display name *

Send Approval Email for Opportunity

Add to

◉ Table

◯ None

Table *

Opportunity   ⌄

Start from

◉ Blank

◯ Template

Figure 8-69. *Configuring action*

This will open the Action Designer window. Add a new input argument of type string called Special Notes. Figure 8-70 shows the input arguments in action.

Figure 8-70. *Input arguments in action*

In the Action panel, add a new step and choose Send Email. In the Send Email step, click Set Properties and use the form assistance to assign dynamic values to the respective fields. Figure 8-71 shows sending the email configuration in action.

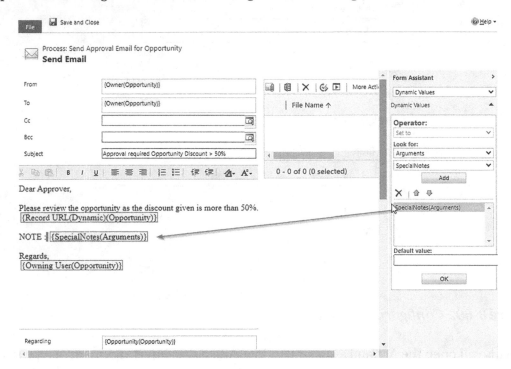

Figure 8-71. *Sending email configuration in action*

Click Save and close. Activate the action. Now you can call the custom action from a workflow. Custom actions don't run independently.

Create a workflow named Send Approval and configure the trigger as a record field change. Select the field opportunity discount. Add a new step called Perform Action and select the action you created in the previous step. Figure 8-72 shows this process.

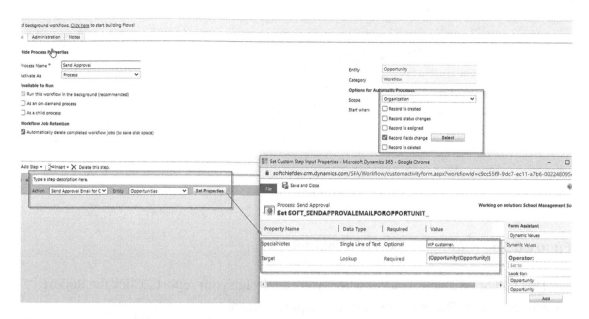

Figure 8-72. *Assigning an input argument value*

To test this workflow and action, open an opportunity, change the opportunity discount to more than 50, and save it. The workflow will trigger and the action will call, which will send an email.

Configure Reports in Power Apps

Reports are well researched, planned, and organized documents that are written for a purpose. Strategic-level personals need reports to redefine proper business strategy. You can create Dynamics 365 Power Apps reports by selecting the correct data items from one or more entities, as needed.

Use the following steps to configure a report for accounts.

Step 1: Add a Report Component to the Solution

Open the Power Apps solution and click Add New Component. Choose Report. Figure 8-73 shows the process of adding reports to the solution.

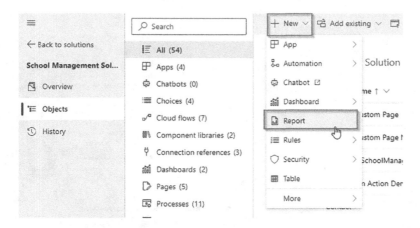

Figure 8-73. *Adding a report to a solution*

This will open a new window where you can design your reports. Click the Report Wizard to open it. Figure 8-74 shows the Report Wizard.

Figure 8-74. *The Report Wizard*

Click the Start a New Report radio button and then click Next. Figure 8-75 shows the Report Wizard option to choose a new or existing report.

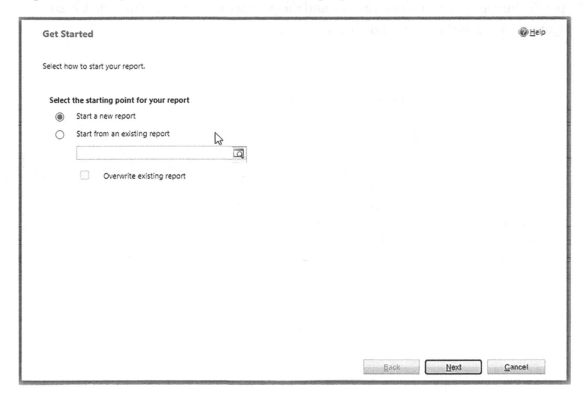

Figure 8-75. *The Report Wizard option to choose a new or existing report*

Step 2: Configure the Report

Specify the report name, a description, and the primary record type. Then click Next. Figure 8-76 shows the report properties.

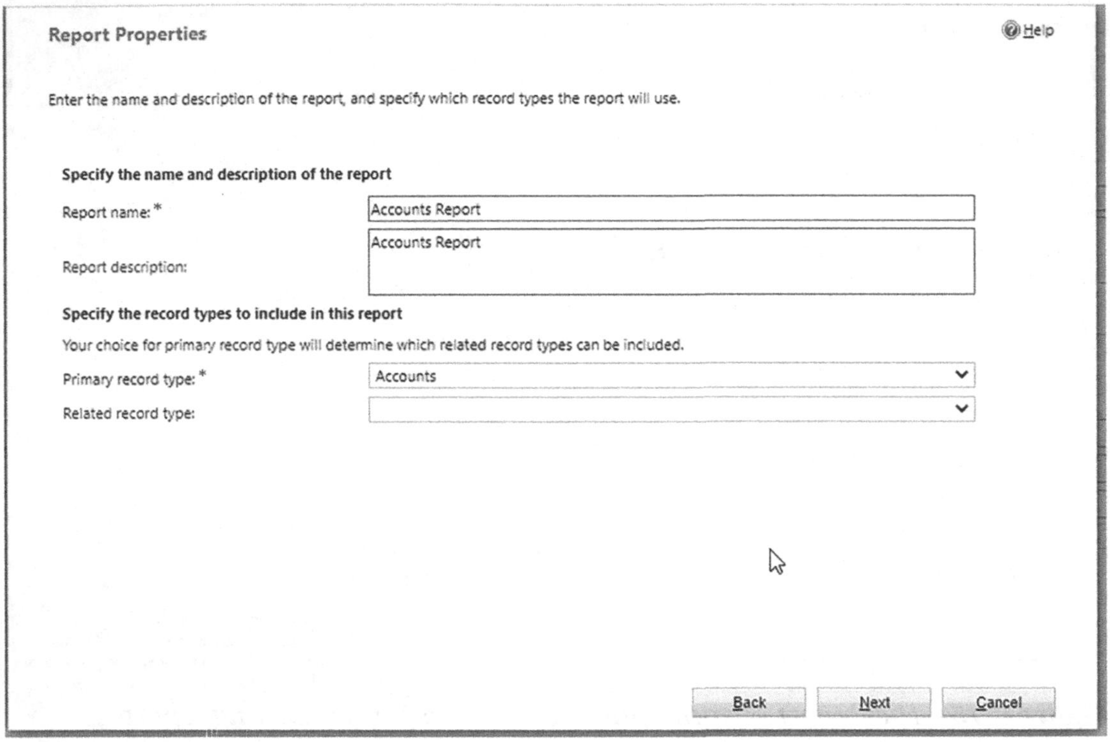

Figure 8-76. *Report properties*

Step 3: Configure the Criteria

Configure the report criteria using the Report Filtering criteria. Figure 8-77 shows the filter condition.

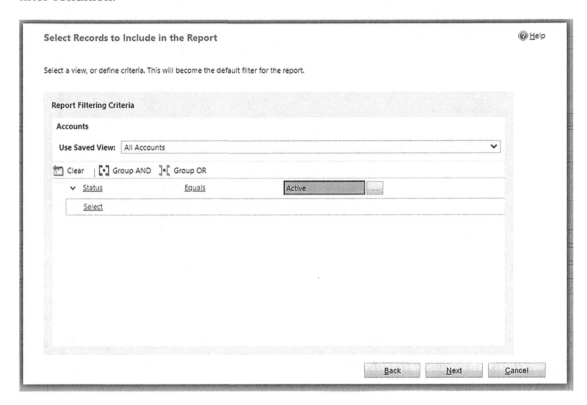

Figure 8-77. *Filter condition*

Step 4: Configure the Layout Fields and Use Grouping

You can configure fields to display on the report and use grouping. Figure 8-78 shows this process.

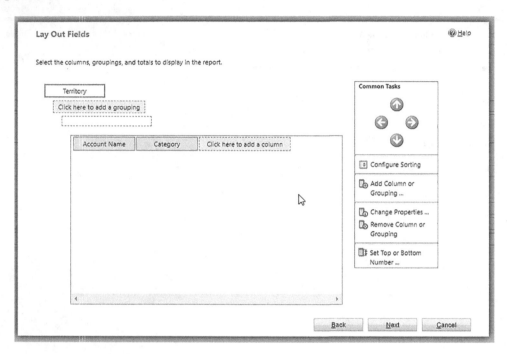

Figure 8-78. *Configure the layout*

Step 5: Configure the Report Format

You can configure the report format using tables only or using charts and tables. If your data contains numeric fields, it's best to use the charts and tables format. Figure 8-79 shows this process.

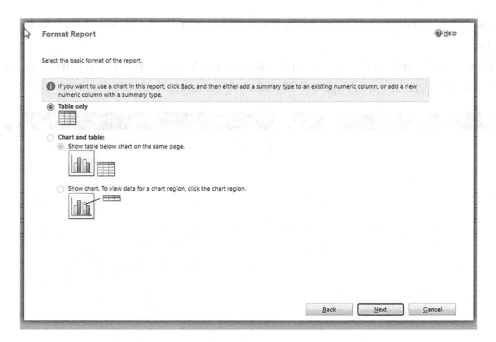

Figure 8-79. *Choosing the report format*

Finally, click Next in the report summary. Figure 8-80 shows the summary of the report.

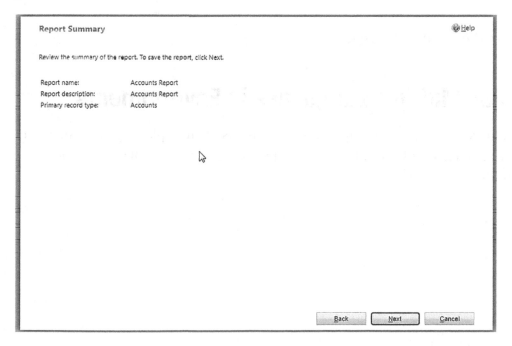

Figure 8-80. *Report summary*

Next click Finish. Your report will be successfully created. Click Run Report to render the report.

The report is rendered as per your configuration. You can run the report from entity view in model-driven apps. Figure 8-81 shows the rendered report.

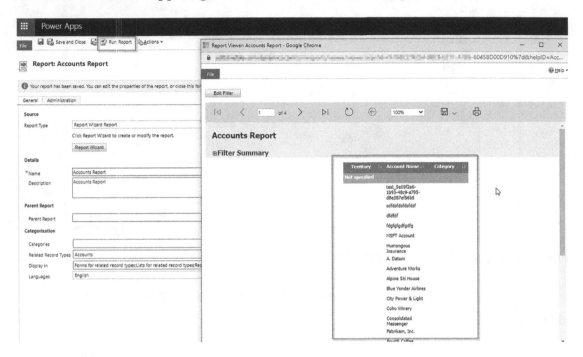

Figure 8-81. *Rendered report*

Install Multiple Languages in Environments

Dynamics 365 supports multiple languages. To install multiple languages, navigate to the advanced settings and click the System Settings. Figure 8-82 shows the Administration option.

Figure 8-82. *The Administration option*

Choose Languages. Select the desired languages and click Apply. Figure 8-83 shows the language settings.

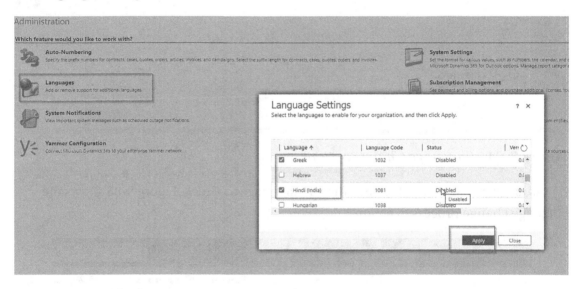

Figure 8-83. *The language settings*

It will take some time to install all the selected language packs. After the packs are installed, you can navigate to the personalization settings. In the Languages section, you can select your language and click OK. This will change your User Interface language to the desired language. Figure 8-84 shows the Language Change options.

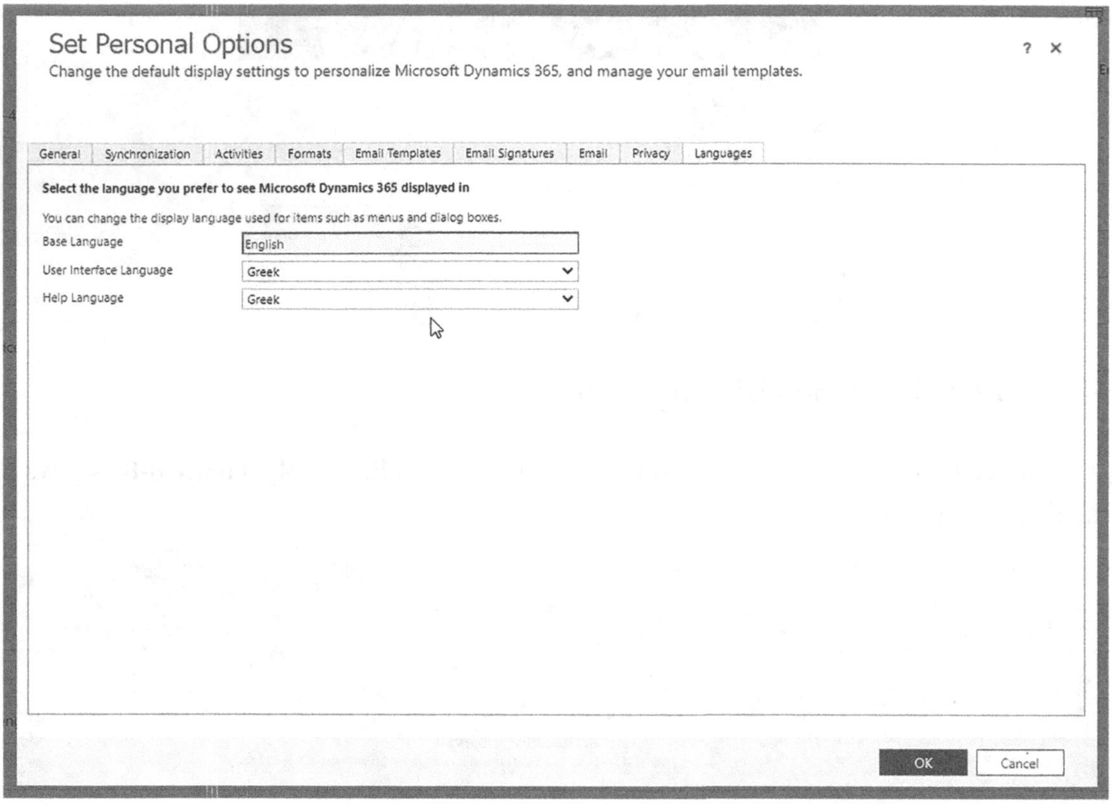

Set Personal Options
Change the default display settings to personalize Microsoft Dynamics 365, and manage your email templates.
General
Synchronization
Activities
Formats
Email Templates
Email Signatures
Email
Privacy
Languages
Select the language you prefer to see Microsoft Dynamics 365 displayed in
You can change the display language used for items such as menus and dialog boxes.
Base Language
English
User Interface Language
Greek
Help Language
Greek
OK
Cancel

Figure 8-84. *Language Change options*

As an example, this will change the UI's language to Greek. Figure 8-85 shows the language change process in action.

Dynamics 365
Sales Hub
Αναζήτηση
Εμφάνιση γραφήματος
Δημιουργία
Navigate To
Αρχική
Πρόσφατες
Καρφιτσωμέ...
Η εργασία μου
Δραστηριότητες
Επιταχυντής πωλ...
Dashboards
Students
Όλοι οι λογαριασμοί
Όνομα λογαριασμού
test_5e09f2e6-1b93-48c9-a795-d8e387ef56b5
sdfdsfdsfdsfdsf
dfdfdf
fdgfgfgdfgdfg
MSFT Account

Figure 8-85. *The language change in action*

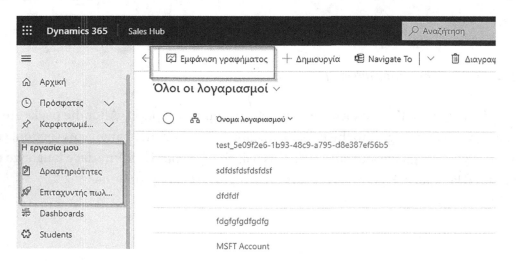

All the sections are not updated yet to Greek, so you'll need to update the translations.

Working with Translations

When you upload translations, you need to export them from the Power Apps solution. Open the Power Apps solution and add the necessary components that require translation.

Select Solution Overview. Click the Export Translation command to export the translation template. For more details, see `https://docs.microsoft.com/en-us/ dynamics365/customerengagement/on-premises/customize/export-customized- entity-field-text-translation?view=op-9-1`.

Figure 8-86 shows the export translation process.

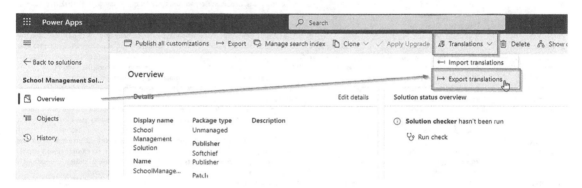

Figure 8-86. *The export translation process*

Export Translation will prompt you to download the file so that you can open it and define specific translations of English words.

Extract the ZIP file and open `CrmTranslations.xml` using Microsoft Excel. Figure 8-87 shows the Extract Translation package

Name	Date modified	Typ
[Content_Types].xml	4/30/2022 1:45 PM	XMI
CrmTranslations.xml	4/30/2022 1:45 PM	XMI

sktop > CrmTranslations_SchoolManagementSolution_1_0_0_0

Figure 8-87. *Extract Translation package*

In the Display strings, you will see the English and corresponding Greek translations. Figure 8-88 shows this process.

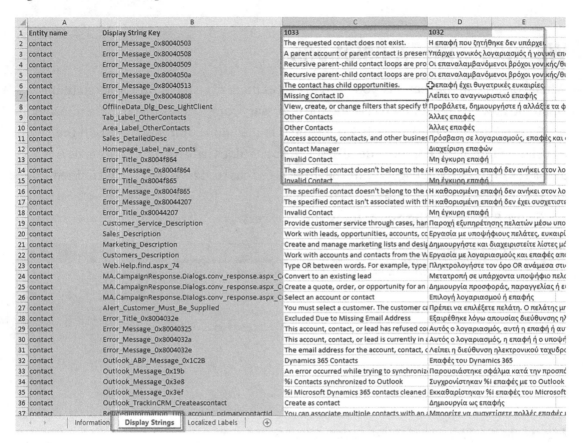

Figure 8-88. *Updating the corresponding language translations*

But for the Localized Label, some English words don't have Greek translations. Open that sheet and update the corresponding Greek words to English ones. Figure 8-89 shows the Update Corresponding Language Translation in the Localized Labels.

	A	B	C	D	E
1	Entity name	Object ID	Object Column Name	1033	1032
2	Solution	4d739b98-9c9a-ec11-b3fe-000d3a30a0fb	friendlyname	School Management Sol	
3	Publisher	870a308c-9c9a-ec11-b3fe-000d3a30a0fb	friendlyname	Softchief Publisher	
4	Publisher	870a308c-9c9a-ec11-b3fe-000d3a30a0fb	description	Softchief Publisher is ow	
5	soft_vehicle	8e3431b5-2298-ec11-b400-000d3a300c9c	LocalizedCollectionNa	Vehicles	
6	soft_vehicle	8e3431b5-2298-ec11-b400-000d3a300c9c	LocalizedName	Vehicle	
7	soft_vehicle	0e6766f2-312d-4896-a667-81e841b9b8bd	Description	Unique identifier for ent	
8	soft_vehicle	0e6766f2-312d-4896-a667-81e841b9b8bd	DisplayName	Vehicle	
9	soft_vehicle	0b7340cf-5c9c-4a09-86c1-af8a13c9dbd0	Description	Unique identifier for the	
10	soft_vehicle	0b7340cf-5c9c-4a09-86c1-af8a13c9dbd0	DisplayName	Owning User	
11	soft_vehicle	5ab1da3c-2d1b-4a95-97bc-a79c872e4ae5	Description	Status of the Vehicle	
12	soft_vehicle	5ab1da3c-2d1b-4a95-97bc-a79c872e4ae5	DisplayName	Status	
13	soft_vehicle	ee3431b5-2298-ec11-b400-000d3a300c9c	DisplayName	Status	
14	soft_vehicle	ee3431b5-2298-ec11-b400-000d3a300c9c	Description	Status of the Vehicle	
15	soft_vehicle	ea3431b5-2298-ec11-b400-000d3a300c9c	DisplayName	Active	
16	soft_vehicle	ec3431b5-2298-ec11-b400-000d3a300c9c	DisplayName	Inactive	
17	soft_vehicle	a03a0707-a047-4b40-9636-cd5d4e769e4f	Description	Name of the owner	
18	soft_vehicle	a582bf75-ec54-4d9e-9670-15f2248d4dd6	Description	Unique identifier of the	
19	soft_vehicle	a582bf75-ec54-4d9e-9670-15f2248d4dd6	DisplayName	Created By (Delegate)	
20	soft_vehicle	57ccaf34-6910-4d85-8279-77aa1d598db6	Description	Sequence number of the	
21	soft_vehicle	57ccaf34-6910-4d85-8279-77aa1d598db6	DisplayName	Import Sequence Numbe	
22	soft_vehicle	ea3983a2-3717-415b-bdb0-2cc9ed15216f	DisplayName	Student	Μαθητης σχελειου
23	soft_vehicle	1cc122db-3747-49f3-af03-17c1d4bcc479	Description	Time zone code that was	
24	soft_vehicle	1cc122db-3747-49f3-af03-17c1d4bcc479	DisplayName	UTC Conversion Time Zo	
25	soft_vehicle	d8d29346-c42e-4ca5-9abb-be5253049a17	Description	Unique identifier for the	
26	soft_vehicle	d8d29346-c42e-4ca5-9abb-be5253049a17	DisplayName	Owning Business Unit	
27	soft_vehicle	2120fb34-4d8d-4773-98fe-018a1960f247	Description	Unique identifier for the	
28	soft_vehicle	2120fb34-4d8d-4773-98fe-018a1960f247	DisplayName	Owning Team	
29	soft_vehicle	a42abd91-7957-4bbb-8bea-c3ffd757a25e	Description	Unique identifier of the	
30	soft_vehicle	a42abd91-7957-4bbb-8bea-c3ffd757a25e	DisplayName	Modified By	
31	soft_vehicle	317fb0a9-d6bb-4cc8-9c5f-02fa360de1dc	Description	Unique identifier of the	
32	soft_vehicle	317fb0a9-d6bb-4cc8-9c5f-02fa360de1dc	DisplayName	Created By	
33	soft_vehicle	69c21efe-567d-497a-ba77-5cc09a969dff	Description	For internal use only.	
34	soft_vehicle	69c21efe-567d-497a-ba77-5cc09a969dff	DisplayName	Time Zone Rule Version	
35	soft_vehicle	331f1a83-e1a4-46f6-8320-de78e2ce01d6	Description	Owner Id Type	
36	soft_vehicle	8f3431b5-2298-ec11-b400-000d3a300c9c	DisplayName	Name	
37	soft_vehicle	cd3431b5-2298-ec11-b400-000d3a300c9c	Description	Yomi name of the owner	

| Information | Display Strings | **Localized Labels** | ⊕ |

Figure 8-89. *Update the corresponding language translation in the
Localized labels*

After all these changes are done, sav the file and ZIP it. Import the translation.
Refresh the screen; you will see the new translations.

Working with a Document Template

You can use Word or Excel to generate documents that contain values from records in
Dynamics 365. To create a template, follow these steps.

Step 1: Download a Template

Go to the advanced settings and click Templates. Choose Document Templates.
Figure 8-90 shows the Document Templates option.

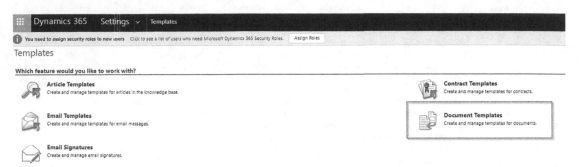

Figure 8-90. *Document Templates option*

Click +New. Choose Word Template and filter the results by the Quote entity.
Figure 8-91 shows the download template.

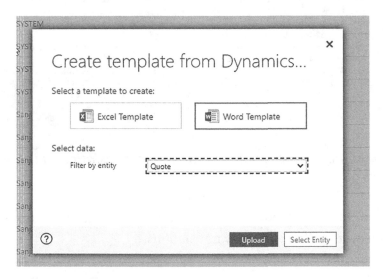

Figure 8-91. *The download template*

Click Select Entity. Choose 1: N Relationship Quote Line Details and download the
template. Figure 8-92 shows the select entities.

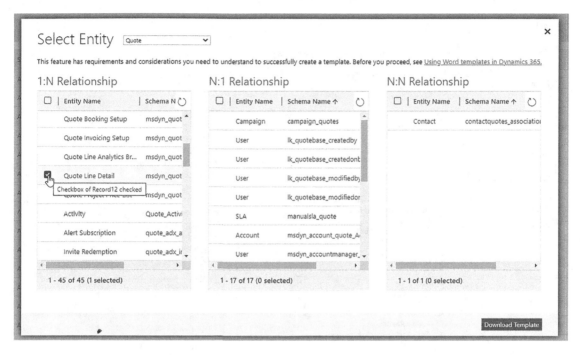

Figure 8-92. *Select entities*

Step 2: Edit the Template Using Developer Mode

Open the downloaded template in Microsoft Word. Go to the Developer tab. If the
Developer tab is not visible, go to File ➤ Options and select Customize Ribbon. Then
enable the Developer option and click OK. Figure 8-93 shows the process of enabling the
Developer option.

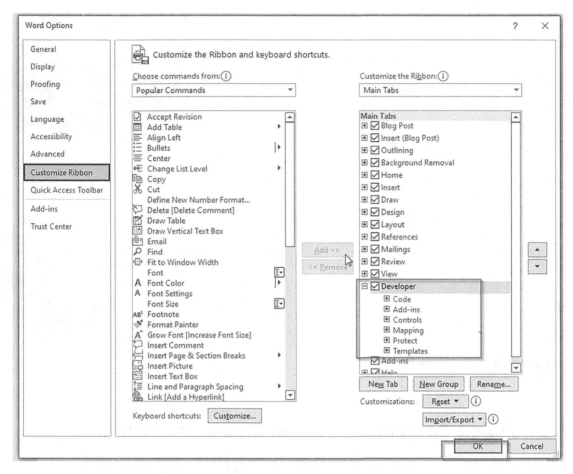

Figure 8-93. *Enabling the Developer option*

In the Word document, design the template as needed, such as adding headers and footers, and so on. After that, select the Developer tab and Click XML Mapping. In the right panel, choose the Quote option. Figure 8-94 shows the use of the XML mapping option.

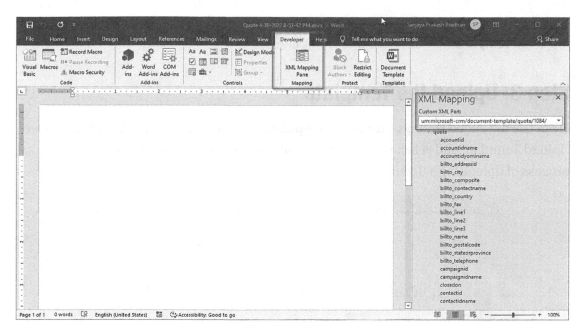

Figure 8-94. Using the XML mapping option

You can insert dynamic values into the template using XML mapping fields. Figure 8-95 shows the process of adding fields to the document from mapping.

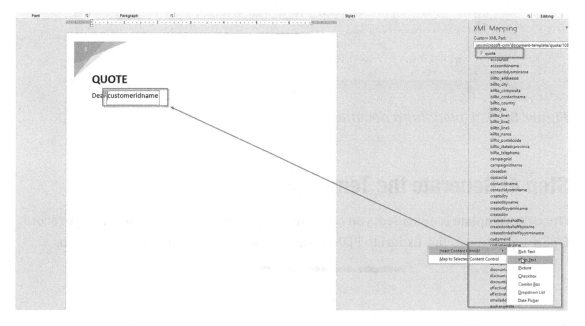

Figure 8-95. Adding the fields to a document from mapping

After the dynamic values are prepared, you can upload the final template. Rename the Word template My Custom Quote Template.

Step 3: Upload the Template

From the advanced settings, choose ➤Templates ➤ Document Templates. Then choose Upload Template and select the document you just prepared. Figure 8-96 shows the process of uploading a document template.

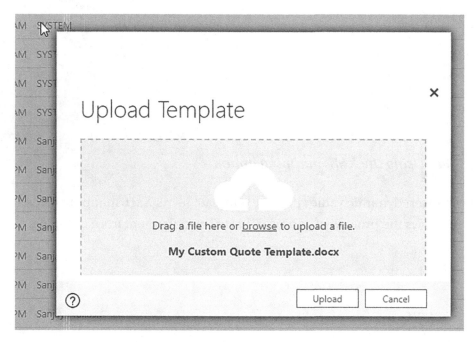

Figure 8-96. *Uploading a document template*

Step 4: Generate the Template

Once the template is uploaded, you can generate this document in a quote entity record. Open a quote and click Export to PDF. Figure 8-97 shows the Export to PDF option.

Figure 8-97. *Export to PDF option*

Choose the template you uploaded. You will see that the fields are dynamically generated. Figure 8-98 shows the Export to PDF option, which renders a PDF.

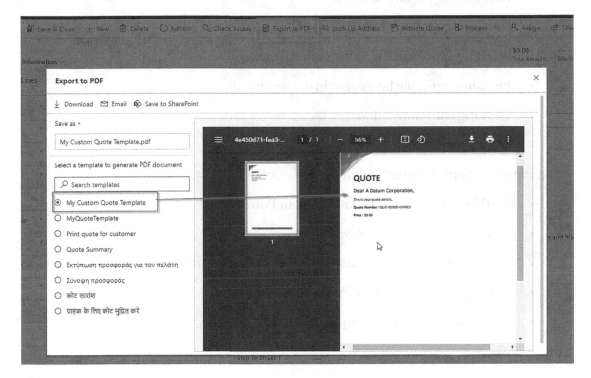

Figure 8-98. *The Export to PDF option renders a PDF*

Now you can download or send emails with attachments.

Summary

In this chapter, you learned about the following concepts:

- Admin Centers and their uses

- Importing data into Power Apps

- Configuring duplicate detection rules

- Configuring the auditing feature in Power Apps

- Adding users to environments

- Using the security matrix and configurations

- Configuring workflows and concepts

- Configuring custom actions

- Configuring reports in Power Apps

- Working with email templates and signatures

- Installing multiple languages in environments

- Working with translation

- Working with document templates

In the next chapter, you will learn about the following:

- Working with client-side JavaScript in Power Apps

- Developing plugins for Power Apps

- Developing custom workflow activities in Power Apps

- Editing command bars in Power Apps

- Business scenarios and implementations

CHAPTER 9

Working with Power Apps Customizations

Power Apps provides many customization components so you can customize it based on your business needs. The following customization components can be developed for Dynamics 365 Power Apps:

- Client scripting (JavaScript)
- Server-side code (plugins)
- Server-side code (custom workflow activities)
- Edit the command bar

Working with Client-Side JavaScript in Power Apps

Microsoft Dynamics 365 allows you to write scripts for dynamic behaviors that can run in a browser or client side.

You can develop scripts for the following purposes:

- Get or set column values
- Show and hide user interface elements (columns, sections, and tabs)
- Reference multiple controls per column
- Access multiple forms per table
- Manipulate form navigation items
- Interact with the business process flow control
- Perform CRUD operations in a server table using Web API

© Sanjaya Prakash Pradhan 2022
S. Prakash Pradhan, *Power Platform and Dynamics 365 CE for Absolute Beginners*,
https://doi.org/10.1007/978-1-4842-8600-5_9

- Show notifications on forms

- Open popup screens from entity forms

Events

There are many events available in model-driven power apps:

- Form events: On Save and On Load

- Field events: On Change

- Tab events: On Tab State Change

You can call JavaScript from any event that is supported in Dynamics 365.

Event Handlers

Event handlers are JavaScript methods that are called against an event. You can call multiple event handlers against a single event.

Libraries

Libraries are JavaScript files included in specific forms that contain methods that you can call as event handlers.

Form Context

The Client API form context contains a reference to the form or to a specific item on the form, such as a quick view control or a row in an editable grid, against which the current code is run. You can pass form context objects to your event handler so that you can refer to form elements in your JavaScript.

Microsoft provides many client script objects that you can use to interact with Dynamics 365. There are four main client APIs available. The following table explains the Client APIs:

Object	Description
ExecutionContext	In model-driven apps forms and grids, this property represents the execution context for an event, which can be used to extract form field information with the help of the Form Context method.Read more about client execution context at `https://docs.microsoft.com/en-us/power-apps/developer/model-driven-apps/clientapi/clientapi-execution-context`. Figure 9-1 shows the process of passing an execution context from a form to an event handler.

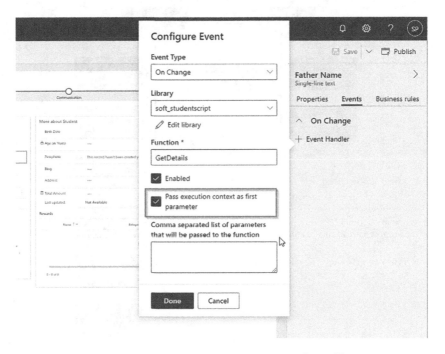

Figure 9-1. *Passing an execution context to an event handler*

(*continued*)

Object	Description
formContext	Form context provides a reference to a form against which the current code executes. To get the formContext object, you have to use the getFormContext method. Figure 9-2 shows the form context object hierarchy.

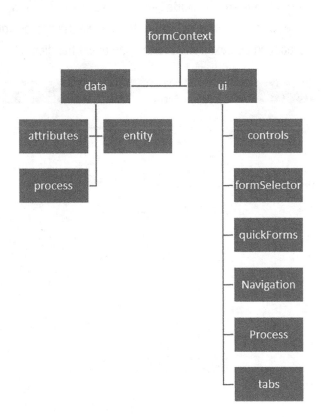

Figure 9-2. *Form context object hierarchy*

gridContext	This object provides a reference to a grid or a sub-grid on a form against which the current code executes.

(continued)

Object	Description
Xrm	This object provides a global object for performing operations that do not directly impact the data and UI in forms, grids, sub-grids, controls, or columns. For example, you can navigate through forms and create and manage records using the Web API. Figure 9-3 shows the Xrm objects.

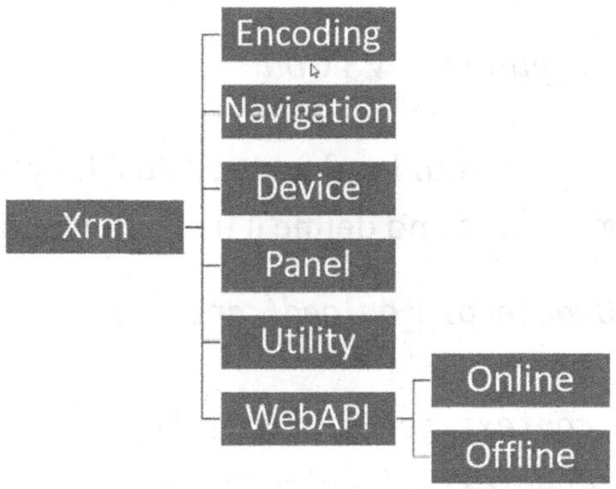

Figure 9-3. *Xrm objects*

Business Scenario

Write JavaScript to disable a mobile number if the contact form type is Update on Load of Contact Form. Follow the steps in the next section to write and upload the script as a web resource to complete the scenario.

Step 1: Write the Script

Use your Power Apps solution to add a contact entity and its main form. Open any of your favorite JavaScript editors. This example uses Visual Studio code. You can download it free from `https://code.visualstudio.com/download`.

After the installation complete, open VS Code and choose File ➤ New File. Choose JavaScript for the language. Figure 9-4 shows the process of choosing a language in VS Code.

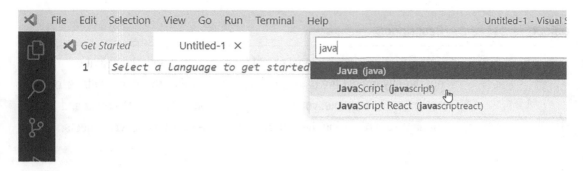

Figure 9-4. *Choosing a language in VS Code*

Save the file as `contact.js` in your local folder. Add a function called `disableMobileUpdateForm_onload` and define it using the following code snippet:

```
function disableMobileUpdateForm_onload(context)
{
    var formContext = context.getFormContext();
    var formtype = formContext.ui.getFormType();
    if(formtype == 2)
    {
        formContext.getControl("mobilephone").setDisabled(true);
    }
}
```

In this script, the method has a parameter called `context`. This parameter value will be passed from the entity form while calling the method. The context parameter is used to extract form context, which is required to communicate with the form fields.

A form type variable is assigned a value using the `getFormType` method. This method gives the form mode. Form modes are given as follows:

Value	Form Type
0	Undefined
1	Create
2	Update
3	Read Only
4	Disabled
6	Bulk Edit

Since the scenario is to find the Update form type, only disable the field so a condition checks the form type value. Using the `getControl` and `setDisabled` methods, the field mobile number is disabled. The logical name of the field is used in JavaScript.

To get the complete form script syntax, see https://docs.microsoft.com/en-us/power-apps/developer/model-driven-apps/clientapi/reference.

Step 2: Upload the Script as a Web Resource

Open the Power Apps solution and add a new component called *Web resource*. Figure 9-5 shows the process of adding a web resource.

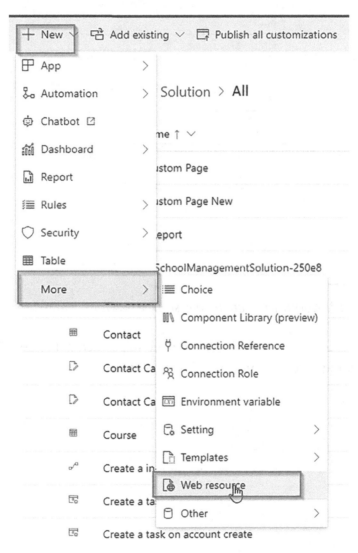

Figure 9-5. *Adding a web resource*

Click Upload File and select the contact.js file you saved.

Specify display name, name, and description. Type is automatically identified by file type. Click Save. Figure 9-6 shows the details about this new web resource.

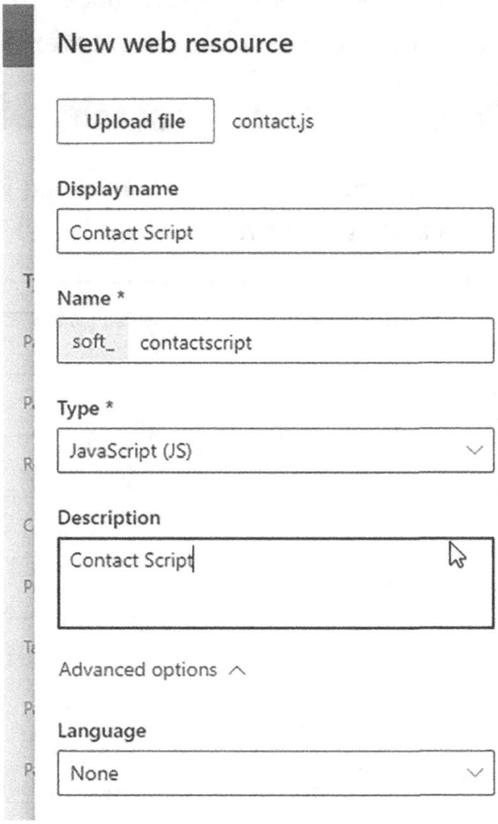

Figure 9-6. *Details about the new web resource*

The web resource will be now saved. You need to publish it. Figure 9-7 shows the process of publishing a web resource inside the solution.

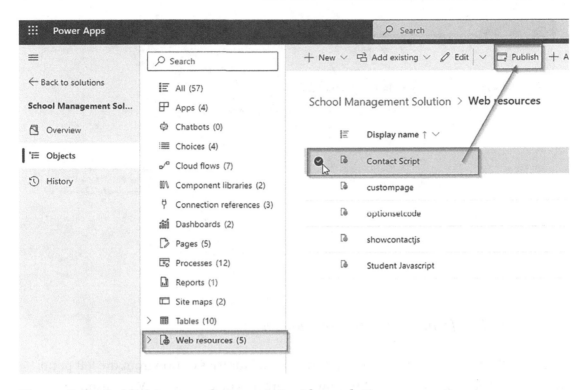

Figure 9-7. Publishing a web resource inside a solution

After the publishing process is successful, you need to add an event handler for the contact form.

Step 3: Add an Event Handler

Open the contact main form. Click Edit in a new tab. Figure 9-8 shows the Edit form that adds an event handler.

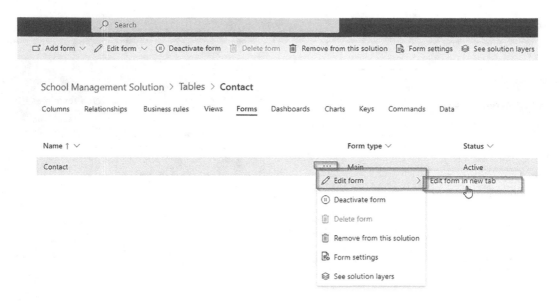

Figure 9-8. *Edit form to add an event handler*

In the Form Designer window, select the Form Libraries option from the left panel and choose Add Library. Figure 9-9 shows the process of adding a JS Web resource inside a form.

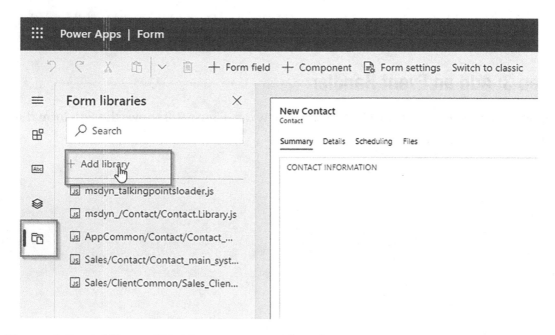

Figure 9-9. *Adding a JS Web resource inside a form*

From the Add Library window, search your JavaScript and click Add. Figure 9-10 shows the process of selecting the JS Web resource.

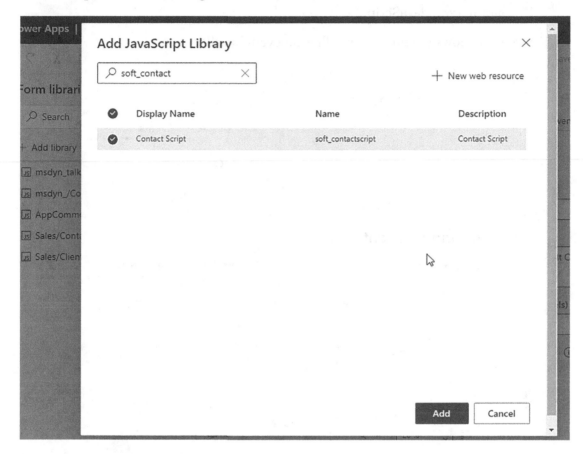

Figure 9-10. *Selecting the JS web resource*

Because you want to call the method On Load event, go to the Events option on the right panel and expand the On Load event.

1. Click +Event Handler to add a new event handler.

2. From the popup panel, select the On Load event.

3. In the Library dropdown, choose the JS Web resource.

4. In the Function textbox, choose the function you defined in your JavaScript.

5. Enable the Enabled checkboxes.

6. Pass the execution context as the first parameter. This execution context parameter must be enabled, as you are using a context parameter in JavaScript.

Figure 9-11 shows the process of calling an event handler event.

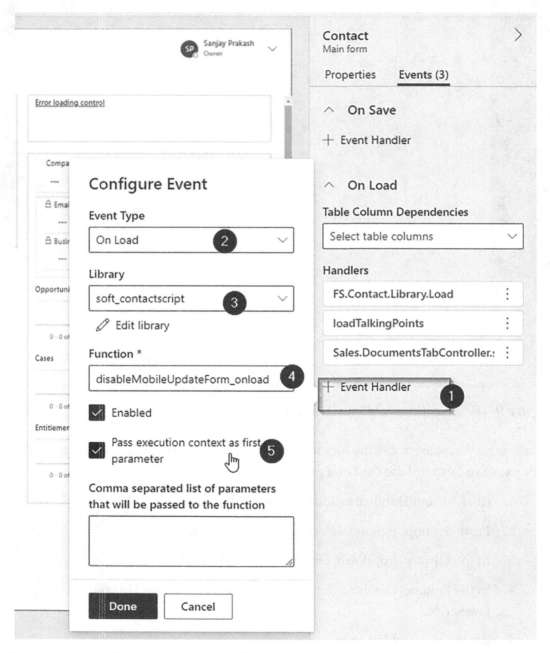

Figure 9-11. *Calling an event handler event*

After the settings are complete, click Done. Save and publish the form.

Now you can test. Refresh the form by pressing Ctrl+F5. The browser page will reload with fresh data from the server and will clear the cache memory and open an existing, active contact. The mobile number field is disabled. Figure 9-12 shows the disabled mobile number.

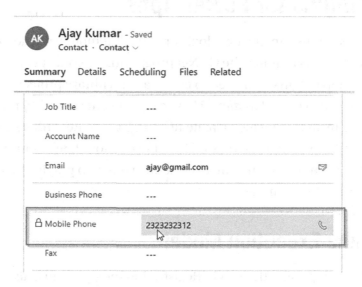

Figure 9-12. *Disabled mobile number in the update form*

If you create a new contact record, you can edit the mobile number. Figure 9-13 shows the enabled mobile number in the Create form.

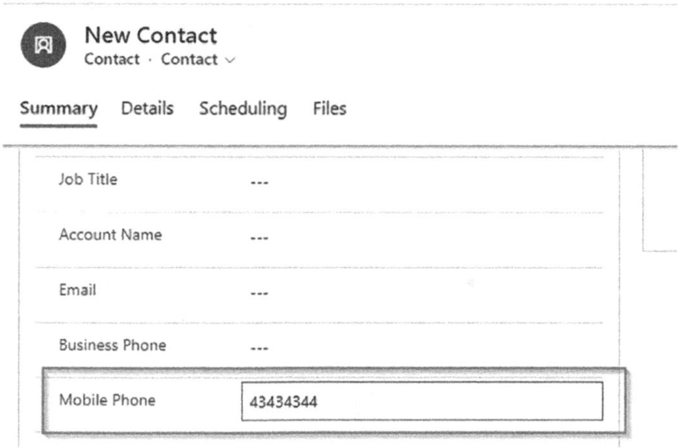

Figure 9-13. *Enabled mobile number in the Create form*

This way, you can write JavaScript methods to customize forms. You can add multiple methods to one JavaScript file. Multiple event handlers can be called against the save event.

Develop Plugins for Power Apps

Plugins are server-side custom business logic or code that modify the default behavior of the CRM platform. This requires the C#.Net programming concept and knowledge of CRM SDK. To develop plugins, you need to create a class library project.

Plugin are also called *event handlers*. They react to events raised by the CRM platform. Events or messages include Create Record, Update Record, Retrieve Record, Delete Record, and so on. Plugins follow an Event Execution Pipeline model. Plugins go into timeout after two minutes. That means you must develop plugins that can complete their execution within two minutes.

Event Pipeline Execution Model

When you register a step using the Plugin Registration tool, you must also choose the event pipeline stage called Execution. Each message is processed in a series of four stages, as described in the following table. Figure 9-14 shows the event pipeline stages.

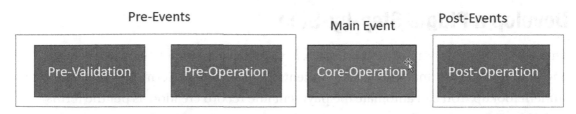

Figure 9-14. *Event pipeline stages*

Name	Description
Pre-Validation	This stage occurs before the primary system operations, such as Create, Update, Delete, and so on, for the initial operation.
	This gives you the option of including logic to cancel the operation before it goes to the database. Subsequent actions triggered by extensions registered in previous stages will also pass through this stage, but they will be included in the calling extensions' transaction.
	This stage occurs before any security checks to ensure that the calling or logged-on user has the appropriate permissions to conduct the desired action. This stage does not allow for rollback .
Pre-Operation	This stage occurs before any core operation. Using this stage, you can add or change values for an entity included in the message passed to the plugin.
	Pre-operation supports rollback.
Main-Operation	Main operation is the system stage where the core operations, such as Create, Update, and Delete operations, occur. You cannot register any plugins during this stage.
Post-Operation	This stage occurs after the core operation. This stage supports rollback. You can register plugins as asynchronous modes in post-operation. This stage is part of the post event. If you want to achieve a business need after the data pushed to the database, you can use this stage.

You can register plugins synchronously or asynchronously. Synchronous plugins execute immediately with the core operation as one transaction. Asynchronous plugins queued during the Async process execute in the background in a different execution thread.

Develop a Plugin Step-by-Step

This section considers a business scenario. Say you have a payment entity that stores payment header information for each student, such as amount, term, and due date with student lookup. You can automate the payment line record creation as per the terms available. For example, if term is set to 3 and the amount is $600 USD, as soon as the payment header is created, three payment lines should be created, each with an amount of $200 USD. The due date of the first payment should be the current date and the rest will be incremented by one month. The following steps explain how to develop a plugin for this scenario.

In this chapter, the late-bound programming concept is used, but you can use early-bound for your plugin projects if you prefer. I personally prefer writing plugins with late-bound, but take a look at this article to learn more about the early-bound and late-bound options: `https://docs.microsoft.com/en-us/power-apps/developer/data-platform/org-service/early-bound-programming`.

Step 1: Create a Class Library Project

Open Visual Studio and create a new project of type Class Library. Figure 9-15 shows the process of creating a new project in Visual Studio.

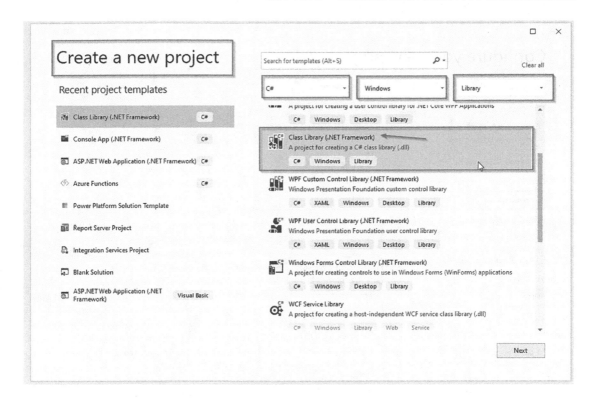

Figure 9-15. *Create a new project in Visual Studio*

Make sure you choose Class Library (.NET Framework). Click Next. In the next screen, specify the project name and choose 4.6.2 for the framework. Then click Create. Figure 9-16 shows the process of configuring a new project.

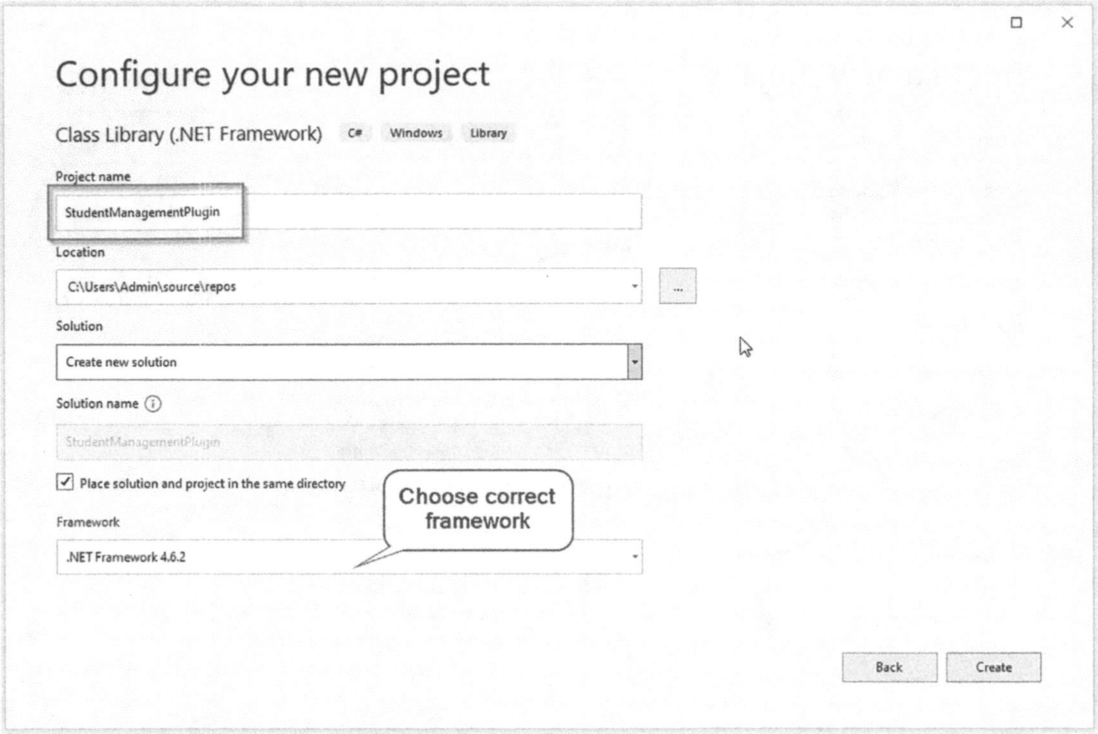

Figure 9-16. *Configure a new project*

This will create a project with a class file called Class1.cs. Right-click the filename and rename it from Class1 to CreatePaymentLineafterPaymentcreate. If it supplies a prompt to update all the references for this name change, click Yes. Figure 9-17 shows the process of renaming this class file.

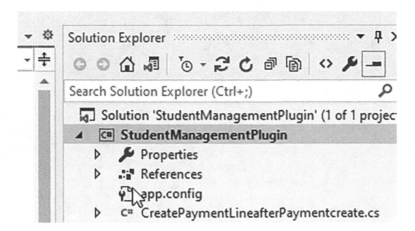

Figure 9-17. *Renaming a class file*

After that, the class name will change. You now need to add the required Microsoft libraries.

Step 2: Add the Required Microsoft SDK Binaries

Right-click the project and choose Manage NuGet Packages. Figure 9-18 shows the Managing NuGet Package option.

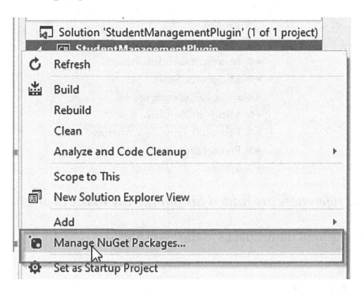

Figure 9-18. *Managing a NuGet package*

On the NuGet screen, browse to Microsoft.CrmSdk.CoreAssemblies, select an older version such as 8.0.2.1, and click Install. You can choose the latest stable version of assemblies, but sometimes the project has compatibility issues with other assemblies. There is no harm in using the latest assembly version. Click Accept in the prompt screen. Figure 9-19 shows the process of choosing the Microsoft Core Assemblies version.

Figure 9-19. *Choosing the Microsoft Core Assemblies version*

After a couple of seconds, the binaries are installed in the project. You can see inside the References folder in the project. Figure 9-20 shows all the references that have been added automatically to the project.

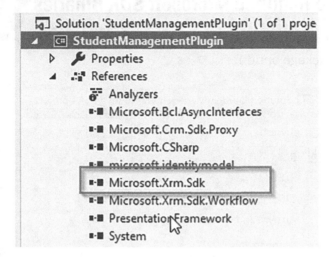

Figure 9-20. *All references are added automatically to the project*

Now add the required namespaces to the class file:

```
using System;
using System.Activities;
using System.Collections.Generic;
using System.Linq;
using System.Text;
using System.Threading.Tasks;
using Microsoft.Xrm.Sdk;
using Microsoft.Xrm.Sdk.Query;
using Microsoft.Xrm.Sdk.Workflow;
```

Every plugin must inherit from the IPlugin interface. You must implement the method of the interface called Execute.

```
namespace StudentManagementPlugin
{
    public class CreatePaymentLineafterPaymentcreate : IPlugin
    {
        public void Execute(IServiceProvider serviceProvider)
```

```
      {

      }

   }

}
```

The `Execute` method has an `IServiceProvider` interface object, which will be used to extract other objects for the plugin.

Now you need to define the required object for your plugin. Every plugin contains those common objects.

Step 3: Define the Required Objects

Define the context object, the tracing object, the service factory object, and the service object. The following code snippets show the required objects:

```
        //define required plugin object
IPluginExecutionContext context = (IPluginExecutionContext)
             serviceProvider.GetService(typeof(IPluginExecutionContext));

ITracingService tracingService =
             (ITracingService)serviceProvider.GetService(typeof(ITracing
             Service));

IOrganizationServiceFactory serviceFactory =
             (IOrganizationServiceFactory)serviceProvider.GetService
             (typeof(IOrganizationServiceFactory));

IOrganizationService service =
             serviceFactory.CreateOrganizationService(context.UserId);
```

The `Context` object defines the contextual information passed to a plugin at runtime. It contains information that describes the runtime environment that the plugin is executing in, information related to the execution pipeline, and entity business information. Read more about the `Context` object at `https://docs.microsoft.com/en-us/dotnet/api/microsoft.xrm.sdk.ipluginexecutioncontext?view=dataverse-sdk-latest`.

The `Tracing Service` object is used to log information from the plugin, so that you can debug or troubleshoot the plugin's issues and behaviors.

The Service Factory object is used to extract a service object. The Service object is used to perform actions such as Create Record, Update Record, Delete Record, and so on.

Next, you need to check whether the input parameter is a type of entity or not. The following condition checks for this:

```
//your code goes here
if (context.InputParameters.Contains("Target") &&
    context.InputParameters["Target"] is Entity)
{
    Entity studentpayment = (Entity)context.InputParameters["Target"];
```

If it is entity type, assign it to an entity object, then you can extract field information from the entity object.

Step 4: Implement the Core Logic

The requirement is to create payment lines as per the term. So, you need to extract the term, the amount, and other required fields from the entity object. The following variables are declared to extract the amount, due date, and term.

```
Entity studentpayment = (Entity)context.InputParameters["Target"];

var amount = studentpayment.GetAttributeValue<Money>("soft_
totalamount").Value;
var duedate = studentpayment.GetAttributeValue<DateTime>("soft_duedate");
var term = studentpayment.GetAttributeValue<OptionSetValue>
("soft_terms").Value;

tracingService.Trace("pline create plugin");

var actualvalue = 0;
if (term == 408260000)
    actualvalue = 1;
else if (term == 408260001)
    actualvalue = 2;
else if (term == 408260002)
    actualvalue = 3;
```

Now you need to add loop logic to run a loop through the term and create payment line records.

```
for (int i = 0; i < actualvalue; i++)
{
    Entity studentpaymentline = new Entity();
    studentpaymentline.LogicalName = "soft_
    studentpaymentline";
    studentpaymentline["soft_name"] = "Payment line "
    + (i + 1);
    studentpaymentline["soft_installmentamount"] = new
    Money(amount/ actualvalue);
    studentpaymentline["soft_installmentdate"] = DateTime.
    Now.AddMonths(i);
    studentpaymentline["soft_studentpaymentparent"] =
        new EntityReference(studentpayment.LogicalName,
        studentpayment.Id);
    service.Create(studentpaymentline);
}
```

The final code will look like this:

```
using Microsoft.Xrm.Sdk;
using System;

namespace StudentManagementPlugin
{
    public class CreatePaymentLineafterPaymentcreate : IPlugin
    {
        public void Execute(IServiceProvider serviceProvider)
        {
            //define required plugin object
            IPluginExecutionContext context = (IPluginExecutionContext)
                serviceProvider.GetService(typeof(IPluginExecution
                Context));
```

```
ITracingService tracingService =
    (ITracingService)serviceProvider.GetService(typeof(ITracing
    Service));

IOrganizationServiceFactory serviceFactory =
    (IOrganizationServiceFactory)serviceProvider.GetService
    (typeof(IOrganizationServiceFactory));

IOrganizationService service =
    serviceFactory.CreateOrganizationService(context.UserId);

//your code goes here
if (context.InputParameters.Contains("Target") &&
        context.InputParameters["Target"] is Entity)
{
    Entity studentpayment = (Entity)context.InputParameters
    ["Target"];

    var amount = studentpayment.GetAttributeValue<Money>
    ("soft_totalamount").Value;
    var duedate = studentpayment.GetAttributeValue<DateTime>
    ("soft_duedate");
    var term = studentpayment.GetAttributeValue<OptionSetValue>
    ("soft_terms").Value;

    tracingService.Trace("pline create plugin");

    var actualvalue = 0;
    if (term == 408260000)
        actualvalue = 1;
    else if (term == 408260001)
        actualvalue = 2;
    else if (term == 408260002)
        actualvalue = 3;

    for (int i = 0; i < actualvalue; i++)
    {
        Entity studentpaymentline = new Entity();
```

```
studentpaymentline.LogicalName = "soft_
studentpaymentline";
studentpaymentline["soft_name"] = "Payment line " +
(i + 1);
studentpaymentline["soft_installmentamount"] = new
Money(amount/ actualvalue);
studentpaymentline["soft_installmentdate"] = DateTime.
Now.AddMonths(i);
studentpaymentline["soft_studentpaymentparent"] =
    new EntityReference(studentpayment.LogicalName,
    studentpayment.Id);
service.Create(studentpaymentline);
                }
            }
        }
    }
}
```

After the code is complete, you need to sign in to the assembly.

Step 5: Sign in to Assembly

To sign in, right-click the project and choose Properties. Select Signing. In the dropdown, select New. To learn more about strong names of the assembly, read https://docs. microsoft.com/en-us/dotnet/standard/library-guidance/strong-naming. Figure 9-21 shows the assembly sign in process.

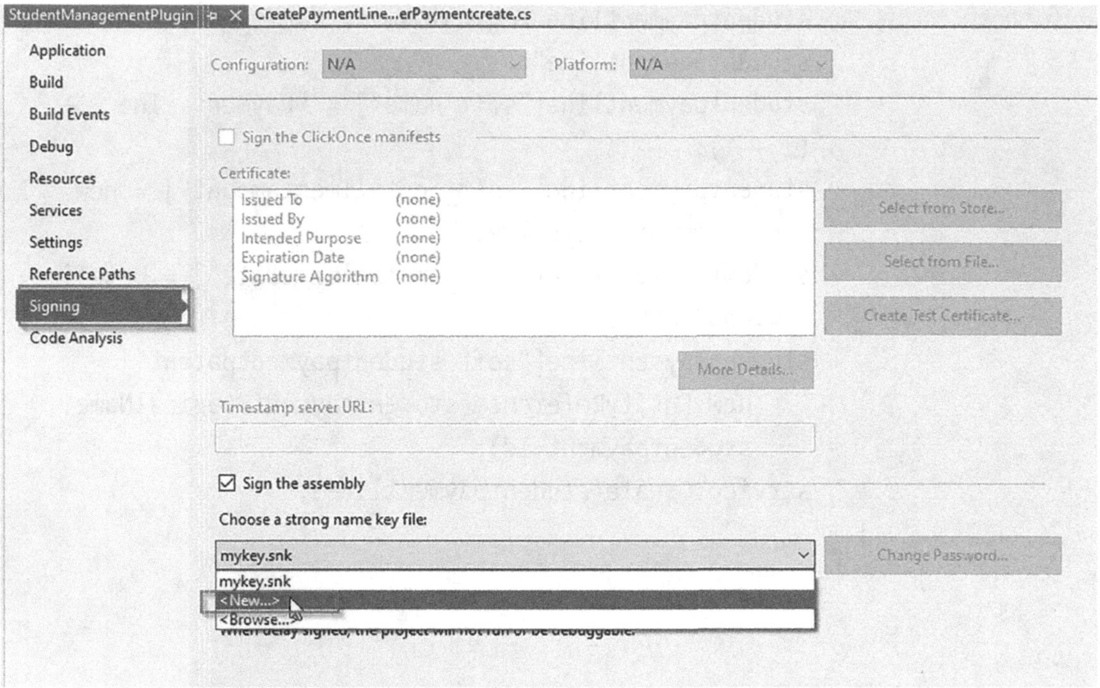

Figure 9-21. *Signing in to the assembly*

In the Strong Name screen, provide a name and click OK. Figure 9-22 shows the process of specifying a key name.

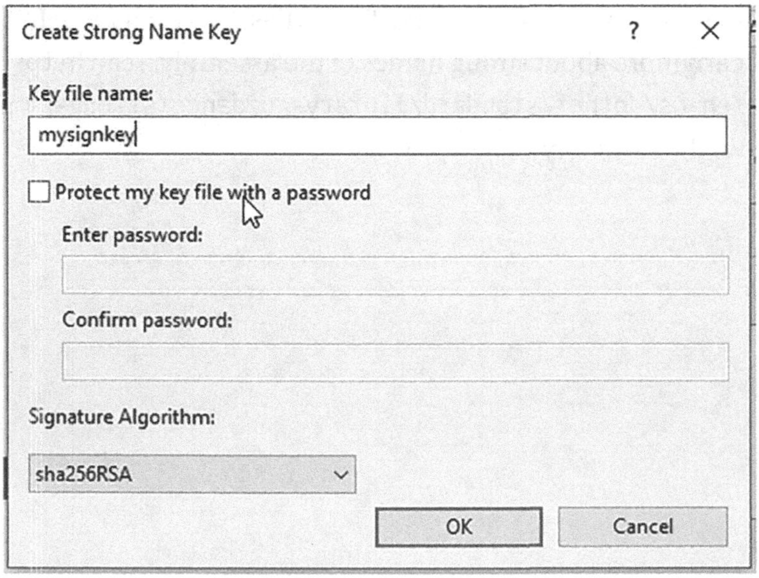

Figure 9-22. *Specify a key name*

After that, save the project. You are now ready to register the plugin.

Step 6: Register the Plugin

To register a plugin, you need to download the Plugin Registration tool using the NuGet Package Manager. Right-click the Plugin project and choose Manage NuGet Package. Figure 9-23 shows the process of managing a NuGet package.

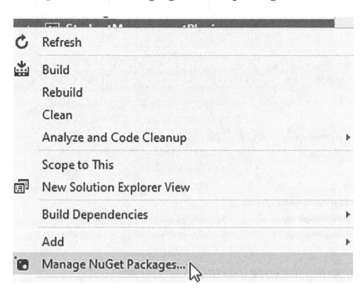

Figure 9-23. *Managing a NuGet package*

In the Browse tab of the NuGet Package Manager panel, search the Plugin Registration tool. Click the highlighted tool and install it. Figure 9-24 shows the process of choosing the core assembly.

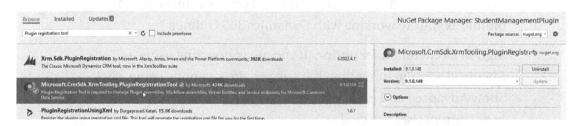

Figure 9-24. *Choosing the core assembly*

After the tool has been successfully installed, navigate to the project's physical directory by right-clicking the project and choosing Open Folder in File Explorer. There, you will see a package folder. Open the folder and navigate to the Plugin Registration tool. Open PluginRegistration.exe tool. Figure 9-25 shows this process.

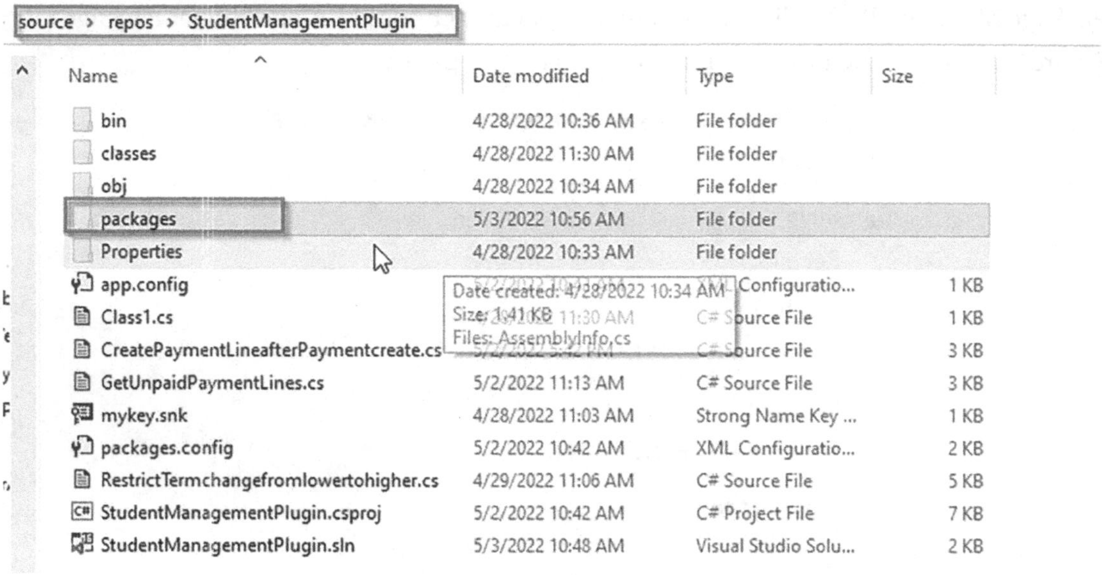

Figure 9-25. *Choosing the core assembly*

The Plugin Registration tool requires a connection to your environment. Click the + Create a New Connection option and provide your credentials. You need to supply the following information:

1. **Deployment type**: This specifies whether you want to connect to an on-premise deployment or online. For this demo, choose online, as you are working with Dynamics 365 Online.

2. **Sign in as current user option**: If you are connecting using a Microsoft account other than the one you are currently using, click Show Advanced and enter your credentials. Otherwise, leave Sign in as Current User selected.

3. **Display list of organizations**: Enable this if you want to see the list of organizations after the connection is successful.

4. **Show advanced**: Select this option to provide a username, password, and online region. Choose Don't Know if you don't know in which cloud region your Dynamics 365 instance is deployed.

Figure 9-26 shows the Create Connection in Plugin Registration tool.

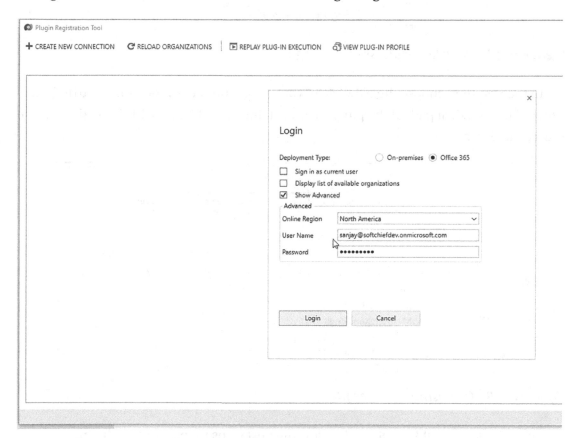

Figure 9-26. *Create Connection in Plugin Registration tool*

Click Login. This will connect your environment and load all the plugins in your environment. Click Register New Assembly. Figure 9-27 shows the Register New Assembly page.

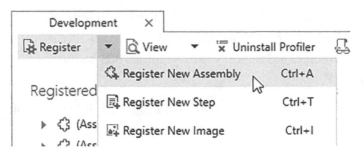

Figure 9-27. *Register New Assembly page*

In the first step, choose the .DLL file of your plugin project by locating the bin Debug folder of the physical path of the plugin's project directory. Figure 9-28 shows the Choose Source file process.

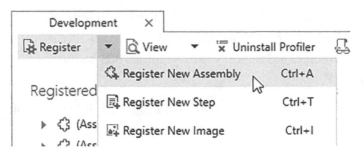

Figure 9-28. *Choosing a source file*

Once the source DLL is selected, follow the next steps to register the plugin. Figure 9-29 shows the Register Plugin options.

1. Select the plugin assembly.

2. The plugin activities are automatically selected.

3. Choose Isolation Mode as Sandbox for all plugins. You can read more about plugin storage and isolation at https://docs. microsoft.com/en-us/dynamics365/customerengagement/on-premises/developer/register-deploy-plugins?view=op-9-1.

4. Choose a location to store the assembly. Choosing Database will store the DLL inside the Dataverse.

5. Use this information for log purposes.

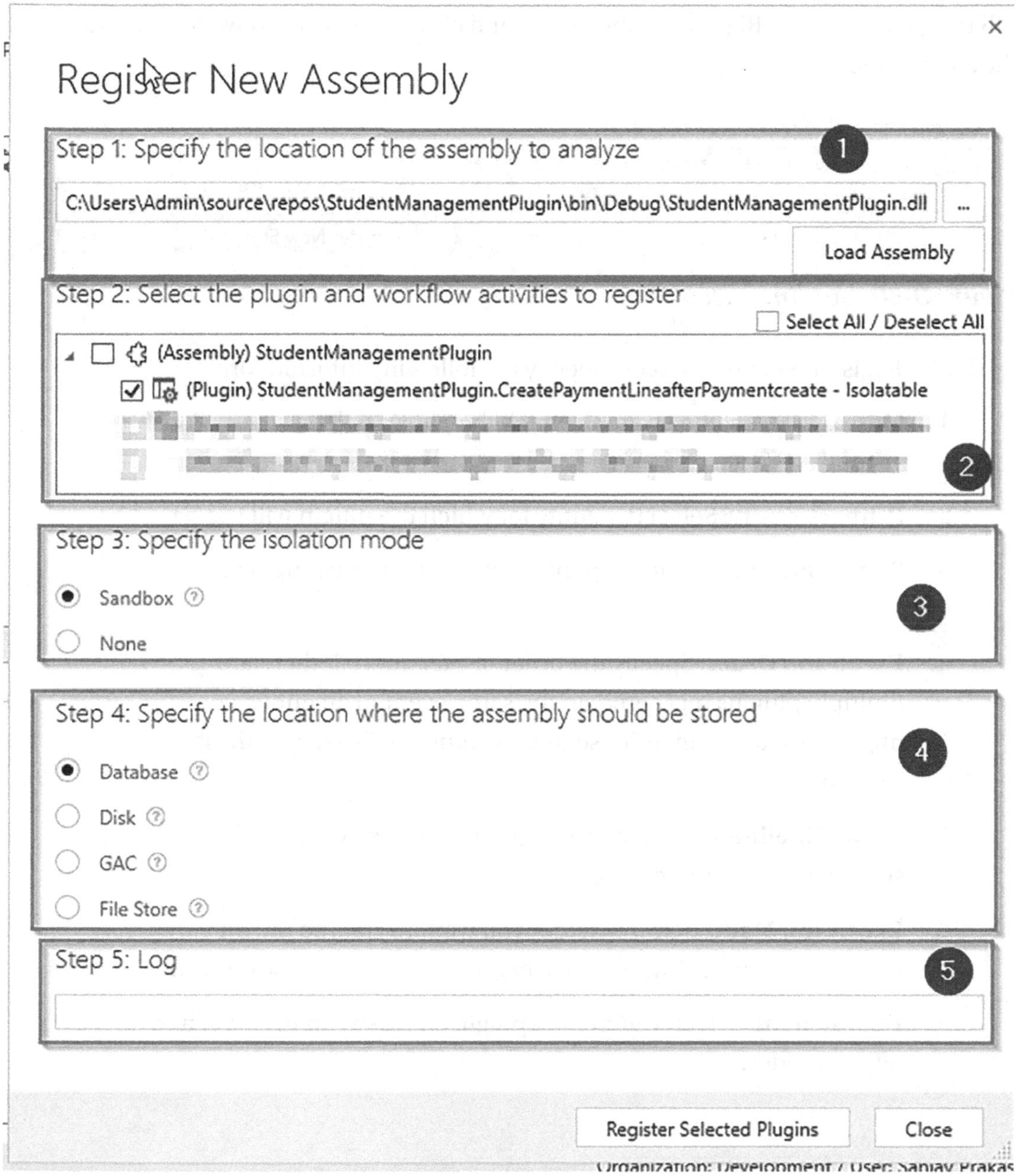

Figure 9-29. *The Register Plugin options*

The plugin is now registered.

Step 7: Add the Plugin Steps

After the plugin has been registered, you need to add a step to define which message will trigger the plugin. Right-click the plugin and choose Register New Step. Figure 9-30 shows this step.

Figure 9-30. *Adding a step*

In the Register New Step screen, specify the following information:

1. **Message**: Select the event on which the plugin will be called. For example, Create.

2. **Primary entity**: Select the entity for which the plugin will trigger.

3. **Step name**: Automatically populated based on the plugin and step name.

4. **Execution Order**: Specify the order of execution. If there are multiple plugins registered on the same event of an entity, you might want to set an order so that the plugin will execute these sequentially.

5. **Event Pipeline stage of execution**: Choose the event pipeline stage, such as pre-operation.

6. **Execution Mode**: Select whether you want to run the plugin synchronously (real-time) or asynchronously (in the background).

7. **Deployment**: Select whether the plugin will also run in server and offline modes.

Figure 9-31 shows the steps for a plugin assembly.

Figure 9-31. *Adding the step details*

Now you are ready to test.

Step 8: Test the Plugin

Open a student payment record and create a payment with terms. Figure 9-32 shows an existing student payment record.

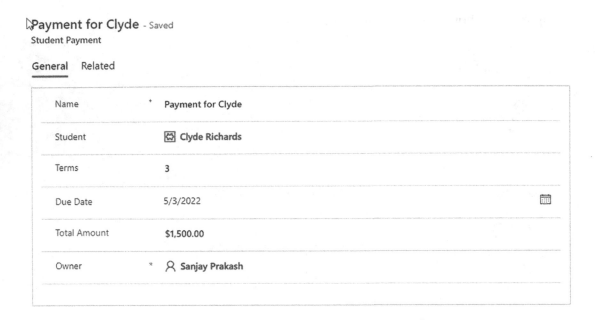

Figure 9-32. *Existing student payment record*

Three payment lines are immediately created with the correct amounts and due dates. Figure 9-33 shows the new student payment lines.

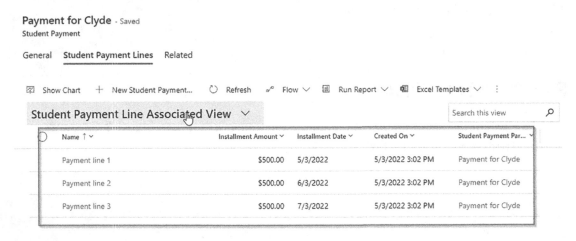

Figure 9-33. *New student payment lines*

Plugin Impersonation

Impersonation is a technique that runs custom code on behalf of a Dynamics 365 CE system user in order to offer the user a desired feature or service. For example, if a user cannot update a student record and the plugin requires some logic to update the student, you can run the plugin under the system admin or any other user context that does have update permissions for students. This way, the business process will not break. For more details about plugin impersonation, see `https://docs.microsoft.com/ en-us/dynamics365/customerengagement/on-premises/developer/impersonation- plugins?view=op-9-1`. Figure 9-34 shows the plugin impersonation tool.

You configure the plugin impersonation in the Plugin Registration tool.

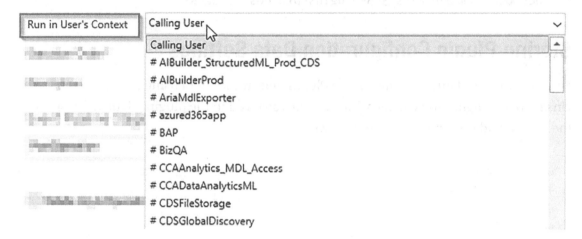

Figure 9-34. *The Plugin Impersonation tool*

Plugin Images

Plugins support pre- and post-images. The pre-image is used to store the attribute values that were present before saving the record in SQL server, while the post-image is used to store the attribute values that are present after saving the record in a QL Database. The pre-image stores an early snapshot of data and the post-image stores updated snapshots of the data.

You can configure images using the Plugin Registration tool. Figure 9-35 shows the Plugin Images screen.

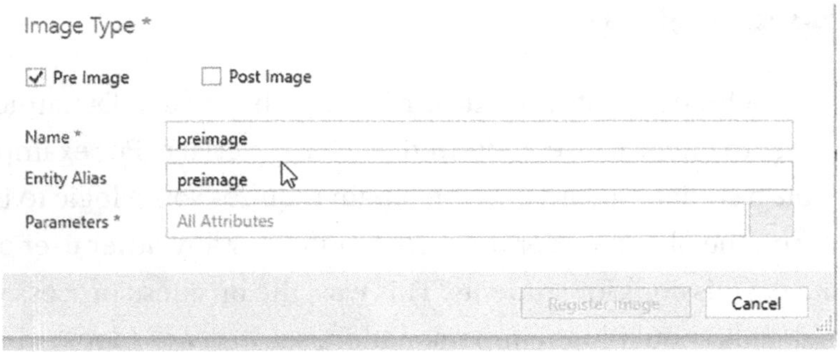

Figure 9-35. *Plugin Images screen*

To learn more about plugin images, see this article from Carl Souza at https://
carldesouza.com/dynamics-365-plugins-pre-post-images/.

Storing Plugin Configuration Data Settings

You can store configuration data in the Plugin Registration tool using the Secure and
Unsecure Configurations panel, which can be retrieved in the plugin. Figure 9-36 shows
the secure and unsecure configuration values.

Figure 9-36. *Secure and unsecure configuration values*

You can read more about secure and unsecure configurations at `https://crmchap.co.uk/what-is-unsecuresecure-configuration-on-a-dynamics-crm365-for-enterprise-plugin/`.

Shared Variables

Shared variables are used to pass data between plugins registered on both pre- and post-events. So, instead of storing values in custom attributes, they can be stored in context variables. You can then read and write data into shared variables of context. Read more about shared variables at `https://docs.microsoft.com/en-us/dynamics365/sales/developer/custom-plugin-handling-shared-variable`.

Develop Custom Workflow Activities in Power Apps

Custom workflow is an extension of the classic workflow for complex logic. If the classic workflow is not enough to meet your business needs, you can configure a custom workflow, which is a .NET class library .DLL like a plugin. Custom workflows can have input and output arguments. The workflow sends parameters to the custom workflows and the custom workflow processes the data and returns the desired result as an output argument, which can be used by calling the workflow.

Use the following steps to configure a custom workflow. As an example, say you want to send an email on demand to a student to indicate to them how many payment lines are unpaid.

For this requirement, the workflow configuration is not enough. You need to develop a custom workflow for this.

Step 1: Create a Class Library Project

Follow the steps explained in the Plugin project to create a new class library project. Rename the default `Class1.cs` file to `GetUnpaidPaymentLines.cs`.

Step 2: Add the Required Microsoft SDK

Use Manage NuGet package to add the required assemblies. You need Microsoft Core Assemblies, Microsoft CRM SDK Workflow Assembly, and the Plugin Registration tools. Figure 9-37 shows the process of adding a core assembly to this project.

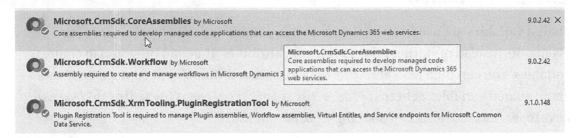

Figure 9-37. *Adding a core assembly to the project*

Use the following namespaces in the class. Namespaces are a logical grouping of types for the purpose of identification. In custom workflows, you also need to use Microsoft XRM namespaces to provide the base classes to interact with Dynamics 365 CE.

```
using System;
using System.Activities;
using System.Collections.Generic;
using System.Linq;
using System.Text;
using System.Threading.Tasks;
using Microsoft.Xrm.Sdk;
using Microsoft.Xrm.Sdk.Query;
using Microsoft.Xrm.Sdk.Workflow;
```

Step 3: Use the Required Objects

You now need to implement CodeActivity for the custom workflow class.

```
public sealed class GetUnpaidPaymentLines : CodeActivity
Define input and out arguments.

  [Input("Student Record")]
```

```
[ReferenceTarget("soft_student")]
public InArgument<EntityReference> StudentRecord { get; set; }

[Output("Count of Unpaid Payment Lines")]
public OutArgument<int> countofunpaidlines { get; set; }
```

Step 4: Implement the Core Logic

Write the core logic. This example retrieves records from the Dataverse. There are many techniques that you can use to retrieve records from the Dataverse, including Query Expression, FetchXML, LINQ, and son. I personally prefer FetchXML and suggest you use it. To read other types of techniques, visit the Microsoft site.

In the following example, the FetchXML reads all the active payment line records for a student. You can use the Advanced Find option to build FetchXML or any helper tool such as the XRM Toolbox community tool to build a fetch XML.

```
protected override void Execute(CodeActivityContext context)
    {
        //Create the context
        IWorkflowContext executioncontext =
            context.GetExtension<IWorkflowContext>();
        IOrganizationServiceFactory serviceFactory =
            context.GetExtension<IOrganizationServiceFactory>();
        IOrganizationService service =
            serviceFactory.CreateOrganizationService(executioncontext.
            UserId);
        EntityReference entStudent = StudentRecord.Get<Entity
        Reference>(context);

        var fetchxml = @"<fetch version='1.0' output-format='xml-
        platform' mapping='logical' distinct='false'>
                    <entity name='soft_studentpaymentline'>
                        <attribute name='soft_studentpaymentlineid' />
                        <attribute name='soft_name' />
                        <attribute name='createdon' />
                        <order attribute='soft_name' descending='false' />
                        <filter type='and'>
```

```
                        <condition attribute='statecode'
                        operator='eq' value='0' />
                    </filter>
                    <link-entity name='soft_studentpayment' from=
                    'soft_studentpaymentid' to='soft_student
                    paymentparent' link-type='inner' alias='ag'>
                        <filter type='and'>
                            <condition attribute='soft_student'
                            operator='eq' uitype='soft_student'
                            value='{0}' />
                        </filter>
                    </link-entity>
                </entity>
            </fetch>";
    fetchxml = string.Format(fetchxml, entStudent.Id);
    EntityCollection ec = service.RetrieveMultiple
    (new FetchExpression(fetchxml));
    var count = ec.Entities.Count;
    countofunpaidlines.Set(context, count);
}
```

This code explains how to fetch all payment lines that are due using the student ID and returning the count in the output parameter.

Step 5: Register the Custom Workflow

Registering a custom workflow activity is the same as a plugin registration. Follow the same steps you followed for the plugin registration process. The only difference is for custom workflow; you don't need the register steps, as the custom workflow will be called by another workflow. A custom workflow cannot run independently, as it is a class library output and the class library output files are DLL files. They cannot be run independently, but are called from other apps to use the logic. Figure 9-38 shows the custom workflow being registered.

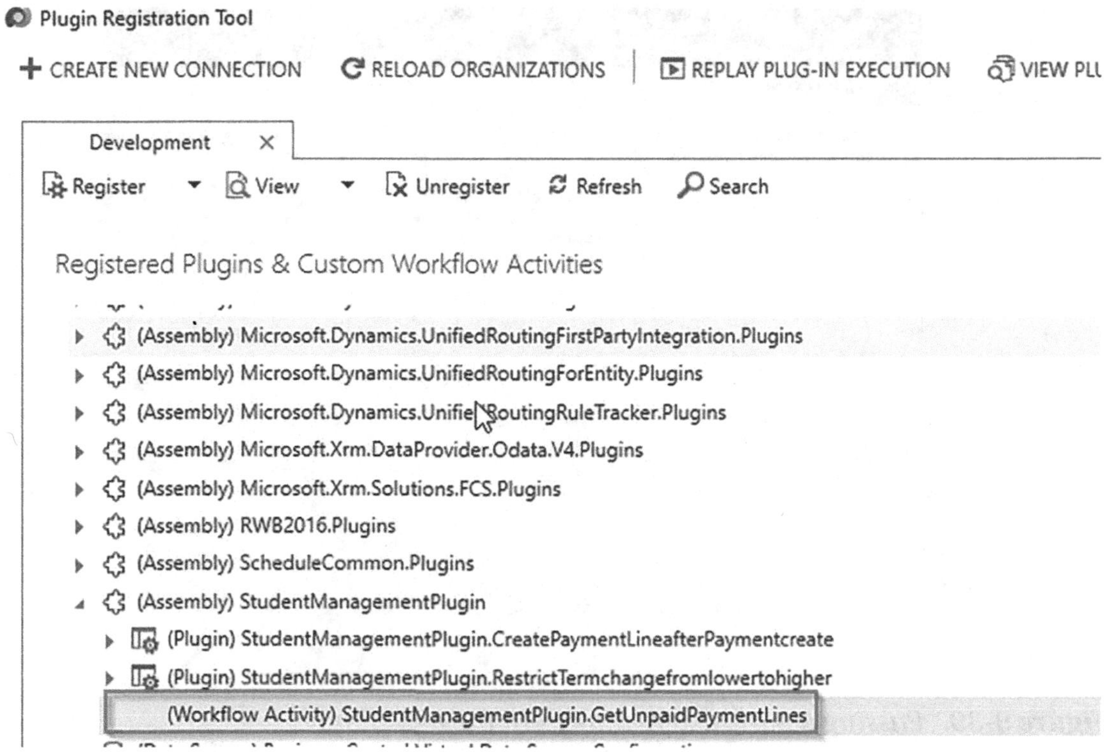

Plugin Registration Tool

+ CREATE NEW CONNECTION   **C** RELOAD ORGANIZATIONS | **▶** REPLAY PLUG-IN EXECUTION   **⊡** VIEW PLU

Development   ✕

⊞ Register   ▾   **◷** View   ▾   **⊠** Unregister   **⟳** Refresh   **⌕** Search

Registered Plugins & Custom Workflow Activities

▸ ⟨⟩ (Assembly) Microsoft.Dynamics.UnifiedRoutingFirstPartyIntegration.Plugins

▸ ⟨⟩ (Assembly) Microsoft.Dynamics.UnifiedRoutingForEntity.Plugins

▸ ⟨⟩ (Assembly) Microsoft.Dynamics.UnifiedRoutingRuleTracker.Plugins

▸ ⟨⟩ (Assembly) Microsoft.Xrm.DataProvider.Odata.V4.Plugins

▸ ⟨⟩ (Assembly) Microsoft.Xrm.Solutions.FCS.Plugins

▸ ⟨⟩ (Assembly) RWB2016.Plugins

▸ ⟨⟩ (Assembly) ScheduleCommon.Plugins

◢ ⟨⟩ (Assembly) StudentManagementPlugin

  ▸ ⬚ (Plugin) StudentManagementPlugin.CreatePaymentLineafterPaymentcreate

  ▸ ⬚ (Plugin) StudentManagementPlugin.RestrictTermchangefromlowertohigher

    (Workflow Activity) StudentManagementPlugin.GetUnpaidPaymentLines

Figure 9-38. Registering the custom workflow

Step 6: Create a Workflow to Call a Custom Workflow

Configure an on-demand real-time workflow for the Student entity. In the first step, you can choose the Custom Workflow step from the list. Figure 9-39 shows the process for passing a parameter value from the workflow.

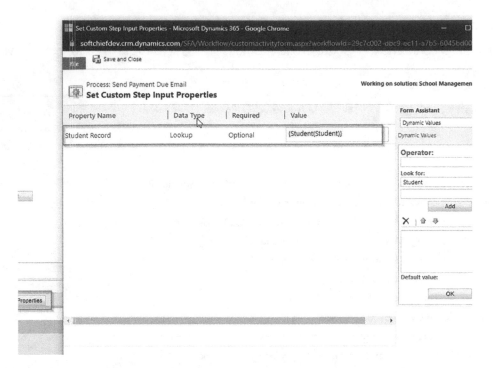

Figure 9-39. *Passing a parameter value from the workflow*

In the next step, add a new step to send an email. In the email body, mention the output parameter received from the previous step. Figure 9-40 shows the process of setting properties of an email record.

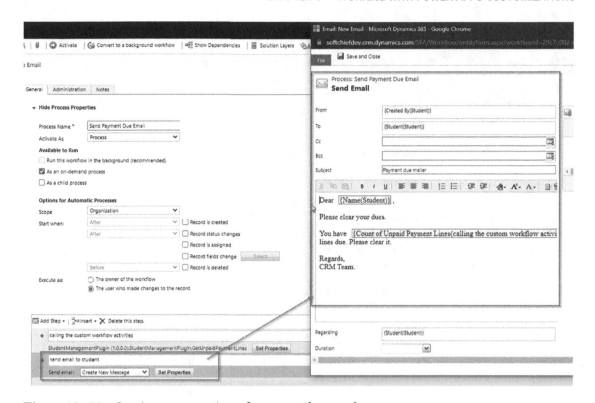

Figure 9-40. *Setting properties of an email record*

The final workflow is shown in Figure 9-41.

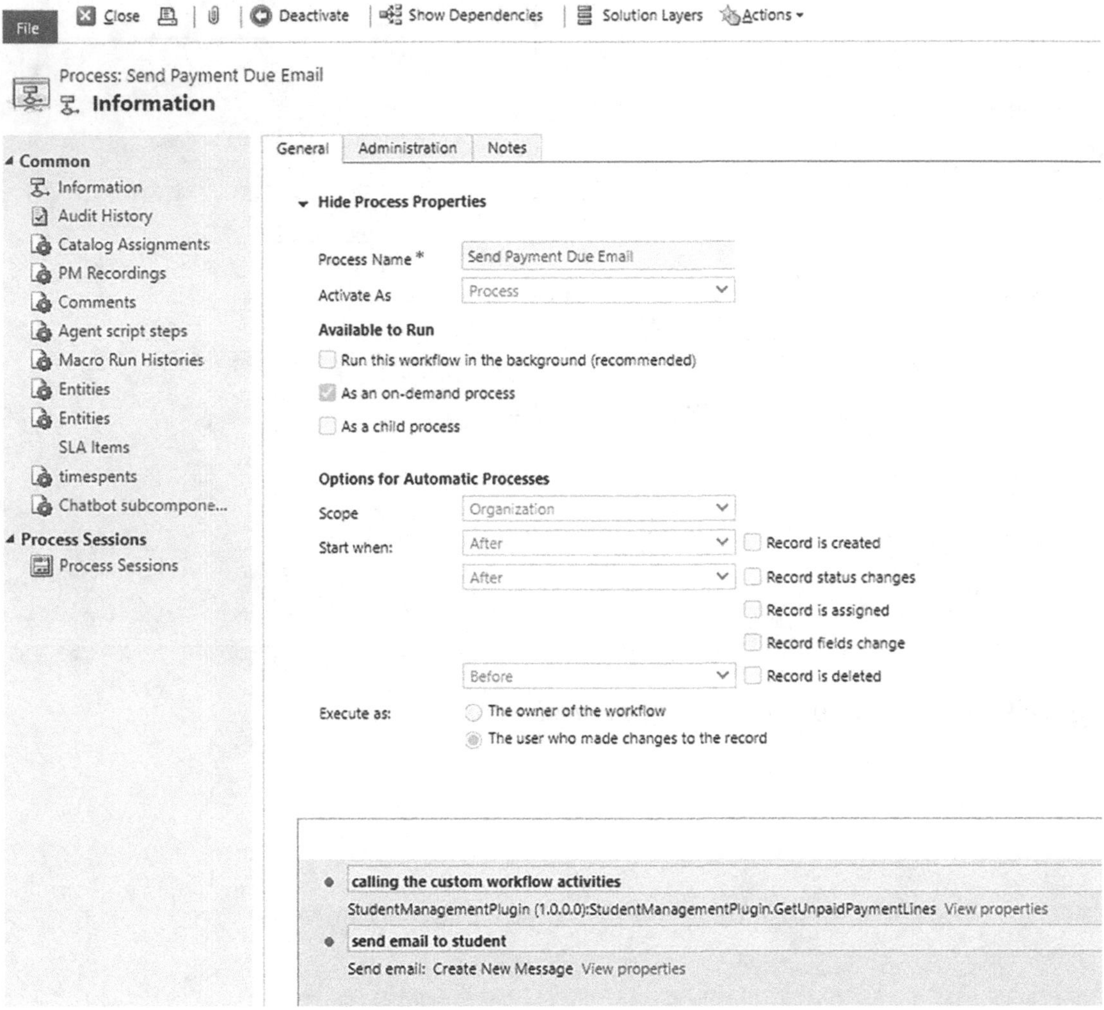

Figure 9-41. *The final workflow screen*

Activate the workflow and go to any student record to test it.

Step 7: Test a Custom Workflow Activity

On the Student form, click the command bar flow option and choose the workflow you just activated. Figure 9-42 shows the process of starting a workflow on-demand.

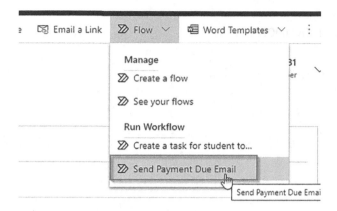

Figure 9-42. *Starting a workflow on-demand*

Figure 9-43 shows the workflow run confirmation box. Confirm the workflow by clicking OK.

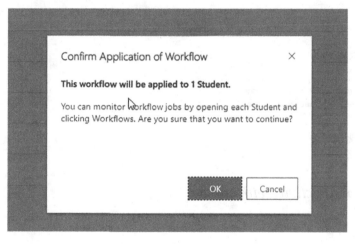

Figure 9-43. *Workflow run confirmation box*

It will run the workflow and will call the custom workflow to get a count of payment lines to be paid and specified in the email. To check this process, go to related activities and open the email activity. Figure 9-44 shows the email activity with content.

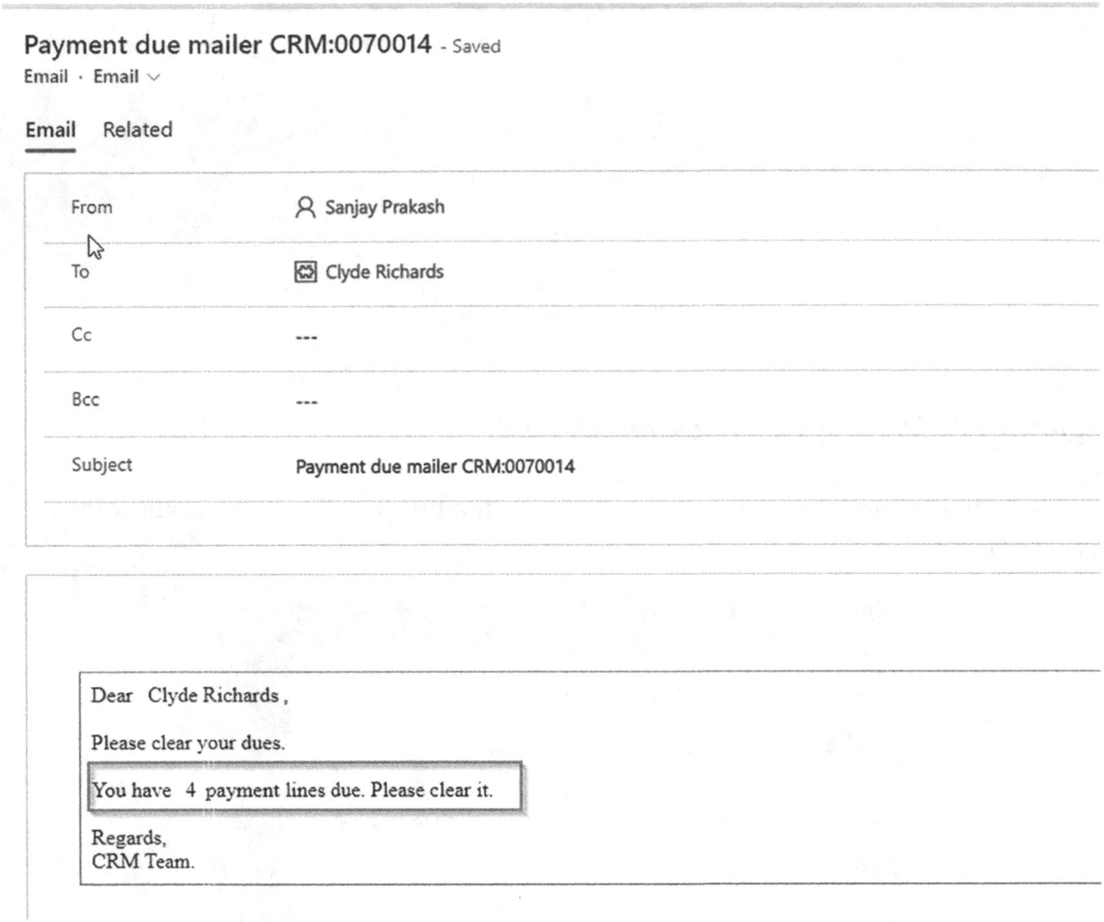

Payment due mailer CRM:0070014 - Saved
Email · Email ⌄

Email   Related

From	𝗔 Sanjay Prakash
To	🖼 Clyde Richards
Cc	---
Bcc	---
Subject	**Payment due mailer CRM:0070014**

Dear   Clyde Richards ,

Please clear your dues.

You have   4 payment lines due. Please clear it.

Regards,
CRM Team.

Figure 9-44. *Email activity with content*

Edit the Command Bar

You can edit command bars in Dynamics 365 Apps or model-driven power apps using the App Editor.

Use Preview Editor to edit the command bar. Add the model-driven app you want to edit inside the Power Apps solution. Click the three vertical dots and select Edit in Preview. Figure 9-45 shows the edit command bar using a modern command option.

Figure 9-45. *Edit the command bar using a modern command option*

Choose the entity that you want to edit. Figure 9-46 shows the Edit Student command bar.

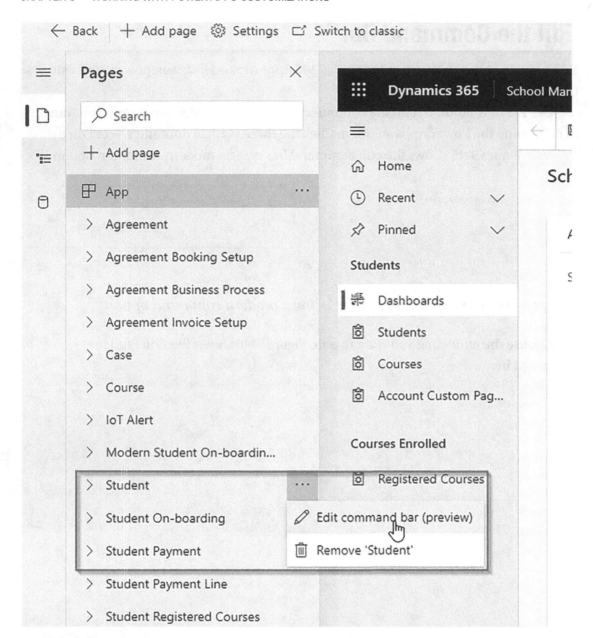

Figure 9-46. *Edit Student command bar*

There are four types of command bar:

1. **Main grid**

    This command bar displays the command buttons from the view
    pages for an entity. Figure 9-47 shows the main home grid.

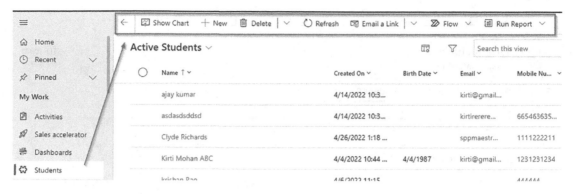

Figure 9-47. *The main home grid*

2. **Main form**

   This command bar is displayed for an individual record of an
   entity. Figure 9-48 shows the main form.

Figure 9-48. *The main form*

3. **Associated view**

   This command bar is displayed for associated views of an
   individual record of an entity. Figure 9-49 shows the associated
   view command bar.

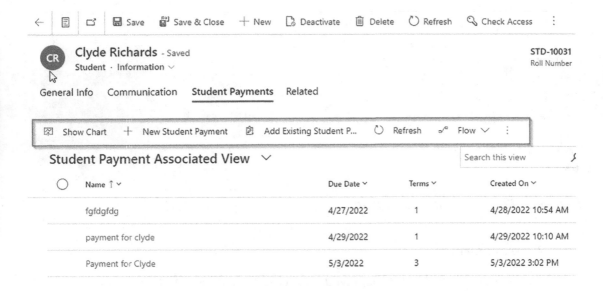

Figure 9-49. *Associated view command bar*

4. **Sub-grid view**

This command bar is displayed for sub-grid view of records of an entity. Figure 9-50 shows the sub-grid command bar.

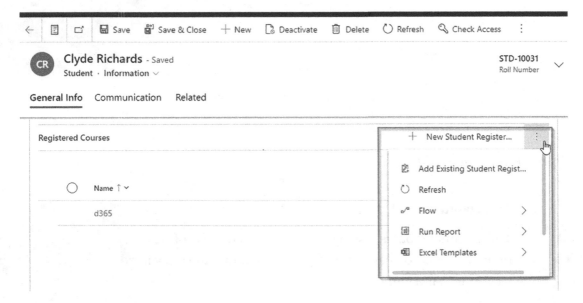

Figure 9-50. *Sub-grid command bar*

You can choose where you want to add command buttons. Here, you will see how to add a command button to a main form.

A command button on the student form must create a student payment record by accepting the required field values and creating a student payment using the client script. Use the following steps to complete this scenario.

Step 1: Add a Command Button to the Main Form

Edit the command bar of the student entity and choose the main form command bar for editing. Click an existing button and choose a new command button from the left panel. Figure 9-51 shows the process of adding a command button.

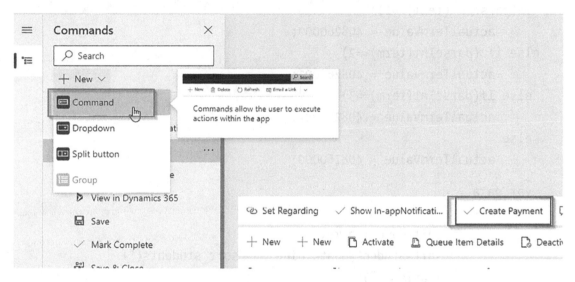

Figure 9-51. *Adding a command button*

Set the command properties for the command button so that the JavaScript method or Power Fx will execute.

Step 2: Create a JS Web Resource to Call on Button Click

Use the following code snippet to call a method when a button is clicked. The following code explains how to prompt users to accept values of different fields such as terms, amount, and so on, and calls a XRM Web API to create a record in the Dataverse. To learn more about XRM Web API, see https://docs.microsoft.com/en-us/power-apps/developer/model-driven-apps/clientapi/reference/xrm-webapi.

```
function CreatePayment(context)
{
    var formContext = context;

    var name ="payment for "+ formContext.getAttribute("soft_name").
    getValue();
    var fees = prompt("Enter Fees");
    var recordId = formContext.data.entity.getId();
    var cleanId = recordId.replace("{", "").replace("}", "");
    var term = prompt("Enter Term");

    var actualTermValue = 408260000;
    if(parseInt(term)==1)
        actualTermValue = 408260000;
    else if (parseInt(term)==2)
        actualTermValue = 408260001;
    else if(parseInt(term)==3)
        actualTermValue = 408260002;
    else
        actualTermValue = 408260000;

    var data =
            {
                "soft_name": name,
                "soft_Student@odata.bind": "/soft_students("+
                cleanId + ")",
                "soft_totalamount": parseFloat(fees),
                "soft_duedate" : new Date(),
                "soft_terms" : parseInt(actualTermValue)
            }

            var confirmStrings = { text:"Are you sure you want to create
            payment for student?", title:"Confirm Payment" };
            var confirmOptions = { height: 300, width: 500 };

                Xrm.Navigation.openConfirmDialog(confirmStrings,
                confirmOptions).then(
            function (success) {
```

```
    if (success.confirmed)
    {
            Xrm.Utility.showProgressIndicator("Wait.. Creating
            Payment");

        Xrm.WebApi.createRecord("soft_studentpayment", data).then(
            function success(result) {

                    var alertStrings = { confirmButtonLabel:
                    "Yes", text: "Payment Created", title:
                    "Message" };
                    var alertOptions = { height: 120,
                    width: 260 };
                    Xrm.Navigation.openAlertDialog(alertStrings,
                    alertOptions).then(
                        function (success) {
                            console.log("Alert dialog closed");
                                    setTimeout(function ()
                                    {Xrm.Utility.
                                    closeProgressIndicator
                                    ();},10000);
                        },
                        function (error) {
                            console.log(error.message);
                        }
                    );
                            Xrm.Utility.closeProgressIndicator();
            },
            function (error) {
                alert(error.message);
            }
        );
    }
    else
        console.log("Dialog closed using Cancel button or X.");
});

}
```

1. In the command property, select Icon for the command button.

2. In Action, select Run JavaScript.

3. Choose JS Web resource in the library dropdown.

4. Specify the JavaScript method.

5. Define the parameters to pass to the JavaScript function. These parameters will be used to interact with the form fields.

Figure 9-52 shows the command properties.

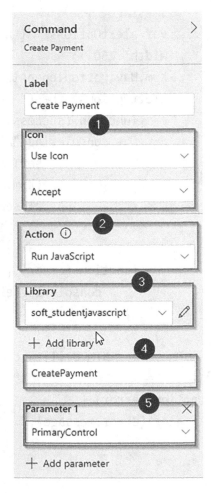

Figure 9-52. Command properties

Publish the command changes and the model-driven app inside the Power Apps solution.

After you publish, test the changes by navigating to a student form. You will see a new button in the command bar. Figure 9-53 shows the command button in action.

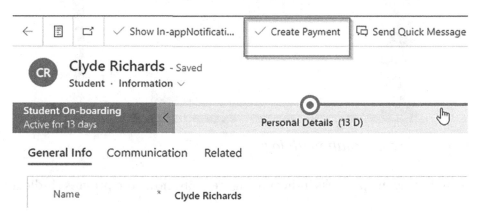

Figure 9-53. *The new command button in action*

When you click the button, it will ask you to provide the amounts and the term. Figure 9-54 shows this testing process.

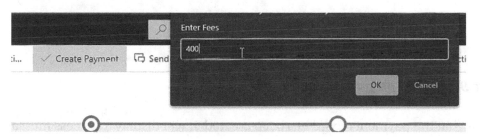

Figure 9-54. *Testing the command button*

After that, it will ask you to confirm the payment creation. Click OK. Figure 9-55 shows the confirmation dialog.

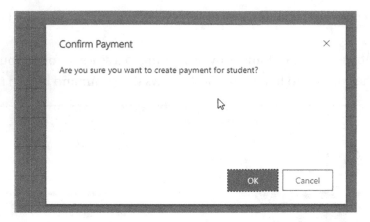

Figure 9-55. *The confirmation dialog*

This will display the progress indicator. Figure 9-56 shows the progress indicator.

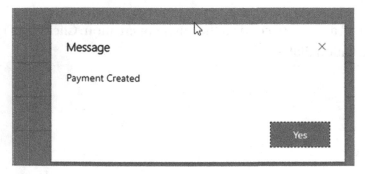

Figure 9-56. *The progress indicator*

Now that the payment record has been created, it will display a success message. Figure 9-57 shows the alert dialog for the success message.

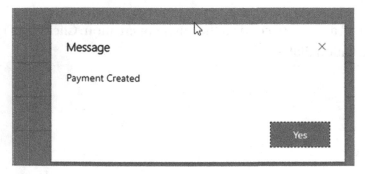

Figure 9-57. *The alert dialog for the success message*

The following payment record has been created for the student. Figure 9-58 shows the result of the button click operation.

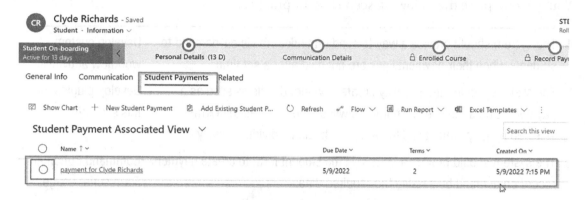

Figure 9-58. *The result of the button click operation*

The amount and term with the student lookup association is correctly added to the record. Figure 9-59 shows the payment record created using JavaScript.

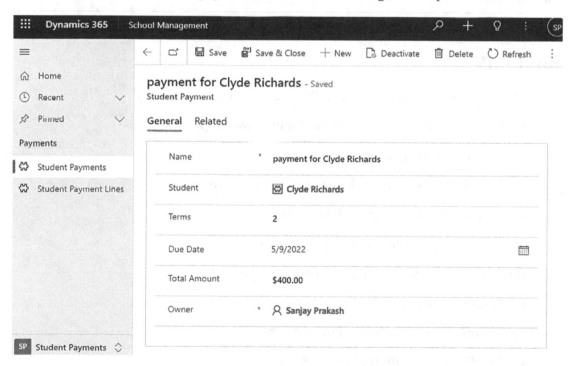

Figure 9-59. *Payment record*

Business Scenarios and Implementations

You can complete the following scenarios for practice.

1	The system should provide a way to send reminder emails on-demand to students when their payment lines are not paid after a set time.	Develop custom workflow activities.
2	The system should automatically create payment details as soon as a payment is created. The line numbers will be the same as the terms selected in the payment and the amount should be divided equally.	Develop plugins for this scenario.
3	The system should provide a button on the student form to create payment record on demand by passing the required data.	Command button and Form script usage.
4	The system should create a reusable action to send emails and create a task for leads on demand.	Configure custom actions.
5	The system should create a report on leads and display the leads by creation date.	Configure reports.

Summary

In this chapter, you learned about the following concepts:

- Working with client-side JavaScript in Power Apps

- Developing plugins for Power Apps

- Developing custom workflow activities in Power Apps

- Editing command bars in Power Apps

- Business scenarios and implementations

In the next chapter, you will learn about the following:

- Outlook integration in Power Apps

- SharePoint integration in Power Apps

- OneDrive integration in Power Apps

- Azure integration in Power Apps

- Business scenarios and implementations

Working with Integrations for Power Apps and Dynamics 365

Integration is very important in all projects. You can integrate Power Apps using Microsoft native apps or third-party systems using the low-code, less-code concept. In this chapter, you learn how to integrate native and third-party apps with model-driven Power Apps and Dynamics 365 Apps.

Integrating Outlook with Power Apps

The following sections outline the steps for integrating Outlook with Power Apps.

Step 1: Determine Whether Your Organization Has an Office 365 Enterprise Subscription

To integrate Office Outlook, you must have an Office 365 Enterprise subscription so that your users can use Outlook. To check for a subscription, log in to the Office Admin Center and go to Billing ➤ Subscription. Figure 10-1 shows the Office 365 subscription process.

411

© Sanjaya Prakash Pradhan 2022
S. Prakash Pradhan, *Power Platform and Dynamics 365 CE for Absolute Beginners*,
https://doi.org/10.1007/978-1-4842-8600-5_10

Figure 10-1. *Adding a subscription*

If you already have a subscription, you can open Outlook. Otherwise, add a subscription to Office 365 E3 and click Trial for Free. Figure 10-2 shows the process of choosing the Office 365 E3 product.

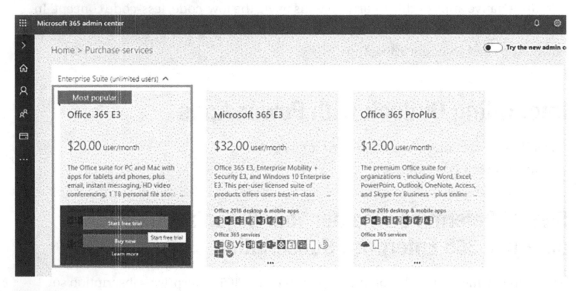

Figure 10-2. *Choosing a product*

Once the trial subscription operation is complete, navigate to Users in the Office Admin Center and select the user you want to assign to the subscription. Click Product License and edit it. Figure 10-3 shows the process of adding a product license for a user.

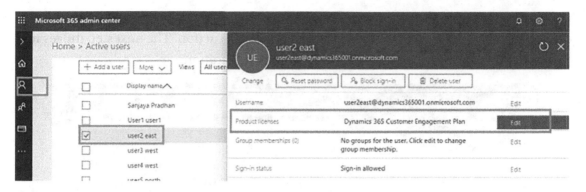

Figure 10-3. *Adding a product license*

Enable the Office 365 license and click Close. Figure 10-4 shows choosing the United States for the location.

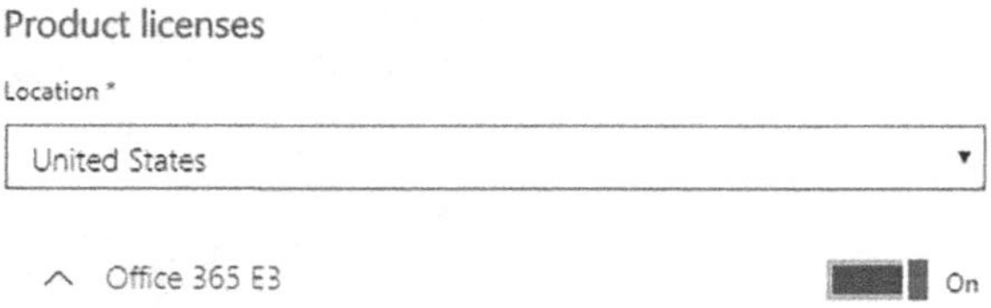

Product licenses

Location *

United States ▼

∧   Office 365 E3   ████ ▌ On

Figure 10-4. *Choosing the location for the license*

Now Open the Outlook app from the dashboard of the Office Portal Center. Figure 10-5 shows the Outlook app on the dashboard.

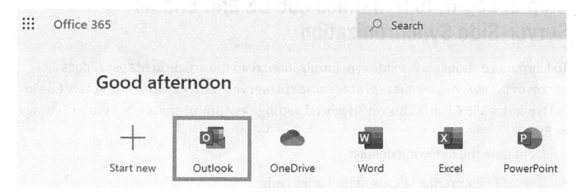

Figure 10-5. *App dashboard*

The system will ask you for your preferred language and time zone and then Outlook will open. Figure 10-6 shows the Outlook app in action. The next step moves to Dynamics 365 for more configuration and Outlook integration.

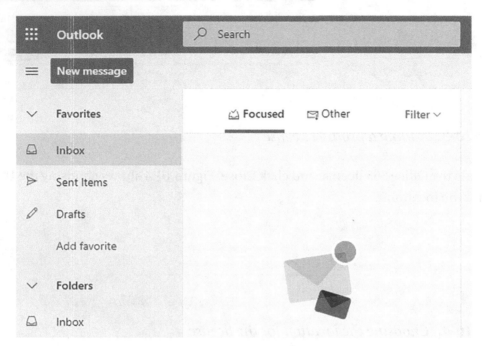

Figure 10-6. *Outlook app*

Step 2: Log In to Dynamics 365 CE and Enable Server-Side Synchronization

To learn more about server-side synchronization, read the article at `https://docs.microsoft.com/en-us/power-platform/admin/server-side-synchronization`. Log in to Dynamics 365 CE and choose Advanced Settings ➤ Administration ➤ System Settings ➤ Email.

Configure the following details:

- Server profile: Microsoft Exchange Online

- Incoming Email: Server-side Synchronization or Email Router

- Outgoing Email: Server-side Synchronization or Email Router

- Appointment, Contact, Task: Server-side Synchronization

Figure 10-7 shows these system settings.

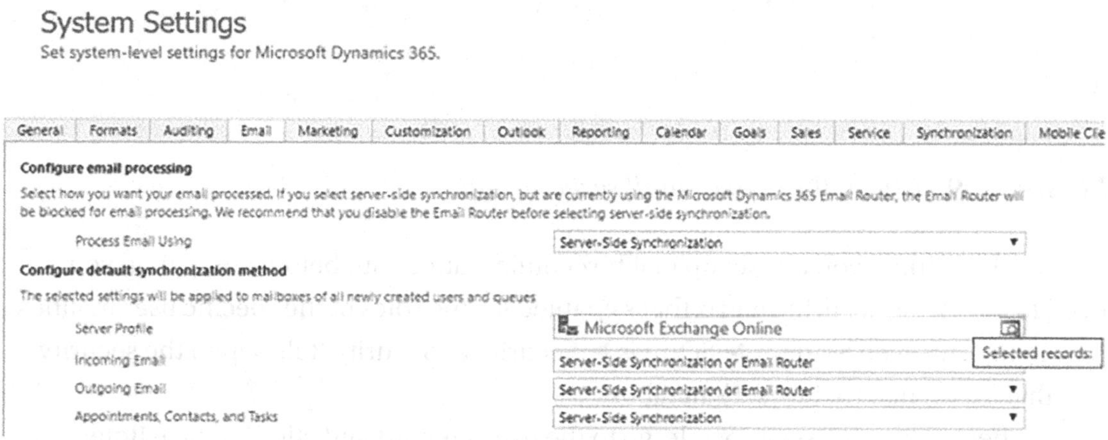

Figure 10-7. *System settings*

Now go to Settings ➤ Email Configuration in the advanced settings area. Figure 10-8 shows the email configuration option.

Figure 10-8. *Email configuration option*

Now click the Email Server profile and verify that Microsoft Exchange Online is shown as the active email server profile, as shown in Figure 10-9.

Active Email Server Profiles ⌄

☐	Name ↑		Email Server ...	Owner
	Microsoft Exchange Online		Exchange Onl...	SYSTEM

Figure 10-9. *Check the active email server profile*

This is the time you can set up mailbox configuration, but before doing that, you need to check the security matrix that's enabled for the roles of the specific user mailbox.

Go to Advanced Settings ➤ Settings ➤ Security ➤ Security Role. Open the security role that's assigned to the user's mailbox.

To check the user's security role, go to the user's record and click Manage Role. Figure 10-10 shows the Manage User Roles window.

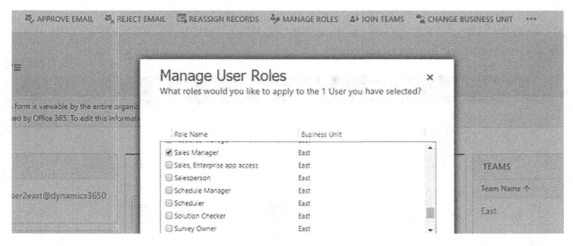

Figure 10-10. *Manage User Roles screen*

In the security role, configure read/write privileges to the following entities in the Security Matrix window: Business management Tab ➤ Mailbox Entity. You need the Dynamics 365 app for Outlook security privilege for the security role.

Go to advanced settings and then choose ➤Security➤ Security Roles➤Pick Security Role ➤ Business Management Tab ➤ Mailbox Entity (this should be a user or a higher level of access). In the Privacy Related Privileges section, choose Use Dynamics 365 App for Outlook for the Organization Access Level. Figure 10-11 shows these mailbox role options.

Security Role: Sales Manager

					Business Management	Service Management	Customization	Missinc
Details	Core Records	Marketing	Sales	Service				
Document Template					○	●	○	○	○
Email Server Profile					○	●	○	○	○
Field Security Profile					○	●	○	○	○
Field Sharing					●	●	●	●	○
Goal					◐	◐	◐	◐	◐
Goal Metric					●	●	●	●	●
Mailbox					◐	◐	◐	○	◐
Mailbox Auto Tracking Folder					◐	◐	◐	◐	◐

Figure 10-11. *Mailbox role options*

Figure 10-12 shows the d365 Outlook app role.

Privacy Related Privileges
Enabling these privileges will allow users to extract customer data from Microsoft Dynamics 365. For more information, review the corresponding user documentation.

Document Generation	●	Dynamics 365 for mobile	●
Export to Excel	●	Go Offline in Outlook	●
Mail Merge	●	Print	●
Sync to Outlook	●	Use Dynamics 365 App for Outlook	●

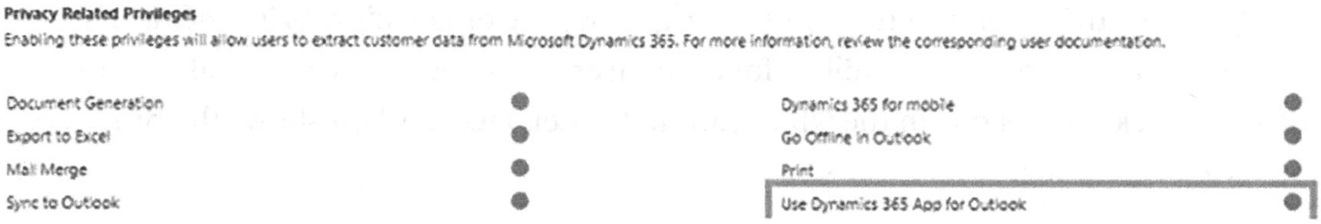

Figure 10-12. *The d365 Outlook app role*

Step 3: Configure the Mailbox

After updating the security matrix for the security role, go to Advanced Settings ➤ Email Configuration and select Mailboxes.

Choose Active Mailboxes view and select the user whose mailbox you want to enable. Open it and configure Incoming, Outgoing, Appointments, and so on, to Server-Side Sync and Server Profile as MS Exchange. Figure 10-13 shows the process of testing a mailbox.

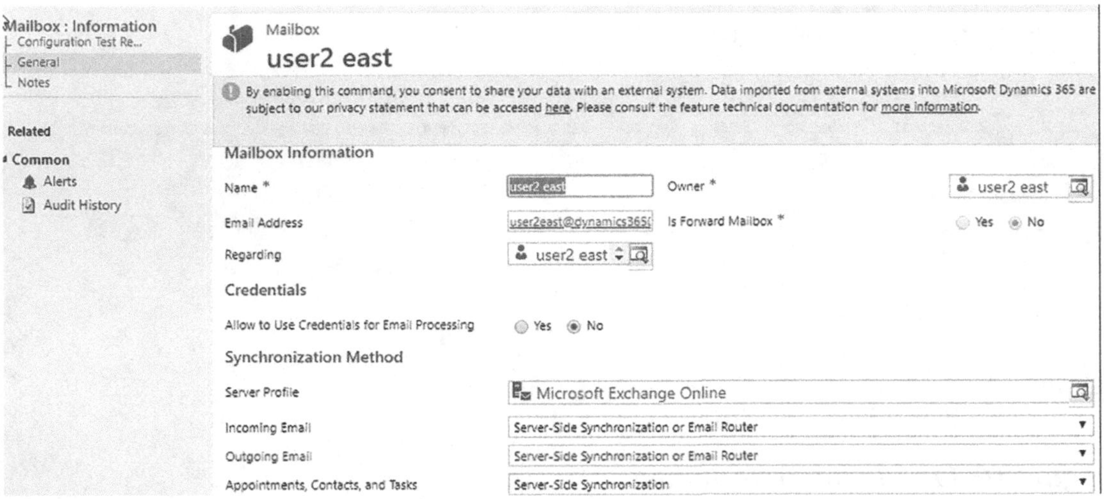

Figure 10-13. *Testing the mailbox*

Then click the Approve Email button to approve the email address for the user's mailbox. Note: To approve a mailbox for other users, you need to be a Global Admin. You can check for this role in the Office Admin Center. Figure 10-14 shows the process of approving a mailbox.

Figure 10-14. *Approving the mailbox*

Click Test and Enable Mailbox. In the popup window, click OK. Wait a bit and then reload the page. Figure 10-15 shows the enable mailbox process.

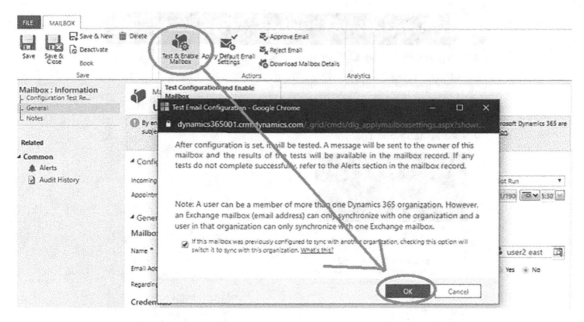

Figure 10-15. *Enabling a mailbox*

After reloading the page, the Configuration Test Results will show Success, as shown in Figure 10-16.

Figure 10-16. *Mailbox status*

Step 4: Install the Dynamics 365 App for Microsoft Outlook by Administer

Log in to Dynamics 365 CE and go to the advanced settings. Choose Dynamics 365 App for Outlook. Figure 10-17 shows the process of enabling the d365 app for Outlook.

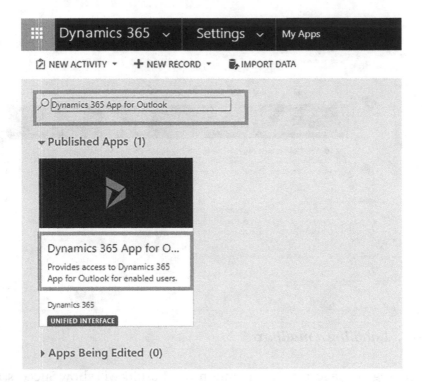

Figure 10-17. *Enabling the d365 app for Outlook*

When you scroll down, you can see the All-Eligible user view, where you can select a user and click Add App to Outlook. Figure 10-18 shows the Add Outlook App to User process.

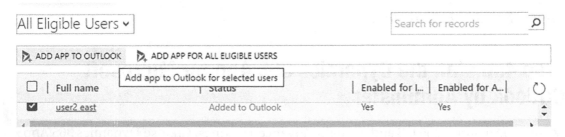

Figure 10-18. *The add app to user process*

Now the user can log in to Outlook. You'll find a link called Dynamics 365 in the Home tab at the end. Figure 10-19 shows the Outlook with d365 option.

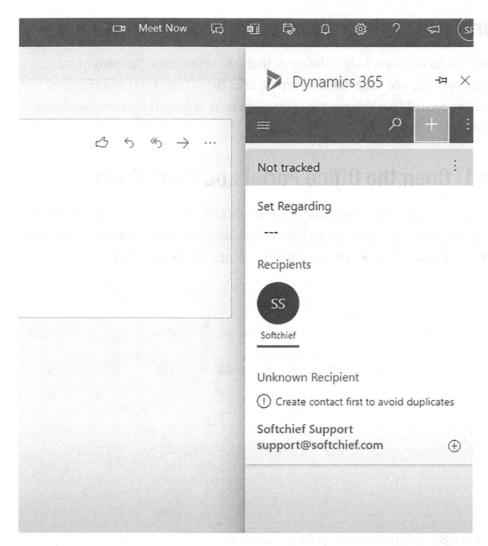

Figure 10-19. *Outlook with d365 option*

Now you can track Outlook email against Dynamics 365 records. To read more about email integration, see https://docs.microsoft.com/en-us/dynamics365/outlook-app/overview.

SharePoint Integration with Power Apps

To integrate SharePoint, follow the steps in the next sections. To learn more about SharePoint, see the Microsoft article at https://docs.microsoft.com/en-us/sharepoint/. In this section, you learn how to integrate SharePoint with Dynamics 365 CE.

Step 1: Open the Office Portal and SharePoint

Browse to the Office Portal with the address office.com. Log in using your Dynamics 365 CE credential. Once you're logged in, click the SharePoint icon from the app dashboard. Figure 10-20 shows the SharePoint app in the dashboard.

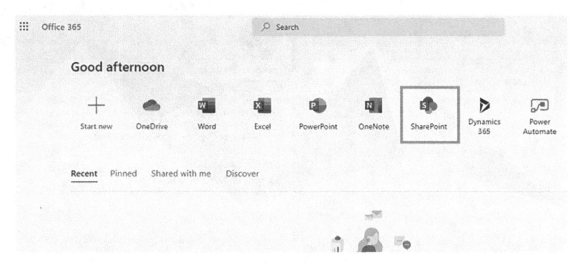

Figure 10-20. *SharePoint app in the dashboard*

Now the SharePoint dashboard will open. From the SharePoint Welcome screen, you can click Next or click the Close icon to go straight to the main screen for editing SharePoint options. Figure 10-21 shows the SharePoint home page.

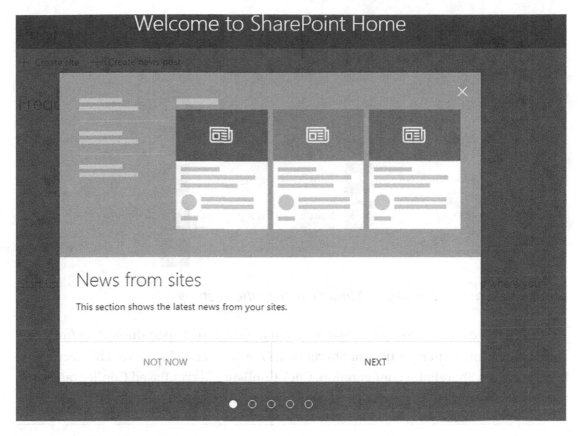

Figure 10-21. SharePoint home page

Step 2: Configure the SharePoint Option in the Dynamics 365 CE Document Management Option

Log in to Dynamics 365 CE and go to the advanced settings. Now Navigate to System ➤ Document Management. Figure 10-22 shows the Document Management Option setting.

Figure 10-22. *The Document Management Option setting*

When you click the Document Management option, it will open the settings for the Document Management option for SharePoint, OneNote, and OneDrive. This section focuses on the SharePoint configuration. Click Configure Server Based Configuration for SharePoint. Figure 10-23 shows the configure server-side integration option.

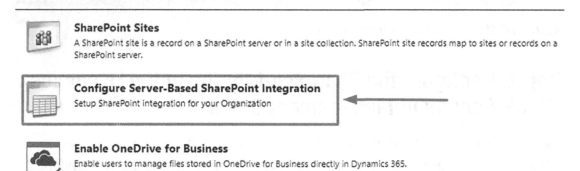

Figure 10-23. *Configuring server-side integration*

Now, in the popup screen, use Online for the SharePoint Site Location. Figure 10-24 shows the Configure Server-Based SharePoint Integration option.

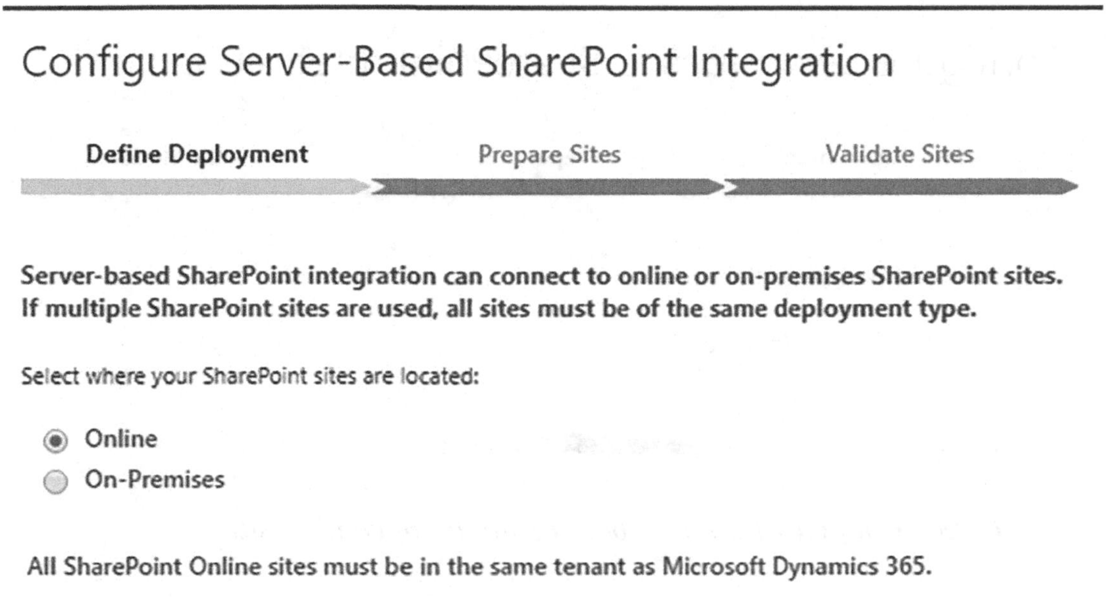

Configure Server-Based SharePoint Integration

Define Deployment   Prepare Sites   Validate Sites

Server-based SharePoint integration can connect to online or on-premises SharePoint sites. If multiple SharePoint sites are used, all sites must be of the same deployment type.

Select where your SharePoint sites are located:

- ⦿ Online
- ○ On-Premises

All SharePoint Online sites must be in the same tenant as Microsoft Dynamics 365.

Figure 10-24. *Configure Server-Based SharePoint Integration option*

Now provide the SharePoint URL. Figure 10-25 shows the configure server-based SharePoint prepare site.

Configure Server-Based SharePoint Integration

Define Deployment   **Prepare Sites**   Validate Sites

No additional setup requirements are required for connecting Dynamics 365 Online to SharePoint Online.

Enter the URL of the SharePoint site for use with server-based integration.

URL | https://██████████1.sharepoint.com/ |

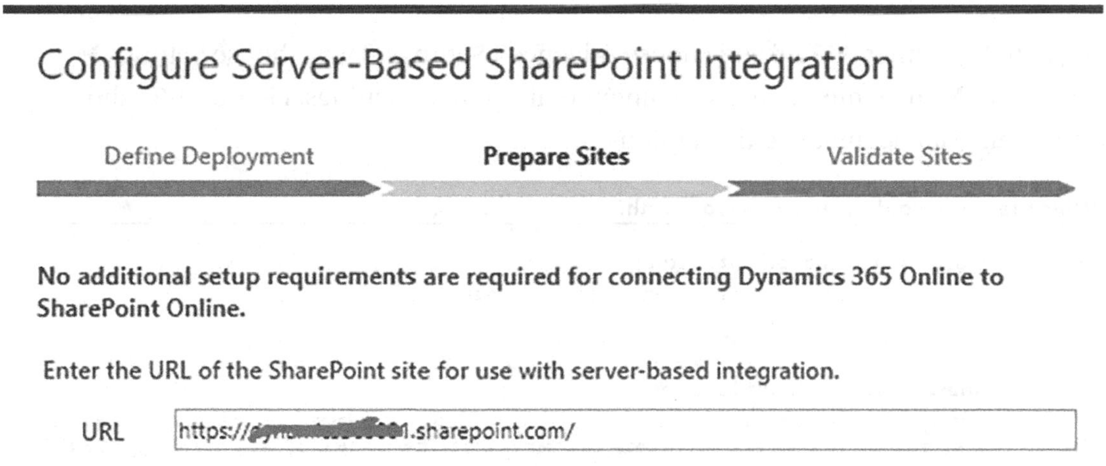

Figure 10-25. *Configure server-based SharePoint prepare site*

On the next screen, validate the information and click Finish. Figure 10-26 shows the configure server-based SharePoint validate site.

Configure Server-Based SharePoint Integration

Define Deployment	Prepare Sites	**Validate Sites**

Validation Status: Complete

Name	Absolute URL	Validation
Default Site	https://dy▓▓▓▓▓▓1.sharepoint....	Valid

Figure 10-26. *Configure the server-based SharePoint validate site*

Once this configuration is complete, it's time to enable the SharePoint document setting for your entities.

Step 3: Enable the SharePoint Document Setting for Entities

Log in to Dynamics 365 CE and choose Advanced Settings. Then choose Settings ➤ Document Management. Click Document Management Settings. Figure 10-27 shows the Document Management Setting options.

Which feature would you like to work with?

 Document Management Settings
Select default document management settings for your organization.

 SharePoint Document Locations
A document location record maps to document libraries or folders on a SharePoint server. They are defined relative to a SharePoint document library record or a document location record. They can be associated with a Microsoft Dynamics 365 record.

Figure 10-27. *Document Management Setting options*

From the popup screen, select the entities that you want to use to manage your SharePoint documents. You will find that some entities like Account, Work Order, and so on, are already enabled. If you want, you can enable other entities. I enabled a custom entity called Blog. Click Next when you're ready. Figure 10-28 shows the enable entities for SharePoint process.

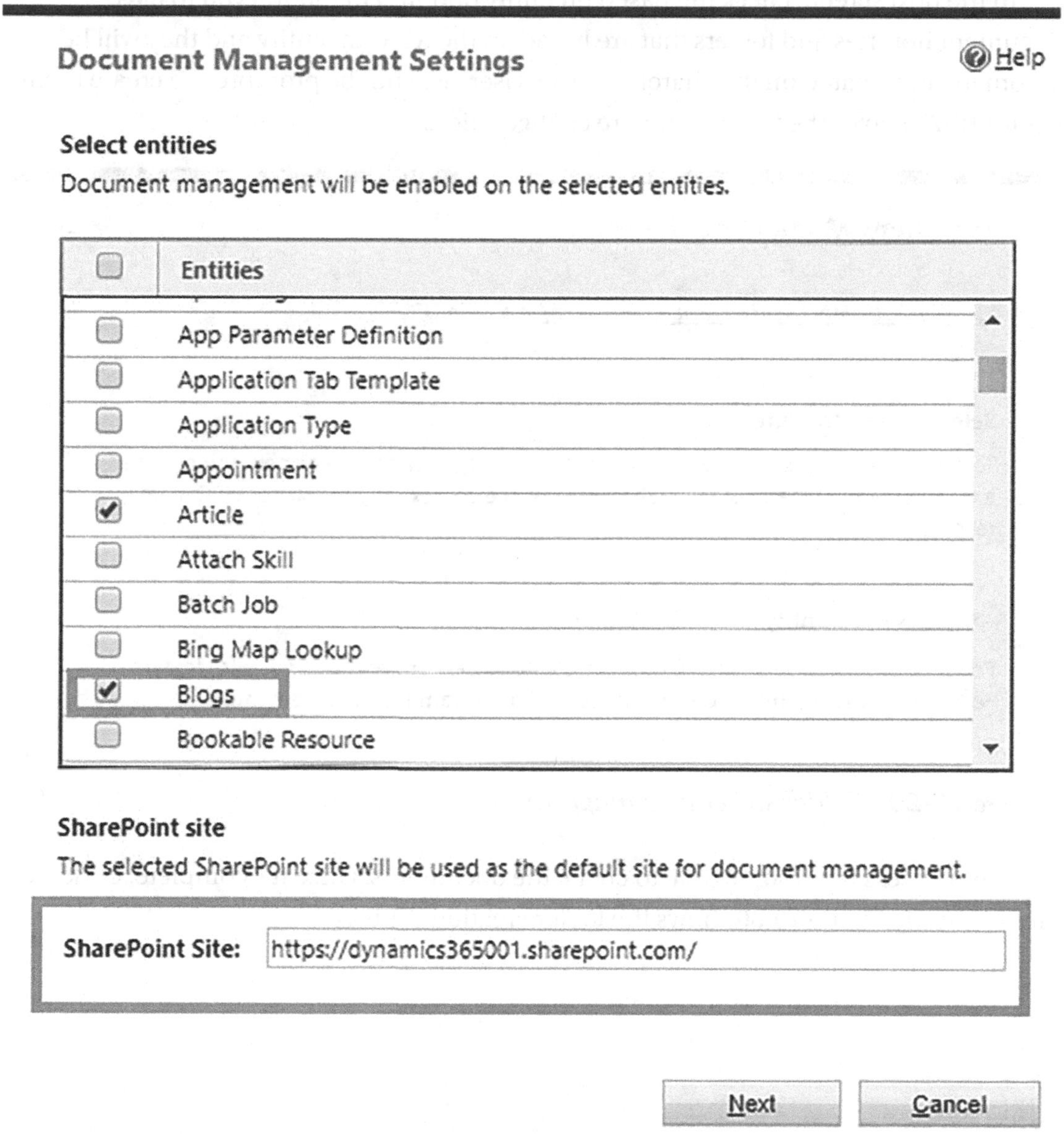

Document Management Settings   ⑦ Help

Select entities
Document management will be enabled on the selected entities.

	Entities
☐	App Parameter Definition
☐	Application Tab Template
☐	Application Type
☐	Appointment
☑	Article
☐	Attach Skill
☐	Batch Job
☐	Bing Map Lookup
☑	Blogs
☐	Bookable Resource

SharePoint site
The selected SharePoint site will be used as the default site for document management.

SharePoint Site: https://dynamics365001.sharepoint.com/

Next   Cancel

Figure 10-28. *Enable entities for SharePoint*

You can see the SharePoint Site field in Figure 10-28. As you have not created a site in SharePoint, you can enter the base URL of the SharePoint site as `https://orgname.sharepoint.com`.

In the next screen, check the Based on Entity option. This allows you to have document libraries and folders that are based on the Account entity and they will be automatically created on the SharePoint site. Users will not be prompted to create them. Figure 10-29 shows the folder structure configuration.

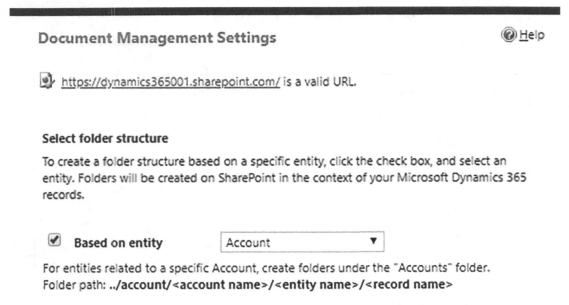

Figure 10-29. *Folder structure configuration*

This process takes some time to create the documents. Once it's complete, click the Finish button. Figure 10-30 shows the folder creation status.

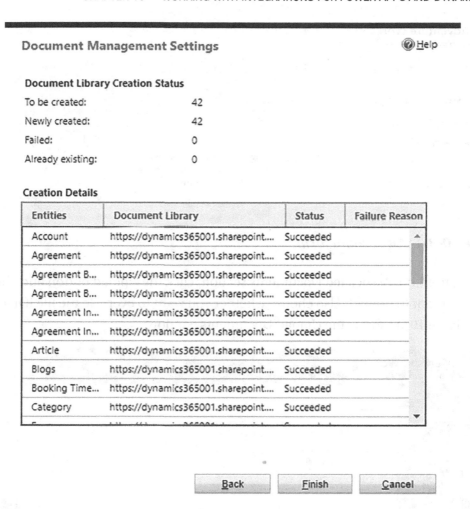

Figure 10-30. *Folder creation status*

Step 4: Store a Document in SharePoint

This section explains how to store a document in the SharePoint account you just configured.

Log in to Dynamics 365 CE and open an account. Click the Related tab to choose the Document option. Figure 10-31 shows an account form.

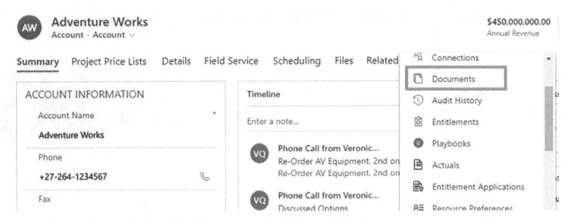

Figure 10-31. *An account form*

Now, from the Associated Documents section, click the Upload button and choose your document to upload. Also choose whether you want to override the file if it already exists. Figure 10-32 shows the Upload Documents window.

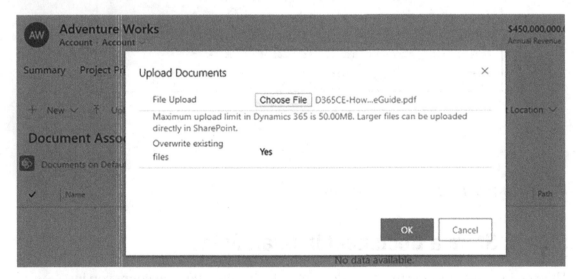

Figure 10-32. *The Upload Documents window*

Now if you log in to SharePoint, the uploaded document will appear inside the account directory with the GUID of the appended record. Figure 10-33 shows the document uploaded screen.

Figure 10-33. *Document uploaded screen*

If you also click the uploaded document from Dynamics 365 CE, it will open in your SharePoint location. Figure 10-34 shows the item uploaded view.

Figure 10-34. *Item uploaded view*

When you click the document, it will open, as shown in Figure 10-35.

Figure 10-35. *The uploaded document has been opened*

If you want to edit the SharePoint sites, go to Advanced Settings and then to Document Management. Select the SharePoint Sites and Document Management settings and edit them.

OneDrive Business Integration with Power Apps

Integrating OneDrive with Dynamics 365 is straightforward. Use the following steps to work through the process of integration.

Step 1: Enable the Integration Settings in Dynamics 365 CE

Log in to Dynamics 365 CE and navigate to Advanced Settings ➤ Settings ➤ Document Management and then click Enable OneDrive for Business. Figure 10-36 shows how to enable OneDrive.

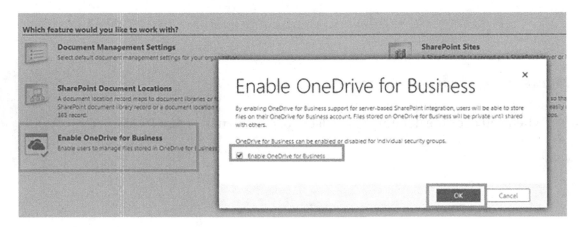

Figure 10-36. *Enabling OneDrive*

Click the checkbox and choose OK to finish. Once this step is done, another option becomes visible, called OneDrive for Business Folder Settings. At this stage, you can change the name of the folder. The default folder name is Dynamics365. Figure 10-37 shows the OneDrive folder setting.

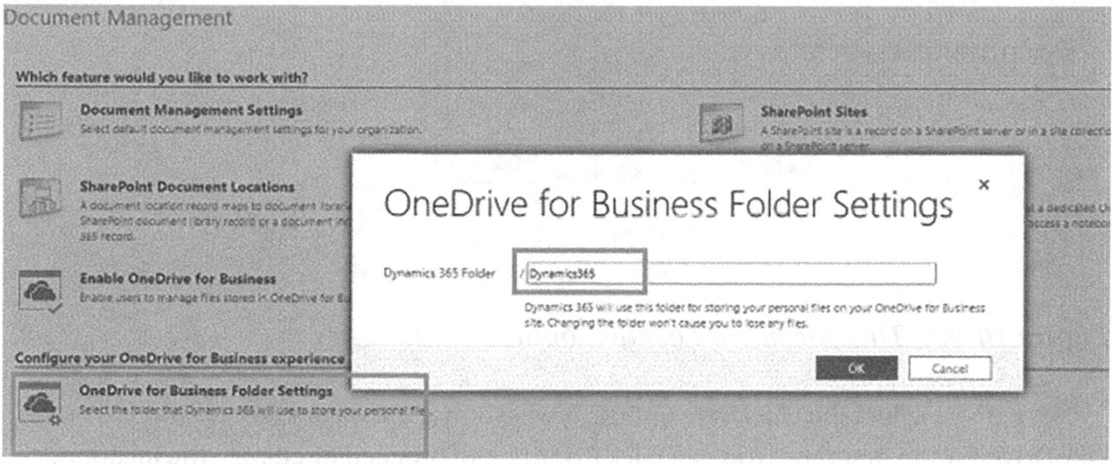

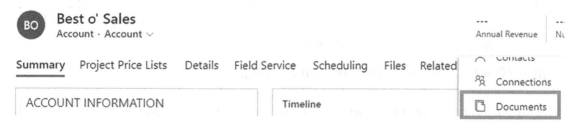

Figure 10-37. *OneDrive folder setting*

Proceed by clicking OK to complete this step.

Step 2: Go to an Account Record and Upload a Document to OneDrive

Log in to the Dynamics 365 Sales app and click an account. Then click the Related tab to choose the Documents option. Figure 10-38 shows the Documents option for the account.

Best o' Sales
Account · Account ⌄

--- Annual Revenue   N...

Summary   Project Price Lists   Details   Field Service   Scheduling   Files   Related   ⌒ Contacts

⌒ Connections

ACCOUNT INFORMATION   Timeline   □ Documents

Figure 10-38. *Documents option for account*

Now you have to choose the Document Location to select OneDrive from the Document Associated view. Figure 10-39 shows the Document Location option.

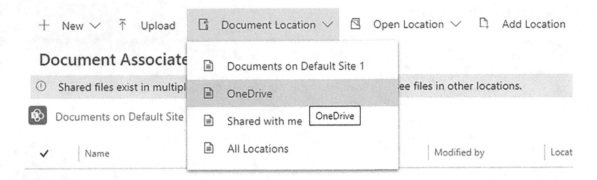

Figure 10-39. *The Document Location option*

When you select the OneDrive option, it will show a message asking if you are using OneDrive for the first time. You can click Continue to proceed or change the location. Figure 10-40 shows this document location option prompt.

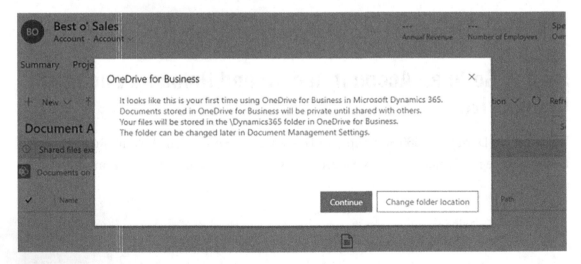

Figure 10-40. *Document location option prompt*

Now you can upload a file using the Upload option. Once the file has been uploaded, it will appear in the list. Figure 10-41 shows the document uploaded in OneDrive.

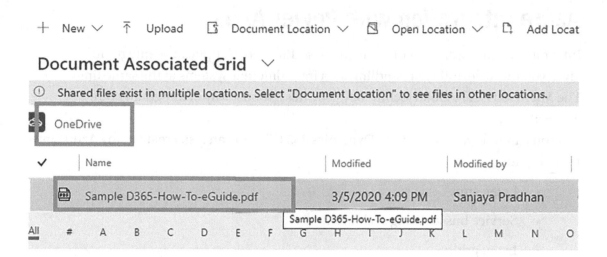

Figure 10-41. Document uploaded in OneDrive

When you click this item, it will open the file in OneDrive. If you go to OneDrive you can see the Dynamics365 folder, as you selected it during the initial configuration. Figure 10-42 shows the document uploaded in OneDrive.

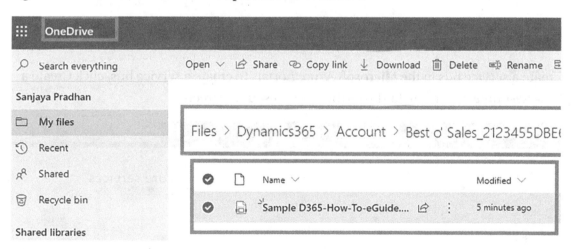

Figure 10-42. Document uploaded in OneDrive

Azure Integration with Power Apps

Integration is an essential part of all business. Enterprise application integration gives you more flexibility in handling data from different systems at the same time. The Microsoft Azure cloud technology provides a robust way of integrating other applications.

You can integrate Azure with Dynamics 365 CE. You can also create many Azure apps for integration:

- Logic apps

- Service busses using Webhook

- Event grids

- Azure functions

- Web API using Client ID and the ADAL concept

Try the following steps to learn how to integrate an Azure bus from Dynamics 365 and read data in using the service bus and queue.

Step 1: Create a Service Bus in Azure

Create a service bus in the Microsoft Azure portal. To create a service bus, click Create a New Resource. Figure 10-43 shows the Azure resource screen.

Figure 10-43. *Azure resource screen*

On the New screen, choose Integration and select Service Bus, as shown in Figure 10-44.

436

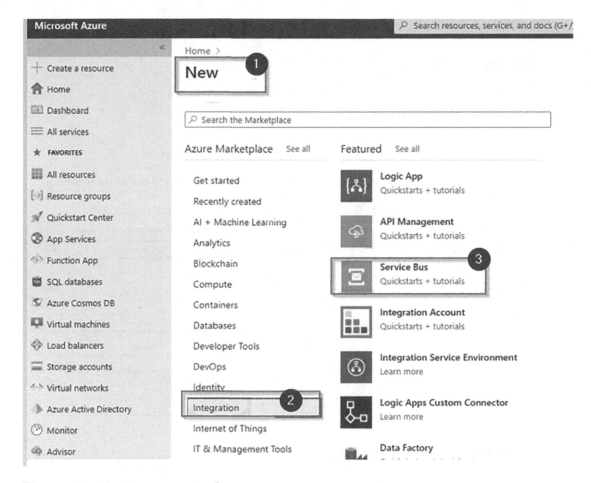

Figure 10-44. *Azure service bus app*

The next screen will prompt you to provide the subscription, resource group, namespace name, location, and pricing tier. To read more about Azure subscriptions, see https://docs.microsoft.com/en-us/azure/azure-resource-manager/management/azure-subscription-service-limits. Follow these steps:

1. Choose your Azure subscription correctly.

2. Select a resource group if one has already been created or create a new resource group.

3. Provide a unique namespace for the service bus.

4. Choose a location.

5. Choose the appropriate pricing tier. For this example, I use Basic.

Figure 10-45 shows the Create Resource review page.

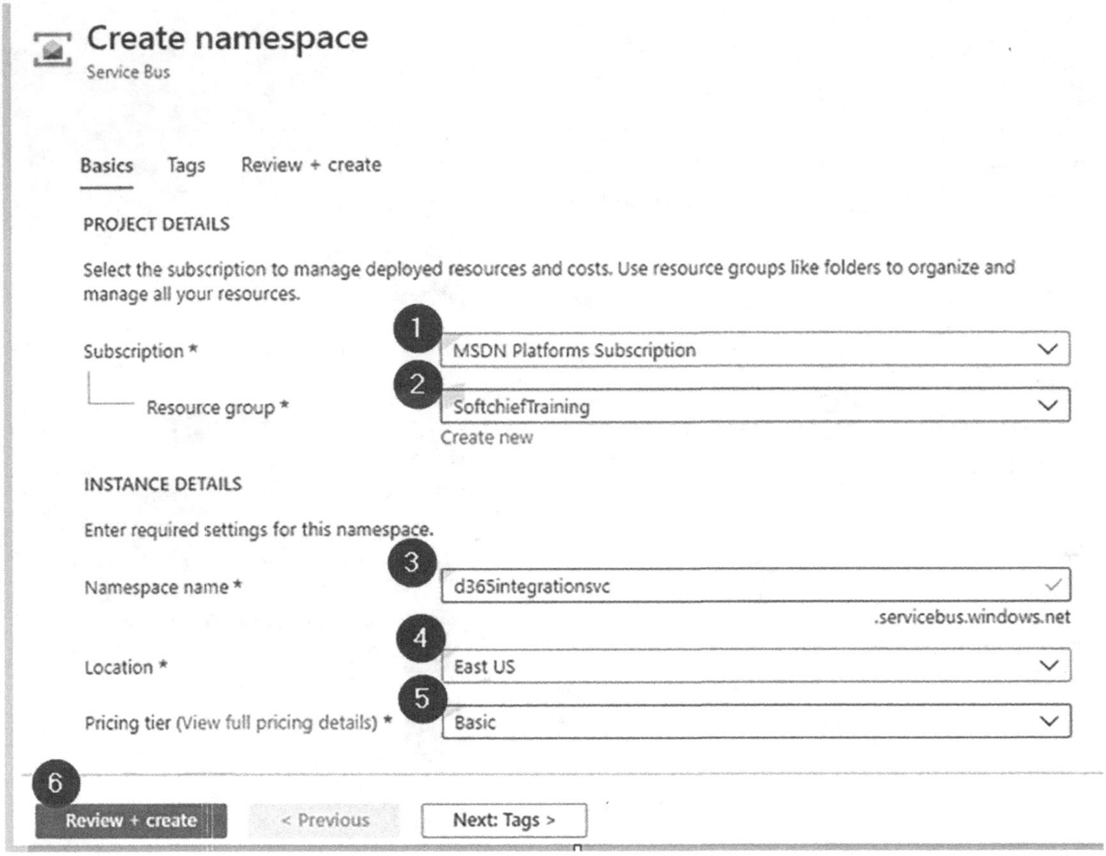

Figure 10-45. *Create Resource review page*

Click Review + Create. This will validate your details and allow you to proceed. Figure 10-46 shows the review resource step.

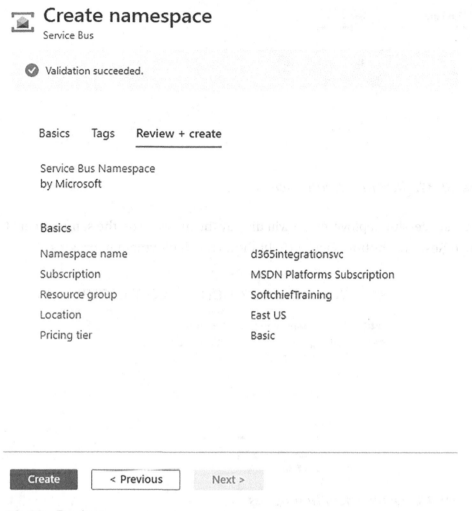

Figure 10-46. *Review resource step*

Now click Create. This will start creating the resource and will display a Deployment in Progress screen. Figure 10-47 shows the resource created screen.

Figure 10-47. *Resource created screen*

After successful deployment, it will display the message on the same screen. Click the Go to Resource button. Figure 10-48 shows the deployment in progress.

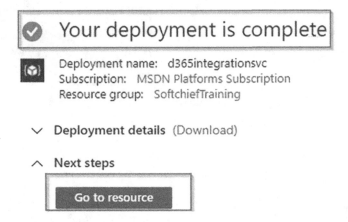

Figure 10-48. *Deployment in progress*

Go to Resource will take you to the service bus resource, where you can do much more. Figure 10-49 shows that the service bus has been created.

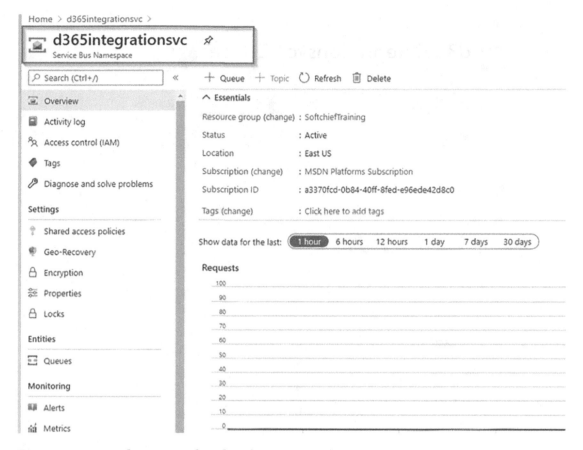

Figure 10-49. *The service bus has been created*

Step 2: Create a Queue Inside the Service Bus

After the service bus has been created, you need to add a queue inside it. Follow the steps in this section to add a queue inside a service bus.

From the Service Bus window, click the Queue option on the left side. Figure 10-50 shows the Queue Creation option.

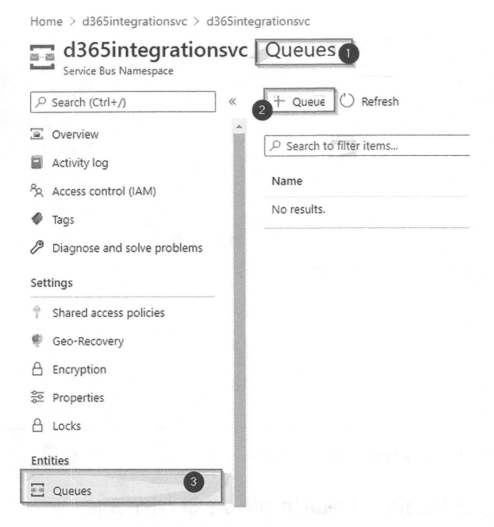

Figure 10-50. *Queue creation option*

In the new Queue Creation window, provide a queue name and click Create. This will create a queue inside the service bus. Figure 10-51 shows the created queue.

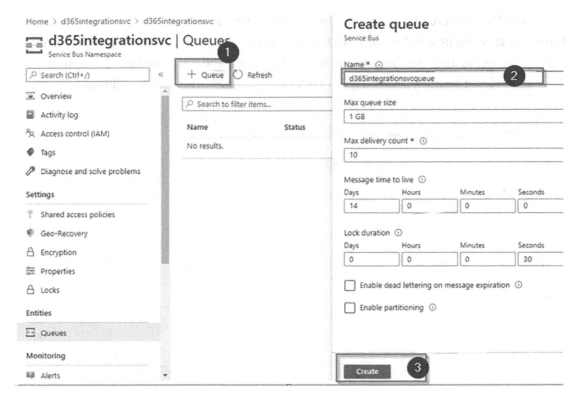

Figure 10-51. *Created queue*

Now you have to click the newly created queue, which will show the details about the queue. Figure 10-52 shows the queue's details.

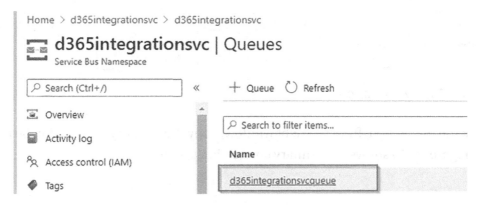

Figure 10-52. *Details about the newly created queue*

In the Details screen, navigate to the Shared Access Policy option. Click the +Add button to create a new SAS policy. An SAS is required to specify the permission that you want to assign to a service bus queue. Name the policy and click the Manage option. After that, click Create to finish. Figure 10-53 shows the shared access policies.

Figure 10-53. *Shared access policies*

You should now see the queue as shown in Figure 10-54.

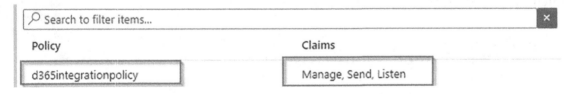

Figure 10-54. *Queue success*

Click the queue and, from the right window, copy the Primary Connection String option. Figure 10-55 shows the primary connection screen.

Figure 10-55. *Primary connection screen*

Paste the copied string to Notepad, as you will use it at a later stage. The connection string looks like this:

```
Endpoint=sb://d365integrationsvc.servicebus.windows.net/;Shared
AccessKeyName=d365integrationpolicy;SharedAccessKey=vMW/
JtON+gsckXB43OK41Uc4zTCIF9Qi4szjAp9q5pg=;EntityPath=d365integrationsvcqueue
```

Figure 10-56 also shows the connection string.

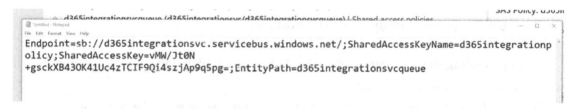

Figure 10-56. *The connection string*

You have now completed the queue creation process. The next step uses the Plugin Registration tool for further integration.

Step 3: Create Steps in the Plugin Registration Tool for Integration

Open the Plugin Registration tool from the NuGet Manager or from the Dynamics 365 SDK. Connect your Dynamics 365 organization using your credentials. Make sure you provide the correct username and passwords to log in, as shown in Figure 10-57.

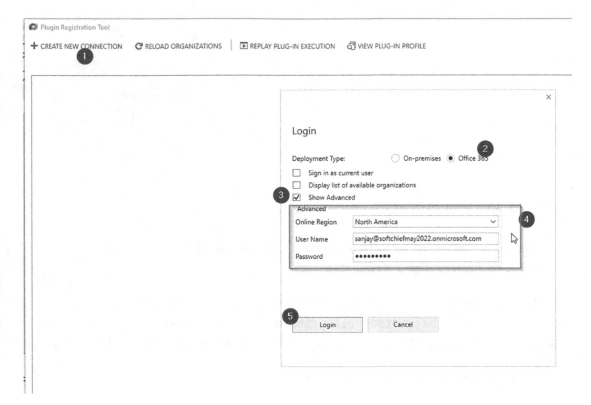

Figure 10-57. *Connect Plugin Registration tool*

After providing the appropriate details, click Login, which will list all the plugins installed in your current environment.

Now click the Register option from the top and choose Register New Service Endpoint. Figure 10-58 shows the Register New Service Endpoint option.

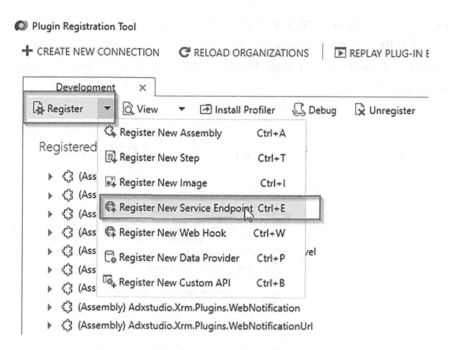

Figure 10-58. *Register New Service Endpoint option*

In the next screen, choose Let's Start with the Connection. Paste the connection string you copied from the queue property. Figure 10-59 shows the connection string inside the Plugin Registration tool.

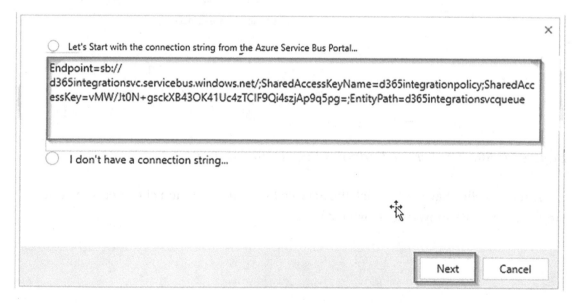

Figure 10-59. *Connection string inside the Plugin Registration tool*

After pasting in the connection string, click Next. In the next screen, you have to set up more details. You have to provide the queue name and set the Message Format to JSON, as well as some other details. Figure 10-60 shows the Service Endpoint Registration option.

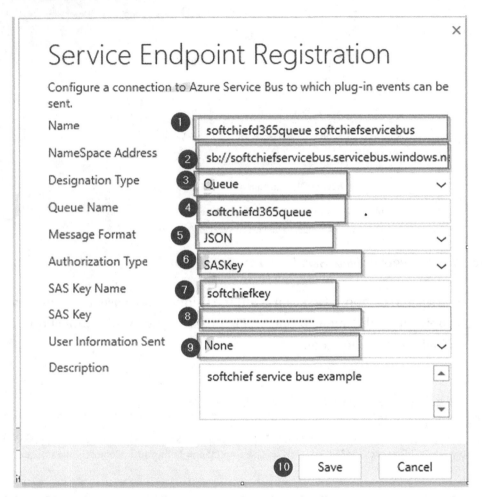

Figure 10-60. *The Service Endpoint Registration option*

After you click Save, right-click the Service Endpoint and then click Register New Step. Figure 10-61 shows the register step.

⊿ ⊕ (ServiceEndpoint) softchiefd365queue so
    ▤ (Step) softchiefd365queue softchiefse
▸ ⊕ (WebHook) AccountPluginHook
▸ ⊟ (Data Source) Available Times Data Sour
▸ ⊟ (Data Source) Case Suggestions Data So
▸ ⊟ (Data Source) Component Layer Data So

✚ Register New Assembly	Ctrl+A
▣ Register New Step	Ctrl+T
▣ Register New Image	Ctrl+I
⊕ Register New Service Endpoint	Ctrl+E

Figure 10-61. *The register step*

Choose Create for the Message and Account for the Primary Entity. The
Asynchronous Server option should be enabled and the stage should be set to
PostOperation. Figure 10-62 shows the register step details.

Figure 10-62. *Register step details*

After providing the details, click Register New Step. Now you are ready to capture
messages and entity contexts in an Azure queue from Dynamics 365 whenever an
account is created.

Step 4: Create a Logic App to Read the Message and Send to Email

Create a Logic app with the following steps in order to receive a message from the queue. Then wait 20 seconds and send the content in an email. Figure 10-63 shows the Logic app.

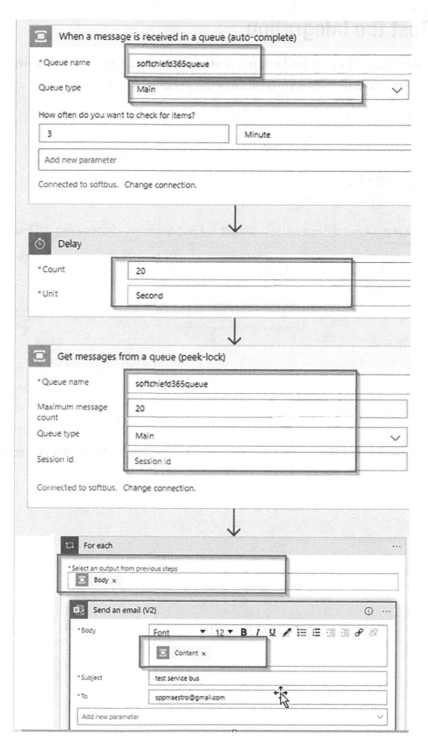

Figure 10-63. *The Logic app*

Step 5: Test the Integration

Open Dynamics 365 and the Sales Hub to create an account. Create an account called MSFT Account and save it. Figure 10-64 shows the account form.

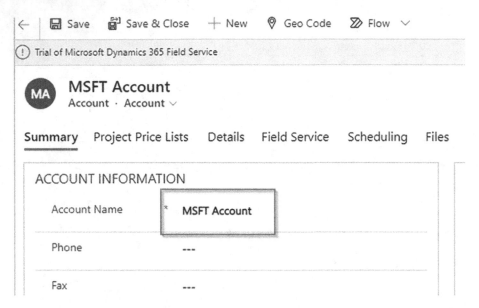

Figure 10-64. *The account form*

Now go to the Azure queue and click Refresh. You will see one message, as shown in Figure 10-65.

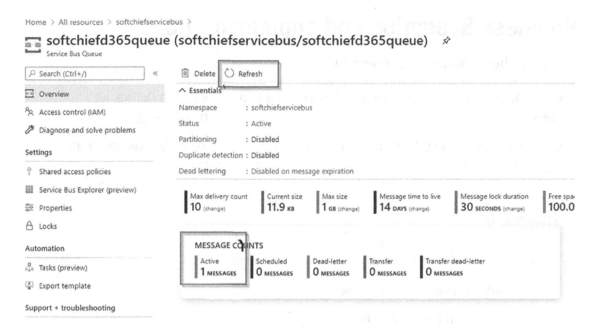

Figure 10-65. *Queue refresh screen*

After a few seconds, you will receive an email with the content, as shown in Figure 10-66.

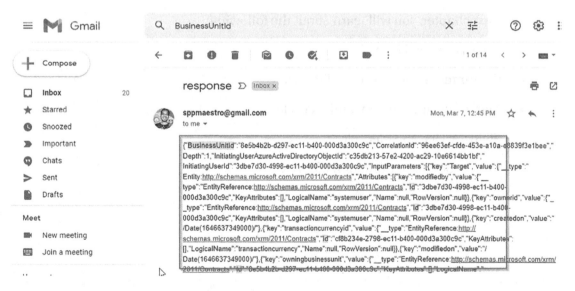

Figure 10-66. *The email received screen*

You can extract further information from JSON.

Business Scenarios and Implementations

Complete the following assignments for practice.

1 Users should be able to track email activities for students in Outlook.	Integrate Outlook with Dynamics 365.
2 Users should be able to upload student documents in SharePoint from Dynamics 365.	Integrate SharePoint with Dynamics 365.

Summary

In this chapter, you learned about the following concepts:

- Outlook integration in Power Apps

- SharePoint integration in Power Apps

- OneDrive integration in Power Apps

- Azure integration in Power Apps

- Business scenarios and implementations

In the next chapter, you will learn about the following:

- Sales Hub app Lifecycle

- Customer Service Hub app lifecycle

- Marketing app concept and lifecycle

- Field Service app lifecycle

- Project Service automation lifecycle

Dynamics 365 CE Core Apps

Dynamics 365 is a combination of CRM and ERP products. Dynamics 365 CE includes the following apps:

- Sales Hub

- Customer Service Hub

- Marketing app

- Field Service app

- Project Service Automation app

In this chapter, you learn about these modules. The Dynamics 365 CE apps are model-driven Power Apps created by Microsoft.

Sales Hub App Lifecycle

This section discusses how the sales process works and the lifecycle of a typical sales process in Dynamics 365 Customer Engagement.

The Sales module consists of the following steps:

1. Lead Capture ➤ Follow-up ➤ Lead Qualification/Disqualification

2. Contact setup

3. Account setup

4. Competitor setup

5. Product catalog

© Sanjaya Prakash Pradhan 2022
S. Prakash Pradhan, *Power Platform and Dynamics 365 CE for Absolute Beginners*,
https://doi.org/10.1007/978-1-4842-8600-5_11

6. Opportunity management

7. Quote management

8. Order management

9. Invoice management

10. Goal MANAGEMENT

Figure 11-1 shows the typical sales lifecycle flow.

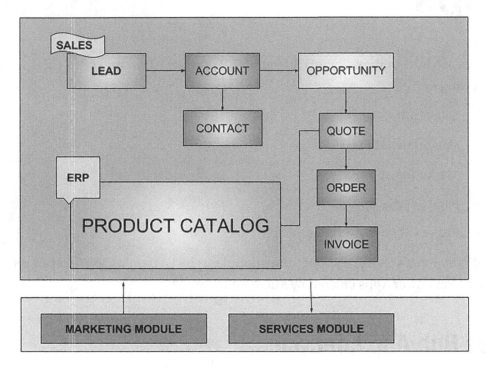

Figure 11-1. *Typical sales process lifecycle*

Lead Capture

You may have heard the phrase, "The customer is the king." Every organization depends on its customers to make a profit. Dynamics 365 CE provides a robust and powerful way to handle sales process-related activities.

The sales process in Dynamics 365 Customer Engagement (CE) starts with a lead record entry in the system. A *lead* represents any person or organization that a company might have the potential to do business with. In other words, a lead is a prospective customer (individual/business organization), created when an individual or business shows interest and provides contact information for communication purposes. Businesses capture leads through advertising (online/offline), trade shows, direct mailings, and other marketing campaigns. The Dynamics 365 Marketing app handles all marketing department activities. Figure 11-2 shows the Open Leads page.

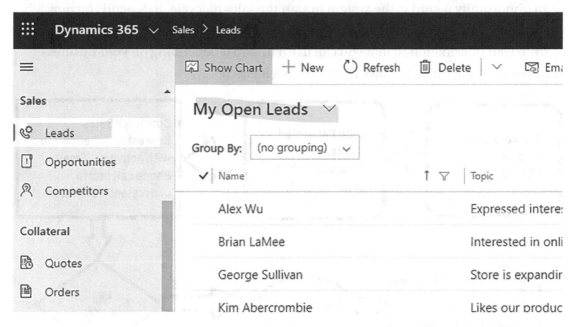

Figure 11-2. *The Open Leads page*

A salesperson enters the lead's information in the Lead entity available in Dynamics 365 Customer Engagement. You only need a first name and last name and a topic describing the lead in order to create an entry in the system. Users can provide additional information as well.

An example of a lead is: TOPIC: 100 Laptop for Contoso Corp. Last Name: Robert Clay.

After a lead record has been created in the system, the salesperson performs the follow-up activities by sending emails, creating appointments, and making phone calls. This way, they can capture more information about the lead's interest and proceed with the next process, called lead qualification/disqualification. Microsoft Dynamics 365 stores these follow-up activities in the Activities record (Email, Task, Meetings, and Appointment) of the system.

Leads can be qualified or disqualified. All qualified leads automatically have a default contact and an opportunity record in the system. When a lead gets disqualified, the system stops the sales process. But the system stores this information for future campaigns as a future prospect.

Some organizations do not follow this lead-creation process but use the creation of an opportunity record in the system to start the sales lifecycle. It depends on how you want to organize your sales data. Lead is an out-of-the-box entity that allows you to store lead information so that you can use it or skip it depending on your business requirements. Figure 11-3 shows the marketing lifecycle.

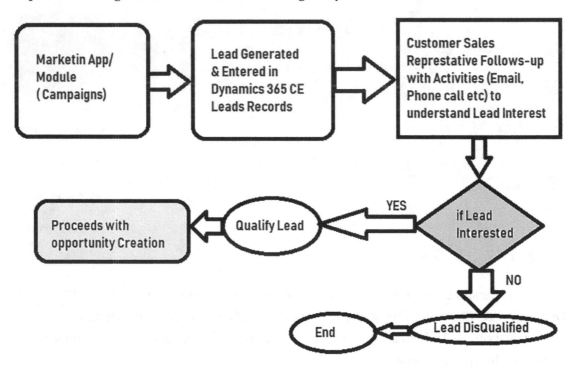

Figure 11-3. *Marketing lifecycle*

Contact Setup

Contacts are individual people with whom you have a relationship. Generally, these are customers or contacts of customers. Contacts are often related to an account, but certain organizations and businesses may serve or sell to individual consumers, and so most of the contacts will not be under accounts.

You can create a contact in the system independently or through a lead qualification process. A contact is automatically created after a lead is qualified, which creates an opportunity record in the system.

Contacts integrate with the contacts in Microsoft Outlook, so it is important to understand that when fields on the contact record are updated, that change may synchronize to Outlook for one or more users, depending on the synchronization settings. Figure 11-4 shows the active contacts.

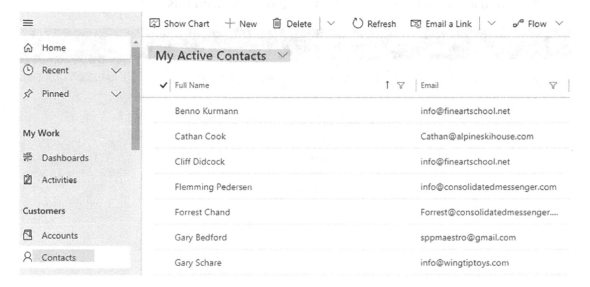

Figure 11-4. *Active contacts*

Contact records are normally created for individual people, but accounts are created for organizations.

Notes

- A contact can be a parent to every other entity except accounts and contacts.

- A contact can have only one account as its parent.

- A contact can be marked as the primary contact person for an account.

Account Setup

Accounts are organizations with which you have a relationship. Since Microsoft Dynamics 365 is a customer engagement solution, this is where customers reside in your database. However, accounts can also contain other types of records, including prospects, vendors, business partners, and other organizations that interact with your organization. Businesses generally store customer data in a contact record and vendor information in an account. Figure 11-5 shows the active accounts.

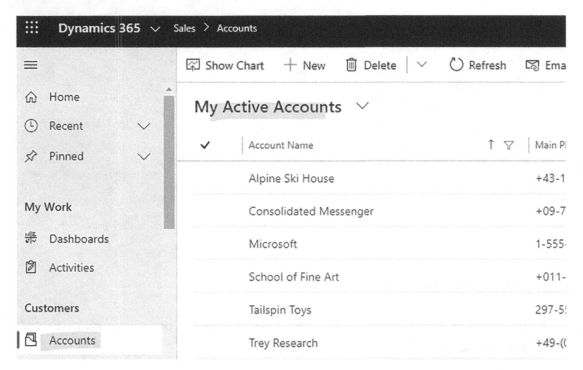

Figure 11-5. *Active accounts*

Example: Lead: 100 laptop Required by Peter from Wipro, Contact: Peter Parker, Account: Wipro.

Notes

- An account can be a parent to almost any other entity. This includes another account.

- An account can be a stand-alone entity.

- An account can have only one account as its parent.

- Accounts can have multiple children accounts and children contacts.

Competitor Setup

During the sale process identification stage, salespeople may add competitors for that specific sale so that at a later stage it can help generate reports for campaign activities. Figure 11-6 shows the active competitors.

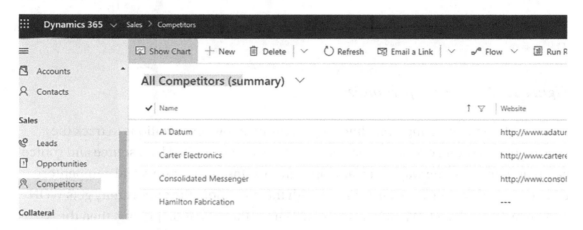

Figure 11-6. *Active competitors*

These represent third-party organizations that are competing with the organization for the services required by the customer.

Opportunity Management

The lead qualification process automatically generates an Opportunity record in the system. Users can also manually create an opportunity in the system.

Opportunities in Microsoft Dynamics 365 are the core record types in the sales process used by the sales team. Opportunities represent a potential sale for a specific customer. Creating an opportunity adds this potential sale to the sales pipeline and therefore puts it on the radar of the sales manager, who may be holding the team responsible for the progress of opportunities. Figure 11-7 shows the active opportunities.

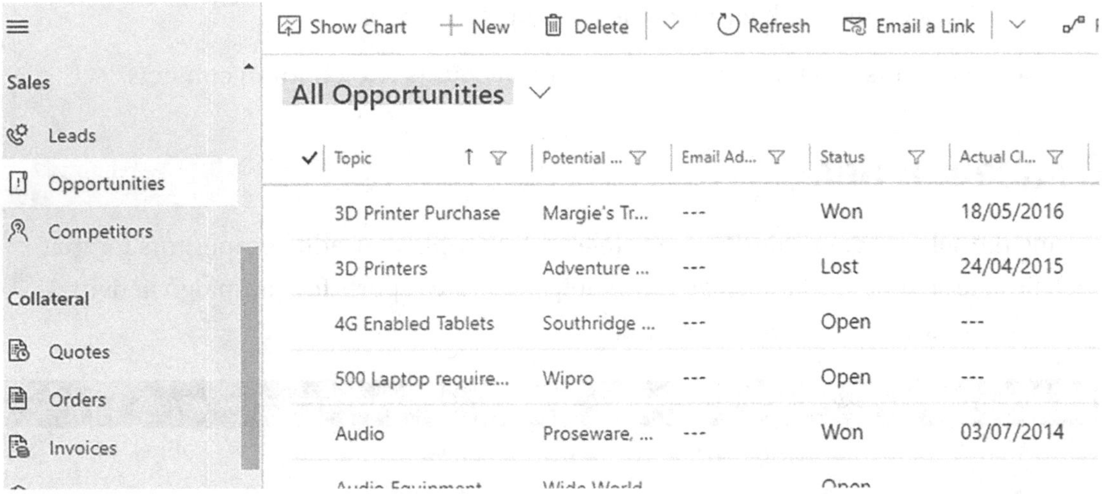

Figure 11-7. *Active opportunities*

In addition to creating a pipeline, opportunities allow organizations to track the success of marketing efforts by tracking sales back to the original lead source and source campaign. In the same way, when an opportunity is lost, lost reasons and competitors can be tracked. When a customer agrees with the quotation, the opportunity gets WON and an order is placed. When a customer disagrees the quotation pricing, then the opportunity becomes LOST and the Sales lifecycle stops.

In Dynamics 365 CE, the sales process is guided by an out-of-the-box Business Process Flow (BPF), called Opportunity Sales Process, by which all salespersons follow to close a sale, starting from lead qualification to invoice creation. The business process involves stages, such as Qualify, Develop, Propose, and Close. You can change or customize the Business Process Flow according to your business's process. Figure 11-8 shows the opportunity form.

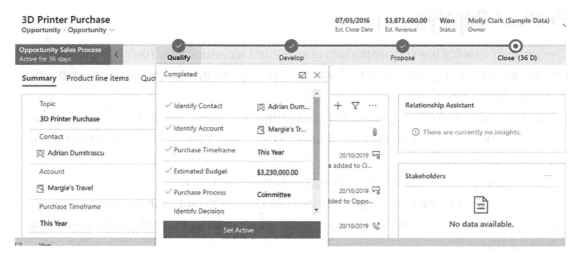

Figure 11-8. *Opportunity form*

Opportunity contains all products lines items selected by the customer. At this stage, the user provides discounts, promotions, and other entitlements to the customer to prepare a final cost. Figure 11-9 shows the product lines inside the opportunity.

Figure 11-9. *Product lines inside an opportunity*

Price List and Revenue are also associated with the opportunity at this phase. For proper opportunity management, the product catalog setup is required.

Product Catalog

The *product catalog* is a very important concept in Dynamics 365. You can configure products with pricing information, discount lists, unit groups, price lists, and products and their families.

In Dynamics 365 CE, the Inventory entity from the Operation and Finance module syncs with the product catalog of the Sales module. Otherwise, you can create products in Dynamics 365 CE.

This configuration can be done using the Settings ➤ Business Product Catalog option. After the product Catalog Setup, you can use the products in Opportunities when creating an opportunity. You can watch the full product catalog configuration using the following URL:

```
https://youtube.com/playlist?list=PLUOornfOhw6eO41NdWCBayObopPsLQ_b4
```

Quote Management

After the opportunity is created in the system with identified product lines and pricing information details, a quote can be created. A quote contains the products or services that the customer is interested in and the proposed price. After the customer review, they agree to continue placing the order. The quotation contains the product or service items with the defined price list, discount list, and so on.

Dynamics 365 CE captures the list of product line items, which the company offers to the client as a quote. The products are associated with the quote line. Along with the product information, this also captures the contact details of the prime contact, shipping information, and discount, if any. Figure 11-10 shows the new quote.

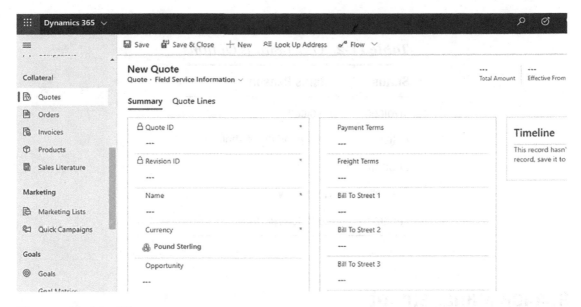

Figure 11-10. *The new quote*

An active quote is WON if the customer agrees with the proposed quotation information and pricing; otherwise, it is LOST. The Quote Status options are listed in Table 11-1.

Table 11-1. *Quote Status Options*

Status	Status Reason
DRAFT	In-progress
ACTIVE	In-progress / Open
WON	Won
CLOSED	Lost/Cancelled/Revised

Order Management

Orders are sale confirmations that need to be placed and invoiced for further logistics. Dynamics 365 Sales may also offer product bundles or product families to make it easier for you to choose products for upsell and cross-sell. If you've already prepared a quote for your customer, you can create an order from that quote. A quote is converted into an order if it is WON.

465

The Order Status options are listed in Table 11-2.

Table 11-2. *Order Status Options*

Status	Status Reason
Invoiced	Invoiced
Active	New/pending/on-hold
Submitted	In-progress
Cancelled	No money
Fulfilled	Complete/partial

Invoice Management

After an order is placed successfully, the invoices are generated in the system. Payments are collected using the Dynamics 365 Finance system. Figure 11-11 shows a new invoice.

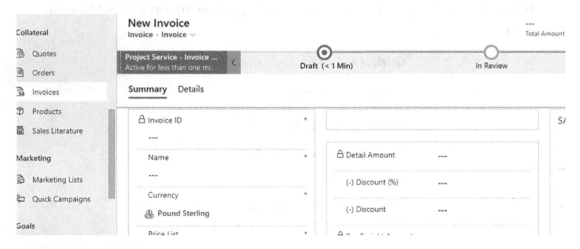

Figure 11-11. *A new invoice*

When the customer accepts the terms and conditions in the quote, the quote is converted into an invoice. Dynamics 365 CE captures the same information as the quote; however, it acts as a formal contract between the organization and the customer.

The sales process diagram is shown in Figure 11-12.

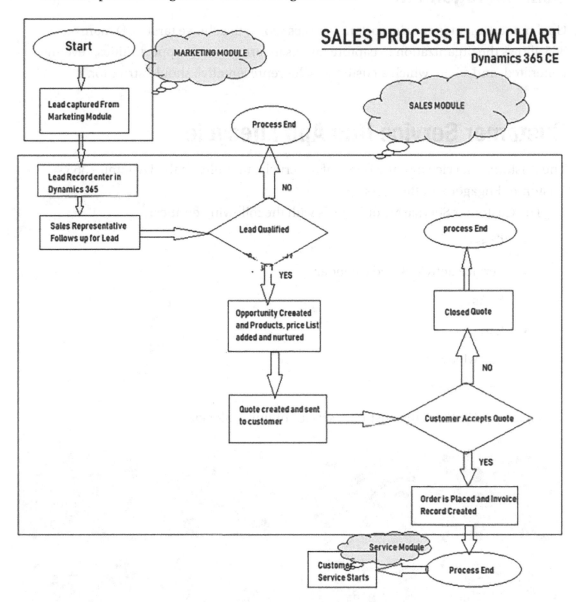

Figure 11-12. *Sales process flowchart*

Goal Management

Goal management is very important for salespeople to achieve targets. Dynamics 365 allows the organization to capture targets in terms of won opportunities, revenue generated, and so on, which a customer sales representative should strive for.

Customer Service Hub App Lifecycle

The Customer Service module is one of the crucial modules in the Dynamics 365 Customer Engagement Business app.

The Customer Service Module deals with the following entities:

- Cases

- Service activities and calendar

- SLAs

- Queues

- Knowledgebases

- Entitlements

Figure 11-13 shows the customer service building blocks.

Figure 11-13. *Customer service building blocks*

Every organization must have a process to deal with customer issues and complaints. Dynamics 365 Customer Engagement provides a streamlined and robust customer service module that addresses all the needs of the customer service operations.

Cases

A *case* in Dynamics 365 CE represents a record of a customer complaint or a query regarding a product or service. When customers call a Business Customer Service Representative (CSR), the CSR creates a case in the system to capture the information. Figure 11-14 shows a case record.

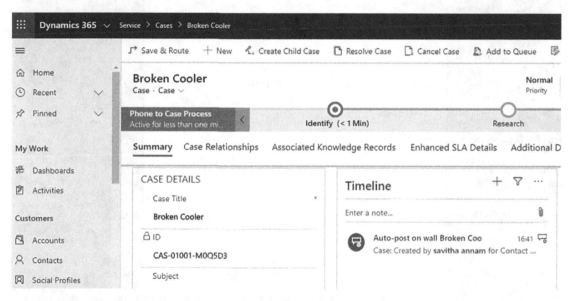

***Figure 11-14.** Case record*

Creating a case record includes the customer query or service-related information and the saved record.

At this stage of case creation, the CSR adds the related information about the current case, such as any similar cases, child cases, knowledgebase records, SLA information, and the type of the case (problem/question/request).

After recording all the required information from the customer, the CSR routes the case to a concerned engineer to look into the matter. Activities like emails and phone calls are created during the research stage of the case.

The user can convert the case to a work order so that the site engineer will visit the customer's site for troubleshooting.

Finally, with proper research, the user will resolve the case by clicking the Resolve Case button. At this stage, the user has to note the Resolution type as problem solved/ information provided. Figure 11-15 shows a resolved case.

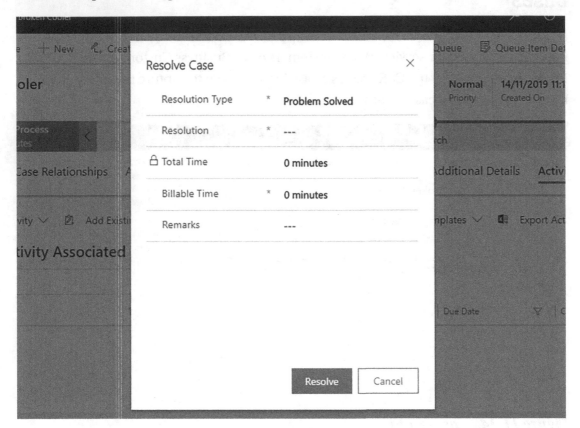

Figure 11-15. *Resolved case*

After giving all this information, the case is resolved and will be read-only. In some cases, a resolved case can be reopened/reactivated.

Service Activities and Calendar

This is a scheduling component in Dynamics 365 and it's used to view and manage the service activities. Service activities are activity records created against a case in the system.

SLA (Service Line Agreement)

These represent the features of Dynamics 365 that can be used for configuring metrics to attain a service level. An SLA is the time taken to solve a support request. Every customer request or complaint must be resolved by a certain time limit, which is predefined by the organization using SLA records.

Queues

Queues act as holding containers for work items; for example, you can queue the cases that are to be resolved.

Knowledgebase

This provides a process for submitting, approving, and publishing articles about an organization's products and services. They help the customer service representatives find information about products and services and find solutions for customers.

Entitlements

Entitlements represent the level of support that is available to an eligible customer.

Marketing (Legacy) App Concept and Lifecycle

Most organizations spend a lot of money marketing their business products and services. Dynamics 365 CE provides a very flexible way of handling all marketing issues for all types of businesses. It provides built-in entities to store marketing data and robust insight for salespeople to make decisions during the lead-capture process.

The Dynamics 365 Marketing app provides the following entities to hold marketing related data for the lifecycle:

- Marketing lists
- Campaigns
- Campaign activities
- Targeted products
- Sales literature

- Campaign responses

- Lead capture/opportunity creation

Figure 11-16 shows the marketing lifecycle.

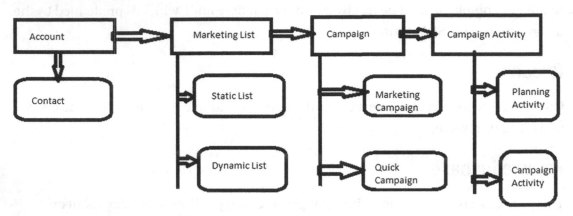

Figure 11-16. *Marketing lifecycle*

This is the most important module of all. Sales depend on the marketing department. The lifecycle of a Marketing module is explained in the following section.

Marketing List

The first and most important decision is creating marketing segments to organize contacts/accounts from the database into logical groups that match a company's marketing strategies.

In Dynamics 365, you can create a collection of segments to target the right audience—those you already know in some scenarios. For example, you can create a segment called "Customers who are frequently calling overseas calls" or "Customers who visited our boot camp". Segments like these, which you define by using a set of rules and conditions, are called *dynamic segments* (dynamic marketing list), because membership in these segments changes constantly and automatically based on information in your database. (Static segments—in the static marketing list—are populated by adding contacts explicitly, one at a time.) Figure 11-17 shows an active marketing list.

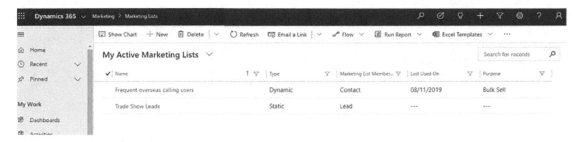

Figure 11-17. *Active marketing list*

Based on the List type (Dynamic/Static), the Member tab will be displayed and you can click the Manage Member button from the command bar. By selecting Look, you can select Accounts or Contacts and then add query rows, as shown in Figure 11-18.

Figure 11-18. *Dynamics marketing list query*

Click Find to see the results and then click Use Query to add the members to the Marketing list.

Note   Keep in mind that since this is a dynamic list, in the course of time, any contacts satisfying the criteria will automatically be added to it.

Campaign

After creating a marketing list, the organization creates the campaign. A *campaign* is a process of promoting products or services by setting up events such as trade shows and boot camps, creating flyers, and so on. Figure 11-19 shows an example campaign list.

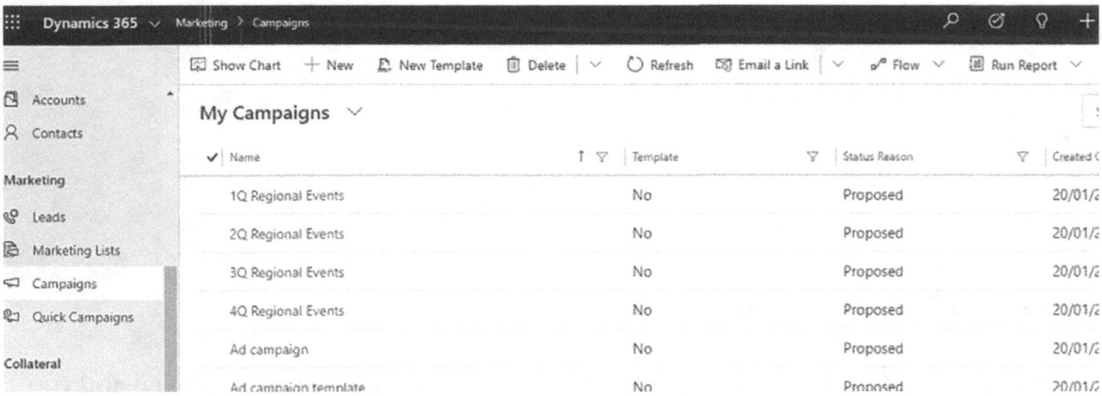

Figure 11-19. *Campaign list*

A marketing list is associated with a campaign to target the list of customers for that campaign. For example, a company may create a marketing list of the customers who are older than 40. This campaign provides a special discount on new products/services and sends campaign mailers to these customers in hopes of making new sales.

You can also create a quick campaign in Dynamics 365 CE, which is the same as a marketing campaign, but with limited functionality. Quick campaigns only support a single activity type and target only one list of customers.

Campaign Activities

During a campaign event, sales and marketing department users create many activities regarding the campaign to let customers know about it. These could be phone calls, emails, and so on. These are called *campaign activities*. Figure 11-20 shows the process of creating campaign activities.

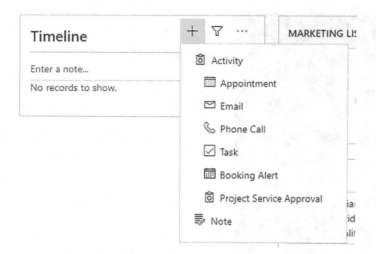

Figure 11-20. *Creating campaign activities*

You can create different types of campaign activities, including appointments, emails, phone calls, tasks, booking alerts, project service approvals, and so on.

Targeted Products

In the process of a campaign, you can associate products with the campaign that are required for discount and promotional offers. Figure 11-21 shows the process of adding a target product.

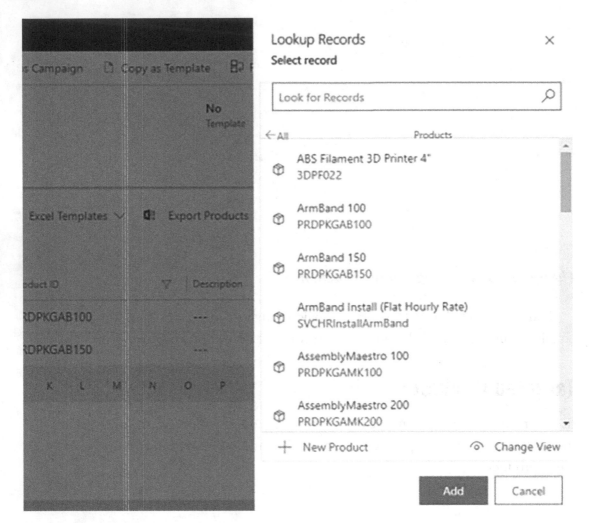

Figure 11-21. *Target product*

Sales Literature

Sales literature is the repository information about the products and services that are targeted for a campaign. Sales users can refer to sales documents when dealing with customers to help close a sale. Figure 11-22 shows example sales literature.

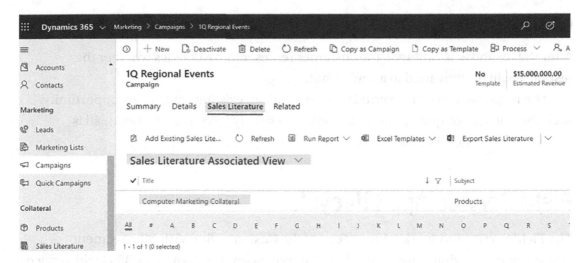

Figure 11-22. *Sales literature*

Campaign Response

A campaign response is the information or response captured from customers as a result of a campaign. Organizations capture the customer response and convert it into a potential sale. Figure 11-23 shows a campaign response.

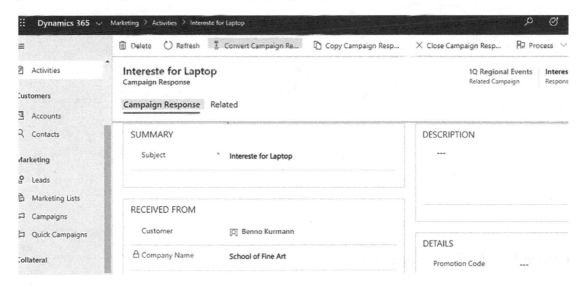

Figure 11-23. *Campaign response*

Lead Capture/Opportunity Creation

After the response is captured, the customer representative decides whether the response will be converted to a lead or not.

The response can be converted to a new lead, an existing lead, a new opportunity, account, contact, or quote. Or the response can simply be closed. If a new lead is generated, the sales lifecycle starts.

Field Service App Lifecycle

The Field Service module is a basic need of the Customer Site Visit Management system. In this module, businesses deal with processes. The Dynamics 365 Field Service business application helps organizations deliver onsite service to customer locations. The application combines workflow automation, scheduling, and mobility to set mobile workers up for success when they're onsite with customers fixing issues.

The first thing is to configure the Field Service in Dynamics 365 using the Dynamics 365 Field Service settings. Figure 11-24 shows the field service settings.

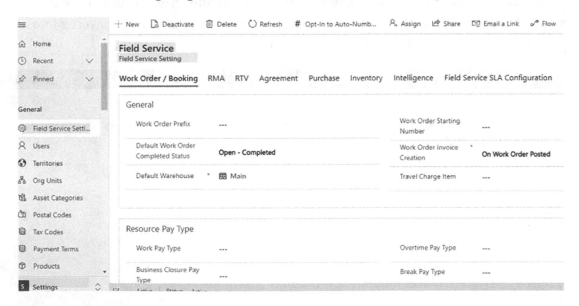

Figure 11-24. *Field service settings*

Fill in the details and save. The following entities are involved in the Field Service module:

- Work orders

- Bookings

- Schedule board

- Resource requirements

- Requirement groups

Figure 11-25 shows the work order form.

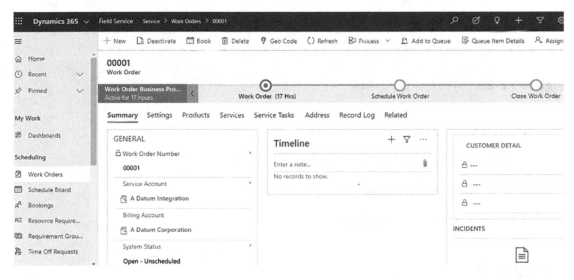

Figure 11-25. *Work order form*

Work Orders

Work orders contain the first bit of information captured from a customer query/
complaint through a case record. According to the information provided in the work
order, the site engineer visits the client location. A work order stores very important
information, as follows:

- Service account and billing account for the work order

- System status (unscheduled/scheduled/in progress/completed/
  posted/canceled)

- Type of work order

Figure 11-26 shows the work order types.

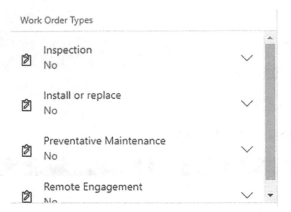

Figure 11-26. Work order types

- Work order pricing information

- Customer details and info address

- Products in discussion

- Other related information

Bookings

After successfully creating a work order with the required information, the customer representative can schedule the work order using the booking process. Geo Code and Bing Map can be used to identify the exact longitude and latitude of an address. Once the Booking button is clicked against a work order, the Schedule Board window opens, where you can provide additional info for the booking. Figure 11-27 shows the booking screen.

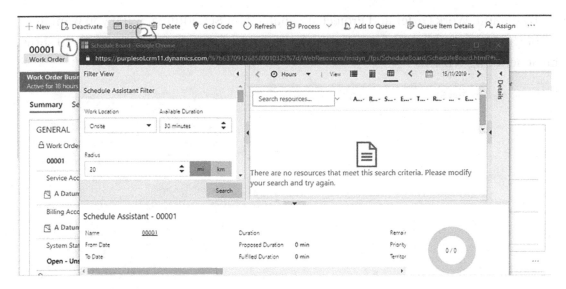

Figure 11-27. *Booking screen*

Using the Booking area, you can create records for bookable resources. A bookable resource is a person, equipment, or a physical place (the facilities).

Schedule Board

This is an interactive view of the booking resources for work orders. This is the one-stop screen for viewing all resources, with many parameters. Figure 11-28 shows the schedule board.

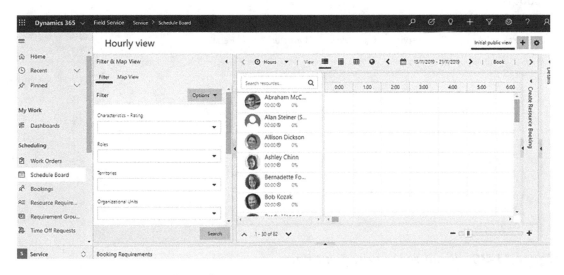

Figure 11-28. *Schedule board*

By default, Work Order and Project are enabled for Scheduling. But if you want to enable for more entities, you can do so using the Scheduling Wizard. Figure 11-29 shows the Scheduling Wizard.

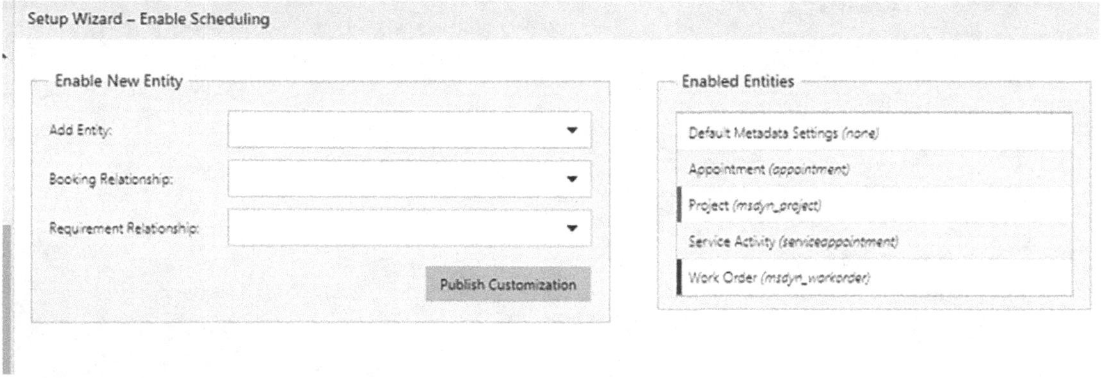

Figure 11-29. *The Scheduling Wizard*

Resource Requirements

Before using the schedule board for booking, you need to set up a resource requirement. Figure 11-30 shows the resource requirement page.

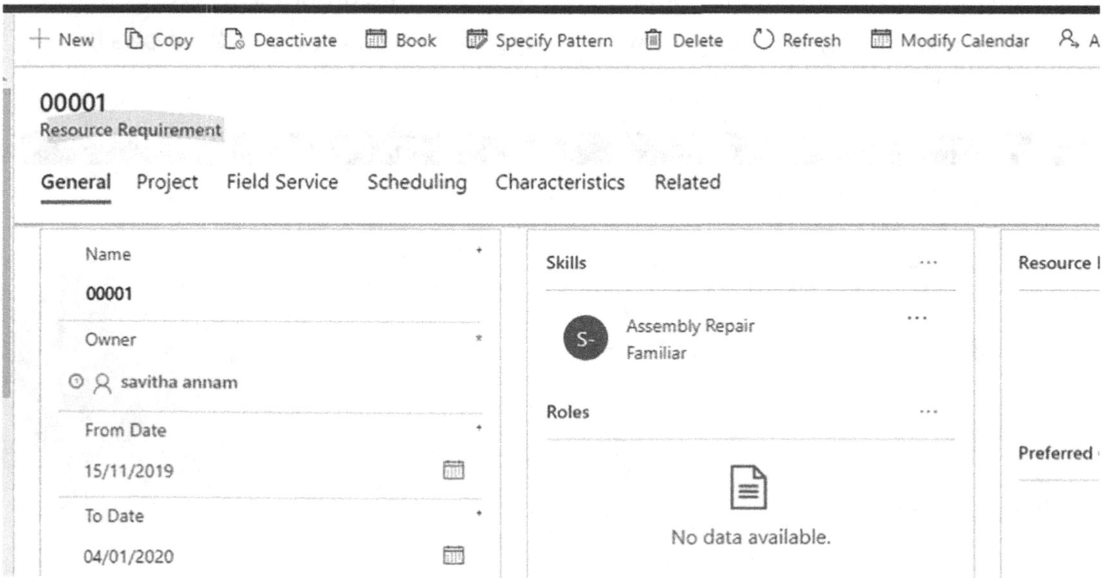

Figure 11-30. *Resource requirement page*

Requirement Group

Requirement groups allow you to define groups of resources that would be appropriate for a job and then schedule all those resources with a single search. With requirement groups, you can mix and match different types of resources, such as individual field technicians, a whole crew, equipment, or facilities needed for a job.

Say you want to use a requirement group to find resources for a work order that requires one field technician with skill X and skill Y or two field technicians, one with skill X and the other with skill Y. Figure 11-31 shows this requirement group.

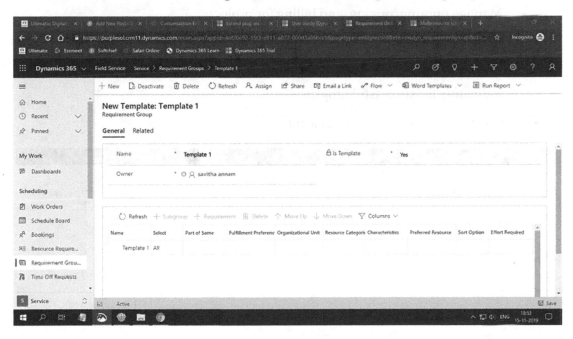

Figure 11-31. *Requirement group*

Project Service Automation Lifecycle

The Project Service Automation (PSA) module helps organizations efficiently track, manage, and deliver project-based services, from the initial sale all the way to invoicing. Project managers rely on software applications to track and manage the delivery of projects. Typically, the first step after finalizing the project charter is to build the work breakdown structure. The popular tools for this are Microsoft Project, which allows you to mold your work breakdown structure into a project plan, where you can assign

483

dependencies, resources, durations, and dates. While it is a very powerful tool, Dynamics 365 PSA (Project Service Automation) offers a more robust end-end solution that also links the sales team to the delivery team. The module enables you to:

- Plan projects, create estimates, and make work schedules

- Estimate and track project cost and revenue

- Forecast resource requirements for projects in the pipeline

- Track project progress and cost consumption

- Manage quoting, pricing, and billing for projects

- Assign and manage resources

- Use reports and interactive dashboards to monitor key performance indicators for successful projects

Figure 11-32 shows the New Project form.

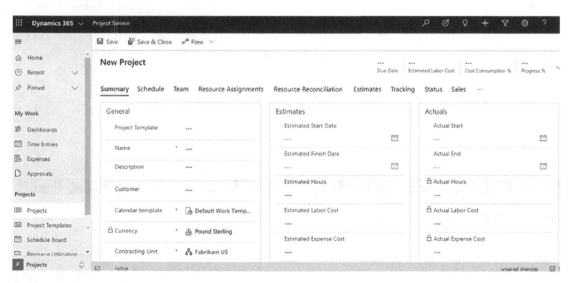

Figure 11-32. *The New Project form*

Project Service Automation Capabilities

This section contains a list of capabilities of the PSA app in Dynamics 365 CE.

Efficient Project Management

The PSA application enables businesses to efficiently organize and deliver project services from start to finish, earning customer trust. With its extensive project planning tools, including Microsoft Project integration, you can precisely forecast cost, effort, and income. You may analyze and track all costs and time using straightforward dashboards.

Resources Optimization

The PSA offers you real-time visibility to resources, and you can optimally utilize those to streamline your scheduling process. It is easy to accurately measure resource utilization, from real-time dashboards, to intelligent decision making and billing purposes. The PSA also empowers consultants to hone their skills and put those to use in the project conceptualization and implementation phase.

Forecast Project Profitability

The PSA gives a unified overview of the product and project-based opportunities that help you prioritize deals. It also enables you to interact directly with customers on the resource needs, the scope of the project, and so on. It ensures seamless sales collaboration and helps you monitor labor rates, creating work statements and more.

Facilitates Innovation

The PSA expedites time to market, unifies your service environment, and transforms your customer interactions, all powered by artificial intelligence (AI). It reduces the cost and protects your data.

Summary

In this chapter, you learned about the following concepts:

- Sales Hub app lifecycle

- Customer Service Hub app lifecycle

- Marketing app concept and lifecycle

- Field Service app lifecycle

- Project Service Automation lifecycle

Next Steps

Your next steps are to go through the advanced scenarios of different configurations and customizations with more Power Apps concepts. You can increase your skill level with the following topics, so you can be a pro at Dynamics 365 CE and Power Apps.

- Power Apps code component framework (PCF)

- Azure DevOps ALM for Power Apps solutions

- More on Azure Integration and Web API calls

- More business scenarios

- Power Platform recent topics

Best Learning Links

You can get more information related to Dynamics 365 and Power Platform using the following links:

- Microsoft Docs: https://docs.microsoft.com/en-us/

- Microsoft Learn: https://docs.microsoft.com/en-us/learn/

- Microsoft Learn TV: https://docs.microsoft.com/en-us/learn/tv/

- Microsoft Shows: https://docs.microsoft.com/en-us/shows/

- Microsoft Events: https://docs.microsoft.com/en-us/events/

- Code Samples: https://docs.microsoft.com/en-us/
  samples/browse/

- GIST GitHub: https://gist.github.com/maestrotex

- My Official Blog: https://softchief.com/

Index

A

Account Manager, 321
Accounts, 460–462
Accuracy score, 272
Active marketing list, 473
Activity tables, 39
Add Node option, 202, 203
Admin Centers, 412
    add a user, 309–316
    advanced settings, 293
    default currency setup, 286
    default pane option, 285, 286
    email templates and
        signatures, 287–293
    links, 283, 284
    personalization settings, 284
    records count per page, 285, 286
    time zone, 286
Advanced settings, 293, 329, 346, 415,
    416, 419
AI Builder, 3, 4
    Canvas apps, 272–274
    concepts, 259
    Form Processing model, 260–272
    models, 259
    Object Detection model, 275–278
    in Power Automate, 272–274
    types, 259, 260
AI model's accuracy score, 272
Alternate keys, 75
App dashboard, 413

Application Lifecycle Management
    (ALM), 29
Approval action type, 184, 185
Approval connector, 184
Approval email, 189
Approvals, 183
Approval taking action, 189
Approval types, 185, 186
Artificial intelligence (AI), 3, 485
Associated view command
    bar, 402
Auditing feature
    advanced settings, 304
    business needs, 305
    entity level, 306–308
    global audit, 306
Auto-number columns, 49, 50
Azure Bot Framework tool, 193
Azure integration, 8
    applications, 436
    logic app, 450–453
    Plugin, 445–449
    service bus, 436–445
    test, 452, 453

B

Booking, 480, 481
Business
    event handler, 361–366
    implementation, 410
    script as web resource, 359–361

E

Printed in the United States
by Baker & Taylor Publisher Services

Printed in the United States
by Baker & Taylor Publisher Services